AMERICAN METEMPSYCHOSIS

AMERICAN METEMPSYCHOSIS

Emerson, Whitman, and the New Poetry

JOHN MICHAEL CORRIGAN

Fordham University Press

NEW YORK   2012

Fordham University Press has no responsibility for the persistence or accuracy
of URLs for external or third-party Internet websites referred to in this
publication and does not guarantee that any content on such websites is, or will
remain, accurate or appropriate.

Fordham University Press also publishes its books in a variety of electronic
formats. Some content that appears in print may not be available in electronic
books.

Library of Congress Cataloging-in-Publication Data

Corrigan, John Michael.
    American metempsychosis : Emerson, Whitman, and the new poetry /
John Michael Corrigan. — 1st ed.
        p.   cm.
    Includes bibliographical references and index.
    ISBN 978-0-8232-4234-4 (cloth : alk. paper)
    1. American literature—19th century—History and criticism.   2. Self-
consciousness (Awareness) in literature.   3. National characteristics,
American, in literature.   4. Emerson, Ralph Waldo, 1803–1882—Criticism
and interpretation.   5. Whitman, Walt, 1819–1892—Criticism and
interpretation.   6. Transmigration in literature.   I. Title.
PS217.S44C67   2012
810.9'353—dc23

                                                                    2011042866

Printed in the United States of America

14 13 12   5 4 3 2 1

First edition

THE
AMERICAN
LITERATURES
INITIATIVE

A book in the American Literatures Initiative (ALI), a collaborative
publishing project of NYU Press, Fordham University Press, Rutgers
University Press, Temple University Press, and the University of Virginia
Press. The Initiative is supported by The Andrew W. Mellon Foundation.
For more information, please visit www.americanliteratures.org.

Contents

Acknowledgments   vii

Introduction   1
1   The Metempsychotic Mind   11
2   The Double Consciousness   39
3   Reading the Metempsychotic Text   73
4   Writing the Metempsychotic Text   104
5   The New Poetry   135
    Conclusion   167

    Notes   177
    Bibliography   225
    Index   237

Acknowledgments

I have benefitted from the support and friendship of numerous people while writing this book—and I would have been unable to persevere without them. I begin by thanking Alan Ackerman for his sure-sighted counsel and steadfast belief in this project; Malcolm Woodland whose warm words of confidence and encouragement I will not forget, coming as they did in times of difficulty and transition; and John Reibetanz whose fidelity to poetry has been an inspiration throughout. I also thank the faculty and administration of the English Department at the University of Toronto and acknowledge the funding of the Ontario government.

Portions of this book have appeared previously: sections of Chapters 4 and 5 in the *Walt Whitman Quarterly Review* (2011); parts of Chapter 1 in the *Journal of the History of Ideas* 71.3 (July 2010); and one section of Chapter 2 in *Dionysius* (2009). I gratefully acknowledge their permission to reprint. For the use of William Blake's "Jacob's Ladder" for the cover art, I thank the British Museum.

I thank Fordham University Press and the American Literatures Initiative, particularly Helen Tartar, Thomas C. Lay, Kathleen Sweeney, Tim Roberts, and Alex Giardino. I am also indebted to many others, Tony Brinkley, Betsy Erkkila, Jay Bregman, Elspeth Brown, Robert Berchman, Kodolányi Gyula, and Sally Wolff-King.

To my parents, Kevin and Elena Corrigan, I owe a deepest debt of gratitude; my brother Yuri for his friendship and the many hours he spent reading and editing my writing; Maria and Sarah Corrigan for their love and support; and Jesse Archibald-Barber, a true friend. I would also like to thank Greg Glazov, Francis and Tess Corrigan, and their families. To my uncle Jamie Glazov, whose brotherhood has made me a better man, and to my grandmother Marina Glazov, our family's poet, I am truly grateful. Peggy Lee, who stayed by my side at the close of this project, thank you for your love and support.

I dedicate this work to my family, both the Corrigans and the Glazovs, and particularly to the memory of my grandfather Yuri Glazov.

Introduction

In the painting *Jacob's Ladder* (1800), William Blake illustrates the nature of the Romantic reconception of human consciousness. At the bottom of the canvas, Jacob lies sleeping, his head resting by the foot of a spiral stair that circles upward through the star-filled sky and finally into the sun itself. Upon the stairway, the souls of angels and human beings pass each other, either descending to earth or ascending to heaven. In the Book of Genesis (28: 11–22), Jacob's dream is a divine revelation: "And, behold, the LORD stood above [the ladder], and said, I am the LORD God of Abraham thy father, and the God of Isaac: the land whereon thou liest, to thee will I give it, and to thy seed." Informed by centuries of mystical practice, Blake's ladder is not only an epiphanic event; it is a figurative map of the human psyche. Indeed, Blake foregrounds Jacob's sleeping body; in the background behind Jacob's head, the staircase rises upward, becoming in its climb the focal point of the watercolor. Jacob reclines, moreover, in the posture of crucifixion, the horizontal plane of the material body intersecting with the vertical dimension within or behind consciousness, which the ladder is intended to represent. Here, upon the ancient architecture of ascent, Blake plunges a whole spiritual cosmology into the internal life of consciousness, powerfully demonstrating the extent to which mysticism underpins the development of the modern self.

Blake's painting also exhibits a decisive Platonic influence, for his ladder is explicitly a ladder of love, much like the ladder of ascent from Plato's *Symposium*. Midway on Blake's staircase, two lovers meet face to face, ascent and descent, the way up and the way down, united in their mutual embrace. By placing the lovers so centrally on the ladder, Blake underscores

a whole tradition of ascent, which viewed the ladder as a structure of me-
tempsychosis or reincarnation.[1] From this perspective, souls descend into
bodies, while others transcend the material world. As early as the first cen-
tury, the ladder had become the site upon which a number of spiritual tra-
ditions intersected. Philo of Alexandria, the Hellenic Jewish philosopher,
interpreted Jacob's ladder as the *anima mundi,* or world soul, the making
of which by the Divine Demiurge Plato depicted in the *Timaeus.* It is this
tradition that Philo incorporated into Judaism, recasting the ladder as a
model of metempsychosis, as "the ascent and descent of souls," and "in-
terjecting a common theme from Platonic writings into the Biblical narra-
tive."[2] Consequently, Jacob's ladder becomes a mystical symbol not only of
ascent and ascent, but of metempsychosis or reincarnation, one of the old-
est and most predominant Hellenic beliefs running through the Pythago-
rean and Orphic traditions into the later (or broader) Platonic heritage and
eventually into esotericism and alchemy with the Golden Chain of Homer,
which Anton Joseph Kirchweger documented and published in 1723 and
which Friedrich Hölderlin and Johann Wolfgang von Goethe studied to-
ward the end of the century.[3]

Where Blake followed certain esoteric and alchemical forms of thought
by clothing spiritual mysteries in secret symbolism, Ralph Waldo Emerson
made these mysteries not simply available to a wider audience;[4] he directly
mapped them onto the idea of American selfhood with its accompanying
emphases on self-reliance and individualism. At the heart of Emerson's
vision lies a conception of consciousness very similar to Blake's mysti-
cal map of the human psyche in "Jacob's Ladder"—except that Emerson
much more fully and systematically develops metempsychosis in terms
of the cognitive capacity of a single self. Emerson's various depictions of
metempsychosis are not occasional portraits; they form part of a lifelong
discourse upon the volatile life of the soul in relation to the evolutionary
sequence of history. James Freeman Clarke, Emerson's close friend, dedi-
cated much of his book *Ten Great Religions Part II* (1884) to arguing that
there is an "essential truth" in the ancient belief of metempsychosis when
seen alongside evolution. "The modern doctrine of the evolution of bodily
organisms is not complete," he states, "unless we unite with it the idea of a
corresponding evolution of the spiritual monad, from which every organic
form derives its unity. Evolution has a satisfactory meaning only when we
admit that the soul is developed and educated by passing through many
bodies."[5]

In "History," the leading essay of the *First Series of Essays* (1841), Em-
erson declares that the "transmigration of souls is no fable,"[6] yet he does
not mean this in any simple, reductionist sense—as an established fact
of the grander arc of soul's journey through bodies. Instead, he uses "the

metempsychosis of nature" (*W* 2: 8) as a figurative model for conscious-
ness' temporal experience of itself. Indeed, following James Hutton's
geologic discovery of deep time in the late eighteenth century, German
Idealism had reinstated much of the mystical knowledge of the past in an
entirely new way, based upon a new awareness of time. According to this
new notion of consciousness, an individual, aided by the correct spiritual
knowledge, could transform himself by concentrating on his own tempo-
ral development—the mystical science of alchemy transposed onto the hu-
man body, the goal not gold, but the creation of a new and more perfect
Adam. Adapting a diverse mystical heritage, both Western and Eastern,
Emerson follows these attempts to intertwine the idea of immanence with
new notions of history that were emerging in the sciences. In so much of
Emerson's oeuvre, the individual realizes that he is part of a series—he per-
ceives the historical sequence like geological strata propping up his present
consciousness. But this realization, epiphany even, is only the beginning of
a self-reflexive process, the goal of which is ultimately self-transformation.[7]

In "Self-Reliance," the essay that immediately follows "History," Em-
erson writes that power "resides in the moment of transition from a past
to a new state, in the shooting of a gulf, in the darting to an aim" (*W* 2:
40). Harold Bloom remarks that "nothing is more American, whether cata-
strophic or amiable, than that Emersonian formula concerning power,"[8]
and Jonathon Levin has used Emerson's "paradoxical poetics of transi-
tion"[9] to analyze the emergence of pragmatism and American literary
modernism. Yet contemporary criticism has largely ignored the fact that
Emerson's very depiction of power as the soul's transition from a past to a
new state resides explicitly within a metempsychotic purview. Emerson's
attempt to collapse a whole mystical cosmos into the individual mind is
not as unlikely an intellectual preoccupation as it might seem. New Eng-
land's Unitarian movement in the early part of the nineteenth century
prepared for it by championing the domain of a new spiritual self capable
of recognizing *the God within* through daily activity and self-reflection.

In his most famous sermon, "Likeness to God" (1828), William Ellery
Channing, the most prominent voice of New England Unitarianism, ar-
gues that to "grow in the likeness of God we need not cease to be men.
This likeness does not consist in extraordinary or miraculous gifts, in
supernatural addictions to the soul, or in anything foreign to our origi-
nal constitution; but in our essential faculties, unfolded by vigorous and
conscientious exertions in the ordinary circumstances assigned by God."[10]
For the generation of transcendentalists that preceded Emerson and his
contemporaries, this notion of a unified, complete individual who draws
together the spiritual and the physical into one stalwart frame constitutes
the continuing Protestant ideal of a new American Adam, capable of

redeeming the failures of the Old World in the promise of America. While
this notion of a unified self partially arose in the early nineteenth century
in relation to German Idealism and English Romanticism, it also pos-
sesses an unmistakable Neoplatonic and esoteric character. In "Oration
on Genius" (1821) and *Observations on the Growth of the Mind* (1826), two
foundational texts of American transcendentalism, Sampson Reed infuses
his writing with the Swedenborgian and larger esoteric teaching that "the
science of the mind" will arise out of "all the other sciences."[11] Because of
this transition to a new framework for consciousness, Reed contends, the
"moral and intellectual character of man has undergone, and is undergo-
ing a change; and as this is effected, it must change the aspect of all things."
In opening itself up to a greater spiritual and material union, the indi-
vidual mind can learn to transform itself into something entirely new: "As
subjects are presented to the operation of the mind, they are decomposed
and reorganized in a manner peculiar to itself, and not easily explained."[12]
Here, Reed anticipates Emerson's metempsychotic mind in his depictions
of how the self witnesses its own cognitive succession and comes to enact
death and rebirth in the process.

While Reed does not fully clarify the nature of this mental transfor-
mation, he insists that the tabula rasa conception of the mind so central
to John Locke's epistemology (derived in part from Aristotle[13]) is indel-
ibly flawed:[14] "There prevails a most erroneous sentiment, that the mind
is originally vacant, and requires only to be filled up." "The mind," Reed
counters, "is originally a most delicate germ, whose husk is the body;
planted in this world, that the light and heat of heaven may fall upon it
with a gentle radiance, and call forth its energies."[15] In *Representative Men*
(1850), Emerson argues that this idea of the mind as "a germ of expansion"
comprises the very heart of a great intellectual tradition of representative
figures, a tradition whose principal value is the Platonic or Neoplatonic
Intellect. Plato "is more than an expert, or a schoolman, or a geometer or
the prophet of a particular message," Emerson writes. "He represents the
privilege of the intellect, the power, namely of carrying up every fact to
successive platforms, and so disclosing in every fact a germ of expansion"
(*W* 4: 46). In the accompanying essay, "Swedenborg; or the Mystic," Em-
erson identifies Intellect's expansion in terms of metempsychosis, argu-
ing that Swedenborg's best work "was written with the highest end, to put
science and the soul, long estranged from each other, at one again" (*W* 4:
63). Here, as in the *First Series of Essays*, Emerson does not advocate a lit-
eral metempsychosis; rather, he argues for its "subjective" character, which
"depends entirely on the thought of the person" (*W* 4: 70).

Emerson's various depictions of the metempsychotic self do not nec-
essarily present a soothing doctrine of the soul's immortality through

successive incarnations—nor an optimistic humanism based upon a spiritual foundation. In *Orphic Sayings* (1840–41) and *Table-Talk* (1877), Amos Bronson Alcott, another close friend of Emerson, indicates how metempsychosis was being interpreted as a pattern of identity, rather than a cosmic vision of soul's immortality. The very transition, Alcott writes, between the sleeping and waking periods of life provides a record of succession that an individual must realize in himself so that metempsychosis operates not simply between lives, but within one single life: "I am sure of being one and the same person I then was, and thread my identity through successive yesterdays into the memory out of which my consciousness was born, nor can I lose myself in the search of myself." Alcott transcribes the soul's continuity and shaping influence upon a series of bodies onto the daily pattern of waking and sleeping so that a whole cosmic vision of soul's eternal life is collapsed into one being: "Every act of sleep is a metamorphosis of bodies and metempsychosis of souls."[16]

Unlike his Unitarian precursors or transcendentalist contemporaries, Emerson unequivocally champions the metempsychotic self as a dynamic part of a radically unsettled cosmos. "I unsettle all things," he affirms. "No facts to me are sacred; none are profane; I simply experiment" (*W* 2: 188). At times, he extols "the firm nature" underneath "the flowing vest" (*W* 3: 21), while elsewhere he contends that "there are no fixtures to men, if we appeal to consciousness" or to the "soul" (*W* 2: 182). These statements are neither random nor arbitrary flights of metaphysical phrase. Instead, they, like many of his dualities, denote the problem of the "double consciousness" (*W* 1: 213; *W* 6: 25), a carefully conceived and highly coherent dialectical philosophy that Emerson initially employs to problematize the prospect of a unified self. In "The Transcendentalist" (1841), Emerson laments a deep schism within the consciousness of human beings—one side the recognition that consciousness unfolds in the temporal present and the other side a hunger for the soul whose life is in the future. In his later writing, Emerson ceases to lament this polarity within the human frame and comes rather to celebrate it. Consciousness cannot be united—and its very oscillation underscores the eternal vicissitudes of an unsettled universe. As he expresses in his fourth lecture of the series *Natural Method of Mental Philosophy* (1858), the "*va et vient*, the ebb and flow, the pendulum, the alternation, the sleeping and waking, the fits of easy transmission and reflection, the pulsation, the undulation, which shows itself as a fundamental secret of nature, exists in intellect."[17] Such a conception is similar in outline to Hegel's dialectic, but without the overarching drive for an absolute *telos* wherein everything foreign will have been sublated in the final experience of self-knowing.

From another vantage point, Emerson's double consciousness can be understood in relation to the redefinition of science in the early modern era. The emergence of modern science from out of the practice of alchemy, magic, and the occult was not the kind of clean break that many would suppose; rather, much of our contemporary conception of science relates to the discovery of deep time in the eighteenth century and the accompanying invention of the idea of evolutionary history, culminating in Charles Darwin's *On the Origin of Species* (1859). Before James Hutton's discovery of geologic time, which initiates the temporal revolutions, one of the chief aims of scientists was to restore the human being to God's grace. In the seventeenth century, Francis Bacon understood scientific progress as a means of attaining salvation. Bacon's "view of the future of science was not that of progress in a straight line. His 'great instauration' of science was directed towards a return to the state of Adam before the Fall, a state of pure and sinless contact with nature and knowledge of her powers."[18] Bacon's aim, moreover, was itself a natural extension of the sixteenth-century occult writings of Cornelius Agrippa and John Dee who served as a scientific adviser to Elizabeth I. As was the aim of many occult scientists during this period, Dee "believed that he had discovered a combined cabalist, alchemical, and mathematical science which would enable its possessor to move up and down the scale of being from the lowest to the highest spheres," a discovery suggesting not simply the perfectibility of the human being on the ladder of ascent and descent, but a new science that could allow the human being mastery over the celestial chain connecting earth and heaven.

In the figure of the double consciousness, Emerson attempts to balance these two corresponding, yet radically different scientific aims: first, the perfectibility of the human being through spiritual science; second, the idea of material evolution, which irrevocably displaced the Enlightenment conception of the human being. Emerson thereby maps the older desire for salvation onto the evolutionary pattern of history, repeatedly portraying the chronological sequence of time as a ladder or stairway linking earth and heaven. In "Love" (1841), which accompanies his depiction of the metempsychotic self of "History," he depicts the Platonic ladder of ascent as a foundational model taught by all great teachers throughout the ages. The "lover ascends to the highest beauty," he writes in the essay, "to the love and knowledge of the Divinity, by steps on this ladder of created souls" (*W* 2: 106). Like Philo's ascending and descending biblical ladder, this "ladder of created souls" possesses two opposing gravities, first the downward fiery procession of the soul from the One and second the upward education of the soul as it attempts to convert itself back to the One. Here, the Neoplatonic triad of procession, conversion, and self-constitution underlies Emerson's description of how a celestial fire falls from heaven and eventually learns to realize itself in the emergent complexity of material consciousness, which evolves from a preconscious state to the self-reflexivity of poetic creativity. As in "History," Emerson uses metempsychosis as a model for this cognitive ascent, as a way to invert the mimetic movement away from the One and to reachieve an affinity with the fire of creation, followed by a synthesis into light itself.

Emerson's double consciousness with its downward mimetic gravity and upward metempsychotic progression forms an open template of incessant self-constituting change that draws the Idealist philosophies of the past as well as the revolutions of modern science into the depiction of one single being, psychologically limited in its vision, yet seeking nonetheless to extend its range by virtue of a Neoplatonic second sight to renew the material world. As with German Idealism and later Romanticism in general, Emersonian metempsychosis unfolds as a patently phenomenological project. Metaphysical values—particularly Plato and Plotinus's conception of an ensouled eyebeam that constitutes itself in what it sees—underlie the very act of reading so that the relationship between perceiver and page both retains the classical focus of the Platonic tradition and simultaneously questions the steps by which we arrive at this splendid metaphor. In "Circles," which continues the metempsychotic emphasis upon perception in the *First Series of Essays*, Emerson depicts the conversion of dead statues into fiery men as a phenomenological process that the eye enacts in its attempt to overcome mimetic reality: "Then cometh the god, and converts the statues into fiery men, and by a flash of his eye burns up the veil which shrouded all things, and the meaning is manifest" (W 2: 184). Emerson's depiction of the flash of the eye powerfully captures the theme of theurgic reanimation of statues in the Neoplatonism of Iamblichus and Proclus,[19] while also recalling the later mystical and alchemical emphasis upon achieving the resurrection of the body. In *The Signature of All Things* (1621), for instance, Jacob Böhme portrays the death of Adam after eating of the tree of the knowledge of good and evil as a process by which the divine light withdrew from the corporeal body, taking with it the fire of the soul. Later inspiring Emerson, Böhme's mysticism powerfully, if not surreptitiously, describes the alchemical process by which the "soul must help itself with the sun's light" so that the body is restored. With the infusion of God's desire, incarnated in the image of fire, the body becomes "again capable of the divine sunshine,"[20] a process of restoration wherein the divine comes to know itself more fully.

In Emerson's oeuvre, the flash of the eye and the restoration of the material world come to evoke a poetic crisis of American nationhood. In "The Poet" (1844), Emerson heralds the future American poet not as a solution, but as the central dilemma of the age: "The breadth of the problem is great, for the poet is representative. He stands among partial man for the complete man, and apprises us not of his wealth, but of the commonwealth."

Here as well, Emerson employs metempsychosis to evoke this future poet, for the attainment of commonwealth sends the individual on a journey to account for every partial, transitory object and to unite all of these objects in his own greater vision. The poet thereby "uses his eyes" to follow the soul's journey through successive forms and, in doing so, "flows with the flowing of nature" (W 3: 13). Perceiving not simply one vantage point, but with "all eyes" (W 3: 21), the poet reachieves an affinity with the natural world not simply by observing the sequence of its animation, but by infusing the world with the fire of new creation. At the same time, Emerson consistently problematizes this venture, for perception upholds a succession of experience that being itself cannot. Thus, in "Experience," which follows "The Poet" in the *Second Series of Essays*, he writes, "I am ready to die out of nature, and be born again into this new yet unapproachable America I have found in the West" (W 3: 41). Indeed, the wish to be *born again* underlies the bulk of Emerson's writing, yet it is also a desire that he repeatedly questions, for an individual may perceive a new vista of experience opening before him and still be unable to approach it.

Emerson's conception of metempsychosis thereby provides the site upon which the shaping forces of ancient philosophy and mysticism, particularly Hinduism, Pythagoreanism, Platonism, Neoplatonism, and Christian esotericism can be recombined with a new awareness of the historical series of being and the individual's provisional place in, and negotiation with, that series. In the era leading up to Charles Darwin, this emerging awareness of series—especially geological and biological sequence—offered a prospective reintegration of metaphysics and science. For Emerson, both poet and scientist engage the same problem: they attempt to understand how the series establishes itself and the direction it will take in the future. Discovery, in this sense, becomes a method of observation, a way of perceiving how life enacts a sequential order through time. Emerson's repeated call for a finely adapted human being, a poetic reconciler, synthesizes these various strands of influence, from the ancient Platonic lover climbing the ladder of being to contemplate a single science and the vision of the Beautiful itself, to the nineteenth-century religious portrayal of a complete American individual who uses his own contemplation and self-reflection to achieve heightened consciousness.

Emerson repeatedly portrays the metempsychotic relationship between perception and the succession of its experience as a foundational pedagogy for consciousness. While the ceaseless fluctuations underlying and involving all individual and universal motion overwhelm the human being's capacity for comprehension, yet does the text—the poetic inscription and mirror for nature's changing order—offer him an activity that may allow him to develop and expand his cognitive capacity to participate in the greater cosmological order. The text, accordingly, does not simply contain a message that must be apprehended and understood; it provides a structure that exceeds its narrative or content. In the movement between eye and word, Emerson insists, the wealth and poverty of history reemerge to teach a lesson to its readers. They may yet come to know themselves and to understand the greater series that runs through and in them; they may yet attain a mastery over their inscribed existence and learn the ever-elusive art of self-transformation, that science for which the alchemists strove and that essential experience which Hegel championed as self-knowing.

While Emerson lays out the transcendental delineations of the metempsychotic self in America, it is Walt Whitman who thoroughly modernizes and formalizes this project in terms of nineteenth-century democratic struggle and situates its work as an expressly poetic activity. In the first edition of the *Leaves of Grass*, Whitman announces the very maturation of expanding individuality as a form of metempsychotic becoming, hinging as ever upon perception: "There was a child went forth every day,/ And the first object he look'd upon, that object he became."[21] Here, most assuredly, is an American drama of selfhood in which the poet must accept his own teeming nation on equal terms and must do so precisely through a metempsychotic phenomenology. Whitman's startling statement in "Song of Myself" that "I am the man, I suffer'd, I was there"[22] further emphasizes that the self in *Leaves of Grass* is one that seeks and potentially possesses a plethora of experience, not simply that of one self or body, but of many bodies. In Whitman's poetry, this self attempts to inhabit all the bodies of American union and does so precisely through a successive pattern of transmigration and metamorphosis. The elusive goal of the effort, as in many of Emerson's depictions of metempsychosis, is to unify the temporal sequence in the experience of consciousness so that "past and present and future are [. . .] joined," a drawing together of history's materials into a new and thoroughly self-referential arrangement, necessarily including the future reader who will assume the sequence and live through each of its coverings.

Although many scholars have depicted Whitman as the poet of the body, Whitman presents a pattern of poetic ascent and descent very similar to Emerson's in character. Indeed, Whitman's soul and body relation is not some amorphic, nebulous one, but a developed and mystically inspired figuration of poetic maturation in which the soul plays a decisive and principal role. In "Song of Myself" and the 1855 preface to *Leaves of Grass*, Whitman develops the trope of the metempsychotic self by depicting his own poetic development with the image of a stairway. In mounting the staircase and sequentially experiencing all the knowledge that each step or age provides, Whitman proclaims his growing power to be the soul's experience of a vast temporal sequence: "All forces have been steadily employ'd to complete and delight me,/ Now on this spot I stand with my robust soul" (44.1168–69). Whitman transforms the ascent of the soul for modern selfhood, formalizing Emerson's metempsychotic project as a textual event, one whose structure rejects traditional poetic form and opens the reader up to a past network of relations and requires him to experience its movement for himself. In this respect, American metempsychosis becomes a methodology of poetic reading and writing, encapsulated in the relation between a reader and a sequence of words that exists before the reader apprehends it, yet that requires our present consciousness to engage and open up its discourse in a heightened act of becoming. Consequently, the advent of modern poetic form is not simply a freedom from past convention, but an effort to understand the past more thoroughly and engage in its reformation more actively.

1 / The Metempsychotic Mind

In the last three decades, the widespread understanding of Ralph Waldo Emerson as a philosopher of metaphysical unity has given way to a more postmodern appraisal. Scholars have come to view Emerson's thought as a contemplative progression where no determination can be final, since the process itself is perpetually ongoing and open-ended.[1] These recent efforts at de-transcendentalizing and revitalizing Emerson counter the long-established tendencies of criticism to portray him as a cheerful mystic who is but an echo—however powerful and influential—of traditional metaphysics.[2] Instead, scholars characterize Emerson as a post-Idealist, a pragmatist, an evolutionist, or a political radical. While these depictions may seem appropriate, Emerson's lifelong attempts to safeguard the idea of the soul in an age of scientific advancement by conceptualizing it as "a volatile essence," ever playful and mysterious, neither a foundation nor a touchstone for being, but an unsettling indeterminacy within the structure of human cognition—this deserves renewed attention. Emerson's recurrent use of the ancient notion of metempsychosis—the transmigration of the soul through successive bodies—is one principal instance of his literary and philosophical inventiveness at work, namely, his search for a figurative blueprint to marry the vast, material sequence of history with the elusive, unsettled activity of the soul.

While older scholarship ignored or tended to dismiss such depictions of metempsychosis,[3] Arthur Versluis makes the case that Emerson "took transmigration seriously" and tended to view it "as a literary conceit first and as a doctrine second," although he was "always seeking to express it in Western terms."[4] Versluis is indeed correct to emphasize the freedom with which Emerson "manipulates" the idea of Indian transmigration and combines it with a Neoplatonic reading, but it is my contention that Emerson adapted the idea of metempsychosis in a much more thorough manner than anyone has previously shown. Like so many of his contemporaries, Emerson used Vedantic and Confucian sources through the filter of Idealistic thought on the esoteric assumption that all great religions and philosophies contain the same universal truths. At the same time, Emerson's use of metempsychosis is more complex and nuanced than this might suppose, for it can be most appropriately understood not simply as an esoteric, exotic, or mystical doctrine, common to both Eastern and Western traditions, but as a figurative template for placing the modern individual within the vast record of history—"in the entire series of days" (W 2: 3). Incorporating the language of metaphysics into the revolutions of science, particularly the new vastness of the geological record and theories of adaptation and evolution emerging in biology, Emerson repeatedly stresses how the structure of transmigration—the soul running through the historical series—can indicate the initial outlines of a greater theory of human cognition and perception.

I begin with Emerson's most detailed description of "the metempsychosis of nature" (W 2: 8) from the leading piece, "History," of his First Series of Essays (1841). Here, Emerson presents metempsychosis not as literal religious doctrine, but as a mode of perception that culminates in an active search for cognitive unity. In the following sections, I outline the principal influences upon Emerson's metaphysics: ancient Greek metempsychosis, especially the Platonic tradition, which I discuss throughout, Hindu reincarnation, Goethean metamorphosis, Hegelian phenomenology, and Christian esotericism. With this diverse array of influences, I show how Emerson transforms metempsychosis into a developmental and evolutionary prototype, a truly volatile poetic power that unsettles the static delineations of history so that an individual can command his or her own self-development. In such a setting, Emerson's metempsychotic mind underscores the prospect of a new humanism, a spiritual science that reconceives of the human being's cognitive and artistic capacity by adapting metaphysics to modern consciousness.

Soul and the Historical Series

Emerson's notion of self-reliance has become a thoroughly American value, although it can be properly understood as an expression of the Protestant faith he both inherited and abandoned. Already in his early lectures, Emerson anticipates the spirit of Representative Men (1850) in his biographies (1835) of Martin Luther (1483–1546) and George Fox (1624–91) who embody, for him, the ideas of immanence, reform, and self-reliance expressing themselves in history. Of Luther, he writes, "No man in history ever assumed a more commanding attitude or expressed a more perfect self-reliance."[5] Luther is thereby more than a man; his very words express a Divine Will that founds nations and refreshes the natural order: "His words are more than brave, they threaten and thunder. They indicate a Will on which a nation might lean, not liable to sudden sallies and swoons, but progressive as the motions of the earth" (*EL* 1: 136). In his notes for these biographic lectures, Emerson wonders whether the indwelling spirit that spoke through Luther resurfaced in Fox: "Did he reappear in George Fox?" (*EL* 1: 118). What may seem idle supernatural speculation of soul's transmigration into new bodies can be viewed in Emerson's oeuvre as a consistent effort to understand how ideas become embodied and adapted in history. Both Luther and Fox, Emerson argues, were poor and humble, yet held fast to the inner voice of conscience and, as a result, they shook the very fabric of Europe's social order and lay the foundation for America's budding democratic enterprise. Yet it is not imitation of these reformers that Emerson desires of his contemporaries; rather, he views their reform as only an emerging, not yet fully expressed example that requires further amelioration. In "Nature" (1836), the essay that brought him fame, Emerson indeed laments an American people who see only through the eyes of tradition and cannot enjoy "an original relation to the universe" (*W* 1: 7). Rather than fall prey to a second-hand, ascribed existence, the American people must learn to think new thoughts; in short, they must learn to think for themselves: "There are new lands, new men, new thoughts. Let us demand our own works and laws and worship" (*W* 1: 7).

The ability to think new thoughts requires, for Emerson, a new way of imagining the human mind and its potential to recreate itself in better form. Over the last two decades, Stanley Cavell has developed a critical context that helps to understand Emerson's distinctive map of human cognition. According to Cavell, the quintessential Emersonian prototype for consciousness is a form of "aversive thinking," the individual *turning away from*, and *toward*, "the dominantly desired virtue of his society." Thinking, in this sense, cannot be understood as a linear enterprise; rather, it is a form of conversation, an engagement with other persons in which one field of possibility is checked and complemented by reversal. Emerson, thereby, "characterizes thinking as marked by transfiguration and conversion" for to "think is to turn around, or turn back [...] the words of ordinary life" so as to change the "present form of our lives that now repel thought." Cavell underscores the Emersonian process of moving through a series, even while necessarily placing all its steps under refutation, "always under criticism (held in aversion)."[6] This brief, general sketch of Cavell's argument can also help to clarify Emerson's repeated depictions of metempsychosis. It is not so much literal transmigration that preoccupies Emerson, but a way of challenging the cognitive capacity of each individual to transform a preestablished tendency into a new, living progression.

In "History," the leading essay in his *First Series of Essays* (1841), Emerson presents his first sustained account of metempsychosis as a direct challenge to his readers. "The transmigration of souls is no fable," he warns. "I would it were; but men and women are only half human" (*W* 2: 18). Emerson confronts his readers with a dilemma that curiously reflects the formation of American individualism: to evolve and become fully human requires not simply self-transcendence, but a way of entering into greater conversation with history itself. Emerson thereby asks his audience not to abide by the definite shape or character of tradition, but to transform by taking on many selves and points of view. To achieve transformation, therefore, an individual must be willing to abandon the single self along with its conventions and ostensible stability and recognize the endless metamorphosis of all living things: "The philosophical perception of identity through endless mutations of form, makes him know the Proteus. What else am I who laughed or wept yesterday, who slept last night like a corpse, and this morning stood and ran? And what see I on any side but the transmigrations of Proteus?" (*W* 2: 18). Here, the dramatic, mythological figure of the ever-changing Greek god, Proteus, points not simply to a metaphysical cosmic order, but to a "perception of identity" whose structure is explicitly metempsychotic.

In "History," therefore, Emerson's portrayal of "the human spirit [which] goes forth from the beginning to embody itself in the entire series of days" (*W* 2: 3) provides a type of metaphysical blueprint radically reenvisioned through the lens of modern selfhood. Transforming Plotinian Intellect under the modern Idealist auspices of historical consciousness, Emerson's portrayal of the metempsychotic mind can be understood as a humanistic expression of the individual's cognitive ability to convert "the whole encyclopedia of facts" (*W* 2: 3) into a living progression. In order to understand the sequence of which he or she is a part, the individual must learn to think metempsychotically: each individual must look within himself to discover that he already contains the whole record of history in his own mind: "Of the works of this mind history is the record. Its genius is illustrated by the entire series of days. Man is explicable by nothing less than all his history" (*W* 2: 3). The universal mind or Intellect already holds all of history within it—and thus the effort to remember, reconstruct, or revitalize necessarily becomes an individual attempt to convert the already created world of brute matter back into living unity.

While affirming the spiritual role of a unifying consciousness in history, Emerson also emphasizes the provisional nature of the vision supplied by the soul's metempsychotic awareness. The individual perceives only parts of the historical series of being, and it is precisely this fragmentary record that inspires his attempts to fit all the pieces of history back into one flowing sequence. The human tragedy is that the individual is incapable of such a feat. The role of genius, however, forcefully intensifies the promise of unity, and for this reason, Emerson's human being of superlative gifts comes closest to unifying history's series: such an individual both recognizes and demonstrates history as a metempsychotic drama in which each stage is a distinct face or embodiment, adopted, and in turn, discarded by the soul that always seeks a new and heightened progression:

> Genius studies the causal thought, and far back in the womb of things, sees the rays parting from one orb, that diverge ere they fall by infinite diameters. Genius watches the monad through all his masks as he performs *the metempsychosis of nature.* Genius detects through the fly, through the caterpillar, through the grub, through the egg, the constant individual; through countless individuals the fixed species; through many species the genus; through all the genera the steadfast type; through all the kingdoms of organized life the eternal unity. (*W* 2: 8; emphasis added)

Characteristically, Emerson does not construct the metempsychotic order in any static, univocal way. In his depiction, the great chain of being has given way to a model in which consciousness itself gives rise to the abundance of nature and its sequential order. The historical series of being exists prior to individual consciousness, but its order and laws are reconstructed by a consciousness that attempts to turn back upon itself and remember the entire history of its amelioration. Equally noteworthy is Emerson's emphasis on perception as the fundamental basis of human knowledge. The order of ascension progresses from "fly," through "caterpillar," "grub," "egg" to "constant individual" because of genius' *perception* or *observation* of the series. The human being observes the principle of life perform "the metempsychosis of nature"; he or she watches the "monad"[7] enacted or performed through all its dramatic masks and, thereby, sees the dispersal of eternal unity into all life's seemingly discrete particulars, from a temporary origin, "the womb of things," into rays that manifest themselves in and through all the world's species, arriving at last at "the steadfast type," a provisional entity that has succeeded in pulling itself together out of the multiplicity of the historical series.

To see the metempsychotic structure of nature, therefore, the individual must go over the whole ground of history not just by relating it to himself and his own experience, but by properly enacting it within his perception and very being. Certainly, the observer receives a historical series, a sequence that exists before and after his individual existence, but this process is never a passive reception. By virtue of his immanent perception, Emerson's superlative individual pierces the external multiplicity of nature to yield its secret law,[8] thereby taking on the power to reorganize the world at will: "He must attain and maintain that lofty sight where facts yield their secret sense [...]. By surrounding ourselves with the original circumstances, we invent anew the orders and the ornaments of architecture" (W 2: 6, 11). Just as consciousness cannot exist without its object(s), the historical series is most real and tangible in the individual's activity of self-constitution.

The individual must make himself the fully self-conscious record of history by using his or her own subjective perception as a receptive and constitutive power: "We are always coming up with the emphatic facts of history in our private experience, and verifying them here. All history becomes subjective; in other words, there is properly no History; only Biography. *Every mind must know the whole lesson for itself—must go over the whole ground. What it does not see, what it does not live, it will not know*" (W 2: 6; emphasis added). Emerson argues for a more concrete conception of historical sequence even while proposing that any knowledge of the truth of this series arises from the individual's own activity in realizing history's progression in himself—in his perception and being.[9] Each active reading reorganizes all the manifold elements of history and gives them a new, contemporary variation, raising the metempsychotic series to yet another heightened step in the universe's ceaseless process of self-renewal:[10]

> All inquiry into antiquity,—all curiosity respecting the pyramids, the excavated cities, Stonehenge, the Ohio Circles, Mexico, Memphis,—is the desire to do away with this wild, savage and preposterous There and Then, and introduce in its place the Here and Now. [...] When he has satisfied himself, in general and in detail, that it was made by such a person as he, so armed and so motived, and to ends to which he himself should also have worked, the problem is solved; his thought lives along the whole line of temples and sphinxes and catacombs, passes through them all with satisfaction, and they live again to the mind, or are now. (W 2: 7)

The problem of the past, its discontinuity with the present and the limitations it imposes—all these can be overcome by means of a perceptive inquiry that enacts a metempsychotic journey, a passage of individual thought through the whole milieu of time—"along the whole line" of history's monuments—so that the materials of the past can be revitalized in the present. Emerson thereby invites his readers to participate in a mode of perception through all the world's abundant facts, from ancient symbols and ruins to the signs and figures of modern day, so as to follow history's grand sequence and unify all its steps in a present act of consciousness.

Apprenticeship in Western and Indian Mysticism

While few critics have paid the metempsychotic mind of "History" much attention, it is by no means an anomalous portrait in Emerson's oeuvre and has a particularly rich prehistory in his thought. In his early college studies in the late 1820s and early 1830s, Emerson began to outline metempsychosis as a pedagogical project to synthesize all of history into modern consciousness, a project drawing heavily upon the post-Kantian Idealist tradition and explaining, to some degree, how Indian thought was assimilated in the West. Emerson's own absorption of Indian mysticism follows such a strategy: he largely studied Hinduism through the lens of English and continental Idealism with the assumption that the spiritual beliefs of the past could be fused into a new and evolving metaphysical order.

Emerson's early journals and notebooks give strong indication of his development from a Christian believer to a transcendentalist who understood education as a spiritual calling, an invitation to the soul to grasp its vocation in the development of civilization and culture. Already at the age of twenty-one in 1824, Emerson sought a dynamic metaphysical model capable of reconciling the ever-widening chasm between religion and science in nineteenth-century America. His 1824 meditations champion spiritual constancy within the flux of nature and provide, in an as-yet-undeveloped manner, the metempsychotic model that comes to prominence in the ensuing decades: "I like the image my fancy presents me of a wise man well bred to a vast variety of sound learning carrying thro' <wind & storm> sun & rain, through his rambles & business, and animal reflections & filthy occupations, thro' visits of ceremony and all the attitudes into which the versatile scene of life may throw him—his soul that rich world of thought."[11] Emerson depicts how "a wise man" learns to carry his soul with him through "all the attitudes" and changes of life. This experience of multiple states of being underscores, moreover, a key motif in Emerson's work: how the human being bears witness to the historical series so that he or she is not simply a spectator, but an active participant in history's development: "Now History is an art (<arranged> devised in correspondence with th<at>e faculty of Memory,)—which multiplies a thousandfold these riches of the soul. Instead of strolling into the world's great fair like ignorant boys wondering at all we see, we are already behind the curtain[;]

we have seen the great series of individuals & nations whose wars & compacts have brought the world into the state we see" (*JMN* 2: 398). Already in 1824, the young Emerson argues that in witnessing the historical series of being, individuals become aware of how the world has been brought into its present state. Intellectual engagement with history is therefore equated with the awakening of the soul's power: individuals perceive the full arc of history's series and cease to be mere observers; instead, they become artists who have a hand in "arranging" and "devising" history's progression in accordance with the "faculty of memory."

While the individual bears witness to the inner, spiritual fire that vitalizes and runs through "the great series," Emerson also indicates that the series itself is a cognitive progression. As the "riches of the soul" are multiplied a "thousandfold," so too does individual consciousness expand to comprise a greater field of interconnection and relation: "Out of these comparisons arise infinite inferences of [the individual's] understanding about which his thoughts are incessantly occupied & which are related to each other by a thousand connexions which make the substance of his intellectual life" (*JMN* 2: 398). As we shall see, this focused attention on cognition only deepens in Emerson's oeuvre as he incorporates both the Platonic and Christian emphases on transcendence[12] into a new ethos of immanence: the educated self does not escape the theater of existence; while it accepts and transcends each historical determinate it sees, such a self never fully abandons its history, instead transforming all the inherited husks of memory into active, living pathways of consciousness.

By 1830, Emerson alludes to metempsychosis with ever-greater frequency in his continuing study of Greek philosophy, from pre-Socratic thinkers such as Pythagoras and Anaxagoras to Platonism and Neoplatonism, as is particularly evident in the copious notes he would make on the subject.[13] Emerson therein highlights soul's recurrent and perpetual journey into and through the material world as both an individual concept— "one single soul ran thro' all being, ordering matter but intimately present to man" (*JMN* 3: 366)—and a universal one: "The soul is an emanation of the Divinity, a part of the Soul of the world, a ray from the source of light. It comes from without into the human body, as into a momentary abode. It goes out of it anew; it wanders in ethereal regions, it returns to visit it; it passes into other habitations for the soul is immortal" (*JMN* 3: 367).[14] As in his 1824 journal, Emerson's emphasis falls not simply upon soul's journey through successive bodies, but also upon the human being's capacity to understand the sequence of which history is a record. Quoting Heraclitus, he writes, "The understanding represents the march of the universe such as it has been preserved by memory; we arrive then at truth when we borrow from memory the faithful tablet of which the deposit is trusted to it.

Wisdom is then accessible to all men" (*JMN* 3: 370).[15] So expressly vital to his *First Series of Essays* in 1841, the concept of memory as a particular kind of reminiscence constitutes the possibility of enacting a chronological sequence,[16] each individual containing the memory of history in his very being—his body is the record—and using memory to understand "the march of the universe" as it unfolds in time.

Living as he did during the "first great period of European Sanskrit scholarship," Emerson also drew from Indian poetry and philosophy during his college years in Harvard.[17] As Arthur Versluis argues, Emerson's "reading of Vedantic and Confucian sources corroborated what he had learned in the Platonic school and, to a lesser extent, from Christian mysticism."[18] From the works of William Jones (1746–94), Henry Thomas Colebrooke (1765–1837), Robert Southey (1774–1843), and Charles Grant (1778–1866), Emerson encountered a Vedantic tradition filtered through the lens of English colonialism. While these writers often lamented the superstition of the East, they nonetheless inherited and, in turn, propounded the widespread belief that Indian thought was one of the historical origins of the Greek philosophical tradition. The ancient account of Pythagoras forming his philosophical system, especially his doctrine of metempsychosis, in his travels to India appears in many of the primary texts from which Emerson established his general sense of intellectual history.[19] In this light, these eighteenth- and nineteenth-century writers were attempting a form of cultural assimilation in which the mysticism of the East could directly correspond to the underpinnings of classical philosophy, a type of early historicism that sought to map out the chronological development of civilization itself.

In the *Restoration of Learning in the East* (1807) especially, which Emerson read during his college years, Charles Grant attempts a vast revision of Hindu thought in terms of a metaphysical methodology of mind and history. Grant's depiction of how the "degradation" of Hindu learning is redeemed through colonial rule serves to illustrate the developing "scientific method" of English and continental Idealism after Kant, which sought to unify the scattered facts of history into a new and current order. Accordingly, Grant portrays India's cultural forms as a "faint emanation of th' Eternal Flame," a "phantom beauty" that can be purified by the "all in all" of Plotinian Intellect.[20] Grant thereby bends Neoplatonism to a very modern purpose: the spiritual progress of the mind is not simply transcendent; rather, it is a type of historical methodology where thought witnesses and, consequently, moves through "every form of vulgar sense," from material signatures to the divine and immaterial nature of God: "Yet whence this progress of the Sage's mind,/ Beyond the bounds by Nature's hand assign'd?/ Whence every form of vulgar sense o'er thrown,/ Soars the rapted thought, and rests on God alone?"[21] While Grant emphasizes transcendence, the historical character that he gives to the mind clearly complements Emerson's 1824 portrayal of an immanent soul that witnesses and enacts "the great series" that has "brought the world into the state we see" (*JMN* 2: 398). For Grant, consciousness ascends through the historical series of being so that, "by smooth graduations," all "systems of belief unconscious[ly]" exhibit the journey of the mind through matter toward its eventual purification in God. The "infinite of nature swarms," Grant writes, "through endless forms" until it is at last freed in the rapture of soaring thought.[22]

After completing his degree at Harvard, Emerson made another important discovery in the work of the French philosopher Victor Cousin (1792–1867). Encountering "an influential account of the *Bhagavad Gītā* in Cousin's *Cours de Philosophie*, which he read in 1831,"[23] Emerson deepened his knowledge of the Vedantic tradition, while also assimilating the attitude of French Idealism along with its Neoplatonic and German Idealist underpinnings. Much like Grant, Cousin calls his audience "to re-collect the true" by drawing together the scattered consciousness of the previous age into a more perfect unity.[24] The "question is not to decree and recommence the work of our predecessors," Cousin states, "but to perfect it in re-uniting, and in fortifying by that reunion, all those truths scattered in the different systems which the eighteenth century has transmitted to us."[25] In *Cours de Philosophie*, Cousin clearly approaches Hinduism with this aim in mind: to transform all scattered belief systems into a sure and present chronology. As Cousin claims, whereas the aim of the ancient Brahmans was to remove the historicity of their religion to make it appear eternal and timeless, the very purpose of modern philosophy lay in reinstating or rediscovering the true chronology of civilization, from the superstitions of Eastern and Western religions to the scientific methodology of modern philosophy.[26]

While Emerson certainly shared the Idealist desire for a new historical self-realization, the *Bhagavad Gītā* itself also helped to shape Emerson's conception of the self.[27] Besides Arthur Versluis's account in *American Transcendentalism and Asiatic Religion*, scholarship has consistently overlooked the specific trajectory of this influence, namely, that the concept of unity in the *Bhagavad Gītā* operates in the explicit context of memory and reincarnation. As Krishna teaches in that sacred text, enlightenment depends on recollection: "When in recollection he withdraws all his senses from the attractions of the pleasures of sense, even as a tortoise withdraws all its limbs, then his is a serene wisdom."[28] In seeking an inner serene wisdom, the soul does not throw off the memory of the material world, but realizes it more fully. Where the tortoise does not abandon its shell, but

draws all its limbs further within itself, so too does the human being real-
ize himself in this movement inward: "Bringing them all into the harmony
of recollection, let him sit in devotion and union, his soul finding rest in
me. For when his senses are in harmony, then his is a serene wisdom."[29]
The ultimate difference between the unaware and the enlightened thus
pivots upon metempsychotic recollection. As Krishna says to the soldier
Arjuna, "I have been born many times, Arjuna, and many times hast thou
been born. But I remember my past lives, and thou hast forgotten thine."[30]

Emerson's nineteenth-century notion of immanent individuality finds
a striking affinity with the Hindu notion of *atman*. The movement within,
achieved through many transmigrations, to the recognition of *atman* re-
veals a unity both beyond and encompassing the external world. In the
Upanishads, "this innermost thing, this self [...] is dearer than a son; it
is dearer than wealth, it is dearer than everything else. [...] When a man
regards only his self as dear to him, what he holds dear will never perish."[31]
This movement within, to the recognition of *atman*, is to an original, un-
differentiated abundance, which in its wealth and reflection also realizes
itself as the world: "In the beginning this was only Brahman, and it knew
only itself (*atman*), thinking: 'I am Brahman.' As a result, it became the
Whole."[32] Consequently, out of these Hindu outlines of selfhood, Emerson
presents a methodology of turning inward, where immanence expands
beyond simply a belief in the indwelling God; it becomes a phenomenol-
ogy of consciousness[33] in which the self seeks to restore the true, external
sequence, not as objective fact, but as a process of becoming.

Transformability of Matter

What made Hindu reincarnation attractive to Emerson, therefore, was
its striking similarity to the Greek classical tradition. Emerson's enthusi-
asm to unite these two traditions into a more perfect model was not simply
an Idealist preoccupation; it expresses both a suspicion of past beliefs and
the resulting hope that these belief systems could be reshaped. In *Ameri-
can Transcendentalism and Asiatic Religion*, Versluis observes a striking
tension in Emerson's assimilation of ideas like transmigration "with which
he did not fully concur."[34] Indeed, while classical metempsychosis and
Hindu reincarnation provided Emerson with a dynamic conception of the
soul's journey through the historical series, they are conceptions none-
theless that he warily adapted to modern consciousness. In much of his
writing, Emerson warns against accepting past beliefs too literally, while
consistently identifying metempsychosis as one of the primary religious
and philosophical foundations for the vital, human activity of think-
ing through a series—and it is precisely upon this ground that Emerson

advocates the domain of modern science. As the German philosopher F. W. J. Schelling so succinctly argues in *The Ages of the World* (1815), "Where there is no succession, there is no science."[35] So, for Emerson, being's series and the eye that follows its course are part of a new scientific inquiry that embraces the older metaphysical models even while necessarily transforming them to address the emerging tensions of the age.

Another distinct and important feature differentiates Emerson's conception of metempsychosis from the classical, Hindu, and esoteric view of an individual soul inhabiting various bodies. While Emerson emphasizes the individual's heightened perception in the enactment of metempsychosis, a perception that ultimately culminates in new creation, the soul's progress entails more than simply inhabiting bodies, which are successively discarded or abandoned by soul. In contrast to the metempsychotic traditions he adapted,[36] Emerson's metempsychosis includes the feature of matter's accompanying adaptation through an ascension of state. As he writes in "History," the "soul's advances are not made by gradation, such as can be represented by motion in a straight line; but rather *by ascension of state*, such as can be represented by metamorphosis,—from the egg to the worm, from the worm to the fly" (*W* 2: 163; emphasis added). Scholars have largely chosen to emphasize metamorphosis in Emerson's thought, but this emphasis ignores Emerson's explicit and recurring espousal of what can only be termed a developmental or evolutionary metempsychosis.[37]

In his early journals and lectures particularly, Emerson's desire for a new synthesis between metaphysics and science is palpable. In fact, one of the key lines in "History" that illustrates how this "metempsychosis of nature" is to be enacted—"Every mind must know the whole lesson for itself" (*W* 2: 6)—was first recorded[38] in an 1837 journal that explicitly contextualizes such activity as part of the "Progress of the species" whereby "the chemical production of a new substance [is made] by the combination of old" (*JMN* 5: 384). Whereas traditional metempsychosis largely presents the transmigration of souls through successive manifestations without apparent material adaptation, Emerson combines the two traditions, those of metempsychosis and metamorphosis, into a more open-ended model, an order capable of encompassing the transmigration of soul and transformation of matter simultaneously. Being's metempsychotic unfolding becomes more than simply a spiritual feat, and Emerson conceives of this process as an implicit criticism and reinterpretation of both metaphysics and science and their relationship to each other, much as the German Idealists had done before and after the turn of the century.

Accordingly, Emerson envisions his adapted form of metempsychosis as a synthesis between seemingly discordant positions, integrating an understanding of material evolution[39] within a new form of alchemy.

Once again, it is possible to trace a prehistory for this new conception of metempsychosis in Emerson's earlier thought. Emerson's emphasis upon the individual's ability to apprehend all the historical series of being in 1841 directly echoes his much earlier concerns regarding eighteenth- and nineteenth-century discoveries of science, particularly those of geology, biology, and physics, and the problems they pose to humanity's place in creation. His earliest lecture on science in 1833 illustrates his desire to re-store the sublimity of "man" in the face of the ever-expanding geological chronicle of the world. If "History" argues that the sublime perception of genius watches the monad as it performs the metempsychosis of nature, in the lecture of 1833, the naturalist's observations of nature directly relate to the memory—and, by implication, power—of God:[40]

> The traveler casts his eye upon a broken mountainside, and sees nothing to detain his attention a moment. Let Cuvier regard the same thing; in the rough ledges, the different shades and superposition of the strata, his eye is reading as in a book the history of the globe, the changes that were effected by fire, by water, by pressure, by friction in ages long prior to the existence of man upon the planet, he is hear-kening to infallible testimony of events whereof is no chronicle but in the memory of God, and taking down minutes of the same for the guidance and confirmation of future inquirers. (*EL* 1: 18)

Foreshadowing the conceptual framework of "History," which presents genius' vision of metempsychosis as a process of inquiry that uncovers the sequence in nature, Emerson's 1833 lecture on science contains the seeds of this concern, reaffirming the human being's perceptual power to unite the spiritual with the world of matter by "reading as in a book the history of the globe" from "ages long prior to the existence of man" and deduc-ing in the present how this "memory" can provide guidance for "future inquirers."

Thus, in the writings of both 1833 and 1841, a trained creative eye gives record where no record could be seen, a record that becomes a guide to fellow human beings, allowing them both a higher perception—"Every fact that is disclosed to us in natural history removes one scale more from the eye" (*EL* 1: 15)—and a knowledge of their own place in creation: "The knowledge of all the facts of all the laws of nature will give man his true place in the system of being" (*EL* 1: 23). By virtue of consciousness' self-reflection, the individual unites separate realities by following out the se-quence of facts chronologically from past to present into the future: "Where is it these fair creatures (in whom an order and series is so distinctly dis-cernable) find their link, their cement, their keystone, but in the Mind of Man? It is he who marries the visible to the Invisible by united thought to

Animal Organization" (*EL* 1: 24). Only by following out the sequence by virtue of self-reflection can a human being achieve his true self. As a result, the individual who necessarily sets out for himself a pedagogical project must pursue it with constancy in order to become himself, following out a project at once metempsychotic—since the combination of soul and matter and the sequence they make are essential to its formation—and scientific, requiring the observation and systemization of a material sequence while never discounting the role of the observer in shaping the reality he sees.

In his emphasis upon the classification of nature, moreover, the young Emerson was influenced by Goethe, particularly his work, *Metamorphosis of Plants* (1790). He found in this treatise what he sought most: the seeds for a higher form of science that could arrive at a "theory of animated nature" that would become "the true Classification" (*JMN* 4: 288–89). As Robert Richardson Jr. observes, this desire for a true classification[41]—hinging not upon a static order, but upon life as process and interrelation—was "a premonition of what Darwin would do" except that Emerson "was interested in a kind of science that was not purely material or mechanical"; he desired to formulate, as Goethe had done, a theory in which "the Actual and the Ideal may again meet together."[42]

In an 1834 journal, this desire for a greater synthesis of spiritual and scientific discovery is distinctly evident in how Emerson begins to align the classical, esoteric and Romantic traditions in relation to metempsychosis. Indicating that Goethe's scientific treatise, Pythagorean metempsychosis and Emmanuel Swedenborg's spiritual system must be "integrated," Emerson argues that each viewpoint provides the materials necessary for progressive observation and experimentation.[43] That same year, in his 1834 address to the Boston Natural History Society, Emerson refined his conception of adapting the metempsychotic prototype. Criticizing the naturalist for "losing sight of the end of his inquiries" and becoming "an apothecary [. . .] in the perfection of his manipulations" (*EL* 1: 79), Emerson also condemns the poet of his age for "los[ing] himself in imaginations and for want of accuracy" (*EL* 1: 79). What is needed, Emerson asserts, is a new adaptation that takes the strengths of both inquiries, spiritual and scientific, and integrates them so that a new combination of truth will arise, capable of renewing the delineations of past metempsychotic theories:

> Men of extraordinary powers of a contemplative mind have in all
> ages pondered this secret: Pythagoras, Swedenborg, Goethe, not to
> mention the Brahmins. These have sought to give an explanation
> of Nature; of beasts, plants, and minerals. [. . .] Pythagoras said
> that the soul of man endured penance in the low forms of ferocious,

gluttonous, obscene beasts. The pig was the purgatory of the glutton. A like faith had the Brahmin. Swedenborg taught that the soul creates evermore the body; that certain affections clothe themselves in certain forms as cunning in the fox, innocence in the lamb, cruelty in the laughing hyena. These opinions have failed to persuade men of their truth *and yet are all valuable as the materials of truth*, as proofs of an obstinate belief in the human mind that these creatures have a relation to itself. (*EL* 1: 79; emphasis added)

Each theory, by itself, fails to persuade the contemporary interpreter, although each serves as a prototype that he or she can convert into a finer formulation. Thus, as all life continuously adapts and reformulates itself to live in the present, so too, according to Emerson, does human thought participate in this evolutionary-like climb—from Pythagorean and Hindu reincarnation to Swedenborg's sequential incarnation of soul[44] to Goethe's attempt to reconcile the actual and ideal, always requiring, as we saw in "Nature," "new lands, new men, [and] new thoughts."

Unlike the earlier Idealism of the seventeenth and early eighteenth centuries, Emerson's depiction of the metempsychotic mind embraces the later Romantic conception that soul and matter are, on one level, in perpetual struggle and that it is precisely this relational conflict and the prospect of future unity that allow the advent of qualitative change. The German Idealism formulated primarily by Kant and Schiller, with which both Goethe and Coleridge struggled, presented the Romantic sublime as man's ability to "transcend the boundaries of the phenomenal world and discover the divine power and freedom of the mind."[45] The later Romantic tradition countered this position by giving priority to the unity of mind and matter, rather than the escape from matter.[46] Michael Lopez correctly situates Emerson's struggle with early Idealist philosophy within its Hegelian context,[47] stating that Hegel's attempt to synthesize contradiction and unify the humanities and sciences into a "single cosmic vision [. . .] roused Emerson's as well as Whitman's interest in him."[48] Indeed, Hegel's philosophical system remains one of the best touchstones for Emerson's metempsychotic mind with its express aim of depicting how consciousness realizes itself from out of the materials of historical progression. In his famous lectures on the *Philosophy of History* (1837), for instance, Hegel argues that Spirit's numerous, successive incarnations through history are "evolved in relation to individual existence" in "the idea of *Metempsychosis* [. . . whereby] Spirit—consuming the envelope of its existence—does not merely pass into another envelope, nor rise rejuvenescent from the ashes of its previous form." Instead, it "comes forth exalted, glorified, a purer spirit" because "in this very destruction it works up that existence into a new form."[49]

Hegel's reconception of Spirit, essence, or soul as a radically indeterminate principle that ceaselessly reconceives itself helps to illuminate the unsettled metaphysical ethos of Emersonianism. For Hegel, a perpetual dialectic between Spirit and its object wherein destruction leads to the advent of new form at once affirms an "inherent principle" in man and yet unsettles its coherence, since Spirit ceaselessly transforms itself in rendering and comprehending the historical series of being: "The result of this process is then that Spirit, in rendering itself objective and making this its being an object of thought, on the one hand destroys the determinate form of its being, on the other hand gains a comprehension of the universal element which it involves, and thereby gives a new form to its inherent principle."[50] Spirit makes itself the object of its determinate thought but, as Hegel argues further in *The Phenomenology of Spirit*, such a consummation of spirit in being is too much for the object to hold—the World-Spirit incarnating and lingering over every moment, embodying "in each shape as much of its entire content as that shape was capable of holding" and then discarding these shapes in pursuit of its future fulfillment.[51] In Hegel, Spirit's activity does not really abandon its object; in that space between objects, the outline of a series can be discerned, since the previous object is passed over or, as we saw above, consumed anew and reformed in its present activity. Spirit's shell, as it were, is discarded, even while its materials are taken up onto a higher level.[52] More properly, the discarded object can be seen in the new pattern that Spirit makes, since in order to understand the progression, one must attempt to inhabit the series as it had been engendered by Spirit.

Emerson himself is adamant in this regard, for each soul must go over the whole ground of history before it can engender unity. In "History," this pattern is one that the mind enacts in and through material organization, not above it. Such an emphasis is decidedly Hegelian, for the German philosopher, in his *Phenomenology of Spirit*, explicitly articulates that this movement of World-Spirit over and beyond its manifestations comprises a pattern of consciousness, whose experience consists of successively embodying and discarding itself in order to know itself on ever-higher levels. Consciousness seeks an object, and in this effort, the object it perceives changes and springs anew as an addition to the series that consciousness undertakes. Because it cannot totally apprehend and grasp its object, at least for now, consciousness carries itself and its aim, to be united with itself without anything alien to it, into the new object, thereby initiating or perpetuating its experience of being's series:

Consciousness knows *something*; this object is the essence or the *in-itself*; but it is also for consciousness the in-itself. This is where the ambiguity of this truth enters. We see that consciousness now has two objects: one is the first in-itself, the second is the *being-for-consciousness of this in-itself*. The latter appears at first sight to be merely the reflection of consciousness into itself, i.e. what consciousness has in mind is not an object, but only its knowledge of that first object. But [. . .] the first object, in being known, is altered for consciousness; it ceases to be the in-itself, and becomes something that is the *in-itself* only *for consciousness*. And this then is the True: the being-for-consciousness of this in-itself. Or, in other words, this is the *essence*, or the *object* of consciousness. This new object contains the nothingness of the first, it is what experience has made of it.[53]

The complexity of Hegel's argument can, for our purposes, be simplified in order to emphasize that being's series—the succession of objects that arises for consciousness—expands to engender a new object that is different from the object before it. Consciousness seeks a purity, a complete self-reflection, that it does not already possess, and this is why at each stage—when consciousness attempts to know itself and, thereby, tries to unite with its object—a new pattern of consciousness emerges; the new object is "what experience has made of it," since this activity changes the material determination:

Herewith a new pattern of consciousness comes on the scene as well, for which the essence is something different from what it was at the preceding stage. It is this fact that guides the entire series of the patterns of consciousness in their necessary sequence. But it is just this necessity itself, or the *origination* of the new object, that presents itself to consciousness without its understanding how this happens, which proceeds for us, as it were, behind the back of consciousness. Thus in the movement of consciousness there occurs a moment of *being-in-itself* or *being-for-us* which is not present to the consciousness comprehended in the experience itself. The *content*, however, of what presents itself to us does exist for it; we comprehend only the formal aspect of that content, or its pure origination. *For it*, what has thus arisen exists only as an object; *for us*, it appears at the same time as movement and a process of becoming.[54]

As one can see, Hegel's logic is always double—at every point, there is a simultaneity of perspectives—but, in simpler terms, Hegel demonstrates that consciousness' understanding of its object inexorably allows the object—its very essence—to change and, therein, become distinguishable from the first object of consciousness, thereby generating not simply a series of objects, but most importantly consciousness' experience of this series. From an individual perspective, one sees creation, the emergence of a new becoming, but from another greater, more expansive perspective, this becoming is a reformation of all the objects that came before it.

Poetry and the New Alchemy

For Goethe, the work of the age was to infuse science with spirituality, and Hegel certainly developed this aim into one of the most fully systematized philosophies of the nineteenth century. Emerson's efforts can be seen in conjunction to theirs; he presents metempsychosis as an ever-restless alchemy, where material elements are mixed together to produce original substances. To perceive "identity through endless mutations of form" (W 2: 18), as Emerson observes in "History," can be understood as an activity that combines elements together as in alchemical formation so that "out of unbeliefs a creed shall be formed" (W 3: 43).[55] Emerson's conception of historical alchemy and evolution, moreover, has its roots in his theory of poetic writing. In his meditations upon the power of poetic genius to overcome the dominion of fate, fully entering into creation becomes the ability to realize nature's progress more completely—not to escape natural laws, but to fulfill their "highest forms" (W 3: 112).[56] Accordingly, poetic creation exemplifies how the universe revitalizes itself by turning inward toward the spiritual, preexistent life that animates the material sequence and uses that creative force to form a new material compound so that the series once more aspires toward a finer metempsychotic organization.

In 1841, the same year that he published his *First Series of Essays*, Emerson lectured at the Concord Lyceum on "Nature and the Powers of the Poet." Here, as in "History," Emerson laid out his formulation of genius, juxtaposing various activities—natural, scientific, and poetic—to show how genius participates most fully in the natural order, not by merely understanding it, but by creating it anew out of the materials of the past through a type of alchemical apprehension:[57]

> The sign of genius is originality: its word cannot be guessed: it is new, yet allies with all we know: it has an expected unexpectedness, a new oldness. The bee flies among the flowers and gets mint and marjoram and makes a new product which is not mint and marjoram but honey; and the chemist mixes hydrogen and oxygen to yield a new product which is not hydrogen or oxygen but water: and the poet listens to all conversations, and receives all objects of nature, to give back, not them, but a new and radiant whole. (EL 3: 360)

Like the natural alchemy of the bee, scientist and poet partake in creation, synthesizing what was hitherto disparate and producing an original whole from the various elements of the natural order. Here, a major shift has taken place; Emerson has clearly rejected the traditionally accepted static chain of being[58] in favor of material adaptation. Where the bee uses nature's most basic elements as does the chemist, the poet extends these natural laws to language; he receives all linguistic formulations and mixes them, and because his activity functions in accordance with nature's laws, he fulfills the universal laws with the explicit social aim of revitalizing the means by which humans communicate and build their social organization.

Emerson thereby attributes the privileged activity of creation to the figure of the poet, viewing poetry as exhibiting not merely spiritual power, though it is that too; the poet, a crucial figure in history's metempsychotic process, is himself a timely, historical adaptation of all the disparate elements of material existence. In one sense, the poet is the contemporary effect of nature's immanent progression, finding himself at the end of an ontological series.[59] As he was created, so too does the poet seek to take part in the work of creation and enact nature's succession—and through him the natural laws have their most explicit social fulfillment:

> The Poet shall yet arrive—the fortunate, the adapted man, the timely man, whose heart domesticated in Ideas sees them proclaimed in the face of the world of this Hour, in the men and women of today, and their institutions and covenants, their houses and shops;—who coupling what we do with what we are, the last effect with first cause, shall search the heart and soul with every word he speaks, and [...] adds with every picture insights and presentiments, hopes and fears, and gives to the old dull track of daily life more than the blush and wonder of a lover's dream. (EL 3: 363)

Emerson employs a type of alchemical imagery integrated with his understanding of metempsychotic transmutations: the sequence of cause and effect—and therein the immanent reorganization of material elements—produces reality anew.[60] The poet's work is not simply creative; but it entails the appropriate amelioration of the very properties that comprise the created world: the proper mixture of being with doing—of aligning an ontological series—so as to connect the present moment or hour (that is, the last effect) with its origin, thus producing an emergent vitality in "the old dull track of daily life."

The poet's activity is Emerson's most direct example of how the process of creation brings together metempsychosis and material development. Emerson wonders "what it is that so charms us in a symbol or trope" and argues that we must look "into the heart of nature" (EL 3: 353) to find that poetic language reflects history's aspiring sequence and anticipates a higher activity that only the dual process of metempsychosis-metamorphosis can engender:

> What does all this love for signs denote, if not that the relation of man to these forms in nature is more intimate than the understanding yet suspects; and that perhaps the *metamorphoses* which we read in Latin or in Indian literature[61] are not quite so fabulous as they are accounted?
>
> Who know but more is meant than yet appears? Every gardener can change his flowers and leaves into fruit, and so perhaps is this man who astonishes the senate of the parlor by the splendor of his conversation, who seems to stride over all limits, — this genius who today can upheave and balance and toss every object in nature for his metaphor, capable in his next appearance in human nature of playing such a game with his hands instead of his brain. An instinctive suspicion that this may befall, seems to have crept into the mind of men. Genius may be dangerous. What would happen to us who live on the surface, if this fellow in *some new transmigration* should have *acquired power to do what he now delights to say*? (EL 3: 354; emphases added)

By employing the analogy of a gardener who can "change his flowers and leaves into fruit," Emerson suggests that the metamorphosis of nature, from one state into another, operates as an evolutionary transmigration of soul whose goal is to produce new poetic power. The poet, who merely speaks today, using symbols as his expression, may acquire the ability for a heightened, poetic activity in his next transmigration. Emerson's combination of metempsychosis and metamorphosis also powerfully exemplifies the modern Idealist value of inwardness, how the immanent life potentially guides the fate of the external series. While most men and women "live on the surface," the poet's "intimate" love of signs anticipates the prospect of deepening and enriching the inner life not just of the individual, but of the species in general. As Emerson observes, genius is truly dangerous for those who fail to participate in its adaptive aspiration; compared with the truly adapted man, they may suddenly find themselves mere beasts on the ever-expanding scale of nature.

Unsettling the Metempsychotic Series

While it has been argued that Emerson's humanistic view of transcendent power "retains Christianity's eschatological focus, only with unity, not salvation, as the new goal,"[62] such a summary of Emerson's thought is only partially correct. Certainly, Emerson's thought resonates with Hegel's dialectical formulation of Spirit's pursuit of complete self-knowledge, but Emerson pushes this formulation one step further. Just as Platonic metaphysics stresses the development and education of the mind as a spiritual undertaking that must overcome itself in each instance of contemplation and be radically open to refutation,[63] so Emerson's metempsychotic mind presents itself as a pedagogical enterprise that seizes hold of the materials of the natural and social orders not as ends in themselves, but as part of an open-ended process of adaptation. Unlike Hegel's goal of final unity, Emerson's eschatology continually undermines itself; no single concluding event can be envisioned as a point of final destination.

While Emerson often champions the ability of the human being to assimilate the historical series, he just as often problematizes any such venture. The opening of "Experience" (1844) famously attests to this, since the individual wakens to find himself already midway on an apparently never-ending stairway; he cannot remember how he arrived in his present place nor can he trace out the greater arc of the ontological series rising upward beyond his perceptual range: "We wake and find ourselves on a stair; there are stairs below us, which we seem to have ascended; there are stairs above us, many a one, which go upward and out of sight" (W 3: 27). Here, Emerson presents a very modern predicament: while the steps of the series may suggest a rational construction running from beginning to end, the individual can neither verify nor understand the nature of its construction; all he knows is his own petty place in the sequence of being, and his sequential movement becomes, during the course of the essay, a poverty that he can never fully overcome.

Just as much as this dilemma demonstrates Emerson's skepticism, it also expresses his underlying mystical sensibility. Reverberating powerfully in Emerson's formulation of soul's experience of the metempsychotic series is the Plotinian *amorphon*,[64] a shapeless, unbounded abundance from which all individuation, including Intellect, soul, and body, emanates and to which all seek to return. In his most Neoplatonic essay, "The Over-Soul" (1841), Emerson argues that the soul has just this nature: "The soul in man [. . .] is not a faculty, but a light." It is "the vast background of our being, [. . .] an immensity not possessed and that cannot be possessed."[65] The soul can be understood as that abundance upon which the origin and the series that flows from it are constituted, an abundance which, in numerous other writings, becomes a vanishing point in being, rather than an immanent superfluity. As he writes in "Experience" (1844), "Like the bird, which alights nowhere, but hops perpetually from bough to bough, is the Power which abides in no man and in no woman, but for a moment speaks from this one, and for another moment from that one" (W 3: 34). While the successive movements of the bird from one material fixture to another clearly relate to a spiritual power or soul that is in a process of reincarnation,[66] the whole process is nonetheless fraught with indeterminacy and uncertainty. Nature provides no stable ground with which to catch the spiritual power moving perpetually through its sliding scale of being. The human form and the faculties it possesses are no exception, for the body is but a temporary abode whose solidity and definite proportions tenuously house an absence that "alights nowhere" and "abides in no man and in no woman" (W 3: 34) even as it enacts its unsettled progression through the material world.[67]

Emerson's later lecture series, "Mind and Manners of the Nineteenth Century" (1848–50) and "Natural Method of Mental Philosophy" (1858) upon which the posthumously published and heavily edited Natural History of Intellect (1893) was based, particularly underscores this tension between the abundance or, conversely, vanishing of soul and the human aim to understand its historical expression. While the human being is made from the "the broad, radiating, immensely distributive action" of "the mystic stream," his attempts to chart the nature and course of the stream of life are simply projections of his own linear progression upon it: "If it were linear, if it were successive, step by step, jet by jet, like a small human agency, we could follow with language, but it mocks us by its ubiquity and omnipotence" (LL 2: 74). Yet, despite its all too apparent limits, Emerson nonetheless upholds the "linear" work of "a small human agency" that gradually learns to follow out the spiritual progression in matter in its own little way. "Many men have taken their first step" along history's series, but, Emerson argues, the "Divine Effort in a man" consists in escaping the tyranny of the singular self and struggling to embody the fuller arc of the material series: "All great masters are chiefly distinguished by the power of adding a second, a third, and perhaps a fourth step, in a continuous line" (LL 1: 157; or LL 2: 92).

Emerson also explicitly imagines the dynamics of extending history's great series of being in terms of metempsychosis, Neoplatonic in its auspices and necessarily open to the prospect of volatile and transcendent transformation. He cautions that "it is very easy to push the doctrine into vagaries and into burlesque. Pythagoras and Plato taught it in grave earnest: The comic Poets and the Hindoo priests exaggerated it into the transmigration of Souls who remembered in one state what befell them in another." Yet despite the difficulty of speaking about the soul, Emerson reaffirms the value of the metempsychotic metaphor for the activity of Intellect:

> But the necessities of the human mind, of logic, and of nature require the admission of a profound identity at the base of things to account for our skill, and even for our desire for knowledge. Somewhere,

sometime, some eternity, we have played this game before, and have retained some vague memory of the thing, which, though not sufficient to furnish an account of it, yet enables us to understand it better, now that we are here. (*LL* 1: 161)

Emerson both reminds his audience not to fix too literal a meaning to the metempsychosis of mind and acknowledges it as a way in which human beings can begin to think about the science of cognition. One can also sense the characteristic caution of Emerson's approach in his insistence that every discovery quickly reveals its limitations and requires another step, even if the inquirer is yet incapable of such a feat. Human beings repeat themselves; the "divine energy," on the other hand, "never rests or repeats itself; but casts its old garb, and reappears, another creature; the old energy in a new form, with all the vigor of the earth, the Ancient of Days in the dew of the morning" (*LL* 1: 179). The soul shuffles off one body only to take another, fitter form, a process clearly metempsychotic, yet new at every moment in a way that evades systematization.

Emerson instills this uneasy tension between soul and consciousness into every level of his subject matter. Even the most "profound identity at the base of things" soon becomes the most treacherous of grounds; it is "an ocean of power roll[ing] and stream[ing] this way and that, through million channels." And the poet who "beholds the central identity" and "following it, can detect essential resemblances in things never before named together" does so because he understands that "his own body also is a fleeing apparition, his personality as fugitive as any type, as fugitive as the trope he employs" (*LL* 1: 163). Thus, the foundation of being is itself transitional, with the mind's poetic power also expressing itself in the movement to new states: "In the instinct of progress, the mind is always passing—by successive leaps,—forward into new states, and, in that transition, is its health and power. The detachment which thought effects is the preparation for this step" (*LL* 1: 168). The mind's ability to detach from its object (*LL* 2: 93) thereby allows consciousness to see itself in succession: "It is the nature of the human mind to see in succession the facts or laws of nature as the eye looks at one or another object" (*LL* 2: 77).

How Emerson depicts such succession, however, is complex, at once echoing his earlier portrayals of metempsychotic and metamorphic transformation and broadening their scope within the context of Neoplatonic hierarchies, developed from Plotinus (and, of course, earlier from Plato's *Symposium*) through Iamblichus and Proclus. "It is a steep stair down from the essence of Intellect Pure to thoughts and intellections," writes Emerson, situating his subject within the Neoplatonic triadic structure of abiding, procession, and conversion as a "science of degrees," which he also

maps onto natural phenomena, arguing that the creation of the planets fol-
lows the mystical emanation of "the first mind."[68] Reaffirming his life-long
desire for a fuller, emergent philosophy of mind in which metaphysics and
science are united, Emerson depicts how "the perceptions of a soul" *enact*
creation, passing from one mind and body to the next incarnation, while
carrying the original purpose that caused them to proceed into thought
and matter: "They are detached from their parent, they pass into other
minds; ripened and unfolded by many they hasten to incarnate themselves
in action, to take body, only to carry forward the will which sent them out"
(*LL* 2: 95–96). Emerson's description resonates with both a Neoplatonic
worldview and one of the main principles of Hegelianism, for, as he makes
clear, the soul does not simply make the body; in its transformative experi-
ence, the soul changes by learning to grasp itself, however incompletely,
on higher levels of being: "The thought buries itself in the new thought of
larger scope, which sprung from it—its new creations and forwarder tri-
umphs, whilst the old instrumentalities and incarnations are decomposed
and recomposed into new" (*LL* 2: 96).

As much as this metempsychotic structure helps to clarify Emerson's
"science of mind," one should not discount his persistent desire for inspi-
ration or illumination to transform mere structure into living reality. For
Emerson, the systematizing of mind as metempsychotic, metamorphic, or
evolutionary only reduces a way of thinking that must be radically open
to the possibility of inspiration and, thus, to miracle and transformation.
Emerson's admiration for the Christian esotericism of Jacob Böhme (1575–
1624) and Emmanuel Swedenborg (1688–1772)[69] particularly attests to this
value of mystical illumination over systemization. In "Swedenborg, or the
Mystic" of *Representative Men* (1850), Emerson emphasizes the mystic's
power to gain "access to the secrets and structure of nature, by some higher
method than by experience" (*W* 4: 54). Comparing the two men, Emer-
son finds Böhme "healthily and beautifully wise"; "he is tremulous with
emotion, and listens awestruck with the gentlest humanity to the Teacher
whose lessons he conveys, and when he asserts that, 'in some sort, love is
greater than God,' his heart beats so high that the thumping against his
leathern coat is audible across the centuries" (*W* 4: 76).[70] While Emerson
admires Swedenborg's mysticism as a "path [that] is difficult, secret and
beset with terror" (*W* 4: 55), he nonetheless disapproves of it for being far
too orderly:[71] "The more coherent and elaborate the system, the less I like
it" (*W* 4: 76). Once realized, Swedenborg's doctrine of correspondences,
the Neoplatonic-inspired belief that "the mental series exactly tallies with
the material series" (*W* 4: 66), serves only to systematize oppressively, since
it is entirely predetermined by the spiritual power that manifests itself in
being.[72]

Accordingly, Emerson criticizes Swedenborg for attempting "to reanimate" the past, "by attaching [himself] to the Christian symbol" (*W* 4: 76) and making a temporary form the fixture of truth: "Yet Swedenborg after his mode pinned his theory to a temporary form" (*W* 4: 72). Still, in Emerson's view, Swedenborg was the first truly modern thinker, the "first [to] put the fact [that the spirit pervades the living body] into a detached and scientific statement" (*W* 4: 66). And it is precisely this metempsychotic formulation that redeems the Swedish mystic in Emerson's eyes and makes him a representative man of history. The true secret of Swedenborg's mystical intuition lies in remembering the lives that the soul has hitherto inhabited and reuniting this historical knowledge in present consciousness:

> If one should ask the reason of this intuition, the solution would lead us into that property which Plato denoted as Reminiscence, and which is implied by the Bramins in the tenet of Transmigration. The soul having been often born, or, as the Hindoos say, "traveling the path of existence through thousands of births," having beheld the things which are here, those which are in heaven, and those which are beneath, there is nothing of which she has not gained the knowledge: no wonder that she is able to recollect in regard to any one thing what she formerly knew. "For, all things in nature being linked and related, and the soul having heretofore known all, nothing hinders but that any man who has recalled to mind, or, according to the common phrase, has learned one thing only, should of himself recover all his ancient knowledge, and find out again all the rest, if he have but courage, and faint not in the midst of his researches." How much more, if he that inquires be a holy and godlike soul. (*W* 4: 54–55)

Emerson once again gives one of his most straightforward presentations of metempsychosis as a courageous endeavor or quest, relying on the traditions of West and East—Greek and Hindu—that tell of the soul's path through numerous forms and of the higher, sacred ability to recall the soul's passage through the material world. The interconnected objects of nature take on a rational and knowable sequence within such a metaphysical context, and this is precisely why Emerson so highly esteems Swedenborg's science of metempsychosis, which presents the individual with the specific task to "recover all his ancient knowledge."

In his assessment of Swedenborg, therefore, Emerson clearly expresses his own thought and champions the "subjective" element in the metempsychosis of nature: the individual begins by reading history, soon learning to propel himself through its material sequence and to unify its disparate, dying structure into a new, living whole. Here, the process of willing[73] the series toward a new form "depends entirely upon the thought of the person".[74]

> That metempsychosis which is familiar in the old mythology of the Greeks, collected in Ovid and in the Indian Transmigration, and is there objective, or really takes place in bodies by alien will,- in Swedenborg's mind has a more philosophic character. It is subjective, or depends entirely upon the thought of the person. All things in the universe arrange themselves to each person anew, according to his ruling love. Man is such as his affection and thought are. Man is man by virtue of willing, not by virtue of knowing and understanding. (*W* 4: 70)

Emerson explicitly transforms the chain of being—from vegetative and animal life to human sentience and beyond to celestial consciousness—into a self-propelling evolution of consciousness. Every step in the series of being signifies not just traditional metempsychosis, where the spirit inhabits successive bodies, but an adaptive and evolutionary transmigration that values the subjective element directing and willing the material world to adapt.

Here again, nineteen years after the *First Series of Essays*, we see the precise brushstrokes of the metempsychotic mind of "History"—although Emerson's desire to unsettle the relation between soul and consciousness is now even stronger. Emerson at once criticizes the "magnetic sleep" of Swedenborg's spiritual universe and redeems the Swedish mystic by imagining him as a transmigrating Indian votary situated in a sea-storm where the only foundation to which men cling is sinking, forcing the pilot to choose "with science" and adhere to his "brave choice":

> In the shipwreck, some cling to running-rigging, some to cask and barrel, some to spars, some to mast; the pilot chooses with science, — I plant myself here, all will sink before this [. . .]. Nothing can keep you, not fate, nor health, nor admirable intellect, none can keep you but rectitude only, rectitude forever and ever! And with a tenacity that never swerved in all his studies, inventions, dreams, he adheres to this brave choice. I think of him as of some transmigrating votary of Indian legend, who says, though I be dog, or jackal, or pismire, in the last rudiments of nature, under what integument or ferocity, I cleave to right, as the ladder that leads up to man and to God. (*W* 4: 81)

Emerson reprises the metempsychotic order not as a fixed series running from beginning to end, but as a protean sequence, which at once threatens to strip the individual of everything he is and yet affirms his own aspiring passage on the ladder of creation.[75] Consequently, Emerson advocates not so much Swedenborgian metempsychosis, but his own adapted version of this individual and cosmic order that at once threatens and sustains the inquirer of knowledge with its oscillation of presence and absence, continuity and disruption.

The Idealist desire for a single cosmic vision certainly influenced Emerson's metempsychotic depictions, but just as surely as Emerson expresses a desire for a unifying system, he consistently unsettles any straightforward correspondence between soul and body, signified and signifier. With this uneasy tension between systematization and transformative illumination, Emerson captures part of the character of Neoplatonism itself, for though later Neoplatonists like Iamblichus and Proclus elaborately systematized the mystical tradition they inherited, they always stress the overarching importance of the *beyond*, an opening in thinking that uses the hierarchy of Intellect, but is willing to abandon it in the ecstasy of the spirit.[76] From the vantage point of modern subjectivity, this value consists in the mind opening itself up, rather than in its constrictive ability to grasp and control—and Emerson gives this process emphatic lyrical expression in "The Sphinx," a poem he considered his most important achievement. What was in the *First Series of Essays* the conversion of a metempsychotic sequence into a living reality becomes, in "The Sphinx," a riddle that has no absolute answer and can only be addressed by learning the elusive art of living through a thousand natures in pursuit of an open-ended question:

> "Thou are the unanswered question;
>   Couldst see thy proper eye,
> Always it asketh, asketh;
>   And each answer is a lie.
> So take thy quest through nature
>   It through thousand natures ply;
> Ask on, thou clothed eternity;
>   Time is the false reply."[77]

Much like the "whole line of temples and sphinxes and catacombs" in "History" that must be lived through so as to reinvigorate the mind in the "Now," the Sphinx has to awaken herself from stony slumber by conversing with her soul. The dynamics of this awakening again modify the metempsychotic metaphor that Emerson so prominently adapted throughout his career: consciousness awakening into living being through the experience of its own succession. The Sphinx's self-transcendent experience hinges upon purifying perception so as to see with "proper eye" the unfolding of eternity in time or the spiritual in the material but without overly determining their relationship.

The Sphinx's quest through a thousand natures thereby resonates with the metempsychotic procession into, and conversion out of, matter, but is in no way limited to it. We see, already prefigured in Emerson, the transformation of metaphysics into the modern paradigm of metatextuality, for "The Sphinx" is not simply metempsychotic, but a figurative method of bridging the gap between selves. In realizing that she is the unanswered question of being, the Sphinx rises up, "crouched no more in stone," and yet scatters herself into a "thousand natures" so that she will be able once again to evoke the question of being with all the experience she has gained from her repeated dissolutions and self-constitutions:

> Uprose the merry Sphinx,
>   And crouched no more in stone;
> She melted into purple cloud,
>   She silvered into the moon;
> She spired into a yellow flame;
>   She flowered in blossoms red;
> She flowed into a foaming wave;
>   She stood Monadnoc's head.
>
> Through a thousand voices
>   Spoke the universal dame:
> "Who telleth one of my meanings,
>   Is master of all I am."

Here, illumination paradoxically arises out of, and yet threatens, all of Intellect's various self-constitutions. We no longer have one self operating in "The Sphinx," but a dynamic scattering of the self and a resulting openness beyond the confines of lyrical expression. Inasmuch as perception is an individual, self-constituting activity, the opening of "the proper eye" to its own manifold succession also represents, for Emerson, the abandonment and simultaneous recovery of the self in the absent or not-yet living reader. The Sphinx's final address is both authoritative—she speaks with the experience of a thousand lives—yet the question she evokes demands a response that now falls squarely on the shoulders of the audience. The metempsychotic pattern that opens itself to illumination implicitly points beyond itself not to an eternal repetition[78] of the same structure, but to *other* consciousnesses not yet present in the poetic play of abandonments and self-constitutions, other selves who will ask the question in new ways and under different auspices.

2 / The Double Consciousness

According to many contemporary scholars, Emerson does not accept any preestablished philosophical position, but exercises a type of radical, individualistic freedom by taking various views in hand and escaping them. He is consistent only in one venture: he takes "the risk of exalting transition for its own sake."[1] Indeed, Emerson does not offer an absolutist portrait of either consciousness or cosmos with his conception of the metempsychotic mind. On the contrary, "the metempsychosis of nature" or the spirit in "transition" from being to being thwarts our desire for order. As Emerson writes in "Circles" (1841), "The soul looketh steadily forwards, creating a world before her, leaving worlds behind her. She has no dates, nor rites, nor persons, nor specialties, nor men. The soul knows only the soul; the web of events is the flowing robe in which she is clothed" (W 2: 163). As the soul looks forward beyond the present into an unknown, unwritten future, the world that flies out behind the soul to be incorporated into a new manifestation of being has to be radically discarded: "In nature, every moment is new; the past is always swallowed and forgotten; the coming only is sacred. Nothing is secure but life, transition, the energizing spirit. No love can be bound by oath or covenant to secure it against a higher love. No truth so sublime but it may be trivial tomorrow in the light of new thoughts. People wish to be settled: only as far as they are unsettled, is there any hope for them" (W 2: 189).

While Emerson so often makes his audience "feel delight with him in the spectacle of contrariety,"[2] this radical unsettling of any experience is not an end in itself. From the early 1830s onward, Emerson conceives of metempsychosis as part of a tradition of knowledge that has been, and continues to be, successively adapted by "great men" who perceive more ably than their contemporaries the ontological sequence running through history and the secret spiritual law animating its order. Emerson's consideration of Western and Eastern metaphysics is consistent with a larger intellectual project: to approach the idea of metempsychosis, the journey of the soul through matter, as a way of depicting an emergent conception of consciousness. In order to elucidate both the roots and the character of Emerson's unsettled consciousness, this chapter will examine his refiguring of the Platonic ladder of ascent and emphasize his depiction of the lover's progress to "substance,"[3] as a highly precarious journey, especially since the "perfect beatitude" sought by each lover and enacted by "the progress of the soul" must "be succeeded and supplanted [...] for ever" (W 2: 110). In pursuing this emergent structure, Emerson interweaves two independent, but resonating systems, which he terms in 1841 and 1860 "the double consciousness,"[4] on the one hand, consciousness grounded materially in time and space and, on the other, the life of the soul in the future. These two patterns, one experiential and the other transcendent, are not simply in conflict. In their interaction, they compose a cohesive, but tenuous cosmology that operates according to two gravitational forces, an aspiring, upward metempsychotic activity and a corresponding downward mimesis.

Emerson's ingenuity is perhaps most pronounced in his adaptation of Platonic mimesis; he is able to establish and interweave two contradictory values into the fluctuating pattern of double consciousness. On the one hand, he maintains the univocal power of the soul over the material world in *the order of genesis*; on the other hand, he argues that the soul and the body are equal in *the order of time*. Unlike Swedenborg, Emerson maintains that true marriage is only possible in time and, thus, the material world is not a copy of divine essence, but a necessary feature in the soul's eternal development. In this way, he preserves the metaphysical, Neoplatonic tradition he so admired, while arguing for a transcendental "reconciler" capable of embracing a pervasive equality in order to marry incongruent properties.[5] Emerson's depiction of the soul's recurrent upward and downward progression with its fluctuating values provides an interpretative key to Emerson's poem "Uriel" and its intertextual dialogue with the philosophy of Hegel. Here and elsewhere, Emerson advocates the essential circularity of the double consciousness, a complex intermingling of gravitational forces that compose their unsettled play not simply in the larger circuits of the universe, but in "the eye and brain of every man."

Consciousness Divided

From his earliest lectures to his mature writings, Emerson's use of dialectic[6] draws attention to one of the most vital, yet elusive features of his thought: *the double consciousness*.[7] First termed so in the lecture, "The Transcendentalist" (1841), delivered the same year as the publication of the *First Series of Essays*, the double consciousness denotes an implicit, unsolvable dilemma for the maturing thinker. No matter how much he may desire unity, the human being is an entity divided between his own present, embodied understanding and the urge of the soul, which evades time and space and stands, as it were, beyond material consciousness in the future: "The worst feature of this double consciousness is, that *the two lives, of the understanding and of the soul*, which we lead, really show very little relation to each other, never meet and measure each other: *one prevails now, all buzz and din; and the other prevails then, all infinitude and paradise*; and with the progress of life, the two discover no greater disposition to reconcile themselves" (*W* 1: 213–14; emphases added). Emerson outlines the conflict of the double consciousness and laments the fact that the understanding and the soul will not "reconcile themselves." Human consciousness in time and the soul's future privilege become two principles of order, one prevalent in the ontological present, "now," and the other in the spiritual future, "then." For Emerson, these two paradigms represent "two states of thought [that] diverge every moment, and stand in wild contrast" (*W* 1: 213), indicating that neither the physical nor the metaphysical can attain absolute preeminence over the other. Both perspectives must be entertained, for they form the oscillating character of the universe, a dialectical cosmos that aspires toward ever-greater complexity and interconnection, without apparent beginning or end.

One of the most decisive influences upon Emerson's double consciousness was Samuel Taylor Coleridge's rejection of Lockean epistemology. In *The Transcendentalists*, Barbara Packer recounts the influence of Coleridge's thought on Unitarianism and the development of the transcendentalist movement in New England. In 1829, James Marsh, the president of the University of Vermont, published an American edition of Coleridge's *Aids to Reflection* (1825), which won Marsh "converts among the very Unitarians he had made no effort to attract. The young Boston liberals had little interest in Marsh's attempt to place the doctrines of the Trinity or the Atonement upon firm metaphysical grounds. But they loved his attack upon the philosophical system they detested."[8] In *Aids to Reflection*, Coleridge's distinction between Reason and Understanding helped to salvage the idea of the soul from the philosophical legacy of John Locke. For Coleridge, "*Reason* is the supersensuous, intuitive power, at once the source of morality and of the highest kind of intellection," and "the *Understanding* is the humbler servant which works by combining and comparing ideas derived from sensation."[9] While Emerson's double consciousness is nearly identical to Coleridge's model, there is one very significant difference. Emerson does not insist upon Coleridge's hierarchy where the understanding is the "humbler servant" of the immaterial, higher consciousness. Instead, these two sides of the self are equal, each claiming one side of the human being, one prevailing now, while the other achieves ascendency in the future.

Emerson's notion of double consciousness has direct implications for the psychological makeup of nineteenth-century American individuality not simply because it divides the self into two parts, but because it imagines the soul as an as-yet-unattainable principle of radical otherness. Where Locke makes the soul an unnecessary aspect of intellection, Emerson's desire to validate the soul—the living spark that, according to traditional metaphysics, initiates the material series and invigorates it—becomes the preoccupation of temporal consciousness, which wishes to overcome itself strangely enough through experiencing its own nature. In much of his oeuvre, Emerson depicts metempsychosis as a cognitive attempt to heal the two sides of the self, to bring consciousness together in acts of perception and self-knowing. In the "Sphinx" (1848), for instance, he outlines a poetic methodology whose aim is not simply to achieve a grand metempsychotic assimilation of "a thousand natures" into the domain of consciousness, but to heal the psychic fragmentation to which consciousness is prone. The Sphinx learns to answer its own question—learns, in order words, to become human and self-directing, unfastening itself from a static incapacity, a mimetic entrapment that only a heightened act of consciousness can overcome.

In the opening lines of "Experience" (1844), Emerson invokes the metempsychotic self of "History" as just such a site of spiritual and psychic crisis. Directly addressing his readers, he declares that we, like the souls in Plato's Myth of Er in the last book of *The Republic*, have been purged of all our knowledge of past lives by Lethe's waters. Metempsychosis, in this case, evokes a dilemma of consciousness not easily answered, for doubt permeates human awareness. Consequently, we glide ghostlike through nature in search of self-knowledge so as to answer a most basic question:

> Where do we find ourselves? In a series, of which we don't know the
> extremes, and believe that it has none. We wake and find ourselves
> on a stair: there are stairs below us, which we seem to have ascended;
> there are stairs above us, many a one, which go upward and out of
> sight. But the Genius which, according to the old belief, stands at the

door by which we enter, and gives us the lethe to drink, that we may tell no tales, mixed the cup too strongly, and we cannot shake off the lethargy now at noonday. [...] Ghostlike we glide through nature, and should not know our place again. (W 3: 27)

Like the transmigrating individual of "History" who is only *half-human*, the self in "Experience" wakes to find himself *midway* on an apparently never-ending stairway of ascent. Although he cannot remember how he arrived in this present place on the stair that rises upward beyond his perceptual range, he must attempt to recollect the greater arc of the ontological series so as to "know [his] place again." While every object is potentially capable of self-constitution, of drawing itself together into a living conscious whole, the individual finds in the course of time that he "lacks the affirmative principle" and has "no superfluity of spirit for new creation." "Ah that our Genius were a little more of a genius!" Emerson writes. "We are like millers on the lower levels of a stream, when the factories above them have exhausted the water. We too fancy that the upper people must have raised their dams" (W 3: 27). Indeed, the search for the unity that the soul can potentially bestow is a decisive theme. As he had done with cognition in the *First Series of Essays*, Emerson implicitly maps the metempsychotic dilemma of consciousness onto the emerging modern industrial character of America itself. Somehow, he implies, the relation of the individual to the world about him is disproportionate; the citizen yearns for a new nation, capable of yielding the creation of new men with new thoughts. Nonetheless, the individual is barred from entering this new land not simply because others have prevented him, but because he cannot fully or freely constitute himself anew. The description of the millers on the lower levels of a stream subtly contextualizes economic and social inequality in direct relation to the individual's inability to comprehend his greater social relations. We "fancy" that those above us have brought us to ruin, but we cannot know for sure, since the gap between our present doubt and the prospect of future certainty remains the unbridgeable divide that the double consciousness imposes upon the self.

What is at stake in the structure of this divided self is no less than the discovery of American nationhood. "I am ready to die out of nature and be born again into this new yet unapproachable America," Emerson declares later in "Experience," reinstating both the desire and doubt that haunts the opening of the essay in yet another figuration of metempsychosis.[10] Emerson's pronouncement is representative, moreover, of a far larger literary and cultural anxiety that permeated antebellum America. In *The Sketch Book of Geoffrey Crayon* (1819–20), Washington Irving anticipates Emerson's mixture of mysticism and doubt in a meditation upon the art of bookmaking and proposes the structure of metempsychosis as a potential solution.[11] At first awed by the "extreme fecundity of the press" and puzzled "how it comes to pass that so many heads, on which nature seemed to have inflicted the curse of barrenness, should teem with voluminous productions," Irving's narrator finds a fantastical answer to the "mysteries of the bookmaking craft."[12] He puts "an end to [his] astonishment" by realizing that bookmaking itself "submit[s] to the great law of nature, which declares that all sublunary shapes of matter shall be limited in their duration, but which decrees also that their elements shall never perish":

> The beauties and fine thoughts of ancient and obsolete writers, are caught up by these flights of predatory authors, and cast forth again to flourish and bear fruit in a remote and distant tract of time. *Many of their works, also, undergo a type of metempsychosis and spring up under new forms.* What was formerly a ponderous history, revives in the shape of a romance—an old legend changes into a modern play, and a sober philosophical treatise, furnishes the body for a whole series of bouncing and sparkling essays.[13]

Metempsychosis provides a raison d'être for the bookmaking craft, giving spiritual continuity to the modern advent of mass production. Certainly, Irving's use of metempsychosis is inescapably part of the humorous, fantastical, and gothic aspect of his writing, but it also reflects a way in which the individual can exert a type of mastery over the invention that initiated not simply the industrial age, but the Enlightenment itself. With the rise of American transcendentalism, moreover, such mastery becomes an unstable enterprise; it does not indicate control; on the contrary, it suggests a displacement of the possibility of a unified self, a split in the psyche, one side recognizing temporality, finitude, and sequence and the other hungering after spiritual illumination and continuity.

The most famous poem of Emerson's contemporary, Bayard Taylor, precisely illustrates how the theme of metempsychosis offered the site upon which the dissolution of the idea of the self is posed in relation to bookmaking and industrialization. In "The Metempsychosis of the Pine" (1851), Taylor adeptly uses the notion of transmigration as a grand analogy for the problem of poetic creation and reception in the age of industrialization. He begins simply enough with the conventional Romantic trope of nature suddenly revealing the hidden spiritual element that animates it:

> As when the haze of some wan moonlight makes
>   Familiar fields a land of mystery,
> Where, chill and strange, a ghostly presence wakes
>   In flower, bush and tree[14]

With a scheme similar to Emerson's notion of metempsychosis in "History" (1841) where consciousness recollects and sequentially journeys through its own evolutionary history, Taylor depicts this ghostly wakening as a form of cognitive quickening in which reliving the past indicates the precepts of poetic ritual:

> Another life, the life of Day o'erwhelms:
>> The Past from present consciousness takes hue,
> And we remember vast and cloudy realms
>> Our feet have wandered through[15]

Reemerging with poetic prominence, the inner, ghostly life of the soul is freed from the rationality of daylight. The wandering feet—metric units of the poem—become the nighttime, inner path that consciousness takes in its metempsychotic recollection of the historical sequence that leads into the present. Looking back into the past, therefore, the speaker of the poem recollects a time in which he had no formal name. In this primordial, natural, and as-yet-preconsciousness realm, the speaker sees around him "many a nameless sign" and remembers that "once in time, somewhere in the world/ I once was a towering Pine."[16]

In this evocation of nature as a pure original source, Taylor's Romanticism is evident. However, Taylor formulates this more conventional aspect as part of the poem's own historical development, a metempsychotic series arising out of nature, yet developing itself into the industrialized processes that make the poet's printed medium possible. Like Irving's metempsychotic art of bookmaking, Taylor's "Metempsychosis of the Pine" ends with a pronounced modern twist where the towering pine eventually becomes the raw materials for the paper upon which the poetic medium is fixed. The speaker recollects his growth as a natural entity through countless years until his own untimely death where either nature hurls him into "a wild abyss"[17] or the "hands of men" saw "through his heart" and turn him into the materials on which a poem will be inscribed. The confusion of the speaker in the last four stanzas of the poem—he is not entirely sure how he dies or even what form he transmigrates into—underscores a present dilemma that the poetic medium at once consoles and yet reinstates. As Taylor indicates, although an individual seeks self-awareness, he is irrevocably scattered into the metempsychotic series that constitutes his very being. The speaker's mental acuity is at best discontinuous once he has been sheared of his former incarnation as the pine: "All sense departed, with the boughs I wore."[18] Accordingly, the last three stanzas evoke a sense of lament for a natural entity that cannot now achieve a full self-constitution, but consoles itself nonetheless with the spiritual flourishes of its own poetic body:

Yet still that life awakens, brings again
    Its airy anthems, resonant and long.
Till Earth and Sky, transfigured, fill my brain
    With rhythmic sweeps of song.

Thence am I made a poet: thence are sprung
    Those shadowy motions of the soul, that reach
Beyond all grasp of Art,—for which that tongue
    Is ignorant of speech.

And if some wild, full-gathered harmony
    Roll its unbroken music through my line,
There lives and murmurs, faintly though it be,
    The Spirit of the Pine.[19]

The confusion of the speaker underscores a pronounced anxiety with modern industrialization, for the towering pine has been transformed into an object, a mass-produced product. Taylor thereby presents the Romantic idealization of nature as the fear of losing natural origins or being separated from nature. Here, the art of poetry achieves a self-reflexive aesthetic, while posing a pertinent dilemma for consciousness. The speaker dimly realizes that his identity has been scattered into various selves—the poet, the page of pine, and the reader whose eyes project an ensouled eyebeam through the fixed lines of the verse—whose coherence can only come when "earth" and "sky," body and soul transfigure themselves anew. Several selves thereby prospectively coexist in the transmigratory medium of poetic expression and reception, retaining a spiritual allure, even if it can only be intermittently invoked through the reader's present act of discernment. At the same time, while the speaker entertains multiple configurations of his being, he speaks as if he were the page itself, a product of industrialization that yearns to overcome its mimetic nature, longs to be more than the "shadowy motions of the soul," so as to reachieve the capacity of "wild, full-gathered harmony."

In the confusion of his speaker, Taylor captures both the modern promise of metempsychotic consciousness and the fear that was present at its inception, namely, that consciousness cannot help being overwhelmed by the material vastness of the historical record. In short, the conscious self cannot help being a product of history. At the same time, this self also wishes to be something entirely different from what it is; it desires a radical otherness beyond its material time-bound existence. Within the purview of Hegelianism and its scheme of self-knowing, a new problem accordingly arises. As Stanley Bates clarifies, it is a "form of historicism—the option known to some historians of [the Romantic] era as 'dialectics without a system.' [...] This would accept the Hegelian notion that all of our categories and concepts, along with our social practices and institutions, are historically conditioned—changeable and changing—but deny that there is a result of this process, a privileged end-state."[20] Emerson both embraces this view and wrestles with it, attempting to preserve the Neoplatonic and esoteric heritage that he so admired. In the posture of his double consciousness, he expresses something quite definitive about the notion of selfhood that came to prominence during the modern era, a predicament for consciousness that reflects the anxiety that permeated the age of industrialization—both a belief in human material progress and a simultaneous yearning after a lost spiritual origin.

Refiguring Platonic Ascent

In "The Idea of Hegel's Logic" (1973), Hans-Georg Gadamer argues that Hegel did not reject the Platonic tradition, but "achieves his objective of reinstating the Greek logos on the new foundation of modern, self-knowing spirit."[21] Emerson certainly entertained a similar desire for unifying the ideal and the actual, but his wariness of systematization led him to consider a much more precarious way of conceiving of either consciousness or cosmos. On the one hand, Emerson consistently embraces the Platonic notion of Forms;[22] on the other hand, he argues that matter is not simply a copy or derivation of the ideal, but a principle that has its own internal validity and organization. For Emerson, moreover, the delineations of double consciousness propose an unsettled ontology in which two different ways of explaining cognition are not simply at play, but intimately intertwined.

In "Love" from the *First Series of Essays* (1841), Emerson most clearly portrays the precarious vicissitudes of the double consciousness by adapting the ladder of ascent from Plato's *Symposium*. In the ancient dialogue itself, Plato supplies what has become the most definitive model of the transcendent: the lover's path from earthly material beauty to metaphysical Forms. As Diotima tells Socrates, "He who has been instructed [...] in the things of love [...] has learned to see the beautiful in due order and succession" and "when he comes to the end will suddenly perceive a nature of wondrous beauty" and so transcend "growing and decaying, or waxing and waning" for what is "everlasting."[23] This final goal of Platonic ascent, which has influenced a great deal of metaphysical writing throughout history,[24] is drawn by Diotima and repeated by Socrates as eternal, unmixed with "anything that is of the flesh," and unchanging: "Nor will this vision of the beautiful take the form of a face, or of hands, or of anything that is of the flesh. It will be neither words, nor knowledge, nor a something that exists in something else, such as a living creature, or the earth, or the heavens, or anything that is—but subsisting in itself and by itself in an eternal oneness, while every lovely thing partakes of it."[25]

In "Love," Emerson manages to remain true to Plato and yet alter the character of the journey. While clearly accepting the Platonic conception of the ladder of ascent as a prototype that articulates the upward course of the individual's eternal progress, he succeeds at each point to unsettle any easy grasp of his subject matter: the love that he expounds is not simply Platonic; nor, strictly speaking, is Plato the exclusive teacher of love's ascent. As Emerson observes, "The truly wise [have] told us of love in all ages. The doctrine is not old, nor is it new. If Plato, Plutarch, and Apuleius taught it, so have Petrarch, Angelo, and Milton" (*W* 2: 106). Already in this remark, Emerson's description possesses a carefully balanced complexity that can be easily missed. By rejecting established or newly invented truth in Plato and his successors, Emerson implicitly illustrates that the lover's divine ascent cannot rest upon any steady foundations expressed by one thinker of the past; it must instead partake in an evolutionary process in which each thinker had a part, however significant in itself.

Emerson's description of Plato's ladder, while remaining faithful to Plato, possesses an intricate alteration in its emphasis that every step of the journey is a continuous, but never accomplished process of separating the eternal from the world's taint so that the lover perpetually proceeds through a "ladder of created souls." Nor does this progress in Emerson entail a journey transcending—for the sake of thought—the things of the earth that had been used only temporarily on the lower rungs of the ladder. The contrast between the two ascents is both striking yet highly subtle:

Plato:

> Next he will grasp that the beauties of the body are as nothing
> to the beauties of the soul, so that wherever he meets with spiri-
> tual loveliness . . . he will find it beautiful enough to fall in love
> with and cherish [. . .]. And from this he will be led to contem-
> plate the beauty of laws and institutions [. . .]. And next his atten-
> tion should be diverted from the institutions to the sciences, so he
> may know the beauty of every kind of knowledge. [. . .] Whoever
> has been initiated so far in the mysteries of Love and has viewed
> all these aspects of the beautiful in due succession, is at last draw-
> ing near the final revelation. And now, Socrates, there bursts upon
> him that wondrous revelation that has been the very soul of beauty
> he has toiled so long for. It is an everlasting loveliness which neither
> comes, nor goes [. . .][26]

Emerson:

> And, beholding in many souls the traits of divine beauty, and sepa-
> rating in each soul that which is divine from the taint which it has
> contracted in the world, the lover ascends to the highest beauty, to
> the love and knowledge of the Divinity, by steps on *this ladder of cre-
> ated souls*. (W 2: 106; emphasis added)

Emerson's lover looks upon the beings of nature and sees the divine and
earthly together; he then begins to separate soul and matter from each
other so that he can ascend to the highest beauty, but each step in his as-
cent involves both soul and matter, and the lover's task lies in reuniting
and separating them in each successive step he takes. On his ascent to the
highest beauty, therefore, the lover never abandons the material, although
he purifies the soul "from the taint it has contracted in the world," and his
very activity through the rungs of "created souls" restlessly engages in a
soul/body dichotomy, a metempsychotic process that never ends and from
which the lover never escapes.[27]

By recasting Plato's whole movement from the individual to the divine
as a powerful impulse that repeatedly establishes itself on a never-ending
ladder of ascent,[28] Emerson strongly affirms ancient wisdom, even while
arguing that the process itself always "awaits a truer unfolding" (W 2: 106).
Since the soul never fully cleanses itself of the material world, soul's tran-
scendence from matter comprises a simultaneous reintegration in matter.
In this respect, Emerson complicates the upward movement of soul to the
divine by contrasting it with a simultaneous, corresponding downward
movement toward matter. Emerson thereby never abandons the Platonic
concept of undiluted Forms, which he characterizes in "Love" as the mind's
"overarching vault, bright with galaxies of immutable lights" (W 2: 110) that
exists "wholly above" ontological consciousness. This metaphysical prin-
ciple "foresees and prepares" the "purification of the intellect and the heart"
(W 2: 109) in matter so that "the celestial rapture fall[s] out of heaven [and]
seizes" (W 2: 102) upon human beings, making them dissatisfied with their
present state[29] and more desirous of ascending toward a "perfect beatitude"
(W 2: 108). Consciousness, in this respect, is truly dialectical, since it is both
a divine force pouring itself into matter and a material pattern seeking to
perfect itself in the ideal. In "Love," this polarity repeatedly emphasizes the
ceaseless oscillation between the primacy of a metaphysical system and the
ontological status of material reality: between the divine that is untainted
of materiality and "foresees and prepares" its development "from the first
wholly above [. . .] consciousness," on the one hand, and the perfect equal-
ity or inseparability of soul and matter so that the "soul is wholly embodied,
and the body is wholly ensouled" (W 2: 107), on the other.

Emerson thereby preserves the metaphysical formulation that "soul makes the body" (W 3: 9), even while presenting ontological consciousness as an alternative methodology that explains how the universe produces and arranges itself. Unlike the Platonic Form, this ontological alternative grounds itself in space and time, preparing for the emergence of consciousness not as a replication of the divine mind, but as a principle whose validity resides in the web of material relations of which it is composed. In "Love," a dialectical pattern develops not simply between the lover and the divine or between body and soul, but within nature itself so that a network of material relations slowly establishes interconnectivity and complexity to produce the advent of the human—and divine—mind. In his 1838 lecture, "Love," which forms the basis for the later 1841 essay, Emerson is even more explicit in delineating how inorganic matter strives in polarity toward ennobling itself, first, in a state of preconsciousness and, eventually, in consciousness itself:

> The power of Love is indeed the great poem of nature which all brute matter does seem to predict from the affinities of chemistry—and of crystals upward. The dualism which in human nature makes sex, in inorganic matter strives and works in polarity, showing itself in elective affinities,[30] in explosion, in flame, in new products. In the vegetable kingdom it solemnizes in the springtime the marriage of the plants, with the splendid bridal apparel of those sons and daughters of beauty, in whose sibylline leaves we read the approach of man. (EL 3: 52)

The ladder of ascent—"the great poem of nature" that aspires "upward"—figures as the predominant structure upon which all material beings, even those as-yet preconscious, cling and grope, at first, blindly and, then, with greater ease, assurance, and complexity. In the above passage, the dialectical pattern expresses itself as a "dualism in organic matter [which] strives and works in polarity," already exemplifying in its dumb state the seeds of speech and poetry, presenting in all this the power of generation from below. Emerson, therefore, emphasizes the growing interconnection of material objects empowered by love, which means that matter's maturation depends not only upon moving upward, but upon its own internal organization—an emerging material complexity. Certainly, a spiritual subtext exists; love as an intermediate spirit serves as a type of immanent or relational principle within the material world, allowing there to be connection and mutuality, as in Plato's *Symposium*, but Emerson's depiction underscores the moral interconnection of material elements, rather than materiality's dependence upon an all-controlling divine source. In this respect, "Love" develops somewhat further the metempsychotic order of

"History," which preceded it in the *First Series of Essays*. In "History," the individual's cognitive unity is depicted as the attempt to draw together the disparate material signs of history into a new and vital interrelation—and so in "Love," Emerson clarifies that the individual proceeds not just through rational manipulation, but by virtue of his desire and passion to marry nature's properties so that their growing interrelation alchemically produces new material forms, preserving all the information of their history, but with an additional creative combination.

In "Love," therefore, nature emerges as a distinct, yet corresponding source to the Platonic Form. Consequently, the highest pattern, "the real marriage" of heaven and earth (*W* 2: 109)—that future state in which the divisions of the self are healed—is discernable in the rudimentary dualism of nature, in her blind and dumb preparations for a more complex arrangement of signs and meaning. Nature's material awakening and subsequent order cannot be understood simply as an imprint of a higher reality or its reflection. From the perspective of consciousness in time, nature as a material source provides a foundation upon which the spiritual may be realized, and Emerson emphasizes how material relations awake to each other and begin to form the structures that will support consciousness:

> The passion operates a revolution in the youth. It quickens all things, and makes all things significant. Nature grows conscious. The bird who sung unheeded yesterday on the boughs of the tree, as the boy whistled by,—himself as gay as the bird, sings now to his heart and soul. Almost the notes are articulate. The clouds almost have faces, as he looks on them. The waving bough of the forest, the undulating grass beneath, the peeping flowers have grown sympathetic; and almost he fears to trust them with the secret which they seem to invite. (*EL* 3: 58)

Where, in the 1841 essay "Love," Emerson only slightly amends this passage, similarly stressing how "passion rebuilds the world for the youth" (*W* 2: 103), here, in this 1838 lecture, he is even more specific in how all relations undergo a qualitative change. As all things approach consciousness under the influence of love's attraction, nature begins to express herself in a language almost recognizable, almost articulate; its structure, in other words, yearns for a more complex arrangement, and the youth whose awakening corresponds with the stirrings of consciousness in nature begins to perceive how "the stars [are] letters, and the flowers ciphers" (*W* 2: 103).

Emerson does not simply map the doctrine of correspondences onto the relationship between the divine and the natural world. Rather, one spark, one potential seed for consciousness, enters from above into the world of material relations, and from this "wandering spark"[31] that is caught in the individual's "private bosom" proceeds another spark that lights up others until all relations share the flame of love: "For it is a fire that kindling its first embers in the narrow nook of a private bosom, caught from a wandering spark out of another private heart, does glow and enlarge until it warms and beams upon multitudes of men and women, upon the universal Heart of All, and so lights up the whole world and all nature with its generous flames" (*EL* 3: 54). The enlargement of nature corresponds to the individual's material growth and expansion; he "dilates; he is twice a man; he walks with arms akimbo; he soliloquizes; he accosts the grass and the trees; he feels the blood of the violet, the clover and the lily in his veins; and he talks with the brook that wets his foot" (*W* 2: 103). The language of nature possesses its own aspiring material arrangement, which soon becomes a new language, inclusive and expansive, arising from signs, at first without express human meaning, yet coming to possess significance in the new interconnectivity of nature itself.

Emerson's emphasis on nature, so prominently displayed in "Love," is hardly characteristic of Diotima's ladder of ascent, but rather catches something of the developing interconnectivities in Plotinus's descriptions of natural development, reflected much later in Goethe and Coleridge.[32] The arising interconnectivity in nature also presents itself in the relationship between lovers, for Emerson illustrates that the duality that existed in preconsciousness arises in the union of two individuals, as they serve to educate each other about all the different material combinations that arise in time. As in love's initial stage where the lover realizes the awakening multiplicity of the world, so too is this the case in love's more advanced stages: "As life wears on, it proves a game of permutation and combination of all possible positions of the parties, to employ all the resources of each, and acquaint each with the strength and weakness of the other" (*W* 2: 108). To experience the whole, Emerson argues, one must actively attempt to experience every possible variation in nature. Here, the lover's growing experience of "all possible positions" in relation to the beloved points toward the growing influence of the early probability theory of Pierre-Simon Laplace (1749–1827) and its sociological adaption by Adolphe Quetelet (1796–1874). Truth is not a matter of one possibility, but rather the sum total of every perspective, even those trajectories that prove incorrect.[33] Unlike the material determinism of probability theory, however, the lovers' experience of every material combination and position in their relation to each other is a preparation for spiritual insight.

Emerson thereby recapitulates Plato's ladder of ascent in a very specific key, emphasizing a new awareness of both nature and history and the human being's place therein. The contrast between the final stages of the ascent in Plato and Emerson is striking. For Plato, the lover uses the material world as steps on which to ascend upward, but once he has contemplated each material step in due order and succession, he no longer needs the body:

> And from this he will be led to contemplate the beauty of institutions and laws. And when he discovers how nearly every kind of beauty is akin to every other he will conclude that beauty of the body is not, after all, of so great a moment. And next his attention will be diverted to knowledge. [. . .] And, turning his eyes towards the open sea of beauty, he will find in such contemplation the seed of the most fruitful discourse [. . .] (210c –e)

Emerson, however, is much more explicit in describing how, at each moment, the lover's movement upward necessarily presupposes a turning around toward matter, every step toward a higher reality requiring a reintegration of every step that came before. In contrast to Plato's depiction of the contemplation of beauty, Emerson's notion of ascent portrays consciousness' active, backward apprehension of the series that issued it: "In looking backward, they may find that several things which were not the charm, have more reality to this groping memory than the charm itself which embalmed them" (W 2: 102). In the higher stages of love's progress, Emerson reasserts the type of metempsychotic intensity through recollection that he advocated in "History." Consciousness is both awakened and ennobled by seeking to understand the "metempsychosis of nature" as it proceeds through a historical series to the present moment in being. Faithful to this insight, Emerson again observes that it is not the spark of love alone that awakens nature and human consciousness and makes them expansive, but also reminiscence[34] that allows the youth to go from blind idealism to a richer conception of himself and his experience.

Whereas Plato describes the human being's ascent as a transcendent process, Emerson does not abandon the body. The spark of love has engendered a "rebuild[ing of] the world" (W 2: 103) and, at every moment, the individual's effort to develop himself necessarily includes recollecting and integrating his whole material past. At the same time, Emerson does not reject the Platonic value of transcendence; in fact, his conception of the double consciousness indicates that the human being must look not only to his historically founded and evolving consciousness, but to the understanding of the soul in the future. So a new phase in consciousness' development begins, admitting the fragmentation and sorrow of a fuller experience—of losing the initial fire that pulled all these material relations together—and the need of a new guide, prayer to "Eternal Power":

But the lot of humanity is on these children. Danger, sorrow, and pain arrive to them, as to all. Love prays. It makes covenants with Eternal Power, in behalf of this dear mate. The union which is thus effected, and which adds a new value to every atom in nature, for it transmutes every thread throughout the whole web of relation into a golden ray, and bathes the soul in a new and sweeter element, is yet a temporary state. (W 2: 108)

Looking backward at all the material entities that arise in time and then running their course from the beginning of the series toward the unrealized future—from self-reflexive recollection to prayer—the lover makes a new covenant, this time not with the past, but with "Eternal Power," transfiguring the previous material interrelations that comprise nature and emergent consciousness therein. One should also observe Emerson's own deeply personal experience in these lines of prose. Having lost his first wife to illness in 1831, he indicates that educating oneself will not alleviate the burden of loss; instead, he gestures toward an elusive spiritual power not yet manifest in the material chain of causes, one that will act from without on the human being and transform his daily rituals and activities. In this context, the human being must offer up himself and those he loves to an unknown, as-yet-unrealized future power that "adds a new value to every atom in nature" and "transmutes every thread throughout the whole web of relation into a golden ray." The human being's material consciousness changes by recollecting all its previous incarnations, and in approaching the end of sequence, it begins to achieve a new unity in confronting an elusive power beyond the system of being, one that "bathes the soul in a new and sweeter element."

The Platonic image of ascent, reshaped in "Love," remains an early, not fully formed, but already highly significant testament to the double consciousness that Emerson laments in 1841, even while using it as a template to understand the unsettled nature of the universe. For Emerson, the human being's double-orientation to the past and future comes to admit the precedence of the Platonic Form as an expressly tenuous process. Not only is every new unity that arises out of consciousness' growing interconnectivity "a temporary state" (W 2: 108), but its achievements must all be "succeeded and supplanted" (W 2: 110). As a result, the fluctuation of opposites and the provisional precedence of each part of this dialectic—the cognitive, historical consciousness whose movement runs from the past toward the future and the inverse movement of Eternal Power bathing the embodied "soul in a new and sweeter element"—become the unsettled, focal point of "Love." Emerson's conclusion to the essay bears this out by crystallizing two recurrent patterns: on the one hand, there is the more conventional description of how at the end of his journey the human being quits the senses and learns to appeal to the divine: "There are moments when the affections rule and absorb the man, and make his happiness dependent on a person or persons. But in health the mind is presently seen again,—its overarching vault, bright with galaxies of immutable lights" (*W* 2: 109–10). On the other hand, Emerson immediately undercuts his own depiction of this immutable celestial world at the end of the same paragraph. He adjusts his earlier emphasis upon the "overarching vault" of the divine with an insistence upon further expansion, instructing his readers that this immutability and the ascent to it, "so beautiful and attractive [. . .], must be succeeded and supplanted only by what is more beautiful, and so on for ever" (*W* 2: 110). Thus, he signals, here and elsewhere, two contrasting directions at once: first, consciousness constituting an upward series of material relations in time; second, the Platonic Form generating the universe's sequence downward. Together these provide the context for dialectic and its metempsychotic order as an ever-uncharted path by which consciousness and its emerging poetic character may continue to evolve.

The Order of Time, the Order of Genesis

Emerson's metempsychotic mind with its conception of sequence, recurrence, and advance never assumes a superficially systemized intellectual progression where Plato is exceeded or supplanted by Swedenborg, Goethe, or Hegel. Inasmuch as Emerson believed in sequential unfolding, he presents the metempsychotic formulation of history as an unsettled and unsettling model for depicting a larger intellectual tradition always in the process of unrestrained and disruptive development. Continuing the major emphases of the *First* (1841) and *Second* (1844) *Series of Essays* in *Representative Men* (1850),[35] Emerson places Plato at the heart of this tradition, arguing that while he was the first to embrace these mysteries in an intellectual way, he still remains one of the most powerful guides for the study of the natural series and its dynamic openness to self-generating unity and unsettled expansion:[36]

> Plato's fame does not stand on a syllogism, or on any masterpieces
> of the Socratic reasoning or on any thesis, as, for example, the immortality of the soul. He is more than an expert, or a schoolman, or
> a geometer or the prophet of a particular message. He represents the
> privilege of the intellect, the power, namely of carrying up every fact
> to successive platforms, and so disclosing in every fact a germ of expansion. (*W* 4: 46)

Emerson's Plato is a type of looking glass, providing a context for Emerson's own impulses and desires. Accordingly, Plato can never be a systematizer nor a doctrinaire;[37] he is the first advocate of an expansive cognitive undertaking, which transmits "a germ of expansion" so that the historical series of being can be perceived not as a static order, but as a way of going that questions, transforms, and revolutionizes each step that came before it.[38]

In Plato, therefore, Emerson locates his own circular and indeterminate metaphysics. Plato's conception of spiritual or second sight, Emerson insists, is neither linear nor univocal, but a method of discovery by which the human being extends his consciousness beyond its natural capacity to follow the arcing, rounding path of the universe: "These expansions or extensions consist in continuing the spiritual sight where the horizon falls on our natural vision, and by this secondsight discovering the long lines of law which shoot in every direction. Everywhere he stands on a path which has no end, but runs continuously round the universe" (W 4: 46). Emerson thereby asserts that Plato is among the first to apprehend the endless, circular structure of the universe, and he attributes to this Platonic activity a chiastic cosmology: what "comes from God to us returns by us to God" (W 4: 47). Here, Emerson draws the greater Neoplatonic arc of abiding, progression, and conversion, the procession of Intellect and the soul from the One into matter and from matter back to the One, signaling that both sides of this chiastic figure open up into "the long lines of law which shoot in every direction" to run "continuously round the universe" so as to express the unsettled figure of the double consciousness.

If in 1841 Emerson lamented the ceaseless divergence of consciousness and the soul, in 1850, he forcefully depicts the prospect of an enlarged human consciousness that expands itself by successively splitting apart only to find itself once again united in the circular course of history's series. For Emerson, this ongoing double activity signifies much more than individual conquest; it reprises all the efforts of heightened individuals throughout history, for "the highest minds of the world have never ceased to explore the double meaning" (W 3: 3) and to expand its enigmatic duality to comprise the "quadruple, or the centuple, or much more manifold meaning of every sensuous fact" (W 3: 3–4). Such an ongoing exploration of the double consciousness thereby unites the individual to humanity, while also permitting him or her to experience the metempsychotic series in a state of greater awareness. It is not so much that he or she has lived before, but that his or her activity repeats each previous effort in a new and open-ended way.

Developing his earlier adaptation of the ladder of ascent, Emerson indicates that the ever-mounting series is composed of a double, conflictual order—two patterns, side by side, perpetually falling into each other and oscillating in their reoccurrence, even warlike in their opposition, yet pursuing a grander conception, a greater multiplicity, and an expansive, uneasy unity. What is particularly striking is that Emerson neither prioritizes nor abandons Platonism or the values inherent in Platonic thought; rather, he reorganizes them alongside the new emerging, scientific awareness of chronological series that comprises all the information of the past, thereby anticipating a type of genetic code that continues to adapt itself and encode its changes in every new circumstance. In his essay "The Poet" (1844), published three years after "Love," Emerson returns to this unsettled picture of metaphysics in conflict by renaming the two opposing patterns—consciousness in time and the atemporal Platonic Form—*the orders of time and genesis,* arguing throughout for two conflicting positions at once: first, the equality of soul and body and, second, the soul's power over the body: "The thought and the form are equal in the order of time, but in the order of genesis the thought is prior to the form" (*W* 3: 7).[39] Emerson contends that immaterial thought and material form can be understood in two ways, foregrounding two separate, yet interdependent models that operate as part of a dialectic of creation. Emerson's emphasis upon equality in the order of time presents the budding Romantic fascination with the prospect of new creation and its achievement of unity. In contrast to the above conception of consciousness in time and space, the soul's priority over matter in the order of genesis operates according to traditional Platonism: the material object is derivative, bearing only a mimetic relation to its ideal Form[40] since the universe is an externalization of a perfect spiritual Form.

In 1844, Emerson assigns the role of "reconciler" (*W* 3: 21) not to the scientist or philosopher, but to the poet whose art bridges these two metaphysical models. On the one hand, the poet or creator synthesizes disparate elements into a new, embodied, and ensouled unity and does so within the order of time. The notion of equality of all elements in the creative process is already evident in his early essay "Nature" (1836), where Emerson argues that a "man conversing in earnest, if he watches his intellectual processes, will find that always a material image, more or less luminous, arises in his mind, contemporaneous with every thought" (*W* 1: 20–21). True poetry then, Emerson writes in 1844, requires the value of equality, for the soul and body are born together; one does not follow the other: "In true poetry, the thought and the metre are not painfully adjusted afterward, but are born together, as the soul and the body of a child" (*EL* 3: 359). However, Emerson also adapts the Platonic notion of mimesis, maintaining Plato's famous criticism of poetry in Books 2, 3, and 10 of *The Republic.* In "The Poet," for instance, Emerson appears to contradict his emphasis on the equality of all elements as he examines the mimetic character of poetry's structure and argues that the poet's work is only a reflection or a miswriting of a perfect Form that exists outside the order of time:

> For poetry was all written before time was, and whenever we are so finely organized that we can penetrate into that region where the air is music, we hear those primal warblings, and attempt to write them down, but we lose ever and anon a word, or a verse, and substitute something of our own, and thus miswrite the verse, and substitute something of our own, and thus miswrite the poem. The men of more delicate ear write down these cadences more faithfully, and these transcripts, though imperfect, become the songs of the nations. (W 3: 5–6)

Following Plato's critique of poetry[41] in *The Republic*, Emerson argues that the poet is simply a translator who penetrates into the region beyond time so as to copy—or at least to divine in sudden glimpses, however fragmentary—a preexistent, perfect poem. In so doing, the poet undertakes steps that are inevitably and necessarily deficient and will *substitute* something of his own and, thereby, *miswrite* the poem. Even the most faithful scribe is fated to such imperfect imitation for the very reason that his activity is derivative and places into matter what was only perfect beyond the scope of matter.[42]

Two orders exist, therefore, in the context of poetic activity: one, the simultaneous bringing together of all elements into a unity that defies hierarchical structure, and the other, the implicitly hierarchical order in which a perfect poem "before time" is reflected in its faulty material copy. By bringing these two orders together and making them resonate indeterminately with each other, Emerson offers a new cohesive cosmology, employing the notion of mimesis throughout his essays, first as an explanation for fallen nature[43] and later as a vital feature of how the orders of genesis and time interweave their disparate structures into an unsettled, yet highly organized order. In "The Poet," for example, the order of genesis prioritizes its own spiritual value so that the "universe [becomes] the externalization of the soul," which entails that "wherever the life is, that [universe] bursts into appearance around it" (W 3: 9). And because the soul by its presence immediately gives birth to the world of time, the human being comes into life through an externalization of a larger power that has formed him thus. While this theme is operative in Emerson's early work, his essays from 1844 onward are filled with the problem of attaining freedom when everything—even the series of which we are a part—is already constructed with steps running simultaneously upward and downward out of sight, beyond the perceptual range of the individual. The dilemma the individual faces is that he is composed of two varying gravities: the upward metempsychotic inclination to restore the greater transcendent self and the mimetic downward course of nature that overwhelms the confused, experiential self in time.

Intensifying this predicament in "Nature," the essay that follows "The Poet" and "Experience" in the *Second Series*, Emerson presents the order of time as the mimetic wake that the soul flings out behind itself in its continual effort to escape "again into the state of free thought" (*W* 3: 113). The poet who attempts to follow the life of the soul is left behind in the wake of creation; he or she possesses only a "referred existence," like the world of echoes that he or she now inhabits:

> The poet finds himself not near enough to his object. The pine-tree, the river, the bank of flowers before him, do not seem to be nature. Nature is still elsewhere. *This or this is but the outskirt and far-off reflection and echo of the triumph that has passed by, and is now at its glancing splendor and heyday* [. . .]. *The present object shall give you this sense of stillness that follows a pageant which has just gone by.* What splendid distance, what recesses of ineffable pomp and loveliness in the sunset! But who can go where they are, or lay his hand or plant his foot thereon? *Off they fall from the round world forever and ever.* It is the same among the men and women, as among the silent trees; always a referred existence, an absence, never a presence and satisfaction. (*W* 3: 111–12; emphasis added)

In "Nature," the world of time issues a challenge to the poet. Creation has already occurred, and even "the present object," which remains closest to its inception due to its presence or currency, is nonetheless marked by a ruling subsequence, left in the wake of a living "pageant." As a result, the problem that emerges is the loss of immanent splendor following the initial vitality of creation, for both landscape and humanity are left emptied of the triumph that has passed by; they possess only "a referred existence" and yearn to reestablish being's verdant confluence with spirit.

While admitting "the downward tendency and proneness of things" (*W* 1: 216) and dramatizing the immediate dilemma that humanity faces once creation has occurred, Emerson also clarifies that this mimetic expansion away from the soul or Platonic Form is necessary for the individual to realize his power by mixing and marrying various properties to generate new creation. "Marriage, in what is called the spiritual world, is impossible, because of the inequality between every subject and object" (*W* 3: 44), he writes in "Experience," clearly rejecting the doctrine of correspondences. In Swedenborg's mysticism, for instance, earthly union corresponds to a higher spiritual union, but Emerson affirms matter, arguing that it possesses a property that soul does not possess. In the order of time, therefore, equality operates as the dominant value, so marriage and pro-creation are again possible. In this way, the poet can learn to awaken his finer creative impulses in the order of time. If an individual seeks to make himself more than a mimetic object falling away from the original source of creation, he may yet learn to reverse "the downward tendency" that re-sults in the order of genesis because of the prevailing inequality that exists between every subject and object, soul and body. He may learn to fuse the original creative cause with an already created discourse. As Emerson writes in "Nature," this work is "the blending of experience with the pres-ent action of the mind. It is proper creation. It is the working of the Origi-nal Cause through the instruments he has already made" (W 1: 20–21).

Accordingly, two conflicting realities, each with their own distinct value, collide within the human being's own frame. The individual is, Em-erson insists in 1836, "a god in ruins" (W 1: 42), at once a mimetic likeness pushed outward by a greater power and a potential creator, possessing the self-reliance and authority to be more than merely a translator or imita-tor. The double nature of the human being thereby corresponds directly to the unsettled order of the universe, except that in the human frame its polarity and double gravity—the divergence of two principles that run in cosmic circles away and back again to the site of their separation—are potentially more visceral and intense. In "The Poet" (1844), the human being as a "reconciler" is situated in a privileged location where he can see the order of genesis flowing into the order of time so that the One be-comes many and creation becomes the created, the mimetic inevitability to which all creation is prone: "We stand before the secret of the world, there where Being passes into Appearance, and Unity into Variety" (W 3: 9). Human beings, particularly poets, stand in the spot between unity and variety, soul and matter, thought and material form, and because they are themselves a mixture of the two principles—both gods in ruin and higher syntheses in nature—they possess the power to reverse the downward flow of creation and revitalize the dead world of matter. In the terms of "Love," the lover engages in an activity that "transmutes every thread throughout the whole web of relation into a golden ray," but this golden unity is only "a temporary form" (W 2: 108), ever-fated to split itself again and fall from the firmament of an unsettled heaven.

The Fall of Uriel

From 1841 onward, Emerson portrays the ladder of ascent as both an infinitely upward-moving and yet circular progression, established by two intersecting, conflicting orders. In "Uriel" (1846), which Robert Frost would later call "the greatest Western poem yet,"[44] Emerson continues to develop his conception of the double consciousness by reinterpreting the Christian fall as part of creation's ever-rounding arc. As critics point out, Emerson wrote "Uriel" in response to the harsh treatment he received at the hands of the Harvard Divinity Faculty after his address in 1838,[45] and it can be seen as a protest[46] against the Unitarian establishment that his own father had so prominently served in New England as did Emerson before giving up his ministry in 1832. At the same time, such an interpretation fails to explain the specific meditative images of the poem and overlooks altogether that "the lapse of Uriel" signifies the evolution of consciousness as it enacts the "progression of the soul in matter," an explicitly metempsychotic process that bridges the orders of genesis and time.[47]

Interpreting "Uriel" to be Emerson's poetic testimony to the unsettled and yet cohesive orders of the double consciousness also helps to correct current misinterpretations of Emerson's thought. James Guthrie rightly examines "Uriel" as a poetic challenge to established authority—particularly, "a searing indictment of conservative Unitarians' complaisance"—but argues that Uriel's fall "should be seen as falling out of materiality and linearity into ideality and sphericity."[48] According to Guthrie, "it is not Uriel who has lapsed, but rather his fellow demiurges, whose dualistic thinking has generated lines of division where, rightly, none should exist."[49] However, Guthrie ignores Emerson's insistence upon the double consciousness. "Uriel" is not the movement from materiality toward ideality, but the initiation of soul's self-knowledge as a metempsychotic journey that enacts the chiastic circularity of the orders of genesis and time—thereby bridging the Platonic conception of Form with transcendentalism's developing view of ontological consciousness, dependent on, and constitutive of, time and space, as Kant argued in the *First Critique*.[50]

Uriel's avowal of circular duality—an act that revolutionizes paradise and transforms it from an immutable divine eternity into an as-yet-unknown quality—is also a creative reinterpretation of Hegelian dialectic and, more specifically, of the German philosopher's insistence that divine truth is not an absolute on which reality is founded, but a spiritual experience that unfolds in time. For Emerson, as is so typical of transcendentalism in general, there is no need for a genesis myth, only for an account of how consciousness comes to know itself—first, by engendering itself into a downward series and, then, by drawing itself upward toward the divine, which is transformed with each circular transmigration. Emerson's fall, then, becomes the moment of genesis, the Form generating itself outward and downward into a series, which becomes, in turn, the ground upon which consciousness can conceive itself anew. One can also see Emerson's fundamental difference from Hegel. While Hegel developed a circular metaphysics that similarly incorporates the Neoplatonic procession from, and conversion to the One, he nonetheless places a *telos* on this pattern of development. Emerson, by contrast, is much more radical; for him, there is no end to development.

The title of the poem and the name of its protagonist, "Uriel," point to a specific poetic tradition, which Emerson sought to utilize as his immediate point of departure. From this vantage point, the literary context of Uriel denotes the traditional hierarchy of the cosmos, while simultaneously accentuating the power of the deed that undoes its regimented order in favor of circularity and motion. In John Milton's *Paradise Lost*, Uriel is the "sharpest sighted spirit in all of Heaven" and "the Regent of the Sun,"[51] the gatekeeper between the celestial spheres and earth and, as such, he enforces God's hierarchic order. Edward Waldo Emerson notes that his father employs Milton's angel to undercut Milton's own static cosmology and to highlight instead the ascendancy of modern science and its revolutionary way of conceiving of the cosmos.[52] As guardian of the sun and heavenly orbs, Milton's Uriel can best observe the circular motions of the planets. In Emerson's poem, such heightened perception serves a crucial function, for the angel sees a cosmos in circular motion and perpetual upheaval. Uriel's advocacy of circular truth is an implicit testament to an intellectual revolution that overturns older conventions and understands that the earth and the celestial orbs that rotate are all part of a perpetually changing universe. Emerson's "manipulation of the Miltonic universe" thus denotes tradition—God's ordered, hierarchal cosmos—and simultaneously undercuts it, overturning its static character in favor of a dialectical series whose perpetual, yet unsettled recurrence signals the advent of a more enlightened conception of nature.[53]

"Uriel" develops further the core of Emerson's intellectual position as a clash and confluence between Platonic *logos*[54] and ontological consciousness—initially posing their conflict and correspondence as the question of circularity. On the one hand, the "young gods" that inhabit paradise before the fall uphold a highly ordered, linear metaphysics that begins with "Laws of form" and continues with material degradations in existence, mimetic reflections of true substance: "What subsisteth, and what seems." Uriel refuses to acknowledge the regimented separation of soul and body into this spiritual hierarchy; he "solve[s the problem of] the sphere" because he recognizes that the mimetic order that the young gods advocate—from divine Form to mimetic object—is too linear and orderly. By contrast, the position that Uriel proclaims is inherently unsettled and dialectical: "'Line in nature is not found,/ Unit and universe are round;/ In vain produced, all rays return,/ Evil will bless, and ice will burn.'" Uriel's "treason" becomes, in turn, a "sentiment divine/ Against the being of line," a realization that each perspective or vantage point must necessarily pass into its opposite if it is to know and develop itself.

While the younger gods are content in their seemingly benign, albeit undeveloped meditation on the newly created world, Uriel's position represents a deep-seated and developing antagonism (his treason is "too long pent") to established doctrine; he seeks perpetual activity, not a static hierarchy in which the spiritual copies itself mimetically downward to lower forms and, because of Uriel's awakening, the universe also begins to change, to participate in the descent from divine light to the "procession of a soul" in matter:

> And, shrilling from the solar course,
> Or from fruit of chemic force,
> Procession of a soul in matter,
> Or the speeding change of water,
> Or out of the good of evil born,
> Came Uriel's voice of cherub scorn;
> And a blush tinged the upper sky,
> And the gods shook, they knew not why.

Uriel's position, once expressed, sweeps up all the young deities, changing the very fabric of heaven itself so that "all slid into confusion"—and what was once only spiritual is forced to realize itself anew in the "sea of genera- tion." As the gods or spiritual unities are overcome with Uriel's circular realization—they too will have to participate in the fall and subsequent procession in matter—so the material world below is unbound so that "Strong Hades could not keep his own." Emerson thereby does more than retell the narrative of the fall. He signals a profound upheaval of religious tradition, reiterating his conviction that the hierarchal conception of the universe, exemplified in John Milton's *Paradise Lost*, gives way to a more tenuous and indeterminate cosmology whose activity is expressly metem- psychotic and obeys two varying gravities, the soul arcing downward from its heavenly "solar course" to realize itself in matter and the soul's conver- sion of this process on the ladder of ascent, seeking again, as in "Love," to "transmute" itself "into a golden ray" (*W* 2: 108).

In "Uriel," therefore, Emerson's metempsychotic mind emerges as the dominant activity that unites the shuddering heaven and the material world now unbound from a purely mimetic state. These dualities take the structure of a Pythagorean or Neoplatonic loop[55]—the soul proceeding from the One and then converting back to the One through being or be- ings. Uriel's fall and subsequent activity replay the dialectic of the double consciousness, the metempsychotic interrelations of descending, ascend- ing materiality and the understanding of the soul in the future, that golden ray or impossibility that reemerges once the individual has reversed the mimetic gravity of soul's externalization and traversed the historical series to its last step or incarnation: "Whether doom'd to long gyration/ In the sea of generation,/ Or by knowledge grown too bright/ To hit the nerve of feebler sight." Uriel's realization of the sphere thereby presents him as an expression of the double consciousness. He either proceeds through the "Neoplatonic sea of generation"[56] or transcends the series, having grown "too bright" and made himself a golden ray or impossibility that is, as Emerson argues in "Experience," incapable of marriage or attraction and must then reexternalize itself into a mimetic series so as to begin the process of knitting itself back into a conscious material web of relations.

"Uriel" is Emerson's poetic proclamation of this unsettled metempsychotic process, demythologizing the Christian fall so that it is recurrent and enacted each time the soul contemplates its object, which is every moment in experience that combines the soul's downward course into matter in the order of genesis and the metempsychotic experience of history's series in the order of time. "Uriel" depicts precisely this state of consciousness within its very first lines: the poem's first stanza denotes with striking clarity the principal elements of Emerson's metempsychotic order: a soul from above surveys time in its chronological progression; unlike fallen creation, this soul has not fallen, but it broods upon the fall, which is the object of its meditation and, in thinking about its object, enacts the order of genesis, thereby engendering the path of its object into the order of time, into "calendar months and days": "It fell in the ancient periods/ Which the brooding soul surveys,/ Or ever the wild Time coined itself/ Into calendar months and days." In its meditation upon the fall, the soul engenders a self-referential, dialectical relationship that will be realized each time consciousness seeks its object or, in textual terms (since this process is enacted in a poem with a lyrical sequence), the reader perceives the poetic series before him and, like the "brooding soul," surveys a sequence below him that is at once separate from him and yet part of his activity. "Uriel" thereby operates on several levels, at once a creation narrative denoting a past metaphysical history and the emerging tensions and revolutions therein as well as a textual representation of consciousness' circular progression, the subject who must move through a series of word-objects in order to ingest their meaning, undergoing an experience that inevitably reconstitutes the subject and the world around him.[57]

In what can be characterized as precise poetic shorthand, "Uriel" also unpacks the principal features of Hegelian dialectic and makes them available for an American audience. History, according to Hegel, is not a collection of facts or particulars; rather, through experience, consciousness learns to amalgamate and fuse all particulars into a universal unity that is a dynamic evolving present, not a static past. Emerson's depiction of heaven in "Uriel" captures this very same principle. Since Uriel's heaven is only a temporary origin, a point of departure for the soul's journey into matter, this celestial reality lacks any real substance and, as a result, must attempt to experience and develop itself. Thus, when Uriel utters his circular pronouncements, the celestial paradise is encompassed by and transformed into "a sad self-knowledge" that must obey the new law and develop itself within a material series before reachieving the spiritual preeminence of light. Similarly, the soul broods above the series, but in this meditation, it is likewise pulled down into the series and must, as is its nature, pull the series up again, not to become what it was, but what experience has made it.

"Uriel" can be seen as a testament to the philosophical consciousness of its time, most specifically to dialectic. In the *Science of Logic* (1812), Hegel illustrates how the journey of consciousness toward absolute truth progresses through various stages; thought—or what he also calls immediate being—is abstract and lacking in its first stage, but gradually transforms through experience to reveal its underlying, essential character, which was not yet present in its prior state:

> But above all, thought acquires thereby self-reliance and independence. It becomes at home in abstractions and in progressing by means of Notions free from sensuous substrata, develops an unsuspected power of assimilating in rational form all the various knowledges and sciences in their complex variety, of grasping and retaining them in their essential character, stripping them of their external features and [. . .] filling the abstract basis of logic acquired by study with the substantial content of absolute truth and giving it the value of a universal which no longer stands as a particular alongside other particulars but includes them all within its grasp and is their essence, the absolutely True.[58]

Through the lesson that logic provides, the individual educates himself and fills what was once empty of content. In this process of becoming, consciousness assimilates history—"all the various knowledges and sciences in their complex variety"—so that its prior emptiness gives way to a more evolved, actually experienced, independent whole, free of the externality, abstractness, or emptiness to which it was once subject. "Uriel" propounds this idea powerfully, for the celestial paradise lacks substance (the gods do not even understand the principle of a circle) and, therefore, has no choice but to admit and enact Uriel's circular epiphany and pursue a metempsychotic course so as to develop into a new form of spiritual light.

For both Emerson and Hegel, then, consciousness must expand itself by assimilating a complexity of material relations, but this progression is not a univocal one, beginning with a sure origin and proceeding in a linear fashion to establish itself as an absolute end. Instead, Hegel emphasizes that the "essential requirement for the science of logic is [...] that the whole of the science be within itself a circle in which the first is also the last and the last is also the first."[59] Like Emerson's conception of the "double consciousness," one side pushing outward toward the external and the other resisting, yet complementing this outer gravity by turning inward and eventually transmuting its web of relations into a golden ray, Hegel's science of logic pivots upon the chiastic relationship of two perspectives, wherein consciousness advances from the immediacy with which it began only to return and know that immediate beginning in an entirely new way:

> The advance is a *retreat into the ground*, to what is *primary* and *true*, on which depends and, in fact, from which originates, that with which the beginning is made. Thus consciousness on its onward path from the immediacy with which it began is led back to absolute knowledge as its innermost *truth*. This last, the ground, is then also that from which the first proceeds, that which at first appeared as an immediacy. This is true in still greater measure of absolute spirit which reveals itself as the concrete and final supreme truth of all being, and which at the *end* of the development is known as freely externalizing itself, abandoning itself to the shape of an *immediate being*—opening and unfolding itself into the creation of a world which contains all that fell into the development which preceded that result and which through this reversal of its position relatively to its beginning is transformed into something dependent on the result as principle.[60]

The pure immediacy of being at the beginning of the series is abstract and without content; in advancing and, thereby, realizing itself in its journey through the series, consciousness moves back to its "innermost truth." Inversely, at the end of the series, this immanent, essential character externalizes itself and appears again as a shape devoid of content. One cannot separate these dynamic strands or perspectives, for together they comprise the perpetual opening and unfolding of the world, ceaselessly moving toward complete self-knowledge.

For Hegel, then, origin and end embrace each other to form a self-evolving circle that holds within itself all its previous manifestations. As he writes in *The Philosophy of History* (1837), the circular, chiastic pattern— "while death is the issue of life, life is also the issue of death"—is the "grand conception" that the "Oriental philosophers attained" and which "is evolved [...] in the idea of *Metempsychosis* [...] in its relation to individual existence."[61] Using the analogy of the Phoenix to illustrate this grand conception, Hegel argues that Spirit's metempsychotic vitality depends upon consuming itself and using its materials to exalt itself eternally into a new form:[62]

> A myth more generally known, is that of the Phoenix as a type of Life of Nature; eternally preparing for itself its funeral pile, and consuming itself upon it; but so that from its ashes is produced the new, renovated, fresh life. [. . .] Spirit—consuming the envelope of its existence—does not merely pass into another envelope, nor rise rejuvenescent from the ashes of its previous form; it comes forth exalted, glorified, a purer spirit. It certainly makes war upon itself—consumes its own existence; but in this very destruction it works up that existence into a new form, and each successive phase becomes in its turn a material, working on which it exalts itself to a new grade.[63]

In a way strikingly similar to Emerson's metempsychosis of nature where soul draws the dead materials of history into a new, living manifestation, Hegel's phoenix eternally pursues its metempsychotic course in which its own "funeral pyre" becomes the site of its reemergence and exaltation. Like the greater universe, the phoenix progressively divides and unites itself in ever-higher circles, exemplifying Hegel's insistence that there are no categories of being and spirit that exist outside this circle of creation and death.[64] Rather, spirit takes up all the various strands of itself and comprehends them in an "essential now":

> Nothing in the past is lost for it, for the Idea is ever present; Spirit is immortal; with it there is no past, no future, but an essential *now*. This necessarily implies that the present form of Spirit comprehends within it all earlier steps. [. . .] The life of the ever present Spirit is a circle of progressive embodiments, which looked at in one aspect still exist beside each other, and only as looked at from another point of view appear as past. The grades which Spirit seems to have left behind it, it still possesses in the depths of its present.[65]

The metempsychotic sequence perpetually exists in the present moment, for spirit discards its materials only to take them up again. Consequently, the historical series that the absolute spirit embodies is not something external to it that it transcends in its journey toward new creation; instead, spirit draws history's externality into itself and produces history anew. In Emerson's "History," the poet's central objective follows just such an arc: "to do away this wild, savage and preposterous There and Then, and introduce in its place the Here and Now" so that thought "passes through [all the materials of the past] with satisfaction, and they live again to the mind, or are now" (*W* 2: 7).

Like Hegel's self-propelling circle, Emerson's depiction of the circle in "Uriel" presents an evolutionary design, for consciousness emerges within history and seeks a fuller realization in the present moment.[66] Accordingly, Uriel's fall is not a past event, but a present mimetic dilemma with which Emerson challenges his readers and, particularly his fellow citizens, both present and future, with the preeminent American task to revitalize themselves and their nation, for they inhabit but the outlines of a more perfect formation. Uriel's realization of the circle, his entry into the sea of generation and his progression in matter are just a few heightened examples of an individual entity seeking a higher formation based upon anticipating a higher law and enacting it by virtue of self-reliance.[67] The gods in their celestial kingdom shake to the budding, deepening activity stirring in and around them that is the result of Uriel's fall, but they do not yet understand why this should be so. Their similar realization of circular creation is also vital to the individual who, though he propels himself so much farther than his peers, does so in large part to create a precedent for his fellows so that they can learn from him and free themselves in turn.

For Emerson, Uriel's advocacy of the circle constitutes the greatest revelation of modern thought, at once proceeding out of previous traditions and yet revolutionizing them to express the present character of consciousness. What appears, from one perspective, to bear only one—upward or downward—trajectory takes on a circular character in both Hegel and Emerson's respective systems. In Hegel, both origin and end embrace each other and seek, in their intersection, to engender their processes anew. The kind of emphasis upon unity that one may find in Hegel's thought,[68] however, is even more problematic in Emerson's philosophy. As in "Love," Emerson's "progress of the soul" (W 2: 110) which seeks a "perfect beatitude" (W 2: 108) always involves an uneasy interrelation of corresponding, yet incongruent structures. The consciousness that develops itself by being "dependent on a person or persons" (W 2: 109)—on a field of material relations—must enter a time of transition when it has to transcend these material relations by throwing them off and taking them up to another level in which the process of material interconnectivity reemerges as the dominant value only to be succeeded yet again by transcendence. Although this recurrent alteration from temporal consciousness to classical transcendence bears significant similarities to Hegelian dialectic, nonetheless, Emerson reveals his transcendental system to be fundamentally proleptic, revealing its vitality in the essential Emersonian value of perpetual transition.[69]

"Fate" and the Ring of Necessity

In the five years between his first declaration of the double conscious-ness in "The Transcendentalist" (1841) and his poetic articulation of its essential circularity in "Uriel" (1846), Emerson's tone changes, although the underlying structural significance that he gives to this double order remains the same.[70] While in 1841 he laments that human conscious-ness in time and the soul in the future cannot be properly reconciled to each other—since one order dominates now and the other holds prece-dence later—by 1846, the sad self-knowledge of circularity is a triumphant event, representing *the soul* and *the body*'s universal amelioration. In *The Conduct of Life* (1860), nineteen years after his first articulation of the double consciousness, Emerson proclaims that "One key, one solution to the mysteries of the human condition, one solution to the old knots of fate, freedom, and foreknowledge, exists, the propounding, namely, of the double-consciousness" (W 6: 25). Emerson no longer grieves that the po-larity cutting through human nature will not resolve itself; instead, he sees the fluctuating open-endedness of the double consciousness as a "solution to the mysteries of the human condition."

In "Fate," the opening essay of *The Conduct of Life*, Emerson continues his life-long emphasis upon the mimetic, material dilemma that the hu-man being faces in the order of time. Here, as in "Experience" (1844), he begins by asking a question, "How shall I live?," lamenting that "we are incompetent to solve the times. Our geometry cannot span the huge orbits of the prevailing ideas, behold their return, and reconcile their opposition" (W 6: 1). Accordingly, in the order of time, the human being is initially bound to one prevailing gravity, which is not circular in itself, but mimetic and irresistible: "We can only obey our own polarity. 'Tis fine for us to speculate and elect our course, if we must accept an irresistible dictation" (W 6: 2). For the mature Emerson, the mimetic, downward propensity that follows creation's burst outward—the soul's externalization of itself into the universe—is initially the predominant gravity to which the human is subject: "Every spirit makes its house; but afterwards the house confines the spirit" (W 6: 5). Echoing his emphasis in "The Poet," "Experience," and "Nature" (1844) that the human being is only a "far-off reflection and echo of the triumph that has passed by" (W 3: 111), Emerson accentuates this mimetic dilemma in "Fate" by entertaining various deterministic systems of thought. Whereas, in the eighteenth century, Idealist thinkers struggled with empiricism, in the nineteenth century, Idealist thinkers, particularly in America, contended with the emerging influence of material determin-ism, struggling to reconcile some of the dehumanizing facets of indus-trialization, the rise of Probability Theory developed by Pierre-Simon

Laplace and Adolphe Quetelet,[71] the publication of Charles Darwin's *On the Origin of Species* (1859), and the nineteenth-century "science" of phrenology, to give just a briefest sketch. From this vantage point, Emerson begins his argument in "Fate" by outlining how little freedom and grace humanity really possesses. A human being may suppose that he has an inner power—but the external "organization" of life "tyrannizes over [his] character" (*W* 6: 5). When "each comes forth from his mother's womb, the gate of gifts closes behind him [. . .]. So he has but one future, and that is already predetermined in his lobes, and described in that little fatty face, pig-eye, and squat form" (*W* 6: 6).

Emerson looks to history and sees that many civilizations have accepted this material predicament of existence. Believing their "doom is written on the iron leaf in the moment when [they] entered the world," the Turk, the Arab, and the Persian "accept the foreordained fate"—as does the Hindu, who, "under the wheel [of rebirth], is as firm" (*W* 6: 2–3). All "wise men," according to Emerson, have understood that "there is something which cannot be talked or voted away,—a strap or belt which girds the world" (*W* 6: 3). In opposition to the mimetic inevitably in the order of time, Emerson once again heralds metempsychotic ascent, arguing that while many cultures accepted their mimetic doom, some advocated self-determination. Eastern and Western traditions, Emerson insists, have maintained the belief that human beings are a party to their present state:

> It was a poetic attempt to lift this mountain of Fate [. . .] which led the Hindoos to say, "Fate is nothing but the deeds committed in a prior state of existence." I find the coincidence of the extremes of eastern and western speculation in the daring statement of Schelling, "there is in every man a certain feeling, that he has been what he is from all eternity, and by no means became such in time." To say it less sublimely,—in the history of the individual is always an account of his condition, and he knows himself to be a party to his present estate. (*W* 6: 7)

Like his earlier accounts of metempsychosis, Emerson does not proclaim it as an absolute truth or structure; rather, metempsychosis is the first "poetic attempt" to resist the "irresistible dictation" of the mimetic dilemma in the order of time. Emerson thereby progresses from the Hindu and transcendentalist conception of transmigration and karma to scientific objectivity: "All we know of the egg, from each successive discovery, is, another vesicle; and if, after five hundred years, you get a better observer, or a better glass, he finds within the last observed another" (*W* 6: 7). Thus, all one arrives at is a "vesicle in new circumstances, a vesicle lodged in darkness" (*W* 6: 8)—a material object locked within a living and dying sequence.

No matter the character of the sequential model, Emerson persistently applies metempsychosis to understand how the individual transforms his activity within a mimetic sequence so as to realize the eventual circularity of a line of successive objects. The individual, Emerson insists, is more in the "order of nature" than "sack and sack, belly and members, link in a chain"; the human being is a "stupendous antagonism, a dragging together of the poles of the Universe" (W 6: 12). In the words of "Experience," the human being can become "a golden impossibility" if he recognizes that he is, in fact, composed of the double consciousness, the chiastic circularity to which Emerson returns yet again in "Fate": "Fate follows and limits power, power attends and antagonizes Fate" (W 6: 12). In this respect, the human being lives more than a second-hand existence; he participates in the continual refinement of the power that antagonizes the material structures of life:

> As we refine, our checks become finer. If we rise to spiritual culture, the antagonism takes a spiritual form. In the Hindoo fables, Vishnu follows Maya through all her ascending changes, from insect and crawfish up to elephant; whatever form she took, he took the male form of that kind, until she became at last woman and goddess, and he man and a god. The limitations refine as the soul purifies, but the ring of necessity is always perched at the top. (W 6: 11)

Again, Emerson draws upon Hindu reincarnation to elucidate the ringlike structure that manifests itself everywhere in the universe—the soul purifying itself upon the ladder of ascent, rising upward and away from matter to find that, at the very top when it has become "the golden ray" of "Love" or "golden impossibility" of "Experience," the ladder arcs back down into the elemental order, so that both sides of the double consciousness meet: "On one side elemental order, sandstone and granite, rock-ledges, peat-bog, forest, sea and shore; and on the other part thought, the spirit which composes and decomposes nature,—here they are side by side, god and devil, mind and matter, king and conspirator, belt and spasm, riding peacefully together in the eye and brain of every man" (W 6: 12).[72] By realizing the two orders side by side, the human being has emptied "his breast of windy conceits" to "show his lordship by manners and deeds on the scale of nature" (W 6: 13). He obeys neither the metaphysics of soul nor the materialism of the body, but finds himself composed of a more precarious and unsettled structure. In this respect, Emerson reveals the vitality of his system to be more than just a continual deferral of meaning or perpetual transition so that no final claim can be made. Instead, he once again adapts metempsychosis to show how metaphysics can be incorporated into the modern map of human cognition and corporeality.

From this vantage point, the modern self does not necessarily brace himself upon a literal ladder of ascent—nor dive from one body into another; rather, Emerson uses metempsychosis as a deep structure, built into humanity's very physiology, enabling self-awareness in "the eye and brain of every man."[73]

3 / Reading the Metempsychotic Text

In the last three decades, scholars have come to appreciate some of the complexity of perception in Emerson's thought, questioning the earlier consensus that his notion of sight expresses primarily a desire for unity. Indeed, Emerson's very first published pronouncement of the eye's transcendent power evokes critical uncertainty because of its contradictory evocations: "I become a transparent eye-ball. I am nothing. I see all. The currents of the Universal Being circulate through me; I am part or particle of God" (*W* 1: 10). As the "currents of the Universal being circulate through" it, the eye fluctuates between nothingness and fullness, transforming itself into the medium through which the spiritual expresses itself. As Harold Bloom observes, "In Emerson, the power of the mind and the power of the eye endeavor to become one,"[1] and David Jacobson helps to illuminate this union by arguing that Emerson's "metaphors of vision" depict the process of "the soul's becoming."[2] Even with these clarifications, the Emersonian eye still resonates with an expressly unsettled allure—and Barbara Packer, for one, sees Emerson's characterization of the eyeball cited above as "chiefly composed of paradoxes," not at all a stable, unifying principle that bestows a clear, ready-made order onto the world it perceives.[3]

While greatly expanding the field, Emersonian criticism has failed to draw out some of the most important consequences of the unsettled confluence of the soul and the eye. Harold Bloom is possibly the most illuminating in arguing that "where the eye dominates, without curtailment, *askesis* [practice or purgation] tends to center on the self's awareness of other selves."[4] But the dominating image of the eye[5] purifying itself in its awareness of other selves requires much greater elucidation, especially since it directly signals a metempsychotic ethos that has gone unexplored. In this chapter, I show how the Emersonian eye enacts metempsychosis in each and all of the objects it observes, ever-attempting to reorganize itself into a fuller and more abundant form of vision, despite the limits of its optic gesture. To a great degree, Emerson's metempsychotic self with the power of perception at its core arises out of the eighteenth- and nineteenth-century Protestant emphasis upon immanence and subjectivity in the Romantic figure of the divinely inspired artist who does not copy or imitate, but works according to an inward, self-reflexive turn upon the created world.[6]

From his early lectures to his most mature writing, Emerson repeatedly characterizes the life of the spirit as an "upspringing perception" (*EL* 1: 73), which bursts forth from within the body of the poet through the organ of his eyes, giving him the necessary vision to continue the work of creation.[7] The opening sentence of "Circles" (1841) strikingly depicts the incessant figuration of the immanent eye throughout creation:[8] "The eye is the first circle; the horizon which it forms is the second; and throughout nature this primary figure is repeated without end" (*W* 2: 179).[9] Three years later in "The Poet" (1844), the poet "uses his eyes" to follow the soul's journey through successive forms, and by learning thus to see, he "flows with the flowing of nature" (*W* 3: 13). Sixteen years later in "Fate" (1860), once heightened by the power of the will, "the glance of [the] eye has the power of sunbeams" (*W* 6: 16),[10] bestowing the promise of freedom on a world ruled by a prevailing mimesis, for as "soon as there is life, there is self-direction, and absorbing and using of material" (*W* 6: 21).[11]

While the eye clearly possesses Romantic features, Emerson's view of metempsychotic perception cannot be reduced to the influence of one period alone. The very idea of emanations from the eyes is an ancient one. Empedocles and the Pythagoreans understood "the eye as an active agent that emitted rays or a visual current toward the object of perception," a view that influenced the Platonic tradition and Euclid's work on optics.[12] Emerson's conception is informed by these traditions of thought. In the sense that the metempsychotic eye ceaselessly reconstitutes itself by looking at the pattern of its own succession, Emerson believed perception to be an evolving historical phenomenon. In order to understand the historicity of the eye's composition, I will explore the models of vision that had a most immediate and significant influence on his thought. I begin my examination by arguing that while Emerson viewed nature as a text open to human perception, he developed his notion of perception as a metempsychotic journey that resonates with a Böhmean conception of vision and undergoes a development similar to the phenomenological development of individual spirit in Hegel. Next, I explore Emerson's engagement of the Greek philosophical tradition, specifically Plato's and Plotinus's conception of perception's tripartite self-constitution as well as Goethe's later, kindred theory of optics and colors, which includes his experimentations with the camera obscura. In these contexts, Emerson synthesizes his metempsychotic perception as a physiologically fettered apparatus that must nonetheless exert itself beyond its limits and thereby divine its own future formation in history. Accordingly, the human being must confront the limits and poverty of perception and seek nonetheless to reconstitute himself or herself into successive and expansive apprehensions not simply of the historical series itself, but of the future poet who will draw the fettered physiology of the eye into new and fuller vistas of vision. Emersonian metempsychosis thereby formalizes poetic structure into an act of phenomenological inquiry, even while questioning itself to underscore the fragility and elusiveness of such a venture.

Ascendancy of the Textual Frame

Emerson's understanding of perception can be seen as a response to a pervasive intellectual ethos after the Enlightenment, which viewed nature in terms of language, emblems, or hieroglyphs. In formulating perception as an unsettled metempsychotic process, however, Emerson moves beyond the idea of straightforward correspondences between nature's emblems and the life of the spirit. Largely influenced by the Neoplatonic tradition, Jacob Böhme's theosophic metaphor of the eye,[13] Goethe's optics and Hegelian phenomenology, Emerson sought to locate the polarity of the spiritual and material in the unsettled constitution of a perceiving individual subject. From this vantage point, perception takes on a privileged currency as the medium through which a human being discovers his own place in history as well as the means to achieve self-transformation. What was traditionally understood as spiritual inquiry is transformed in Emerson into a historical and hermeneutical process of self-fashioning.

In *The Veil of Isis* (2006), Pierre Hadot recounts how nature reemerged in the seventeenth and eighteenth centuries as a living poem or hieroglyphic cipher that expresses the language of God. While the textual analogy of the hieroglyph is an old one with its roots deeply embedded in antiquity,[14] its reemergence in the Renaissance incorporates the Protestant Reformation value of *sola scriptura* into a more holistic enterprise in which nature, not scripture, emerges as the true spiritual authority. For sixteenth-century thinkers like Paracelsus and della Porta, the "codes of Nature's language are presented as 'signatures'" and this soon "took on deeper meanings" in other seventeenth-century works like Jacob Böhme's *The Signature of All Things* (1621) and Thomas Browne's *Religio Medici* (1643) where the hieroglyphic "book written by Nature" emerges as an alternative source to scripture. The "idea of a hieroglyph" comes to stand for "the language of Nature, a language that functions not by means of words or discourse but by means of signs and symbols."[15] Nature thereby "composes not just a poem but a coded poem," which the human being of insight attempts to penetrate so as to understand "the language of God."[16] Some of the foremost thinkers of the eighteenth century responded to and participated in this intellectual ethos. By the eighteenth century, Kant argued that all "living forms [. . .] are the ciphers of nature's 'coded language' [. . .] and seem to be made for the human eye," a conception that Goethe developed as a central idea in *The Metamorphosis of Plants*, namely, the notion that what "natural phenomena reveal to us are not the maxims or formulas of Nature, but configurations, sketches, or emblems, which require only to be perceived."[17]

Emerson responded to the theme of the world as a textual frame in his earliest writings, never abandoning the centrality of this episteme throughout his life. In the lecture, "The Naturalist" (1836), he celebrates this hieroglyphic ethos, emphasizing that nature is an original, divinely inspired text, which requires an active perceiver to elicit its inner law.[18] He directly quotes Goethe's assertion that the "works of nature are ever a freshly uttered Word of God" (*EL* 1: 72) and argues that the poet must search for the "inward Law of Nature" (*EL* 1: 81) in order to place objects into their "true perspective" (*EL* 1: 81).[19] In this setting, the individual's goal is once again "to read the great book" of the natural world (*EL* 1: 26),[20] not merely by accumulating its dead materials, but by comprehending these materials in a living way. In "Nature," also published in 1836, Emerson combines this emphasis on the textuality of nature with that of soul's education. He specifically articulates the "wish to learn [nature's] language" in order to facilitate the "redemption of the soul" and to restore "to the world original and eternal beauty" (*W* 1: 43). The manner in which the human being attempts such restoration is by using "the whole of nature [as] a metaphor of the human mind" (*W* 1: 21) so as to give an external language for the internal, spiritual dimension within the human being: "Words are signs of natural facts. The use of natural history is to give us aid in supernatural history. The use of the outer creation is to give us language for the beings and changes of the inward creation" (*W* 1: 18).[21] The person attuning himself to the law that lies within appearances reads the metaphorical quality of nature and language and sees how the invisible, inner law reanimates being and its historical sequence.

In *American Hieroglyphics* (1980), John T. Irwin contends that an "Emersonian essay is simply the decipherment of a hieroglyph." Emerson's "strategy is always the same: he presents the emblem in all its outer complexity and then, through the doctrine of correspondences, he penetrates the emblem to reveal its inner simplicity, to show the hidden relationship between outer shape and inner meaning."[22] Emerson, indeed, admired the ancient Neoplatonic system of sympathy upon which Swedenborg's doctrine of correspondences was based.[23] Like Goethe before him, he adapted Plotinus's conception of the simplicity of vision, especially the emphasis on "prolong[ing] the vision of the eye by means of the vision of the spirit" in order "to pierce the material envelope of things by a powerful effort of mental vision."[24] However, to assert that Emerson accepts the simple strategy of establishing correspondences is to misunderstand the fuller range of his thought. Irwin is undoubtedly correct in identifying Emerson's acceptance and adaptation of the hieroglyphic emblem, but his assessment of Emerson's "strategy" in employing "the doctrine of correspondences" is, at best, incomplete.

Emerson actually came to reject the doctrine of correspondences, which he particularly disliked in Swedenborg's view that "the mental series exactly tallies with the material series" and criticized it as "not vital, and lack[ing] power to generate life" (W 4: 66, 74). Moreover, Emerson's admiration of spiritual "simplicity" centered on the indeterminacy and fluidity of the Neoplatonic cosmos as well as on Böhme's theosophic insights, strikingly unlike the more coherent order of Swedenborg's cosmology. In "Circles" (1841), for instance, Emerson presents the tenuous relationship between a reader and a "sliding" or "fugitive" text,[25] a depiction that moves decisively beyond the postulation of straightforward correspondences:

> The natural world may be conceived of as a system of concentric circles, and we now and then detect in nature slight dislocations, *which apprize us that this surface on which we now stand, is not fixed, but sliding.* These manifold tenacious qualities, this chemistry and vegetation, these metals and animals, which seem to stand there for their own sake, *are a means and methods only,—are words of God, and as fugitive as other words.* (W 2: 186; emphasis added)[26]

The natural world is a system of signs, words of God on which the polarity of the double consciousness plays, and this is the reason for its "variance" and "sliding." Despite its fugitive surface, language remains the medium through which the human being can explain himself to himself—hence, its ascendancy and privilege in this schema. For though the individual is caught between two gravitational forces whose ground is "not fixed but sliding," the fugitive textual series[27] provides a "means and method" by which the very duality of creation between "the central life" (W 2: 188) and its "dislocation" can be apprehended and, subsequently, addressed.

More specifically, Emerson's adaptation of the Plotinian eye, whose vision can be prolonged by the life of the spirit, serves a vital function in allowing the human being to perceive the greater fluctuations of creation's dialectic and follow them out. In *Representative Men* (1850) particularly, Emerson identifies and foregrounds this Platonic/Neoplatonic context, stating that Plato first recognized the power of "spiritual sight" to continue beyond the "natural horizon" of the eye so as to see the incessant expansions of the historical series of being.[28] In *The Signature of All Things*, Böhme provides an influential model of how this dialectic of vision is centered in the human frame: "The right eye looketh forward in thee toward eternity. The left eye looketh back in thee into time."[29] By depicting the perceptual duality of the material series in time and the future eternal nature of the individual soul in God, Böhme anticipates the uneasy polarity of Emersonian double consciousness as well as the Romantic task of bringing the material and spiritual into proper alignment and eventual unity. Böhme's articulation is well worth quoting in full:

> If now thou sufferest thyself to be always looking into nature, and the things of time, and to be leading the will, and to be seeking somewhat for itself in the desire, it will be impossible for thee ever to arrive at the unity, which thou wishest for. Remember this; and be on thy watch. Give not thy mind leave to enter into, nor to fill itself with, that which is without thee; neither look thou backward upon thyself; but quit thyself, and look forward upon Christ. Let not thy left eye deceive thee, by making continually one representation after another, and stirring up thereby an earnest longing in the self-propriety; but let thy right eye command back this left, and attract it to thee, so that it may not gad abroad into the wonders and delights of nature. [...] However, [...] both eyes may become very useful, if ordered aright; and both the divine and natural light may in the soul subsist together, and be of mutual service to each other. But never shalt thou arrive at the unity of vision or uniformity of will, but by entering fully into the will of our Savior Jesus Christ, and therein bringing the eye of time into the eye of eternity; and then descending by means of this united through the light of God into the light of nature.[30]

Böhme strikingly foreshadows the Romantic enterprise to reunite the created world with the creator, the caused with the cause itself, through the medium of perception. Böhme's belief that the ascent to God must be ordered aright resonates, moreover, with the older Platonic teaching that the soul must order itself properly so as to ascend to the One.[31] In the theosophist's view, the eyes, one that looks backward in time and the other that looks forward to the future, must become united through the light of God, but this ascent through light into that which is beyond light is only one aspect in the process, since unity is decisively followed by another descent into matter, from unity back into spiritual light and then into the light of nature itself. Here, Böhme differentiates between two forms of perception, one that gets lost in the world and the other that is able to renew the light of nature through perceptual transcendence. Thus, Böhme's spiritual hierarchy is not a static chain linking earth and heaven, but a dynamically unfolding process by which many dimensions of time, spirit, and God become present to each other through acts of perception.

From his earliest essays, Emerson also emphasizes the process by which the natural world is renewed by the spirit. In the terms of "Nature," "a man in alliance with truth and God" seeks to restore the world of time by enacting "proper creation," the "working of the Original Cause through the instruments he has already made" (W 1: 20–21). In the *First Series of Essays*, this form of double perception also possesses an explicit mimetic and metempsychotic polarity. Since the eye first perceives shapes long separated from their source and is also initially ruled by this subservience, the eye must become capable of transcending its natural horizon by perceiving "the monad perform the metempsychosis of nature" as it lives in and through each of its dramatic "masks" in an effort to achieve "the eternal unity" (W 2: 8). In a manner similar to that of Böhme, Emerson consistently argues that the human being would become lost if he perceived the succession of natural objects alone. Natural perception, in other words, must be transfigured by second sight so as to be capable of turning itself into the light of the divine and of returning to matter renewed and rejuvenated. After Uriel's fall from ideality, his reascension consists in a metempsychotic conversion or refinement of matter into light. In "Love" as well, the backward apprehension of nature is not an end in itself, but must be offered up to "Eternal Power" so that "every thread throughout the whole web of relation" is transmuted "into a golden ray" (W 2: 108). In Emerson, therefore, consciousness is not simply the subject's apprehension of successive objects, but a future power pouring itself from above into being as being offers itself up from below, the figurative ladder between earth and heaven resonating with the unsettled vicissitudes of perpetual metempsychotic becoming.

In "Circles" and "Art," Emerson expands this metempsychotic focus by depicting a reader observing both the textual sequence of civilization and the future life of the soul. A reader perceives the various gradations of the soul in history as it produces new forms, discards them into determinate, mimetic shapes, and then repossesses them in order to shape them anew. Because every newly created object "will be presently abridged into a word" (W 2: 181), so too are all present forms "already passing under the same sentence, and tumbling into the inevitable pit which the creation of new thought opens for all that is old" (W 2: 180). Despite the falling away of each object from its source, Emerson nonetheless celebrates the mimesis of the created world. Human beings cannot "advance toward their beatitude" without "ordaining" themselves with the mimetic code of language whose deeper, ever-escaping reality they comprehend through perception:

> This circumstance gives a value to the Egyptian hieroglyphics, to the Indian, Chinese, and Mexican idols, however gross and shapeless. They denote the height of the human soul in that hour, and were not fantastic, but sprung from a necessity as deep as the world. Shall I now add that the whole extant product of the plastic arts has herein its highest value, *as history*; as a stroke drawn in the portrait of that fate, perfect, and beautiful, according to whose ordinations all beings advance to their beatitude. (W 2: 210)

Although each material symbol incessantly degrades itself after being created, all words and letters comprise a sequence whose mimetic gravity can be inverted through reading. The historical sequence of being, therefore, reveals history itself, a code whose oldest inscriptions are gross and shapeless, but become clearer as human beings advance to their beatitude through retracing the sequence to its source. The mimetic, historical code that falls away from its source and loses its vitality can be transformed through perception, which inverts the series pushing it back toward its vital, volatile center.

Throughout the *First Series of Essays*, Emerson depicts textuality as the site upon which two fluctuating orders, mimetic and metempsychotic, clash and coalesce. The "flash of the eye" encounters the mimetic text and, in recognizing the greater historical movement from beginning to end, transforms the text into an aspiring metempsychotic sequence: "In common hours, society sits cold and statuesque. We all stand waiting, empty,— knowing, possibly, that we can be full, surrounded by mighty symbols which are not symbols to us, but prose and trivial toys. *Then cometh the god, and converts the statues into fiery men, and by a flash of his eye burns up the veil which shrouded all things, and the meaning is manifest*" (W 2: 184; emphasis added).[32] This passage from "Circles" (1841), characteristic of so much of Emerson's thinking, depicts the conversion of "mighty symbols" into "fiery men"—abstract phenomena into being. In the order of time, every material object, including the human frame itself, is initially ruled by a mimetic gravity that makes each object "cold" and "statuesque." The infusion of a "fiery" essence into every object is not simply the restoration of immanence into a lifeless system. More precisely, "the flash of the eye" initiates material interconnectivity so that the whole sequence and

interrelation of statues and symbols become revivified in the human be-
ing's cognitive act of reading.

The Böhmean conception of the polarity of perception, so influential
for Emerson and Hegel,[33] helps to clarify the mystical underpinnings of
converting the dead material body into a fiery entity. As Böhme writes
in *Forty Questions of the Soul* (1620), "We understand the soul to be a life
awakened out of the eye of God, its original is in the fire and the fire is its
life."[34] In Böhme, as we saw with the two eyes, there is a twofold fire, one
that does not go forth from the eye, consuming itself in wrath, and the
second that pours forth and seeks to gain its essentiality in love and regain
the divine body. In Emerson, the fiery conversion of mimetic shapes into
metempsychotic aspiration represents the second fire of the eye of God,
which goes forth in love to restore the divine body in the flesh so that it
cannot be destroyed. This esoteric mystery, the restoration of the divine
life through perception, becomes, in Emerson and Hegel, an expression of
the illumined ability to enact historical progression. In the preface to the
Phenomenology of Spirit (1807), for instance, Hegel depicts the endeavors
of individual consciousness in terms of the greater arc of history itself. He
begins with the dialectical movement of World-Spirit manifesting itself in
determinate shapes, while progressing beyond them toward further evolu-
tion in history:

> The *length* of this path [Spirit's insight into what knowing is] has to
> be endured, because, for one thing, each moment is necessary; and
> further, each moment has to be *lingered* over, because each is itself a
> complete individual shape [. . .]. the Substance of the individual, the
> World-Spirit itself, has had the patience to pass through these shapes
> over the long passage of time, and to take upon itself the enormous
> labour of world-history, in which it embodied in each shape as much
> of its entire content as that shape was capable of holding.[35]

According to Hegel, the individual spirit who follows in the wake of
World-Spirit must retrace and adopt each discarded shape. In attempting
this motion, the individual passes into shapes that no longer possess the
grandeur of the past, but have been abbreviated and reduced to smaller
determinations of thought. Although the individual "certainly cannot by
the nature of the case comprehend his own substance more easily" than
the World-Spirit, yet "he does have less trouble, since all this has already
been *implicitly* accomplished; the content is already reduced to a possibil-
ity, its immediacy overcome, and the embodied shape reduced to abbrevi-
ated, simple determinations of thought." Each of these shapes, moreover,
has lost its fullness as being and remains now only a recollection that
the individual can convert back into a living entity through the process

of retracing World-Spirit's path: "It is no longer existence in the form of *being-in-itself* [. . .] but is now the *recollected in-itself*, ready for conversion into the form of *being-for-self*."[36]

While Hegel underscores the process by which individual spirit attempts to retrace the World-Spirit's previous steps, Emerson explicitly places the emphasis on textuality, foregrounding the precarious relationship between active perceiver and material text.[37] In "Circles" (1841), Emerson emphasizes that the abbreviated shape, discarded by soul, is a letter or a word. In this respect, the reader finds himself already within a series that has been produced by the soul in the order of genesis, a series made up of steps, each of which "will be presently abridged into a word" (*W* 2: 181). The initial role of individual consciousness is to perceive this sequence of symbols and, with "the flash of the eye," to convert these abbreviated words into "fiery men" (*W* 2: 184)—or in Hegel's words, to convert the recollection back into being: "the *recollected in-itself* [. . .] into the form of *being-for-self*." For both Hegel and Emerson, to know history is to apprehend the textual sequence so as to refill its content and turn the discarded shell of being, the mimetic recollection, into a living tendency. Emerson, however, is even more emphatic in taking Hegel's cosmological dialectic and adapting it to the reading process.

Emerson develops both the esoteric restoration of the divine body and Hegel's phenomenology into a new methodology of transcendental reading, a process of metempsychotic recollection in which the individual receives an already created text and, by using his eyes, enacts a conversion of dead letters into a living and vital interconnectivity. The mimetic inevitability of creation—the discarded shapes of World-Spirit—is not simply a world ruled by imitation, but a world in which every factor including the pathways of individual consciousness has been preestablished as a potential tendency. Emersonian metempsychosis offers the potential to rise beyond such determinism. The individual uses the textual frame to trace his way forward through the word-steps of an established creation to the place where words break off and new creation is needed. As we will see, this reading process cannot be thought of as univocal or static, privileging a stable subject who apprehends immovable objects whose meanings are all pervaded by "an inner simplicity."[38] The reader is only initially a univocal textual signature and, like all other abbreviated shapes, he must learn to transform himself and his relations into an unsettled and living sequence.[39] Accordingly, the work of consciousness confronts not a stable, knowable external order, but the difficulty of achieving the strength with which to prolong its attention so as to trace out the vast open-ended sequence of which it is a part.[40]

Prototypes of Perception I: Plato and Plotinus

In adopting the hieroglyphic ethos of nature, Emerson anticipates a modern emphasis on perception that at once embraces and discards some of the more stable and univocal models of vision that tend to characterize the seventeenth and eighteenth centuries. For instance, Emerson's notion of perception and, more specifically, his transcendental reading of the textuality of nature echo Kant's emphasis upon the mind's essential role in perceiving natural phenomena and the a priori capacity of consciousness to unite the world's disparate signs through apperception.[41] Consciousness, Kant argues in the very beginning of *The Critique of Pure Reason*, apprehends disparate and disunited elements of reality and their synthesis can never be achieved on the level of everyday reality or derived from experience: "There can be no doubt that all our cognition begins with experience [...]. But even though all our cognition starts *with* experience, that does not mean that all of it arises *from* experience."[42] Unification is, nonetheless, accessible, as a transcendental unity of apperception in which "a permanent spiritual substance underlies the fleeting succession of conscious experience."[43]

The obvious indebtedness of Emerson's metempsychotic perception to Kant's transcendental apperception finds its restrictions in the Kantian "pure, original, unchangeable consciousness," a self-contained autonomous principle, discovering its own moral laws as categorical imperatives.[44] As David Jacobson argues, "Emerson is positioned at the point in modern philosophy when the *a priori* structures governing judgment, structures initiated by Descartes and brought to systemic expression by Kant, were coming apart." In contrast to Kant's view of the autonomous character of apperception, Emerson's work underscores the "transformation from a reflective to a self-reflexive methodology,"[45] which signifies, in turn, that the Emersonian eye possesses a closer affinity to the Platonic and Neoplatonic principle of spiritual sight, an ancient structure that underlies the respective methodologies of Böhme, Goethe, and Hegel.

In *Emerson's Life in Science* (2003), Laura Dassow Walls argues that Plato's *Timaeus* offered Emerson "a theory of vision that eventually provided the answer [he] needed" in the midst of the intellectual and religious schisms sweeping early nineteenth-century America.[46] The *Timaeus*'s depiction of the eye's power is by no means the only Platonic or Neoplatonic influence in this regard. Employing Plato's "secondsight" in *Representative Men*, Emerson quotes and utilizes a wide range of Platonic dialogues and Neoplatonic writings, both in Greek and in English, including most prominently Ralph Cudworth's *The True Intellectual System of the Universe* (1678) and Thomas Taylor's first English translation of Plotinus in the eighteenth century. Plato's emphasis on the soul's internal power in the figure of the eye is a singular feature of all his middle dialogues, and Emerson not merely captures this Platonic emphasis, but forcefully upholds this striking feature as the primary influence of Platonism on all subsequent thought.

In the *Phaedrus* especially, Plato outlines how the eyes serve as the organ that opens the inner life of the human being toward the dialectical unfolding of love through the sensuous and, eventually, the intellectual realms of the cosmos. Socrates describes how love "is absorbed within" the lover, pouring in through his eyes until "he can contain no more," then reversing course and going "back to its place of origin [. . .] so the stream of beauty turns back and reenters the eyes of the fair beloved."[47] Even while Socrates points out the sensual delight that the lovers take in apprehending each other, he clearly signals the prospect of ascent by virtue of perception, since the eyes invigorate the sustenance of the inner world: "And so by the natural channel it reaches his soul and gives it fresh vigor, watering the roots of the wings and quickening them to growth, whereby the soul of the beloved, in its turn, is filled with love."[48] The organ of sight, therefore, is the conduit that allows the inner world to absorb and emanate the principle of love. The eyes provide a "natural channel" allowing love to ennoble the inner life of the individual, and if the lover and beloved learn to develop this pattern between them according to the ordered rule of philosophical life, they will transcend the material barbs that have ensnared the soul and, thereby, win liberty and self-mastery.[49]

In Book 7 of the *Republic*, Plato reinforces this conception of the dialectical pathway through perception and equates such vision with conversion. Disagreeing with the popular notion of the day that "true knowledge" can be put into "a soul that does not possess it, as if they were inserting vision into blind eyes,"[50] Socrates contends that the individual must attempt a profound conversion of what he receives if he is to overcome the gravity from without and contemplate essence itself:

> But our present argument indicates, said I, *that the true analogy for this indwelling power in the soul and the instrument whereby each of us apprehends is that of an eye that could not be converted to the light from the darkness except by turning the whole body.* Even so this organ of knowledge must be turned around from the world of becoming together with the entire soul, like the scene-shifting periactus in the theater, until the soul is able to endure the contemplation of essence and the brightest region of being.[51]

Plato advocates the turning of the whole body around through perception so as to enable the soul to see the "brightest region of being." In this manner, Plato's dialectic of perception in which the eyes receive and absorb an intrinsic, but unnoticed power provides a blueprint for the emergent powers of individual consciousness. Through the organ of the eye, the individual receives the light from without, but he cannot see properly without using his eyes to turn his whole body around to the light.[52]

In this movement of the procession of the soul and the subsequent conversion of the soul through the organ of the eye, Plato lays the foundation for the Plotinian concept of the "self-constituting" eye, which is particularly important for Emersonian perception. For Emerson, the order of genesis entails the procession of the soul into matter whereby the human being is a material entity, drawn as a mimetic shape. In order to constitute himself anew and escape the downward, mimetic gravity, the individual converts what he sees through the organ of the eye and turns himself around. Through perception, he becomes more than a mimetic shape; as he was caused, so now he causes himself to be. Perceiving the world, therefore, is analogous to the emergence of individual consciousness itself. In *Representative Men* (1850), Emerson's depiction of the "expansions" of the "spiritual sight" or "secondsight" of Platonism (*W* 4: 46) captures this notion of procession and conversion from the *Republic* and resonates with the Plotinian configuration of abiding, procession, and conversion. Plotinus's triad is one of the principal models for Emerson's precarious, yet cohesive chiasmus of the double consciousness: the soul externalizing itself or proceeding into a mimetic sequence, which, through perception, is inverted and converted into an aspiring metempsychotic series and then into light itself. But this is only one side of Plotinus's triad with abiding, procession and conversion outlining one facet of a causal process: the One emanates forth into being and being converts itself back to the One. Procession, conversion, and self-constitution reflect another side of this process and further emphasize the point of view of being. What is caused comes to posit itself in that conversion: that it *causes itself to be*.[53] In other words, for Plotinus, existence is not simply created by the One; in proceeding from the One and undergoing conversion, it begins to develop its own consciousness and, thus, is able to constitute itself.

Emerson's understanding of self-constitution through perception cannot be fully understood without this context. These two triadic perspectives, (1) abiding, procession, and conversion; and (2) procession, conversion, and self-constitution, often coalesce in Plotinus's accounts, as for example in *Ennead* V 1: intellect "is shaped in one way by the One and in another by itself, like sight in its actuality; for intellection [thought/*noēsis*] is seeing sight and both are one." The language of perception is pronounced throughout, as in *Ennead* VI 7, 16, 16–22: "and in turn it [intellect] came to be all things and knew this in *intimate perception* (*synaesthesis*) of itself and was already intellect, having been filled in order that it might have *what it will see* but *looking at them* with light from that which gives these things." For Plotinus, as for Plato, perception is not just passive sensation (though it can be); it is an active self-constituting energy that grasps sense objects where they are and is capable of bringing intelligibility—a much larger mind—to them.[54] Thus, a perceiving subject participates in a much larger activity: just as the intellect in its perception or intellection bestows a self-constituting power upon the individual, so does that individual mediate intellect's agency to the phenomena that he or she experiences.

Intellect, in Plotinus's thought, cannot be separated from the act of perception, since intellect constitutes the deeper ground of perception's ability to connect things together. In the sensible universe, however, the world is not always illuminated by intellect; thus things are not immediately interconnected. A human being has to work out these connections, and sometimes, things are at variance, hostile to each other. When objects are transformed by intellect, that is, once the triad of perception takes place (procession, conversion, and self-constitution), everything is connected simultaneously so that "in each all are manifest" (V 8, 4). But this triadic movement, as we have begun to see, is not a univocal process by which each object is simply illuminated by a spiritual power. Rather, for entities with different capabilities, each sees only what it can according to the capacity of the recipient. Nonetheless, even though a given object "has the appearance of a part . . . a penetrating look sees the whole in it" (V 8, 4), Plotinus affirms.

For Emerson, the power of the eye, reflecting these stages of procession, conversion, and self-constitution, enacts intellect's interconnectivity, burning away the mimetic, fragmented state of the material world and revitalizing it with new fire. In "Art," the concluding essay of the *First Series* (1841), Emerson forcefully emphasizes that the "flash of the eye" must be much more than mere revitalization. The self-constituting eye enacts neither side of the dialectic alone—neither a scattering of relation (procession) nor a confluence (conversion)—but both together. In this way, the perceiving subject learns gradually to engage intellect in order to elicit an "integrity" and "vigilance" not only in himself, but in the objects he perceives:

> Neither by detachment, neither by aggregation, is the integrity of the intellect transmitted to its works, but by a vigilance which brings the intellect in its greatness and best state to operate every moment. It must have the same wholeness which nature has. *Although no diligence can rebuild the universe in a model, by the best accumulation or disposition of details, yet does the world reappear in miniature in every*

event, so that all the laws of nature may be read in the smallest fact.
The Intellect must have the like perfection in its apprehension, and in
its works. (W 2: 201; emphasis added)

In other words, it is not simply the subject apprehending, nor the objects
that are themselves apprehended, but a greater interconnectivity that
draws all these relationships together so that in each object the whole is
manifest, since it does not possess its meaning in itself but in a larger con-
stitution of reality of which it is a part. In "Art," Emerson once again advo-
cates this Plotinian realization—for in picking up a written text, whether
poetic or prosaic, the reader only ostensibly initiates textual relation. His
act is not a beginning at all, but an extension of a triadic process already
underway. Each word is part of a greater order, which cannot be rebuilt
by either "detachment" or "aggregation," but each word is constituted and
constitutes itself in intellect's expansive activity of procession, conversion,
and self-constitution.

Plotinus thereby provides a model for perception that not only involves
the eye and the object, but allows for greater complexity. In Ennead V 5, 7,
Plotinus maps his triad onto the light-eye medium, arguing that although
"seeing is double" (subject-object), nonetheless, it involves three parts: the
light from above, the eye which perceives, and the objects that are per-
ceived.[55] What makes Plotinian perception so slippery a concept is that
perception takes place not just from the point of view of the eye; instead,
each side of the triad actively participates in the unfolding of vision so that
each has the potential to awaken in itself the whole of which it is a part.
In Emerson's oeuvre, what is ostensibly a double structure—soul and its
metempsychotic masks—becomes a more complex triadic structure, espe-
cially in terms of perception. The triadic act of perception is evident in the
metempsychotic journey of the eye in "Circles." Here, the "god" proceeds
from above, the flash of the eye converts the divine light it receives, and the
statues that are perceived in this conversion begin to constitute themselves
into fiery men: "Then cometh the god, and converts the statues into fiery
men, and by a flash of his eye burns up the veil which shrouded all things,
and the meaning is manifest" (W 2: 184). Once the eye receives the emana-
tion of the "god" that descends into being and constitutes itself into a flash
of light, it then proceeds into the statutes, which, like the eye, receive the
light and become conscious beings. In "Love" as well, this triadic structure
takes place when the perceiving individual is flooded with light. After the
lover and beloved have taken on a "combination of all possible positions"
testing out the "strength and weakness" of each other, the lover prays to a
higher power so that "every thread throughout the whole web of relation" is
transmuted "into a golden ray" (W 2: 108). In both passages, one may hear

the echo of the *7th Letter* where Plato explains that after running through detailed comparisons and "disputations" of names, definitions, sights, and perceptions, "at last in a flash of understanding of each" "the meaning" or the "lesson one has to learn [. . .] blazes up, and the mind, as it exerts all its powers to the limit of human capacity, is flooded with light."[56]

Prototypes of Perception II: Goethe and the Self-Constituting Eye

For Emerson, the self-constituting eye, which has its basis in Platonism and Neoplatonism, undergoes not only a transformation but also a decisive scientific culmination in Goethe's oeuvre.[57] Goethe's venture into optics and experimentation with the camera obscura develop another prototype of perception that Emerson incorporates into his metempsychotic conception of vision. Adapting his 1841 celebration of the genius who sees the protean monad in all its dramatic metempsychotic masks (*W* 2: 8), Emerson champions the process by which Goethe "detected the Genius of life, the old cunning Proteus, nestling close beside us, and showed that the dullness and prose we ascribe to the age was only another of his masks" (*W* 4: 157–58). Accordingly, in *Representative Men* (1850), Emerson depicts Goethe's brilliance in his ability *to see* and then *to exhibit* the historical series of being and, thus, to take part in the formulation of an aspiring historical order, which begins when Plato "first drew the circle" and ends with Goethe the writer "who see[s] connexion, where the multitude see fragments" and is "impelled to exhibit the facts in ideal order, and so to supply the axis on which the frame of things turns" (*W* 4: 153). While most creation "is mere stenography," Emerson sees in Goethe "no permissive or accidental appearance," but a truly "self-registering" event, which "is provided and prepared from of old and from everlasting, in the knitting and contexture of things," and yet becomes, on its own terms, the axis for the wheel of nature to turn once more so as to achieve "the second creation" (*W* 4: 152, 153).

In *Plotinus or the Simplicity of Vision*, Pierre Hadot affirms the mystical basis for Goethe's phenomenology as founded centrally upon Neoplatonism, asking rhetorically, "What is Goethe's 'original phenomenon' (*Urphänomen*) other than Form as Plotinus conceives it?"[58] "Plotinus' Forms [. . .] are hieroglyphs which draw themselves," for "the world of Forms does not carry out a program or plan above and beyond itself; rather, one could say that it invents and posits itself."[59] In other words, the Plotinian system of self-constitution in which everything in nature operates according to an oscillating, dynamically interlinked polarity achieves a modern expression in Goethe's thought.[60] For Emerson, Goethe's essential teaching follows the formulation of Plotinian self-constitution with the human being as the most finely adapted exponent of such incessant "self-registration": "All things are engaged in writing their history" (W 4: 151). Goethe's reinterpretation of this ancient tradition gives a new and striking currency to the senses, for it is in correctly educating the very physiology of perception that theory itself properly arises, not as something beyond the phenomenon, but as something from within the phenomenon. In Goethe's famous words, "Do not search for anything behind the phenomena: They themselves are the teaching."[61] Here, Goethe does not reject Neoplatonic Form; rather, his experimental method emphasizes the process by which an observer comes to understand "the higher-order experience within experience."[62]

Perception as a form of self-constitution is the theme that nourishes Emerson's interest in the German poet. Much like Emerson's individual who undertakes the pedagogy of the metempsychotic series in order to pass through "countless individuals" to "the eternal unity" (W 2: 8), Goethe's experimenter must journey through all the phenomenal effects in order to intuit the *Urphänomen* itself. Instead "of verifying or falsifying a hypothesis conceived ideally, outside of experience, the important thing is to order the experiments in such a way that, in progressing through the series of experiences, the underlying idea becomes immediately intuitive."[63] For Goethe, "each phenomenon in nature, rightly observed, wakens in us a new organ of inner understanding." In undergoing such pedagogy of vision, an individual begins to elicit a fuller understanding of what a phenomenon truly is, for as "one learns to see more clearly, he or she also learns to see more *deeply*."[64]

In his early lectures especially, Emerson meditates upon Goethe's ideal unity of the spiritual and actual. Quoting from the *Metamorphosis of Plants* (1790), Emerson argues that the spirit develops itself through "Animal Organization" so that "every fact that is disclosed to us in natural history removes one scale more from the eye" (*EL* 1: 24, 15). As part of a spiritually aspiring, open-ended system of adaptation, the eye, according to Goethe, increasingly refines itself, thereby undergoing a gradual organic metamorphosis in which it learns to see nature with ever-greater clarity: "The morphological idea prompted Goethe to consider the eye as a simple organic sensitivity to light which has gradually developed in some animals into more refined capacities of physiological response."[65] Underlying Goethe's optics, moreover, is the conviction that the human being constructs visible reality, and the *Theory of Colors* (1810) powerfully articulates the conviction that from "light, shade, and colour, we construct the visible world."[66]

The central Emersonian belief that "man is a center for nature, running out threads of relation through everything fluid and solid, material and elemental" (*W* 4: 6) arises, therefore, out of Goethe's emphasis on vision and subjectivity, which so decisively influenced later German Idealism. Like Schelling, Novalis, Hegel, and the un-idealistic Schopenhauer,[67] Emerson championed the *Theory of Colors* as a definitive remedy to the narrowly constructed empiricism arising after the Enlightenment.[68] Admiring the way in which Goethe foregrounds the creative power of perception, Emerson praises Goethe's ability to enter into the science of optics and to undermine the objective existence of colors, formed in nature without the immediacy of the self-constituting power of perception. "In optics," Emerson writes, Goethe "rejected the artificial theory of seven colors, and considered that every colour was the mixture of light and darkness in new proportions" (*W* 4: 159).

In opposition to Isaac Newton's foundational scientific theory that colors are "the diverse refrangibility" of light,[69] Goethe used the camera obscura to refute "a purely objective correlate of color." Goethe argued that "all color is seen, and thus any comprehensive science of color must reflect this fact by incorporating as a fundamental condition the activity of seeing and the lawful contributions of the eye."[70] While Goethe did not disagree with Newton that color is produced by light under certain conditions, he vehemently and even excessively accused Newton of "sophistry, stubbornness, and shamelessness, even of self-deception bordering on dishonesty."[71] The "greatest evil of modern physics" Goethe writes, is that "one has as it were divorced the experiments from man," wanting "to know nature only in what artificial instruments show, to limit and prove thereby what nature can accomplish."[72] Opposing the fundamental epistemological apparatus of Newtonian optics, Goethe insists instead that color is produced in dynamic relation to the eyes that perceive it: "Colour is an elementary phenomenon in nature adapted to the sense of vision; a phenomenon which, like all others, exhibits itself by separation and contrast, by commixture, and union, by augmentation and neutralization, by communication and dissolution."[73] In other words, color is a tendency that manifests itself through experience—and not one form of experience from which one can extrapolate an objective law, but a multiplicity of predicaments and conditions that are grounded in the ever-shifting experience of a perceiving subject.[74]

In *The Damnation of Newton* (1986), Fredrick Burwick describes the initial difference between Newton and Goethe's use of the camera obscura and argues that, in Goethe's very first experimentation with prismatic color in 1791, he was already radically departing from Newton's methodology. The reasons for this departure from the established tradition of the camera obscura were initially circumstantial. Having to return the borrowed prism he was using while moving to new quarters, Goethe in his haste did not properly outfit his new room to the specifications of the camera obscura, failing to cover properly "the one window with a sheet of metal which would allow sunlight to enter through a small hole of the prescribed dimensions."[75] Instead, Goethe put himself directly into the experiment. Whereas "Newton's experiment was objective" in the sense that "he observed the beam of sunlight enter the prism and divide into rays that cast a colorful spectrum on the opposite wall," Goethe placed the prism directly in front of his eyes and thus made himself the focal point from which colors manifested themselves.[76] Within this subject-oriented schema, Goethe concluded "that color arose on the surface or boundary because of the interaction or tension between light and darkness,"[77] the very polarity of light and darkness eliciting not simply the emergence, but the experience of color.

The haste with which Goethe attempted his first experimentation certainly affected his findings. But his later experiments were anything but hasty or clumsy. Criticizing Newton for not testing his color theory in a rigorous enough manner and for "drawing overhasty conclusions from isolated experiments," Goethe came "to the nucleus of his experimental method" in "the systemic multiplication of experiments,"[78] many of which posed "conditions in which the inescapable physiological components of vision can be artificially isolated and made observable."[79] By instructing his reader to seal the hole of the camera obscura so that color no longer arises within the apparatus, but "belongs to the eye" as an undulating, changing afterimage, Goethe "announces a disordering and negation of the camera obscura as both an optical system and epistemological figure."[80] Goethe thereby frustrates the very structure of knowledge that "the order of the camera obscura" permitted so that "the kind of separation between interior representation and exterior reality implicit in the camera obscura becomes in Goethe's work a single surface of affect on which interior and exterior have few of their former meanings and positions."[81] What replaces the previous order is "the unstable physiology and temporality of the human body,"[82] which demand and reinvigorate, especially in the context of Emerson, a new focus upon self-fashioning and exerting the powers of the individual in order to overcome one's fettered state.

It is not simply Goethe's revolutionary stance against seventeenth-century modes of vision that impressed Emerson, however. Emerson saw in Goethe the dynamic continuation of Platonism and Neoplatonism's express aim to synthesize the polarity of the universe within the thinking individual. Goethe's theory of vision dynamically adapts Plato's dialectic of perception and the Plotinian light-eye medium, thereby making the Neoplatonic tradition the site upon which modern subjectivity itself is possible. In *Theory of Colors*, Goethe explains that his very conception of the metamorphic eye arises directly out of the Ionian school and Plato's *Republic*.[83] Echoing Plotinus's famous dictum that the light of the sun and the light of the eye are cognate,[84] Goethe insists that the "eye may be said to owe its existence to light, which calls forth [. . .] a sense that is akin to itself."[85] Accordingly, the eye is "fit for the action of light; the light it contains corresponding with the light without,"[86] so that color arises out of light through the subject's experience of it both within and outside himself.

Goethe's departure from the order of the camera obscura with its express objectivity arises, at least in part, as a consequence of adapting these ancient structures of vision. Like Plotinus's tripartite system of perception (eye, sunlight, and object),[87] Goethe's *Theory of Colors* establishes an almost identical tripartite phenomenology of color:

> Goethe ultimately worked out a tripartite division that he hoped would elucidate the most basic conditional categories, within which further subdivisions could be carried out. The three main categories comprised the contribution of the eye, the contribution of the medium through which the image-bearing light passes, and the contribution of the illuminated and perceived object—which Goethe named, respectively, the physiological, physical and chemical aspects of color.[88]

Here, the epistemological assumptions of seventeenth- and eighteenth-century science are eclipsed by another arrangement of knowledge in which perception opens itself in a multifaceted way, while always grounding itself in the tangible, yet shifting schema of the human body. It is not simply a subject who sees or an object that impresses itself upon this subject. Rather, the eye opens and forms itself according to the light that calls forth this vision and to the illuminated object that, like the subject himself, begins to transform and constitute itself anew.

Emerson's own dynamic of vision cannot be fully understood without this history. In "Beauty" (1860), for instance, the same tripartite structure of light, eye, and object provides the medium through which a poetic, self-constituting event is made possible. As light from without opens itself and proceeds into the experience of polarity, the "second sight of the mind" is awakened from within and begins to constitute its own deep vision of itself, so that both together they, light and eye, disclose the "secret architecture" or "deep holdings in the frame of things" and an object is not only apprehended, but created and imbued with a form of self-consciousness:

Polarized light showed the secret architecture of bodies; and when the *second-sight* of the mind is opened, now one color or form or gesture, and now another, has a pungency, as if a more interior ray had been emitted, disclosing its deep holdings in the frame of things. The laws of this translation we do not know, or why one feature or gesture enchants, why one word or syllable intoxicates, but the fact is familiar that the fine touch of the eye, or a grace of manners or a phrase of poetry plants wings at our shoulders; as if the Divinity, in his approaches, lifts away mountains of obstruction, and deigns to draw a truer line, which the mind knows and owns. (*W* 6: 162–63)[89]

In his *First Series of Essays* in 1841, Emerson depicts men as dead statues, which require the Seeing Eye to burn away their dislocation and connect them together in a fiery line. Almost two decades later, the same structure is at play in "Beauty" (1860), for the "fine touch of the eye [. . .] deigns to draw a truer line"[90] from out of the ostensibly immoveable pattern creation has taken.[91] This dialectical movement from perception to representation, however, does not adequately illuminate the complex structure of the passage above. It is through the procession of light, the conversion of the eye, and the self-constitution of all these elements into a freshly created object that Emerson synthesizes this unstable, yet highly ordered principle of sight that ever-seeks to write itself.

"Experience" and the Dilemma of Perception

Emerson's praise of Goethe is only matched in intensity by his subsequent criticism. Although Goethe is no imitator, he is not yet an artist (*W* 4: 163). "He is fragmentary; a writer of occasional poems, and of an encyclopædia of sentences" (*W* 4: 165), Emerson concludes at the close of *Representative Men*. The cause of Emerson's disaffection is highly significant. He does not question Goethe's work with eyesight, which remains for him an example of dedication and profound, original discovery. What he criticizes instead is Goethe's failure to recognize fully that in each act of self-constitution, the perceiver also abandons himself to a power from without. While Goethe may scrutinize nature with the finest and most precise eye, "lay[ing] a ray of light under every fact" (*W* 4: 163), he is incapable, Emerson insists, of abandoning himself to the highest unity: "I dare not say that Goethe ascended to the highest grounds from which genius has spoken. He has not worshipped the highest unity; he is incapable of a selfsurrender to the moral sentiment" (*W* 4: 163). As Sharon Cameron rightly argues about Emersonian individuality, "What self-reliance turns out to mean for Emerson is a strong recognition of the inadequacy of any person, other persons or this person. And what the preacher and the American scholar know how to do is break out of the tyranny of egotistical self-enclosure."[92] Emerson thereby criticizes Goethe's egotistical individualism and argues that Goethe evaded the highest metaphysical test: he is unable to let go of the self in each stage of perception. What one finds, accordingly, is Emerson's dedication to metempsychotic vision, a process in which self-constitution is accompanied by self-surrender.

Emerson's criticism of Goethe's inability for "selfsurrender" also possesses a very precise Neoplatonic context. As we have seen, in Plato's *7th Letter*, "the meaning" or the "lesson one has to learn" finds its culmination only after rigorous and self-refuting study by "the mind" exerting itself to its limits and being "flooded with light."[93] Emerson's "Love" (1841) closely follows such a formulation. The process of being "flooded with light" for Emerson is intricately connected with being transformed into a ray of light and, thus, is itself an experience of self-surrender. Only by first perceiving all combinations of the series and then abandoning this developed self can an individual self be "transmuted" into a "golden ray of light" and thereby recover—albeit in a new way—an original, spiritual state. In "Uriel" as well, the fallen god reconstitutes and develops himself in his ascending metempsychotic journey through nature and eventually "grow[s] too bright/ To hit the nerve of feebler sight."[94] In this moment of spiritual brightness, the surrendered self is transformed into a purely creative power, at once overcoming the order of time and yet resubjecting itself into a temporal, mimetic series in which the metempsychotic process can begin again so as to achieve an even finer material adaptation.

In "Experience" (1844) particularly, the dilemma that haunts the metempsychotic order and the double consciousness implicit in its sequence is that the individual is both capable and incapable of this "selfsurrender" and recovery in a new form. On the one hand, Emerson argues that the circular movement of self-constitution and abandonment operates potentially in every moment: "To finish the moment, to find the journey's end in every step of the road, to live the greatest number of good hours, is wisdom" (*W* 3: 35). Through sudden "flashes of light," the perceiving individual in a type of incomplete metempsychotic ecstasy begins to constitute himself into a new self that converts "the love and homage of innumerable ages" into the youth and rigor of a fresh, as-yet-unpeopled land: "I am ready to die out of nature, and be born again into this new yet unapproachable America I have found in the West" (*W* 3: 41).[95] On the other hand, Emerson just as surely argues that such activity is beyond the scope of one individual alone. Using the image of Goethe's color wheel, Emerson reflects upon the nature of light and the problem of spinning the wheel fast enough so that the colors return to their original unity: "It needs the whole society, to give the symmetry we seek. The parti-colored wheel must revolve very fast to appear white" (W 3: 34). Although light throws itself into the experience of polarity and color in each moment, the ability to reunite these colors requires a speed that the human subject cannot quite muster. The very physiology of the eyes, in turn, cannot be trusted, for the focal unity they attain is defective: "Of what use is genius, if the organ is too convex or too concave, and cannot find a focal distance within the actual horizon of human life?" (W 3: 30). The experience of optics, therefore, points to the process in which the self-constituting individual finds his or her limits in vision.

Echoing the image in "Love" of an individual being transmuted into a golden ray of light, Emerson's "Experience" paradoxically answers what is needed to unify the polarity of the created world: "A man is a golden impossibility. The line he must walk is a hair's breadth" (W 3: 38–39). Because a single individual cannot perceive "a focal distance within the actual horizon of human life," he fails to unite the polarity of the double consciousness in himself. Again, Goethe's *Theory of Colors* provides an imagistic structure of colored lenses through which Emerson depicts the individual's inability to constitute or recover himself in his experience of the historical series of being. He or she is simply the experience of light in polarity, thereby becoming a color that cannot escape its own hue. And though this individual may expand himself or herself by experiencing successive steps in the series, he or she cannot attain the speed sufficient to convert all the individual colors of the series back into light:

> Dream deliver us to dream, and there is no end to illusion. Life is a train of moods like a string of beads, and, as we pass through them, they prove to be many-colored lenses which paint the world their own hue, and each shows only what lies in its focus. From the mountain you see the mountain. We animate what we can, and we see only what we animate. Nature and books belong to the eyes that see them. [. . .] Thus inevitably does the universe wear our color, and every object fall successively into the subject itself. The subject exists, the subject enlarges; all things sooner or later fall into place" (W 3: 30, 46).

As both subject and object fall into each other without fully converting or constituting themselves anew, the chiasmus of the double consciousness—the procession of the One and the conversion back to the One—takes on a futile, even absurd luster, pointing to the limits of human perception: "We animate what we can, and we see only what we animate." Accordingly, life's series is not composed of "good moments," in which the individual "find[s] the journey's end in every step of the road" (W 3: 35). The series is a train of moods whose individual colors dominate the perceiving subject who, in turn, colors the world so that the circular series inscribes only the solipsistic, enclosing bond between subject and object: "We have no means of correcting these colored and distorting lenses which we are, or of computing the amount of their errors" (W 3: 43).

While procession, conversion, and self-constitution are the principal features of the greater arc of creation, Emerson anticipates an already strikingly modern (even postmodern) focus upon the perceptual poverty, devolution, or scattering of a self that is unable to posit itself in the existential dilemma of self-constitution or find itself fully in its metempsychotic readings. Consequently, in "Experience," Emerson employs the image of a cat chasing her tail as a fitting analogy for all individual human activity, from scientific investigation, to America's discovery, to the act of reading itself. A human being may expand the dimensions of his circular enterprise to galvanic proportions, but the power to complete the circle is lacking all the same, no matter whether it is a universal circuit or a "solitary performance":

> Do you see that kitten chasing so prettily her own tail? If you could look with her eyes, you might see her surrounded with hundreds of figures performing complex dramas, with tragic and comic issues, long conversations, many characters, many ups and downs of fate,— and meantime it is only puss and her tail. How long before out masquerade will end its noise of tambourines, laughter, and shouting, and we shall find it was a solitary performance?—A subject and an object,—it takes so much to make the galvanic circuit complete, but magnitude adds nothing. What imports it whether it is Kepler and the sphere, Columbus and America; a reader and his book; or puss with her tail? (W 3: 46)

While the passage above denotes an ostensibly futile movement between subject and object, Emerson is, nevertheless, implicitly adamant about situating the circle within the context of the aspiring metempsychotic order. In fact, he instructs his reader not just to recognize the absurdity of subjective perception, but to project his perception beyond himself— into another body: "If you could look with her eyes." Impelling the reader to see with the eyes of the cat eventually requires other metempsychotic perceptions, which come to include the reader's own standpoint: "Kepler and the sphere, Columbus and America; a reader and his book." In this sense, the galvanic circuit of metempsychotic perception requires a type of abandonment and recovery: from the self into another and from that other back into the self and so on repeatedly so that a new creed will be formed out of the metempsychotic experiences of others: "Onward and onward! In liberating moments, we know that a new picture of life and duty is already possible; the elements already exist in many minds around you [. . .]. The new statement will comprise the skepticisms, as well as the faiths of society, and out of unbeliefs a creed shall be formed" (*W* 3: 43). It may not be the full abandonment with which a human being is transmuted into a golden ray of light, but it nonetheless prepares a subject to see more than just himself—to take on, as it were, a society within himself, for to convert colors into light requires, as we saw, an entire society: "It needs the whole society, to give the symmetry we seek. The parti-colored wheel must revolve very fast to appear white" (*W* 3: 34).

Emerson offers, therefore, a vital amendment to the apparent futility of the chiastic, circular relationship between perceiving subject and object. Although the human being cannot fully constitute himself anew or enter the "unapproachable America" he sees shining in the west, he must nevertheless seek a "vigorous self-recovery" by accepting first the impoverished ground of experience:[96] "And we cannot say too little of our constitutional necessity of seeing things under private aspects, or saturated with our humors. And yet is the God the native of these bleak rocks. That need makes in morals the capital virtue of self-trust. We must hold hard to this poverty, however scandalous, and by more vigorous self-recoveries, after the sallies of action, possess our axis more firmly" (*W* 3: 46). Amid such "poverty," the human being must, first, achieve a type of self-reliance or "self-trust" and push every trivial relationship—even if it is simply a puss with her tail—to an "extravagance" so that "the soul attains her due sphericity" (*W* 3: 46). In this way, the subject projects his vision beyond himself and yet recovers himself so that with each activity, he "possess[es]" his "axis more firmly." The principle of this procession, conversion, and self-constitution so much underlies the oscillating movement of "Experience" that Emerson concludes that the lesson of self-constitution will assist the individual in his further passage into new worlds: "In the solitude to which every man is always returning, he has a sanity and revelations, which in his passage into new worlds he will carry with him." If the color wheel is to spin as it should, self-recovery cannot mean an individual's complete self-constitution, for each failure initiates another abandonment of the self in vision so as to realize a new vital self: "Never mind the ridicule, never mind the defeat: up again, old heart!—it seems to say,—there is victory yet for all justice; and the true romance which the worlds exists to realize, will be the transformation of genius into practical power" (*W* 3: 49).

Emerson's conception of vision, therefore, incorporates Goethean perception, but it does so while much more strongly affirming its Platonic, Plotinian roots. Goethe's eye constitutes itself and the world in its vision through the triadic eye-light medium, and Emerson interprets this structure with explicit metempsychotic overtones in "Experience." Sixteen years later in "Fate" (1860), Emerson is even more emphatic; the human being does not necessarily live a thousand times, but he experiences moments of vision so important to his being that he rightly understands that his body is a product of all these moments. Inasmuch as seeing is an individualistic, self-constituting activity, the opening of "the inward eye" to its own succession also represents, for Emerson, the abandonment and simultaneous recovery of the self. Where, for Goethe, the sunlight draws forth a sense akin to itself, which comes to posit and inscribe itself in seeing, for Emerson, the "beatitude dips from on high" so that a human being sees and registers himself in nature by lawgiving, speaking, and divining:

> *We rightly say of ourselves, we were born, and afterward we were born again, and many times.* We have successive experiences so important, that the new forgets the old, and hence the mythology of the seven or the nine heavens. The day of days, the great day of the feast of life, is that in which the inward eye opens to the Unity in things, to the omnipresence of law;—sees that what is must be, and ought to be, or is the best. *This beatitude dips from on high down on us, and we see.* It is not in us so much as we are in it. If the air come to our lungs, we breathe and live; if not, we die. If the light come to our eyes, we see; else not. And if truth comes to our mind, we suddenly expand to its dimensions, as if we grew to worlds. We are as lawgivers; we speak for Nature; we prophesy and divine. (*W* 6: 14; emphasis added)

Each act of perception, then, is a metempsychotic step in the series, accumulating into "successive experiences" so that we are "born again, and many times." But, as I have shown, it is not a univocal or stable methodology; rather, Emerson offers a way of opening the eye toward its own temporality and spatiality, even while insisting that the physiology that reveals these dimensions pivots upon more than materialities in line, row, or relation; it embraces and opens itself up to an abiding volatility that is at once the beatitude that falls from on high, the eye that constitutes itself in seeing, and the words that in being looked at must attain a type of self-constitution as well.

The Emergent Figure of the Poet

The lessons of perception's poverty, as well as the ensuing need to correct the limits of individual vision through the eyes of the other, underlie Emerson's understanding of the process of reading and, more specifically, the highest value he places on poetry. Although Emerson did not fully realize this in his own verse, his work with metempsychotic perception both lays the foundations for a new poetics of reading and sets out a direction for modern poetry. No longer are meter or rhyme essential to the new poetic order; instead, there is a context and form implied that reinterprets and revitalizes past traditions in the very process of reading. The metaphysical structure of dialectic and the metempsychotic motion that it entails become latent characteristics of poetic textuality that the reader draws forth in his activity, even when he or she does not at first comprehend the process in question.[97] Emerson offers his readers a vital visual project where individual perception opens itself up into a polyphonic, fluctuating sphere in which the varying stages of chiastic creation and adjustment of individual vision take place: the movement outward from soul to manifestation and its inversion from manifestation to soul. Soul maintains a distinct privilege as an originative feature in the order of genesis, but the inward turn, arising in the order of time, conflicts with this perspective, prioritizing being and perception as foundations for consciousness and its expanding interconnectivities.

In this expanding and contracting visual process, Emerson establishes an ordered relativity, a truly "volatile essence," which affirms the immanent subject—as a fluctuating perception that continually draws a greater number of relations into its development—and uses the same method to unravel the subject's aspiring centricity in perception's perpetual expansion. There are always more vantage points beyond the optical capability of the subject for which he must attempt to account. Emersonian reading is, thus, carefully worked out. As the eye follows the textual sequence of dead letters and converts them into a living web of relations, the reader possesses some measure of command over what he reads. At the same time, in initiating his eyebeam into the growing stream of successive, interlinking objects, he is inevitably drawn forward by the very structure that his relations take and is forced to confront the inescapable eventuality of the process and admit a certain defeat, since his own physiology "cannot span the huge orbits of the prevailing ideas, behold their return, and reconcile their opposition" (*W* 6: 2). Because Emerson so viscerally creates this personal sense of poverty even in the moment of pervasive perceptual expansion, his celebration of the "coming poet" takes on a startling allure. The future poet promises to reconcile the orbits that we as readers were not quite able to fathom and, as a result, this poet becomes even more real to us since he is our own, as-yet-unreal projection beyond the half-constituted conversion of the self in perception.

Emersonian metempsychosis, as an expanding relationship between reader and text, thereby integrates metaphysics into an open-ended phenomenological inquiry whose limit and simultaneous limitlessness bear an uneasy, although cohesive logic. In this fluctuating body of relations, it is not simply a matter of what we deem noble or ignoble, what we wish to praise or to dismiss—all the similarities and differences that make these concepts meaningful are needed in order to understand the expansive, self-regulating system that underscores every act of cognition, higher and lower alike: "We side with the hero, as we read or paint, against the coward and the robber; but we have been ourselves that coward and robber, and shall be again, not in the low circumstance, but in comparison with the grandeurs possible to the soul" (*W* 2: 81). Emerson's methodology of reading bears some similarity to Laplace's and Quetelet's respective theories on probability that became synonymous with material determinism in the nineteenth century. For Emerson, if one attempts to predict the future, one must consider all the variables that manifest themselves in the functioning of a system in motion.[98]

Unlike this law of errors, however, Emerson consistently invigorates his system with the tenuous prospect of self-direction. Certainly, the individual works himself up from his bare first-person delineations to contemplate and experience the ever-shifting system in which he is set. But if he is to have any value, Emerson insists, he must nurture a hope that in its highest state the soul or animating life can reshape the self into a higher manifestation and interrelation. To perceive the work of art, therefore, is to enter into the promise of creation with no limit in sight, within which human beings must invariably initiate themselves in the way of metempsychosis so as to apprehend their own future reorganization in matter:[99] "But the thoughts which these few hermits strove to proclaim by silence, as well as by speech, *not only by what they did, but by what they forebore to do*, shall abide in beauty and strength, to reorganize themselves in nature, to invest themselves anew in other, perhaps higher endowed and happier mixed clay than ours, in fuller union with the surrounding system" (*W* 1: 216; emphasis added). Aspiration, Emerson insists in the concluding lines of his lecture, "The Transcendentalist" (1841), leaves its mark in the developing code of life. But he is just as emphatic that those few hermits capable of a more complete self-constitution did not achieve their reorganization in nature; nor did they realize a fuller union with the surrounding system. As Emerson writes in "Art" (1841), "Our best praise is given to what they aimed and promised, not to the actual result" (*W* 2: 215).[100]

The act of reading a text is a form of revelation and simultaneous deferral. Reading revivifies a past, dead sequence by drawing it into a new cognitive currency, but the process itself is never wholly present, for the full reorganization of nature and the constitution of an individual self always partially defer themselves. Emerson thereby affirms the prospect of a self that apprehends and draws its relations into the life of individual consciousness. At the same time, this achievement also threatens such unity since it gestures to the dissolution and reconstitution of the individual self in the greater arc of creation, a transmigration that perception upholds, but individual consciousness cannot:

> With what joy I begin to read a poem, which I confide in as an inspiration! And now my chains are to be broken; I shall mount above these clouds and opaque airs in which I live,—opaque, though they seem transparent,—and from the heaven of truth I shall see and comprehend my relations. That will reconcile me to life, and renovate nature, to see trifles animated by a tendency, and to know what I am doing. Life will no more be a noise; now I shall see men and women, and know the signs by which they may be discerned from fools and satans. This day shall be better than my birthday: then I became an animal: now I am invited into the science of the real. *Such is the hope, but the fruition is postponed.* (W 3: 8; emphasis added)

By initiating a textual activity ("I begin to read a poem"), the reader begins to change the poem and convert each of its relations. What were mere "trifles" are now "animated by a tendency." In absorbing, assuming, and passing over the literal characters of the poem, the reader reveals this tendency so that consciousness can "comprehend [its] relations" from another, higher vantage point. In this respect, the relationship between the reader and the poem provides a new ontological event, a drawing together of one's immediate, shifting relations into the self-reflexive work of human consciousness.[101] Emerson sees this aspiration in reading as a potentially divine vantage point, for the spatial positioning of the reader above and looking down on the book he reads takes on an added heavenly symbolism, where a whole host of objects are transformed into a new combination. In Plotinian terms, this polyphonic experience is the "clear perception" of Intellect, a kind of intelligible, metempsychotic power refracted in bodies through the medium of the perceptive soul, as we saw above. Though mediated, such perception apprehends the object—now the text—and begins a process of renewal. At the same time, the whole process is prospective, and there remains an element not wholly present in the multiplicity of being and becoming, since again in the order of embodied, time-bound experience, the indeterminate entity that seeks to posit or constitute itself is not altogether capable of such an feat.

What makes Emerson such a demanding thinker for his readers is precisely this challenge of perception and the deferral of unified sight. In "The Poet," Emerson does not simply announce the coming poet; rather, he asks his readers to see with "all eyes," to consider the greater arc of creation funneling itself from the past to the present to the future, and to ask the age-old, metempsychotic question that the Brahmins and Pythagoras sought to perceive and answer in their time:[102]

> There was this perception in him, which makes the poet or seer an
> object of awe and terror, namely, that the same man, or society of
> men, may wear one aspect to themselves and their companions and
> a different aspect to higher intelligences. Certain priests, whom he
> describes as conversing very learnedly together, appeared to the chil-
> dren, who were at some distance, like dead horses; and many the like
> misappearances. And instantly the mind inquires, whether these
> fishes under the bridge, yonder oxen in the pasture, those dogs in the
> yard, are immutably fishes, oxen, and dogs, or only so appear to me,
> and perchance to themselves appear upright men; and whether I ap-
> pear as a man to all eyes. The Bramins and Pythagoras propounded
> the same question, and if any poet has witnessed the transformation,
> he doubtless found it in harmony with various experiences. We have
> all seen changes as considerable in wheat and caterpillars. He is the
> poet, and shall draw us with love and terror, who sees, through the
> flowing vest, the firm nature, and can declare it. (W 3: 21)

Emerson refigures Plato's dialectic of perception—two lovers exchanging
eyebeams and increasing themselves in the process—into a highly charged
metempsychotic textual event, an unlimited and expansive reading pro-
cess. By divining the future aspiration of the historical series of being, we
perceive the poet and are also perceived by him from his higher, more en-
lightened vantage point, and within this pattern, a host of other binaries
emerge, prehistories of this relationship between perceiver and metem-
psychotic series, positing past arrangements that partially comprise the
present act of discernment, while also pointing to the future textual event.

Even the grammatical structure of Emerson's declaration of the future
poet intensifies the overall transmigratory context. Emerson begins in the
past tense—"There was this perception in him"—and finishes in a present
tense that quickly opens itself to the future: "He is the poet, and shall draw
us with love and terror, who sees, through the flowing vest, the firm na-
ture, and can declare it." As a result, the future, haunting image of the poet
arises as a sublime spectacle that Emerson forces his readers not simply to
consider, but to bring into a type of haunting existence. Readers cannot
isolate or reduce the future poet to any one past or present perspective,
since the poet is already made up of a whole host of vibrant fluctuating per-
spectives, including our own, seeking to unite themselves in nature—as we
saw above in "The Transcendentalist," in a "higher endowed and happier
mix [of] clay than ours, in fuller union with the surrounding system" (W
1: 216). The emergent poet not only combines all these past perspectives,
but also becomes in their prospective unity a separate, emergent act of con-
sciousness, echoing in this the Plotinian triad of procession, conversion,

and self-constitution—an orbit that we, as readers, cannot quite make. Even the assurance of the "firm nature [. . .] beneath the flowing vest" is not at all assuring; by contrast, it signifies our own dissolution since the poet's future activity means that we have become merely the materials that another consciousness now shapes.

In essay after essay, therefore, Emerson presents the tenuous activity between reader and text, which draws the past up to an almost tangible, yet still unknowable realization. The new ontological event has not yet come to be, even in the very presence of its own unfolding, and Emerson's poet is a presence announced and yet characteristically deferred: "I look in vain for the poet whom I describe. [. . .] Time and nature yield us many gifts, but not yet the timely man, the new religion, the reconciler, whom all things await" (W 3: 21). What is particularly prevalent in this process of "look[ing] in vain" is Emerson's desire for his readers to put themselves at risk through reading—to observe the pattern of their own succession, failure, and reconstitution through perception and mental projection.[103] Emerson's visual metempsychotic journey must remain essentially incomplete, yet it exudes a democratizing power where each person through perception becomes a poet: "We are all poets at last, and the life of each has high and solemn moments which remind him of the fact in a manner he cannot choose but understand" (EL 3: 365).

While Emerson offers his readers these visionary outlines of the new American poet who will compel all men and women to achieve their own preeminence, it is Walt Whitman who achieves a truly democratic vision of the poet in which the whole literary, philosophical, and scientific landscape of Emersonianism is plunged headlong into an ever-shifting confrontation and symmetry of perceiving subject and nation. "There was a child went forth every day,/ And the first object he look'd upon, that object he became," Whitman writes in the tenth, unnamed poem of the 1855 edition of Leaves of Grass, transforming the metempsychotic delineations of Emerson's thought into the perceptual framework of American selfhood. The "child who went forth every day, and who now goes, and will always go forth every day" seeks to incorporate the whole universe into himself through the pattern of his own perceptual succession. All these selves— Whitman who inscribed the poem, the present reader, and all those who follow—become part of this democratic fabric of poetic vision. As a result, Whitman's poetic form abandons the conventions of the past to embody the religious, philosophical, and scientific tensions of the nineteenth century. As readers, we no longer receive exquisitely organized eloquence from poetry, but a more formalized and sustained investigation of what it truly means *to see* and *to become*, to perceive a protean series and form ourselves from out of all our perceptions.

4 / Writing the Metempsychotic Text

While there is a propensity to interpret Whitman's poetry in the poetically secular terms of the twentieth century, a number of critics have come to emphasize the mystical and religious tenor of Whitman's writing. Throughout the 1960s and 1970s, for instance, scholars sought to uncover the Hindu influences in Whitman's poetry;[1] in recent decades, critics, like David Kuebrich and Arthur Versluis, have understood it in terms of a "new American religion."[2] Versluis touches upon a major obstacle in assessing the spiritual, mystical, or esoteric underpinnings of Whitman's writing. Such influences, he argues, "were utterly subordinated in Whitman's poetry to Whitman himself and to his own religious perspective."[3] Whitman's art of absorption and expansion, with its roots embedded in diverse metaphysical traditions from ancient Greek and Hindu thought to Christian esotericism and German Idealism, announces such an unusual compound of psychic and bodily union that Harold Bloom equates it with a new American religion "so original we as yet have not assimilated it."[4] Whitman, Bloom declares, is "the American bardic Christ, self-anointed to strike up the cognitive and spiritual music for the New World."[5]

Whitman largely understood his own poetic mission in this way: he was attempting "the Great Construction of the New Bible."[6] In 1872, he wrote that "one deep purpose underlay the others, and has underlain it and its execution ever since—and that has been the religious purpose." Michael Robertson argues that "critics have explained away [this] statement," even though during his own time, Whitman's disciples and admirers "insisted that *Leaves of Grass* should be interpreted in primarily moral and spiritual terms."[7] The spiritual ethos of Whitman's poetic project has not been fully understood; particularly lacking is any systematic treatment of the metempsychotic self in Whitman's poetic project. Indeed, much as Emerson's desire "to die out of nature and be born again into this new yet unapproachable America" (*W* 3: 41) has been interpreted as a process of negotiating constitutional identity,[8] so Whitman's revolutionary visualization of the poetic process is repeatedly understood as a type of individual and national negotiation, "similar to the Constitution in being an outline, a projection forward in time of the conditions of democratic personality and experience, just as the Constitution is a permanent frame."[9] Whitman imagined his mission in slightly different terms, adapting Emerson's metempsychotic vision of history's series and doing so in relation to Emerson's hope for an emergent American poet able to speak for his nation.

While Emerson looked forward to an American poet capable of true creation, he was also keenly aware that his own work failed to achieve anything close to such a feat. He was simply the one who could apprehend or hear "this new, yet unapproachable America," but could not articulate its greater proportions. The "fruition is postponed," he laments in "Experience." By contrast, Whitman announces himself as the future poet, a poeticized adaptation of Emerson's metempsychotic self, imbued with the powers of perception and proclamation. What was always unsettled and proleptic for Emerson—the future poet enacting the metempsychosis of nature to arrive at the end of being's series—becomes for Whitman, as his 1855 preface and "Song of Myself" indicate, the visual site upon which the incarnational drama of the divided self unfolds. While Emerson's depictions are often intellectual and abstract, Whitman draws into the metempsychotic process the visceral characteristics of biological, sexual urges along with their joys and torments, liberations and oppressions. This drama of the divided self with its metempsychotic structure underpins Whitman's poetic vision throughout his entire poetic career, from the boundless enthusiasm of his 1855 edition of *Leaves of Grass* to the isolated spiritualism of his later years.

"A Sort of Emerson Run Wild"

Whitman's 1855 edition of *Leaves of Grass*[10] with its ambitious preface and twelve unnamed poems holds the distinction of being the most unexpected and mysterious creation of the poet's career, perhaps of American poetry in general. Whereas scholarship has been able to map much of the historical context and detail for the later editions, Whitman's 1855 achievement remains all the more spectacular, since it arrives seemingly out of nowhere, rejecting the refinement of past poetry and seeking, as Whitman himself insisted, "to put a whole living man in the expression of a poem, without wincing."[11] While this assessment may well be true for present readers of Whitman's poetry, it was all the more so for the American public of the mid-nineteenth century who had little context for Whitman's radical poetic project other than to equate the "Good, Grey Poet," as he came to be known after the Civil War, with Emerson and New England transcendentalism. For some, Whitman was "a sort of Emerson run wild"[12] whose first two editions of *Leaves of Grass* (1855, 1856) were simply late transcendental attempts to resuscitate what was already a movement considered passé.[13]

The tendency—whether past or present—to understand Whitman in terms of his influential predecessors is certainly reasonable. Whitman for his part provided plenty of material to encourage the Emerson comparison. Even after he had already achieved the status of preeminent American bard, Whitman was not sparing in discussing Emerson as America's first man. In Whitman's conversations with Horace Traubel throughout the 1880s (which became the memoir *With Walt Whitman in Camden*), "Emerson is a constant, almost an obsessive presence in this record; there are over three hundred references to Emerson, many of them extended discussions."[14] These clear lines of influence, however, do not minimize the originality or richness of Whitman's response to either Emerson or the America of his day. The period of poetic development in the thirteen years[15] leading up to the first edition of *Leaves of Grass* was a time when Whitman immersed himself in a wide range of Romantic thought. As Whitman biographer Jerome Loving argues, "The notebooks leading up to *Leaves of Grass* strongly imply that Whitman was awash in romantic ideas about art and the artist and that he owed his vision to nothing in particular, but rather to a broad confluence of ideas and events."[16] While this diverse engagement in Romanticism may be true, Whitman himself preset and established the Emersonian context for the first two editions of *Leaves of Grass*. In 1855, Whitman sent his anonymous collection of poems by mail as a gift to Emerson who was unsure to whom he owed gratitude for "the most extraordinary piece of wit and wisdom that America has yet contributed" and wished to meet his "benefactor."[17] This high praise Whitman soon published without Emerson's permission in the *New York Tribune* for October 10 and again in the 1856 edition of *Leaves of Grass*.[18]

In the 1856 edition, Whitman particularly reveals his eagerness to situate the *Leaves of Grass* within the purview of Emersonianism, not as an artistic debt, but as a grand development of Emerson's call for a new American identity and expression.[19] Having included both Emerson's letter of praise and his own response as a second preface,[20] Whitman repeatedly calls Emerson "Master" and honors him for discovering the shores of the nation, which Whitman and other poets are to enlarge and ennoble.

While Whitman's language is certainly extravagant, his early enthusiasm for Emerson is not simply that of an apprentice for a "Master."[21] Instead, it can be more appropriately understood as an epic response to a poetic challenge that had gone unanswered:

> Those shores you found. I say you have led The States there—have led Me there. I say that none has ever done, or ever can do, a greater deed for The States, than your deed. Others may line out the lines, build cities, work mines, break up farms; it is yours to have been the original true Captain who put to sea, intuitive, positive, rendering the first report, to be told less by any report, and more by the mariners of a thousand bays, in each tack of their arriving and departing, many years after you.
>
> Receive, dear Master, these statements and assurances through me, for all the young men, and for an earnest that we know none before you, but the best following you; and that we demand to take your name into our keeping, and that we understand what you have indicated, and find the same indicated in ourselves, and that we will stick to it and enlarge upon it through These States. (*1856*: 374–88)

Emerson's own failure to become the great poet that he had himself called for only served to reemphasize the momentous achievement of this future individual. Whitman himself was keenly aware of this fact. Although he defended Emerson's verse against criticism, he never regarded Emerson as a great poet or even as a critic capable of recognizing great poetry, although he certainly used Emerson's sanction and praise to his own benefit.[22] As he would later write, "It has been doubtful to me if Emerson really knows or feels what Poetry is at its highest."[23] The desire to exceed, not to imitate, is, Whitman argues, the principal value of worth in Emerson's thought, since Emerson provides the young man with the necessary evolutionary compulsion for self-reliant disobedience: "The best part of Emersonianism is, it breeds the giant that destroys itself. Who wants to be any man's mere follower? lurks behind every page. No teacher ever taught, that has so provided for his pupil's setting up independently—no truer evolutionist."[24]

Presetting Whitman's poetic project in terms of Emersonianism can be misleading, therefore, since the very self-reliance Emerson preached discourages the linearity of an absolute poetic genealogy. In addition, Whitman himself was not part of the culture of New England transcendentalism with its Whig politics and intellectual privileges. Rather, he was raised a Jacksonian Democrat by a family that bordered continually on financial and psychological ruin. It was Whitman's political prowess, not his poetry, which allowed him to escape his family, to enter into the New

York newspaper game and to come to know the city that would figure so prominently in his poetry. Instead of nature and the self-reliant intellectual, Whitman more often celebrates the titanic and always uneasy democratic union of teeming cities, the sacred with the daily lives of American men and women, the transcendent alongside the erotic. Yet when Whitman proclaims in the 1855 preface to the *Leaves of Grass* that the "poets of the kosmos advance through all interpositions and coverings and turmoils and stratagems to first principles" (*1855*: 524–26), implicit in this declaration are the broad brushstrokes of Emerson's metempsychotic mind.[25] Whitman emphatically emphasizes that if the poet is to attain power, he must first pass through all the various coverings and bodies that had come before him. Consequently, Whitman imagines himself as the direct, yet original accumulation of the whole series of being, enveloping the materials of the past in life's all-encompassing push outward toward a democratic future.

While Emerson's figurative depiction of the self as the "metempsychosis of nature" provides a precise prototype for the kind of expansive self Whitman poeticizes in *Leaves of Grass*, such was Emerson's influence in this period that many of the most prominent American transcendentalists were similarly inspired. In *Ten Sermons of Religion* (1853), dedicated to Emerson for his "genius" and "friendship," Theodore Parker describes the progressivism of religion in terms of metempsychosis. The "human idea of God has its metempsychosis," Parker writes, "and transmigrates through many a form, rising higher at every step until this day."[26] For Parker, the human idea of God has it own lineage—with human beings first gazing into nature to describe the divine before attributing the features of man to the deity. As in Emerson's essays, metempsychosis is not simply a doctrine of soul's passage into multiple bodies, but a template for the development of consciousness. Much like Emerson's metempsychotic mind that "passes through [...] the whole line of temples and sphinxes and catacombs" (*W* 2: 7), Parker's metempsychotic consciousness must journey through "sphinxes and pyramids[,]" the "fossil remains of old facts of consciousness[,]" in order to arrive most fully in the present moment.[27]

For Parker, therefore, humanity's comprehension of God is invariably rooted in history and, as such, can be understood as a process of experience and invention, sending the human being on a quest through nature so as to name something for which he has as-yet no name. Here, the individual yearns to taste every conceivable experience without surfeit, for no experience is enough; no one embodiment can fulfill this titanic hunger at the center of the human being's spiritual nature:

> This vague, mysterious, superhuman something, before it is solidified into deity, let me call The Divine. Man does not know what it is. "It

is not myself," says he. "What is it, then? Some outward thing?" He takes the outward thing which seems most wondrous to himself,—a reptile, beast, bird, insect; an element, the wind, the lightning, the sun, the moon, a planet, or a star. Outward things embody his inward feeling; but while there are so many elements of confusion within him, no one embodiment is enough; he must have many, each one a step beyond the other.[28]

With Parker's nod to the metempsychotic mind of Emerson's "History," we can already hear the language of Whitman's 1855 *Leaves of Grass* and glimpse the unmistakable outlines of the swallowing soul of "Song of Myself." "These come to me days and nights and go from me again,/ But they are not the Me myself," writes Whitman in Section Four of "Song of Myself," declaring with metaphysical flair a line later, "Apart from the pulling and hauling stands what I am." Like Emerson and Parker, Whitman celebrates the soul that wants to identify itself fully within embodied experience, but hungers insatiably not only for new bodies, but for perpetual transcendence.

American Consciousness and the Stalwart Heir

In "Song of Myself," Whitman grandly poeticizes the metempsychotic self of Emerson's essays. To "see and hear the whole," the poet must "take part" (33.863) in the larger, human struggle, which means becoming the "hounded slave" (33.838), the "mash'd fireman with breast-bone broken" (33.847), and the "old artillerist" who has to witness the death of his general (33.858) before being able to inhabit the "next fold of the future" (51.1320). Like Emerson, Whitman does not portray the movement into other selves traditionally—as in the Hindu, Pythagorean, and Neoplatonic traditions where the soul endures multiple lives and attempts to free itself from matter. Instead, Whitman conceives of "the interiorizing of objects as an ingestion, a magical incorporation of the world into the body."[29] "I fly those flights of a fluid and swallowing soul" (33.800), Whitman writes in Section 33 of "Song of Myself," repeating the idea with the force of a poetic declaration some lines later: "All this I swallow, it tastes good, I like it well, it becomes mine,/ I am the man, I suffer'd, I was there" (33.831–32). These lines are more than a casual boast; as Philip Fisher argues, "behind Whitman's words [. . .] lies the staggering fact that [they] are spoken not about a proud moment of his own experience, but out of his claim to be able to be someone else."[30]

Donald E. Pease was one of the first scholars to examine Whitman's belief that he could inhabit all conceivable American identities. For Pease,

Whitman's supposition that "everything is itself and on its way to becoming all" is based upon "eradicat[ing] the distinction between the reflections within the mind and things in the world." "Individuals," in Whitman's poetry, "do not reflect upon things but project them into what they can be, thereby extending what we more usually call memory, or the work of reflection, into the future."[31] This "most elusive aspect of Whitman's poetry," Pease argues, consists essentially in "identifying the self with the evolutionary process, rather than any single individual."[32] Whitman's claim to be someone else infuses his epic with a strange combination of mysticism, evolution, and democratic practice, but it is most substantially a claim that directly aligns him with Emerson. While a number of critics have noted that "Whitman's belief in reincarnation [. . .] provided the poet with a structure for his oceanic views concerning selfhood,"[33] no one has observed that Emerson's metempsychotic characterization of the cognitive expansion and accompanying biological adaptation of the individual self provides a decisive prototype for the kind of reincarnation Whitman has in mind.[34]

Harold Bloom argues that Emerson's doctrine of power "resides in the moment of transition from a past to a new state, in the shooting of a gulf, in the darting to an aim" (W 2: 40) —and what is just as "urgent for Walt is the *crossing*, Emerson's metaphor for darting to a new aim."[35] As in Hegel's view of consciousness, such power consists not simply in the transition to a new aim or the transcendence of one self for another, but in the simultaneous integration of what is abandoned in a new vista of heightened being. In the 1855 preface to *Leaves of Grass*, Whitman has already prepared his readers to imagine this form of power in terms of metempsychotic absorption. In the very first sentence of the 1855 preface, Whitman prepares his readers for the heightened, self-reflexive visuality of his poetic form and grandly resituates Emerson's metempsychotic self to portray the formation of one individual consciousness, namely, his own emerging poetic self. Accordingly, Whitman's American "lesson" underscores a visual pedagogy wherein a poetic inheritor "perceives" the historical series of being and approaches its sequence in order to adopt the series and infuse it with new life:

> America does not repel the past or what it has produced under its
> forms or amid other politics or the idea of castes or the old reli-
> gions. . . . accepts the lesson with calmness . . . is not so impatient
> as has been supposed that the slough still sticks to opinions and
> manners and literature while the life which served its requirements
> has passed into the new life of the new forms . . . perceives that the
> corpse is slowly borne from the eating and sleeping rooms of the

house . . . perceives that it waits a little while in the door . . . that it
was fittest for its days . . . that its action has descended to the stalwart
and wellshaped heir who approaches . . . and that he shall be fittest
for his days. (*1855*: 1–11)

In response to Emerson's ardent call for a poet who can work "in wor-
thy continuation" with past creation (*EL* 1: 73), Whitman implicitly de-
clares that he—the approaching "heir"—will inscribe a new character for
America by providing the medium through which such a realization can
take place. At the same time, this opening passage is necessarily open-
ended, for it is not one individual alone, but America itself—the collection
of many consciousnesses—which "accepts the lesson" and seeks to realize
itself as both commonwealth and individual. Whitman, then, provides the
text, but he, like the poet before him, is part of a historical series, which
in each realization seeks another inheritor *to perceive* and *reconstitute* the
series anew.

Whitman is sure to evoke the prospect of his own poetic power within
America's expansive and necessarily incomplete anticipation of its future
identity.[36] After all, the "stalwart and wellshaped heir" only "approaches";
although he "shall be fittest for his days," he has not yet fulfilled his man-
date. Still, his response is already being formulated as a political, rather
than an exclusively meditative awareness, for the prospect of the coming
heir reveals that America requires something fundamental of its citizens.
In "await[ing] the gigantic and generous treatment worthy of it" (*1855*: 50),
the new republic calls for a civic response from the individual member of
its aggregate: "The largeness of nature or the nation were monstrous with-
out a corresponding largeness and generosity of the spirit of the citizen"
(*1855*: 51–53). Only a real correspondence between nation and individual
maintains the health and vitality of the democratic enterprise, while pre-
venting the ever-looming threat of tyranny, by bringing the past and the
future into present communion.[37] "America does not repel the past," Whit-
man insists; it "accepts the lesson" of the past and "perceives" the "new life"
passing into and inhabiting "new forms" (*1855*: 1–7). The nation's present
conception of itself entails an individual citizen "corresponding" in kind
to the expansiveness of his own nation, first by perceiving the metempsy-
chotic circuit of the series from "the eating and sleeping rooms" of the
house to the "doorway" of being and, second, by apostrophizing the future
on this threshold.[38]

In the opening to the 1855 preface, therefore, Whitman specifies the
metempsychotic underpinnings of his poetic project by depicting America
as a series of past incarnations that must be passed through and radi-
cally reshaped. The lesson that America accepts—and that culminates

open-endedly in the figure of the poetic heir—is one, moreover, that perception itself constitutes. In "History," as we have seen, Emerson describes how "Genius *watches* the monad through all his masks as he performs the metempsychosis of nature" (*W* 2: 8; emphasis added). This spiritual, metempsychotic journey is primarily a phenomenological process, which allows the individual to realize the whole lesson of history in his own individual mind by using his perception to live through, and know the past. In the 1855 preface, Whitman also foregrounds the poet's perception of being's series as a "lesson" that culminates in a new and vital incarnation. The process unfolds not merely in the mind, however; it is more grandly situated on the national scene with the poet absorbing and transfiguring everything around him through his own perception and bestowing the ability onto others:

> Who knows the curious mystery of the eyesight? The other senses corroborate themselves, but this is removed from any proof but its own and foreruns the identities of the spiritual world. A single glance of it mocks all the investigations of man and all the instruments and books of the earth and all reasoning. What is marvelous? what is unlikely? what is impossible or baseless or vague? After you have once just opened the space of a peachpit and given audience to far and near and to the sunset and had all things enter with electric swiftness softly and duly without confusion or jostling or jam. (*1855*: 202–11)

Directly addressing his readers, Whitman asks them to imagine the "marvelous" act that fits the vast universe into a minuscule space.[39] His description also provides an implicit metempsychotic context for how this process unfolds—with Whitman welcoming his readers to participate in the construction and reconstruction of perception's continual movement into an individual shape, in this case, the space of a peachpit. The eyesight potentially achieves an "unlikely" temporal union where a power beyond being's series—identities of the spiritual world—is immediately made manifest in the reader's apprehension of language. Here, Whitman intimates, is no book, but a dynamic confluence of ensouled eyebeam and material body.

In "Song of Myself" especially, Whitman celebrates the relationship between perception and language, as though each written word—each metric foot of poetry—were simply the inscription of seeing itself. As Alan Trachtenberg observes, the "aim is to outstretch visibility itself, to bring into view an *emergent* reality accessible only to a certain act of seeing."[40] In Section 25, Whitman accomplishes this conversion of sight into emergent speech by accepting the rays of the sun and converting them through the self-constituting medium of the self into a voice that holds within it "worlds and volumes of worlds":

Dazzling and tremendous how quick the sun-rise would kill me,
If I could not now and always send sun-rise out of me.

We also ascend dazzling and tremendous as the sun,
We found our own O my soul in the calm and cool of the daybreak.

My voice goes after what my eyes cannot reach,
With the twirl of my tongue I encompass worlds and volumes of
    worlds. (25.560–65)

Harold Bloom argues that this passage is "an enormous elaboration of
Emerson." As "the eye's power identifies with the sun, an immense *ask-
esis* is accomplished [in] a voice that sees what even sight cannot reach."[41]
Whereas Emersonian vision "centers on the self's awareness of other
selves,"[42] Whitman's portrayal of the relationship between vision and
speech merges everything, even the future, into the present articulation of
the self. This process is not a deepening Emersonian isolation or even an
American solipsism, as Bloom insists, but a new kind of political and social
self through which present and future readers may engender a visual me-
tempsychotic practice that draws together individual and national forms
of experience. Indeed, Whitman is engaged in sculpting a new order for
democratic experience by seeing himself and making others see through
him, thereby colonizing his nation through the very act of perception: "My
eyes settle the land" (10.7).

To see with "all eyes," as Emerson intones in *The Poet*, is more than a
preoccupation in *Leaves of Grass*; it is a poetic declaration of being, the
realization of which pivots upon the painful fact of human finitude along-
side the desire for a titanic expansion of the self through the medium of
the poetic frame.[43] In the passage above, the eye, the printed word, and
the light that has drawn forth the possibility of this relationship provide
only a sketch of poetic order; Whitman is not after structure alone; he is
evoking something more substantial. "Do you not know O speech how
the buds beneath you are folded?" he asks, concluding at the end of the
section that "[w]riting and talk do not prove me,/ I carry the plenum of
proof and every thing else in my face" (25.579–80). Here, the flatness and
two-dimensionality of the printed page have given way to a multiplicity of
living possibilities, not simply nature in its budding infancy, ever-stirring
beneath Whitman's poetic language, but a face composed of all these inter-
sections of a vaster temporal sequence. Whitman's own face, the type-face
of the poem, which Whitman himself set, and the face of the reader—
all these relations are impossibly interwoven into one discontinuous, yet
flowing system, requiring a present act of consciousness to apprehend and
synthesize a structure that is at once living, dead, and not yet alive.

Whitman's incorporation of Emerson's metempsychotic self into this cohesive, yet unsettled model of textuality thereby emphasizes both perception and inscription with a definite mystical accuracy. Each act of perception requires the reader to assume[44] a new identity or realize a new position in relation to the text and to the poet who has already shaped its proportions and meanings. Within this miniature textual cosmos, Whitman is both an absent creator and yet the textual face itself, the very words and lines into which the reader persistently peers.[45] The speaker's command to the reader—"Look in my face" (51.1322)—at the close of "Song of Myself" does not come as a surprise. Whitman has prepared for it throughout his epic by spatializing and temporalizing the depictions of the reader's relation to the typeface, leaves, grass blades, or pages of poetry.

The reader comes to assume what the poet has assumed in his very apprehension and realization of the shared textual frame. His perception falls like "generous" sunbeams upon the textual face, even while that face of words mysteriously exerts itself on the reader: "Sun so generous it shall be you!/ Vapors lighting and shading my face it shall be you!" (24.538–39). This depiction of the reader lighting and shading the textual face echoes Emerson's metempsychotic perception, adapted from Platonic, Neoplatonic, and Goethean prototypes. For Emerson, "the glance of [the] eye has the power of sunbeams" (W 6: 16), and when it falls upon the textual object, that object becomes capable of "self-direction" (W 6: 21). In absorbing the ensouling eyebeam, that object is not simply caused or inscribed; it becomes its own self-constituting subject. The "flash of the eye" not only reveals the essence within things; it can "convert" dead objects into "fiery men" (W 2: 184). In Section 25 of "Song of Myself," the "sunrise" of the reader's perception initiates the self-constituting energy and vitality of the speaker's textual voice. The abbreviated textual shapes take on greater proportions in being seen so that the speaker of the poem can proclaim that it is not simply words that constitute his being, but the now living textual face itself.

Being's Mimetic Dilemma

Whitman's 1855 preface embraces Emerson's conception of the future poet, who is both an object of perception, since he is constituted by the historical series that leads up to his emergence in time, and a subject preparing to reshape the materials of the past in an act of heightened creation. As the first sentence of the preface indicates, while the corpse of the past is dragged out of the rooms of history and into the doorway, the heir approaches this threshold so that the dead body can be reborn—body and soul coming together in a way that echoes previous metaphysical cosmologies without being reducible to them. Whitman also indicates how organically he has absorbed Emerson's view of double consciousness. Emerson divides creation into two models, the *orders of genesis and time*. In the order of genesis, which is fundamentally based on Platonism and the Neoplatonic tradition, the universe bursts outward from pure idea or origin to individual manifestation and series. As it externalizes itself, the universe loses the spiritual urgency and fire that initiated its creative burst outward. From this perspective, the human being is simply part of this external bursting forth, a mimetic shape falling away from the source that shaped him or her. In this respect, the individual remains subject to this external power and its mimetic dictation; subsequently, his task becomes one that takes place in the order of time as he attempts to reverse the mimetic momentum of genesis. In the order of time, he attempts to overcome the inequality that exists between every subject and object, an inequality that continues to push the universe outward; accordingly, he learns to marry opposites, to establish equality between the spiritual and the material, so as to prepare for new creation.

In "Fate" (1860), Emerson continues to depict this dialectic of genesis and time as a creative challenge for the modern self. The individual becomes conscious of the fact that, although he is but "a link in a chain" and "must accept an irresistible dictation" that propels being's series outward, he holds within himself "a stupendous antagonism" (*W* 6: 12, 2, 12) to the outward flowing of the universe. Similarly, in the 1855 preface, America's vast history flows into the individual and writes his identity, but he nonetheless finds within himself the immanent authority to respond to the vast flowing of his nation. The poetic heir therefore is not simply constructed by an outside force; in being the object of another's perception, he begins to constitute himself on his own ontological ground. Like Emerson, Whitman captures a decisive aspect of the Neoplatonic heritage. Plotinus's triad of procession, conversion, and self-constitution emphasizes that in proceeding from the One and undergoing conversion, what is caused comes to posit itself in that conversion; it *causes itself to be*. In Whitman's cosmos, such self-constitution means that everything can eventually attain intelligence and self-direction.

Whitman's 1855 preface preserves this crucial facet of Neoplatonism, filtered through the lens of German Idealism and American transcendentalism, and transforms it into a drama of identity.[46] The American aggregate seeks to understand itself and, to do so, pours itself into an individual shape, filling him with—as well as extracting from him—its own teeming history, which is the history of America from its original inhabitants, to colonialism to nationhood and beyond:

To him the hereditary countenance descends both mother's and fa-
ther's. To him enter the essences of real things and past and pres-
ent events—of the enormous diversity of temperature and agricul-
ture and mines—the tribes of red aborigines—the weather-beaten
vessels entering new ports or making landings on rocky coasts—
the first settlements north or south—the rapid stature and muscle—
the haughty defiance of '76, and the war and peace and formation
of the constitution. . . . the union always surrounded by blather-
ers and always calm and impregnable—the perpetual coming of
immigrants—the wharf-hem'd cities and superior marine—the un-
surveyed interior—the loghouses and clearings and wild animals
and hunters and trappers. . . . the free commerce—the fisheries and
whaling and gold-digging—the endless gestation of new states—the
convening of Congress every December, the members duly com-
ing from all climates and the uttermost parts. . . . the noble charac-
ter of the young mechanics and of all free American workmen and
workwomen. . . . the general ardor and friendliness and enterprise—
the perfect equality of the female with the male. . . . the large
amativeness—the fluid movement of the population—the factories
and mercantile life and laborsaving machinery—the Yankee swap—
the New-York firemen and the target excursion—the southern plan-
tation life—the character of the northeast and of the northwest and
southwest—slavery and the tremulous spreading of hands to protect
it, and the stern opposition to it which shall never cease till it ceases or
the speaking of tongues and the moving of lips cease. (*1855: 105–31*)

In this long passage, Whitman indicates what will be a principal charac-
teristic of his poetic style: the long list of nouns, clauses, and phrases serves
a vital purpose in the sense that it denotes the vast sweep of history present
to the individual in every moment, a sequence understood by Emerson
as a historical series grounded in cognition. Whitman gives his reader a
more visceral understanding of the metempsychotic lesson that must be
accepted, gone over, and realized by each American citizen, particularly by
the new American poet who inherits this vision and must speak for it.[47] As
America "accepts the lesson" and externalizes itself by pouring itself into
an object or shape ("To him enter the essences of real things and past and
present events"), this object assumes an individual life of its own, reveal-
ing, in this movement, its relation not only as an object or receptor, but
now as a subject free to articulate his "stern opposition" to the societal ills
that plague America's present conception of itself.

For Whitman, the awakening of American poetic consciousness is inter-
twined with the nation shaking off its practice of slavery. The approaching

heir does more than formulate a poem; his activity draws into itself the men and women who labor upon the land—and, thus, nourish its fruitful receptivity and harvest—and provides them with the ability to claim that work for themselves. In this pouring, absorption, and outflowing, the powers of the subject—of the citizen, the approaching heir, and future poet—are developed and exercised, placing him at the center of all the networks of relationships. His powers, thus engaged in dialectical conflict or conversation, come to light, whether of "the haughty defiance of '76," which led to the "formation of the constitution" or the "stern opposition" to slavery. Like Emerson's future poet who becomes a center for nature, Whitman's poet receives his nation and learns to respond to it with newfound energy, shaking off the feudal oppressions and slave masters of the past. The poet does not simply overcome creation's outward flowing; more properly, he makes himself creation's own self-constituting ground, at once responsive "to his country's spirit" and able to "incarnate its geography and natural life and rivers and lakes" (1855: 76–77).

In the very act of observing, listening, or receiving, Whitman's poet begins to realize his own power as potential creator, not simply inscribing a new poetic object, but making himself this new and vital sequence. Whitman's emphasis on a "transcendant" order, an incarnating force, expressly indicates that he consciously confronts the mimetic inevitability of creation, which pulls outward away from the source that gave it birth, and insists instead on the possibility of a poetic voice that leads his readers to "the origin of all poems" (2.33). By means of his metempsychotic perception, the poet participates in the cosmos about him, not simply as an object swayed by a greater force, but as a subject grounded in the domain of his own emergent personhood and individuality. Therein, Whitman responds to Emerson's quandary of art and mimesis—that age-old dilemma—insisting that the poet invert the gravity of creation's preceding burst outward and that he overcome, by virtue of this turn or conversion, the weight of the past. The poet is no longer mediated, no longer drawn outward, away from the original fire of genesis, becoming, as Emerson describes in "History" and "Circles," a mere fossil of consciousness; instead, the poet seeks to retrace the path to the origin, to move through time's chronology to the end of the series, to the place where present and future meet.

Whitman's "Song of Myself" is particularly illuminating in this regard, since Whitman explicitly offers his readers a path by which they may journey to the "origin," inverting the mimetic laws of nature (nature and art's removal, twice or thrice, from reality, according to Plato's *Republic*) by attaining a heightened perception based upon an emergent selfhood or individuality:

> Stop day and night with me and you shall possess the origin of all
>   poems,
> You shall possess the good of the earth and sun, (there are millions of
>   suns left,)
> *You shall no longer take things at second or third hand,* nor look
>   through the eyes of the dead, nor feed on the specters in books,
> You shall not look through my eyes either, nor take things from me,
> You shall listen to all sides and filter them from your self. (2.33–37;
>   emphasis added)

Whitman announces a poetic order through which the reader can learn to transcend his role as an inactive addressee or spectator.[48] The reader "shall no longer take things at second or third hand"; he will learn to see for himself, accept his own emergent individuality, and fulfill the marked goal of the transcendental order, that is, "Nature without check with original energy" (1.13), as the closing line of the first section affirms. To attain this origin, the reader does not strictly return to the past; he is already swept up in the past; instead, he must journey through inversion, retracing the mimetic sequence back to the place where it began. The reader must, in Emerson's terms, see and know the ground for himself and, in doing so, strip himself of the mimetic weight that so obscures his vision.[49]

While Whitman promises this freedom from mimesis to his readers and, by implication, to himself, he also tacitly suggests an unavoidable conflict. The individual may learn to "listen to all sides" of creation and "filter them" through himself, but his attempts—*in his present position*—take place in the wake of creation, not at the forefront of it. Although his perceptive powers may promise a new vista for experience, such power is nonetheless deferred.[50] As a result, the reader currently peers through the eyes of the dead—through the mimetic weight of creation, the "second" and "third hand"—toward an elusive freedom and unity that can be his only if he chooses to absorb the external, historical series and rekindle its creative fire once more. Some critics term the disempowerment of the reader, stemming from his or her complete dependence on the poet, a totalitarian aspect of Whitman's poetic approach. As David Cavitch states, "Unlike any other major poet, Whitman makes his readers feel totally dependent on his speaking voice." Readers "have the sensation that [their] only valid responses are being directed—indeed, conducted with bravura—by Whitman from the page."[51] In "Song of Myself," however, the reader's dependence on the voice of the poet—his very dependence on the typeface that Whitman has already thoroughly visualized in relation to the reader's living gaze—represents a stage of poetic maturation. The reader comes to realize that he has been predetermined by the historical series—that it both props him up in time and writes him, as it were. His task becomes an effort to retrace the poetic sequence—to "stop day and night" with his precursor's materials—in an effort to free himself from his own mimetically mediated vision and assume a self-reliant creative power over the series on which he and his fellow citizens are currently braced.

Although "Song of Myself" exudes optimism, there is an implicit crisis at the heart of Whitman's poetic vision. The poet and reader are always on their way toward the origin of the series; they are presently swept up in the dilemma of mimetic being, a concept decisively tinged with a pre-Darwinian materialism. From this antebellum transcendentalist perspective, the individual is already mapped out, both cognitively and physiologically, by the series he inherits, a series that is much more than a mere conception, but a biological sequence. The human being's freedom is all prospective, never actual—and so he must learn to traverse the greater historical series and experience all the variations that this entails. Thus, Whitman's initial depictions of selfhood strikingly replay being's dilemma as a growing awareness that the prospect of unity, intensified by incarnate joy and love, entails the experience of division and fragmentation:

> I am satisfied—I see, dance, laugh, sing;
> As the hugging and loving bed-fellow sleeps at my side through the
>   night, and withdraws at the peep of the day with stealthy tread,
> Leaving baskets cover'd with white towels swelling the house with
>   their plenty,
> Shall I postpone my acceptation and realization and scream at my
>   eyes,
> That they turn from gazing after and down the road,
> And forthwith cipher and show me to a cent,
> Exactly the value of one and exactly the value of two, and which is
>   ahead? (3.59–65)

Where Emerson lamented that humans possess "always a referred existence [. . .] never a presence or satisfaction" (*W* 3: 111), Whitman reveals that our deepest knowledge of satisfaction includes the larger arc of human experience and embraces loss and absence, not just fulfillment ("Shall I postpone my acceptation and realization and scream at my eyes/ That they turn from gazing after and down the road"). Here, Whitman quickly discloses a pertinent human dilemma by revealing that "satisfaction" spans numerous states of being, explicitly moving from perception to expression (that is, "see, dance, laugh, sing"), mirroring Emerson's own transcendental process beginning in perception and ending in creative expression. The coming together of material bodies in sexual love and friendship cannot be understood by itself—as an isolated experience from only one perspective; rather, the experience of the whole in all its various, congruent, disparate positions informs our profound, albeit temporary "satisfaction."

Whitman's concluding question in Section 3 of "Song of Myself" further characterizes selfhood as a multiplicity of potential perspectives, rather than a discrete entity. The speaker finds himself "gazing after and down the road" where his future development lies not in the past—with the discarded white robes—but in the "value" of things, a quality that will be revealed in the future, in what "is ahead." Accordingly, in these earlier sections of "Song of Myself," the speaker is not a complete being; on the contrary, he remains divided between past and future.[52] Whitman even problematizes perception, the transcendental principle itself, within this scheme, for the speaker "screams at [his] eyes," which look backward instead of toward "acceptation and realization." In this respect, the speaker's satisfaction is constituted in the context of multiple perspectives, spanning the gamut from perception to action and from presence to absence. From the perspective of the dispossessed—in this case both the speaker and his readers who will assume what the speaker assumes (as the second line of the poem declares)—the dawn of present experience, "the peep of day," opens to a mimetic wake, a space and time already evacuated by the lover, who departs into the future and leaves the speaker alone with only the reminiscences of a fleeting union. But this is only one perspective; the mimetic inevitability initiates an inquiry that must pass through a variety of identities in order to achieve the express goal of "original energy without check" (1.13). Later in "Song of Myself," the speaker throws off his dispossession and adopts the perspective of the departed bedfellow:

> A gigantic beauty of a stallion, fresh and responsive to my caresses,
> Head high in the forehead, wide between the ears,
> Limbs glossy and supple, tail dusting the ground,
> Eyes full of sparkling wickedness, ears finely cut, flexibly moving.
>
> His nostrils dilate as my heels embrace him,
> His well-built limbs tremble with pleasure as we race around and
> return.
>
> I but use you a minute, then I resign you, stallion,
> Why do I need your paces when I myself out-gallop them?
> Even as I stand or sit passing faster than you. (32.701–9)

Whereas the speaker was once the self left behind among the white towels (the discarded shells or covers of the transcendent bedfellow), he becomes the one that leaves others behind by out-galloping them. In experiencing both viewpoints of this erotic embrace, he is no longer simply an inheritor of loss, its addressee or passive receptor, seeing through "the eyes of the dead" or "tak[ing] things at second or third hand" (2.35); divided by the orders of genesis and time, he has begun to experience the dialectic's conflict and learn its metempsychotic lesson for himself.

The Divided Self and its Bloody Crowning

In "Song of Myself," Whitman's constitution of the divided self sets a precedent upon which all his other announcements of selfhood play. Not only does this division establish the principal conflict of the poem; the divided self manifests creation's dialectical structure and presents the metempsychotic series as a conflictual path that each individual must undertake and experience for himself or herself.[53] The speaker of "Song of Myself"—and the reader who follows him—must become killer, victim, companion . . . and he must come to a bloody end in order to restore himself as well as the prospect of future unity. Accordingly, one of the principal questions of Whitman's poem has to do with how the individual inhabits the series of which he is a part. As Whitman's speaker asks, "To be in any form, what is that?" (27.611), providing a parenthetical answer that assures his readers that all humanity is bound in the metempsychotic cycle of selfhood: "(Round and round we go, all of us, and ever come back thither)" (27.612). The dialectical cycle of history pivots upon a figurative wheel of rebirth, giving rise to an array of different experiences and viewpoints that underscores the fury and conflict of becoming. In this respect, Whitman explicitly indicates that selfhood involves the construction, destruction, and reconstruction of identity, pointing to a greater unity that encompasses all these disparate forms of experience into one flowing, fluctuating system.

On an apparent level, Whitman's announcement of selfhood appears grandiose and all-encompassing—"Walt Whitman, a kosmos" (24.497)—with an assurance of eternal life and power: "I pass death with the dying and birth with the new-wash'd babe, and am not contain'd between my hat and boots" (7.133). From this perspective, being's series arises as something easily traversed by an assimilating self who moves through the pattern of death and life and does not feel in the least constrained by his material body. In fact, all sensible things have a special meaning for him, which it is his job to discern and realize: "I know I am solid and sound,/ To me the converging objects of the universe perpetually flow,/ All are written to me, and I must get what the writing means" (20.403–5). The speaker accepts the address of the whole, understanding that his purpose cannot be easily offset; he remains steadfast, not just in the present, but for "ten thousand" or "ten million years":

I know I am deathless,
I know this orbit of mine cannot be swept by a carpenter's compass,
I know I shall not pass like a child's carlacue cut with a burnt stick at
     night.
[. . .] And whether I come to my own to-day or in ten thousand or
     ten million years,
I can cheerfully take it now, or with equal cheerfulness I can wait.

My foothold is tenon'd and mortis'd in granite,
I laugh at what you call dissolution,
And I know the amplitude of time. (20.406–21)

Whitman's speaker proclaims the grand whole with one, sure voice; he laughs at his own dissolution because he is assured of his own future. In the larger context of "Song of Myself," however, this perspective is a tenuous one that attempts to take account of the amplitude of the metempsychotic series and to affirm the individual as a spark of certainty within an indeterminate, ever-transforming pattern.

In *Representative Men*, Emerson endeavors to redeem Emmanuel Swedenborg for his "elaborate" (*W* 4: 76) systemizing on just such grounds. For Emerson, Swedenborg assures his place among the other intellectual giants of history for his courageous entry into metempsychotic flux: "In the shipwreck, some cling to running-rigging, some to cask and barrel, some to spars, some to mast; the pilot chooses with science" (*W* 4: 81). Instead of these illusory anchors, the pilot chooses a course through the shipwreck not because of his individual power (this must assuredly be dashed in the storm), but because he recognizes that the series aspires upward and that he himself is part of that progression: "I think of him [Swedenborg] as of some transmigrating votary of Indian legend, who says, though I be dog, or jackal, or pismire, in the last rudiments of nature, under what integument or ferocity, I cleave to right, as the ladder that leads up to man and to God" (*W* 4: 81). In Whitman's "Song of Myself," the assurance of immortality reverberates in just such a context; the speaker does not "laugh" at "dissolution" because he is immune to, or has conquered, death. Instead, he knows that the series necessarily embraces the living, the dying, and the dead, and in this sure embrace, the seeds of the future "cheerfully" wait to come into their "own to-day or in ten thousand or ten million" (20.409). In Section 20, then, Whitman's song of selfhood—with all its metempsychotic transitions during the full "amplitude of time" (20.421)—presents a precarious journey reminiscent of Emerson's Indian votary whose continual metempsychosis is enacted in a sea storm; he has no anchorage; his ship along with its barrels and rigging are all sinking; he may cling to nothing, not to identity nor to its many masks, just to a rectitude whose unsettled impulse propels him onward. Similarly, Whitman does not assure the self's permanence offhandedly at all; instead, he presents it in the context of flux, indeterminacy, and in Section 28, even horror so that this deathless protean persona is recurrently pierced with a deeper division or conflict that manifests itself in numerous expressions of identity, none more powerful than the speaker's fear of losing his individuality and of being absorbed into a new prospective whole.

Whereas Emerson implicitly conceived of the metempsychotic self as a form of cognitive wish fulfillment, Whitman transgresses these ideal bounds to imagine the consequences of the soul's metempsychotic assimilations. What we find is that the "flights of a fluid and swallowing soul" (33.800) do not merely entail reception; they also correspond to a desire for the violent assimilation of the other. Thus, in Section 28 of "Song of Myself," Whitman does what Emerson never attempted to do—to make his audience see through the eyes not of the authorial self, but of the dispossessed:

> Is this then a touch? Quivering me to a new identity,
> Flames and ether making a rush for my veins,
> Treacherous tip of me reaching and crowding to help them,
> My flesh and blood playing out lightning to strike what is hardly different from myself,
> On all sides prurient provokers stiffening my limbs,
> Straining the udder of my heart for its withheld drip,
> Behaving licentious toward me, taking no denial,
> Depriving me of my best as for a purpose,
> Unbuttoning my clothes, holding me by the bare waist,
> Deluding my confusion with the calm of the sunlight and pasture-fields,
> Immodestly sliding the fellow-senses away,
> They bribed to swap off with touch, and go and graze at the edges of me,
> No consideration, no regard for my draining strength or my anger,
> Fetching the rest of the herd around to enjoy them a while,
> Then all uniting to stand on a headland and worry me.
>
> The sentries desert every other part of me,
> They have left me helpless to a red marauder,
> They all come to the headland to witness and assist against me.
>   (28.619–36)

Whitman's extraordinary capacity to imagine how the poetic process unfolds in space and time suggests a greater anxiety in regard to seeing through the eyes of another. Indeed, this stanza plays out the poem's principal conflict: both the desire for metempsychotic expansion, to see eventually with "all eyes," as Emerson intones in "The Poet," and the fear that such assimilation may, in fact, be a form of rape. By charging the scene with a sexual violent energy, Whitman thereby underwrites this transcendental structure of selfhood as an act of plunder, since the "touch" that brings with it a "new identity" is "licentious" and "immodest," possessing "no consideration" for the passive, emasculated, ever-weakening subject being subsumed by the greater whole.

Even as Whitman indicates such violent assimilation to be a social reality, he characterizes the red marauder's advances and the weakening resistance against them as a war raging inside the individual himself. The speaker comes to experience firsthand the fuller panoply of metempsychotic assimilation in the sense that he must endure both sides of its dialectic, not simply the feature of consciousness that reaches out to assume and take in, but the other aspect that reluctantly gives way as a new, empowered entity emerges. Consequently, the speaker comes to experience the metempsychotic lesson firsthand and to understand the pain of sundering and division as a visceral experience of each step in the series that he makes. In this, he is a being divided, not just from the herd that crowds around him, but from himself, for, in this instance, he has no access to the active part of himself, the self realizing its immanent power. On the contrary, he waits helplessly as all his internal vitality is drained from him: "Straining the udder of my heart for its withheld drip."

In *Whitman Possessed*, Mark Maslan emphasizes not simply the act, but the structure of penetration in the violent encounter above, interpreting it in terms of the larger soul/body relationship in "Song of Myself": "Whitman personifies what might ordinarily be considered part of himself—his soul—as an independent agent that takes violent, if amorous, possession of his body."[54] For Maslan, such a structure of penetration and the accompanying subversion of individual identity do not "undermine structures of cultural or political authority," as critics have often argued. "On the contrary, by portraying sexual desire as an invasive, automating force, [Whitman] identifies it with the oldest form of cultural authority in the Western tradition: inspiration."[55] Indeed, in Section 28 of "Song of Myself," because it is forced to accept another's consciousness, the penetrated self ironically becomes the conduit of great power. Just four sections earlier, Whitman has already prepared his readers to understand such penetration in the grandest terms at his disposal: "Unscrew the locks from the doors!/ Unscrew the doors themselves from their jambs!" (24.501–2). Here, "the pass-word primeval," the "sign of democracy" (24.506) opens the sublime doorway or threshold of the body to receive the universe. "Through me the afflatus surging and surging, through me the current and index" (24.506), Whitman intones, announcing himself as the threshold through which all must pass.

Whitman's "stalwart and wellshaped heir" who "shall be fittest for his days" (1855: 10–11) implicitly undertakes a messianic task: he is a spirit made flesh, possessing the capacity to resurrect the corpse dragged from the sleeping rooms of the house into the doorway. Because of Whitman's visceral depiction of embodiment, the new life in running its course—becoming a recipient of America's teeming wealth and eventually offering itself as the material for yet another heir—will have to experience a bloody division, much more violent and terrifying than Emerson's articulations of metempsychotic transformation. While both writers share the bolder strokes of metempsychotic becoming, Whitman's depiction of the loss of individual existence fused with a notion of individual sacrifice reaches biblical intensity. As Section 28 reveals, the speaker's internal struggle echoes some of the events leading up to the death and resurrection of Jesus Christ. The speaker's "flesh and blood" become the sacrifice that the herd demands. People first strip him of his vestments and then bribe each other for pieces of him, actions strikingly reminiscent of Christ's passion on the cross where Christ is stripped naked by the Romans who proceed to gamble for his robes. In order to strengthen the biblical allusion, Whitman evokes the sense of Roman imperial power as part of the crime, for the mob transforms into "sentries" who come "to witness and assist" against the speaker.

While these intertextual, biblical allusions intensify and heighten the drama of this sequence, they do not define it; they reverberate as a past formulation of a present and, therefore, more pressing predicament. Since the conflict functions as an internal one, the speaker cannot represent a Messiah or indicate an undiluted Christian sensibility. Instead, the speaker encompasses both sides of the conflict: he is both a sacrifice of "flesh and blood" and the "greatest traitor," Jesus and Judas made momentarily one and bound up in a pattern that echoes the older drama but cannot be reduced to it:

> I am given up by traitors,
> I talk wildly, I have lost my wits, I and nobody else am the greatest
>   traitor,
> I went myself first to the headland, my own hands carried me there.
> You villain touch! what are you doing? my breath is tight in its throat,
> Unclench your floodgates, you are too much for me. (28.637–41)

Since it is the speaker who undergoes the metamorphosis, the "touch" that "quiver[s]" him "to a new identity" (28.619) is now unequivocally his own. He and "nobody else" is the "greatest traitor" for his "own hands carried [him] there," as he finds himself already being shaped anew, with "his breath [. . .] tight" in another's throat. At the same time, the speaker does not accept the process without resistance; rather, he recognizes it as something alien, as something to which he must submit although he has no power over it. While Emerson writes constantly of metempsychotic transitions, he never shows their actual stripping, body-rending process. However, without ever explicitly naming or identifying the death-rebirth as metempsychosis, Whitman draws it explicitly and dedicates to it some of his most dramatic and intense poetic passages.

The mimetic dilemma, moreover, underlies this problem of reformulating the self out of the materials of the past. In one sense, this self that has had "the udder of my heart [strained] for its withheld drip" is still a feature of the past; his immanent power has been stripped bit-by-bit until he has no choice but to yield to the power of the dialectic to revitalize itself. In these instances, the subsumed self along with its agony and pain is simply a collection of mimetic fragments, past realizations that have lost or are in the process of losing their original potency and, as a result, need to be transformed with original energy. Thus, this subsumed self undergoes a fall from grace; he has lost his immanent power and confronts death not with his immortal vigor intact, but knowing full well that, in his present state, he cannot survive the outcome—very much like Christ who comes to suffer Adam's curse fully before he can redeem himself and humanity, his last cry a lament that he is forsaken by his heavenly father. Unlike the biblical fall, Christ's passion or even the classical, pre-Socratic notion of metempsychosis where the shedding of blood results in a fall from unity,[56] Whitman depicts no explicit fall from grace; instead, he demythologizes the event, illustrating that the fallen world—that of dislocation and pain, of individuation and the loss of it—is always implicit in each moment of becoming, from the biological, sexual urges of the flesh and blood running through the herd and linking the community of animals to the individual seeking to understand and name the agony of having to be swept up in the greater pattern of creation so that a new identity may be formed from out of all the old divisions.

In the context of this suffering, it is understandable why Whitman frequently wonders whether there is an outside to the ever-fluctuating dialectic of existence. As Whitman asks, can the human being stand outside all the "coverings and turmoils" of the "kosmos" (1855: 524–26); may he stand apart from "the riddle and the untying of the riddle" (17.357), or is he fully tied into creation's dialectic?

> Apart from the pulling and hauling stands what I am,
> Stands amused, complacent, compassionating, idle, unitary,

Looks down, is erect, or bends an arm on an impalpable certain rest,
Looking with side-curved head curious what will come next,
Both in and out of the game and watching and wondering at it.

Backward I see in my own days where I sweated through fog with lin-
guists and contenders,
I have no mockings or arguments, I witness and wait. (4.75–81)

Although this self "stands amused" and "looks down" upon creation, he is presently unreal, partly ironic and disbelieving, and yet bracing himself on an "impalpable" or nonexistent "certain" foundation, thus reinscribing duality in the very gesture beyond its circle or arc. Like the approaching heir of Whitman's 1855 preface, this self—this prospect of future unity—has not yet realized himself in being's series; he has not yet stepped into the doorway to revitalize the corpse that has been dragged there in anticipa-tion of his arrival; he remains, therefore, only a possibility. Although, in one respect, Whitman affirms an outside to being "apart from the pulling and hauling," he has repositioned the drama of identity, for the speaker is preparing to absorb the historical series that braces his very being.[57] The speaker must look backward at the signatures of his development: "Back-ward I see in my own days where I sweated through fog with linguists and contenders." With his duality thus reinscribed as a soul assimilating its many bodies, the speaker's perceptive abilities reenact the mimetic burden of previous sections.

Whitman thereby reinforces the dialectic in the figure of being both within and outside the game of being. At the same time, the speaker is more than simply tied to this game; he also has the freedom to enact and live through it. In order to arrive at his true self, the speaker must first watch himself move through all his coverings, the series in which he "sweat[s] through fog," words, and conflicts. He awaits unification and being, yet he is already encompassed, like all the other selves, within one flowing, outward system. This is why Whitman continually clarifies consciousness as ontologically founded, while also suggesting that it stands at a brink or verge into which the future pours: "He learns the lesson. . . . he places him-self where the future becomes present" (1855: 310–11). The self, described above, who waits without "mockings or arguments," has forgotten the "mockers and insults" and must once again experience a "bloody crown-ing" in being: "I discover myself on the verge of the usual mistake./ That I could forget the mockers and insults!/ That I could forget the trickling tears and the blows of the bludgeons and hammers!/ That I could look with a separate look on my own crucifixion and bloody crowning" (38.962–65). The speaker may not look at his own crucifixion with a "separate look"; he must accept the experience of being, not seek to ascribe himself outside of it.[58] At the same time, Whitman has chosen the crucifixion to reinforce the duality of creation. While being traditionally the ultimate expression of embodiment and being, Christ's passion also precedes spiritual transformation, since Christ must undergo a bloody crowning in order to reemerge a glorified heavenly king. Although Christ prays that his suffering may be lifted from him, his bloody incarnation is the necessary passage through which his spiritual power is affirmed. In this context, Whitman's speaker stands at another "verge," other than that of the usual mistake. His trickling tears and suffering are passions of torment, but they prepare him for transcendence, the movement beyond being toward the spiritual, except that, in Whitman as with Emerson, the movement is always one of duality: as being crosses over to soul, so soul becomes being. The movement toward the spiritual reaffirms the metaphysics of creation, which, in turn, reestablishes mimesis as being's dilemma, the created world as copy, which ensures that there is a series through which consciousness must continually pass. The dialectical paradox is accordingly revealed: the very moment of unity where there can be no separation between soul and body (to do so would be the "usual mistake") gives way to duality and, thus, reinscribes the movement outward to new apprehensions and selves.

A Poetics of Personal Transcendence

Whitman's insistence that his poetry bestows the democratic ideal upon its readers implies that what is shared is not merely the excitement and freedom of new expression, but a structure that continually requires reformulation. As Whitman once shaped the poetic text into a particular form, so now the completed text—these dead letters or living blades of grass, depending on one's point of view—requires the new poet to take on the work for himself or herself, to remake the body and revitalize it with the fire of the soul. During the Civil War years, Whitman's poetry and poetics preserve this central metempsychotic formulation, but in Reconstruction America, Whitman comes to lament the absence of an individual equal to the task.[59] The American body that Whitman found so beautiful and perfect through the 1850s has become scarred by the bloody carnage of the Civil War, and Abraham Lincoln becomes, for Whitman, the "fullsized man" capable of infusing the body politic with "his most characteristic, artistic, moral personality,"[60] transfiguring the ugliness of reality into a spirited union. With Lincoln's assassination, however, the vacuum simply cannot be filled—and Whitman both preserves and loses hope in the expectation of "the stalwart and wellshap'd heir" of the 1855 preface. Still, the metempsychotic structure of his poetics does not change, and he continues to long for the ability to reshape the ontological series in a decisive act of spiritual power.

Whitman, in fact, emphasizes that the impetus and certainty that drove him to write *Leaves of Grass* had come to an end. As he writes in his preface to "As a Strong Bird on Pinions Free" (1872), "The present and any future pieces from me are really but the surplusage forming after that volume, or the wake eddying behind it."[61] Being true to the image of textuality as a body undergoing the transitions of life and death, Whitman acknowledges that the exuberance that drove him to write and create a new poetic form for the American experience has served its purpose and, thus, lived its life. The task of taking up "a vast seething mass of materials, ampler, better, (or worse also,) than previously known" and carrying them toward the "crowning stage" falls, for Whitman, to another generation, for the "leading parts" are "not to be acted, emulated here, by us again."[62]

It is not simply aging that affects Whitman's thought, however; his visualization of the American body—both national and individual—undergoes a change that parallels the aftermath of the nation's costly sacrifice to preserve the union of the states and to end slavery.[63] In the 1860s and 1870s especially, Whitman imagines his own aging body as an appropriate symbol of the conflict that had so shaken the country.[64] His initial enthusiasm for the war and his subsequent experience tending tens of thousands of injured and dying soldiers throughout the war accompanied with the breakdown of his own body are for him the conflictual record of the nation, the "vast seething mass of materials" that requires new poets to ensoul this mass once more. The full health and bodily vigor—the idealized body in perfect equanimity with the soul—that he so ardently proclaimed in "Song of Myself" are often replaced, after the third edition of *Leaves of Grass* (1860), with the image of a wounded and dying body—a purely materialistic existence—that has spent the spirit that once animated it and become instead "the highly artificial and materialistic bases of modern civilization."[65]

"Drum Taps" (1866) particularly records the arc between poetic vitality and exhaustion.[66] In "Rise O Days from Your Fathomless Deeps," Whitman idealizes the recruitment for the war of succession with a type of metempsychotic revelry, the soul rising up from the deep with a fierce material hunger: "Rise O days from your fathomless deeps, till you loftier, fiercer sweep,/ Long for my soul hungering gymnastic I devour'd what the earth gave me" (1.1–2). The evolutionary ascent toward a lofty, yet fully material height mirrors the earlier portrayal of the robust soul in "Song of Myself," revealing an *elemental* and *spiritual* force bursting forth toward a "fiercer sweep" with clear metempsychotic delineations. Whitman does not simply indicate that the elemental, protean body increases and strengthens itself according to its consumption; he also depicts a soul whose movements are "gymnastic," jumping from experience to experience, its transcendence from matter and eternal return to it synonymous, almost inseparable. Indeed, the merging of opposites—soul and body—implicitly signals their divergence. While the soul's modifiers are all physical images (its hungers and its proportions are like a gymnast's), the soul itself escapes each experience to feed on more until its crescendo in wartime America. This metempsychotic journey rises up, therefore, at first "hungering for primal energies and Nature's dauntlessness" (3.41) and soon experiencing "true lightning" and "cities electric" until "man" himself "burst[s] forth and warlike America rise[s]" (3.45–46).

In "The Wound-Dresser," perhaps the best-known poem in "Drum Taps," such ideal and boundless enthusiasm significantly gives way so that youth and vigor no longer hold sway; instead, Whitman identifies himself with the infirm, the price exacted for another war of liberty: "Arous'd and angry, I'd thought to beat the alarum, and urge relentless war,/ But soon my fingers fail'd me, my face droop'd and I resign'd myself,/ To sit by the wounded and soothe them, or silently watch the dead" (1.4–6). Whereas others, having already passed through being's series, once "turn'd sideways or backward towards" Whitman "to listen,/ With eyes retrospective towards" (2.35–36) him, as in "Starting from Paumanok" (1860), now in "The Wound-Dresser," Whitman sees himself as the one looking backward toward the young: "An old man bending I come among new faces,/ Years looking backward resuming in answer to children" (1.1–2). The absorption and expansion so prevalent in the first three editions of Leaves of Grass are displaced and echo only in the repeated insistence of individual movement: "I go" (2.26), "I onward go" (2.34), "On, on I go" (3.39). What is left, therefore, is the journey of an old man whose sure purpose is to go "straight and swift to [his] wounded" (2.26) and then to "return" and "resume" the work "through the hospitals" (4.60).

Whereas, in much of Whitman's earlier poetry, the agency of the whole sweeps up the stark, bare proportions of individual bodies, in "The Wound-Dresser," by contrast, the delineations of the whole—the national consciousness that seeks an heir—are repositioned in the drama of an elderly individual tending the injured and dying. Indeed, the poetic power of the speaker in "The Wound-Dresser" is his ability to "pacify with soothing hand" (4.61), his inscription not simply upon the page, but upon the bodies of others, and the response that he receives is the tender, unconditional love of those over whom he watches: "Many a soldier's loving arms about this neck have cross'd and rested,/ Many a soldier's kiss dwells on these bearded lips" (4.64–65). As Whitman portrays himself as the one who waits upon others, toward the end of "Drum Taps," he imagines himself as the one being administered to. For instance, "Spirit Whose Work Is Done" places the speaker in the position of an injured or dying soldier, the Spirit

itself tending and caressing him and preparing his body for burial before
it departs: "Touch my mouth ere you depart, press my lips close" (15). The
drama of the divided self in "Song of Myself"—one side left behind and
the other touching this self, even while out-galloping it—clearly operates
in the poems above, although under different auspices; the body withers
although the steadfast gaze upon it, as well as the desire for it, holds fast.[67]

In "When Lilacs Last in the Dooryard Bloom'd," written following
Abraham Lincoln's assassination on April 14, 1865, and published that
same year and again in the 1867 edition of *Leaves*, Whitman's previous
themes are present, although the poem signals a changing emphasis in
the poetic process. To a large extent, Whitman reclaims his earlier poetic
voice, able yet to speak for the American multitude—and this is due to
the fact that Whitman repositions his own previous project of national
union and individuality in the figure of Lincoln. As he wrote on April 16,
two days after Lincoln's assassination, "UNIONISM, in its truest and am-
plest sense, form'd the hard-pan of [Lincoln's] character. These he sealed
with his life. The tragic splendor of his death, purging, illuminating all,
throws round his form, his head, an aureole that will remain and will grow
brighter through time, while history lives, and love of country lasts."[68] The
American poet, whom Whitman dramatized and whose mantle he elu-
sively accepted in his 1855 preface, culminates, therefore, in the figure of
Lincoln who "leaves for America's history and biography, so far, not only
its most dramatic reminiscence—he leaves, in my opinion, the greatest,
best, most characteristic, artistic, moral personality." In other words, Lin-
coln becomes America's fittest representative man, the poet/redeemer able
to meet his nation on equal terms.

Much like the 1855 preface and "Song of Myself," full of images of the
threshold, Whitman's "Lilacs" uses the image of the doorway to mourn
the dead body of the president and offer it up to another poetic heir who
will take up the body and infuse it with the energy to heal the nation. The
dooryard thus takes on a centrality, forming the symbolic setting for the
elegiac process of national death and rebirth: "in the dooryard [. . .] lilacs
blooming perennial" (1.1, 5). At the same time, Whitman depicts a star-
tling image of spiritual solitariness, suggested in the earlier volumes, but
never so surely articulated. Whitman's evocation of the solitary songbird,
withdrawn completely into itself, away from the mass of men and women
united in grief, offers a distinct contrast to the older, dependable images of
fluid and interpenetrating selves:

> In the swamp in secluded recesses,
> A shy and hidden bird is warbling a song.
> Solitary the thrush,

The hermit withdrawn to himself, avoiding the settlements,
Sings by himself a song.

Song of the bleeding throat,
Death's outlet song of life, (for well dear brother I know,
If thou wast not granted to sing thou would'st surely die.) (4.18–25)

Instead of the stalwart heir of the 1855 preface that approaches the doorway to take up or infuse the body that waits there, the soul, signified by a "shy and hidden bird," stands apart from the current threshold and the activity that surrounds it. Certainly, materiality and the body are still constitutive elements of Whitman's depiction; by the end of the stanza, the bird's song is one that has originated from a "bleeding throat." Nonetheless, the "solitary thrush" and the "hermit withdrawn to himself" enter into "death's outlet song of life"—the duality of which the self is spun—without being present to it. They are wholly beyond the process at hand, yet, as images, they comprise the elegiac formulation itself.[69]

After the 1867 edition of *Leaves of Grass*, Whitman came to believe that the sacrifice of Lincoln, "purging, illuminating all,"[70] had not been properly accepted by the nation. The administrations of Andrew Johnson and Ulysses S. Grant failed to live up to the promise that Whitman perceived in Lincoln's second great war of independence.[71] With these political failures, Whitman's belief in the stalwart, well-shaped heir approaching to take up the national body and revive it also loses its drive, although he continues to write longingly that a spiritual resurrection may yet restore the broken body politic. "Song of Exposition" (1871) powerfully illustrates this effort to "fill the gross the torpid bulk with vital religious fire" as one of the central lessons of "the New World" (1.7,10). As Whitman insists in *Democratic Vistas* (1871), the national body requires resuscitation, a spiritual infusion that confronts the torpid bulk of the nation and restores its lost immanence or reincarnates and reignites—catching the fire of soul—the nation's material body:[72]

> I say all this tremendous and dominant play of solely materialistic bearings upon current life in the United States, with the results as already seen, accumulating, and reaching far into the future, that they must either be confronted and met by at least an equally subtle and tremendous force-infusion for purposes of spiritualization, for the pure conscience, for genuine esthetics, and for absolute and primal manliness and womanliness—or else our modern civilization, with all its improvements, is in vain, and we are on the road to a destiny, a status, equivalent, in its real world, to that of the fabled damned.[73]

The true, emerging poet will no longer simply entertain his nation or reflect its glorious, youthful conception of itself; rather, the "destruction" escaped just "by a hair [...] during the late secession war"[74] still presses upon the national body and threatens it with a fate equivalent to "the fabled damned," those resigned to a soulless existence in Hades, where they beweep their fate with still-human emotions, but have lost the fire that gave these activities any meaning.

What is needed, Whitman argues, are not songs of life—these have already been sung—but poets arising to chant "the songs of death," not only responding to the bloody experience of the nation itself, but also warning it of the peril it presently faces by tending only to its material health: "In the future of these States must arise poets immenser far, and make great poems of death. The poems of life are great, but there must be the poems of the purports of life, not only in itself, but beyond itself."[75] Whitman identifies a shifting tension in the very fabric and growth of American consciousness—and recognizes that the poetry he had written may not be the spiritual infusion that the country now requires.[76] Still, the old assurance does not leave Whitman altogether; he begins to inhabit with sincerity the space of preparation for death, writing the very poems of death, which he sees as the requirement for a new age and nation.

At the same time, *Democratic Vistas* betrays a loss of faith in the future poet who will greet his nation on equal terms and amend it. While the "dream" of a "new, undying order, dynasty, from age to age transmitted"[77] still exists, Whitman increasingly begins to meditate upon a much more personal form of transcendence. He preserves the older structure of moving beyond the series in order to inscribe the future, but with a prevailing sense of isolation:

> I should say, indeed, that only in the perfect uncontamination and solitariness of individuality may the spirituality of religion positively come forth at all. Only here, and on such terms, the meditation, the devout ecstasy, the soaring flight. [...] Alone, and identity, and the mood—and the soul emerges, and all statements, churches, sermons, melt away like vapors. *Alone, and silent thought and awe, and aspiration—and then the interior consciousness, like a hitherto unseen inscription, in magic ink, beams out its wondrous line to the senses.* Bibles may convey, and priest expound, but it is exclusively for the noiseless operation of one's isolated Self, to enter the pure ether of veneration, reach the divine levels, and commune with the unutterable.[78]

Whereas, in Whitman's earlier poetry, the soul is always assimilating, always approaching the ontological threshold, in *Democratic Vistas*, where the songs of death hold sway, the soul's flight away from the material into the alone holds precedence. At the same time, the transcendent movement upward, away from the body, still descends to reinscribe and reinfuse the senses. Only in the "soaring flight" away from dead material structures can the soul or "the interior consciousness" regain its creative fortitude so as to inscribe itself in a "magic ink" that gradually becomes discernible to the body. The metempsychotic order that Whitman so thoroughly infused into his earlier poems thereby reemerges in the solitary movement of the soul outside of the body and its subsequent reconstitution in the written word. However, the goal of this "isolated Self" has less to do with the nation, for the soul's desire is to "reach the divine levels, and commune with the unutterable"—not at all like the intimate earlier portraits of spiritual and physical longing and union.

In Whitman's later poetry as well, this preparation for death and the longing for an ascent that can purify the body in a type of transcendent bliss are essential aspects of a personal vision that he attempts to append to his earlier poetic project of national unity. At the end of *From Noon to Starry Night*, a cluster of twenty-one poems that appeared in the 1881 edition of *Leaves of Grass*, Whitman champions the transcendent movement of soul at the close of day. As in his earlier work, he is still very much aware of how the form of his poetry reflects the metempsychotic entrance into being and beyond it, but the movement has become much more the journey of one individual alone. Beginning the cluster with a plea to prepare this movement—"Prepare the later afternoon of me myself—Prepare my lengthening shadows,/ Prepare my starry nights" (24–25)—so, in "A Clear Midnight," Whitman concludes with the soul launching forth beyond words and the body to ponder "night, sleep, death and the stars": "This is thy hour O Soul, thy free flight into the wordless,/ Away from books, away from art, the day erased, the lesson done,/ Thee fully forth emerging, silent, gazing, pondering the themes thou lovest best,/ Night, sleep, death, and the stars" (1–4). Many scholars have interpreted Whitman's preparation for death and the changing value of his system as particularly weak and ineffectual compared with his earlier poetic vigor.[79] Whitman has not changed as significantly as many would suppose. He still imagines his writing in a metempsychotic manner, each word being a record of the soul's individuation and a vehicle that enables the prospect of renewal. Whitman's wish for release through transcendence, however, dominates much of the tone of his later work, underwriting a much more personal narrative of suffering and decrepitude without the glorious intimacy of the earlier editions of *Leaves of Grass*.

5 / The New Poetry

In "Song of Myself," Walt Whitman portrays his own poetic evolution with the image of a stairway. Standing on the top rung of a flight of steps, the poet has earned, after "trillions of winters and summers," a new power to "launch all men and women forward with [him] into the Unknown."[1] In mounting the staircase and assimilating all the knowledge that each step or age provides, Whitman declares his emergent power to be the culmination of the soul's experience of a vast temporal sequence: "All forces have been steadily employ'd to complete and delight me,/ Now on this spot I stand with my robust soul" (44.1168–69). This notion of gaining the power of the robust soul at the end of history's ontological sequence was similarly essential to Emerson's conception of history. Emerson, like many in his larger New England circle, conceived of the evolution of species as a structure thoroughly intertwined with mystical ascent. "No statement of the Universe can have soundness," Emerson writes in "Fate," "which does not admit its ascending effort." From Bronson Alcott to Theodore Parker to James Freeman Clarke, metempsychosis meant more than simply a doctrine of soul's immortality; it was a way of understanding the idea of history without abandoning the soul. If history comprised the materials for spirit's self-knowing, then history rightly understood was a stairlike structure reaching up from earth into a New World, allowing not only bodily amelioration but also spiritual transformation and power.

Like his New England contemporaries, Whitman attempted to reimagine the relationship between the soul and body and to preserve the privilege of the soul. This effort did not simply consist of a rejection of traditional metaphysics; it was a striking integration of mysticism with new theories of consciousness. This chapter explores Whitman's conception of the "robust soul" in "Song of Myself" and the 1855 preface to *Leaves of Grass* by locating it in a larger mystical tradition and emphasizing an unnoticed feature of Emerson's influence on Whitman. Emerson's adaptation of the Platonic ladder of ascent and his metempsychotic self of "History" inform Whitman's evocation of how the soul educates itself by climbing the ladder of being in an attempt to reach the end of the sequence and to attain the power of creation. Whereas the ancients described the journey of the soul through the natural world over the course of lives and ages, Emerson insisted on understanding the soul's ascent as a metaphor for individual power, a process by which the materials of history could be assimilated by a single, evolving consciousness. Whitman, in turn, incorporates Emerson's conception of ascent into the very structure of his poetics, so that the evolution and expansion of the human self unfolds as a relationship between the reader and the printed page.

This chapter also explores the larger ramifications of the metempsychotic self for modern poetry, charting out the figurative interweaving of an ascending and descending metempsychotic order within the self-reflexive poetry of T. S. Eliot and Wallace Stevens. Many literary and cultural theorists have heralded twentieth-century modernism as a radical break from Idealism, but what one finds instead is a drama of selfhood in which mysticism gives rise to the uneasy delineations of modern identity. Even in the most mystical of Eliot's later poetry, the soul remains a nexus of both doubt and inspiration. "Shall we follow the deception of the thrush?" Eliot questions in "Burnt Norton," indicating that the bird, the spiritual guide into the garden of consciousness, is not at all a source of certainty. Does the bird deceive those who follow in its wake? Does it constitute a pattern of blindness or revelation? These questions cannot be fully answered, for they comprise part of the self-questioning spiritual longing that the modernist assumed when pursuing poetic ritual, as divided as his transcendental precursors were between a hunger for inspiration and the assurance that method can bestow.

Ascent and the "Robust Soul"

In *Upheavals of Thought* (2001), Martha Nussbaum argues against modern rationalist paradigms and asserts instead that emotions shape our mental and social lives, operating as implicit value-judgments with their own nonrational, but cognitive structures. She applies this theory to several quasi-Platonic "ladders of ascent" in the history of thought by examining the tension between the energy of the love for the good and the subversive power of such energy. These "ladders of ascent" (ultimately dependent upon Plato's *Symposium*) are as follows: first, one that focuses upon contemplation of the Good and the Beautiful (Plato, Spinoza, Proust); second, a Christian version of ascent that stresses humility, longing, and grace (Augustine, Aquinas, Dante); third, a Romantic version that rejects a *telos* for ascent (Emily Brontë, Mahler); and finally, a "descent of love" in which human desire sets itself the task of embracing the imperfect with love (Whitman and Joyce). In the case of Whitman, Nussbaum argues that his "descent of love" proposes a new "counter-cosmology" to those "created by philosophical and religious systems."[2] Whitman's focus on the body and his rehabilitation of sex in "Song of Myself" "with its daringly erotic depiction of the relationship between poet and his God and between body and soul" result, in Nussbaum's judgment, in a "cosmology of our finitude and imperfection," a materially adapting process where there is no transcendence, in any traditional sense. Instead, there "is just life, renewing itself; and the only continuity for the human being is the continuity of nature and of human civilization."[3]

Nussbaum is much more adamant than other critics that Whitman replaces "Plato's world of transcendental forms" with a vision in which the only transcendence that makes sense "is the transcendence of partiality and faction in sympathy, of hierarchy in equal respect, of oppression in citizenship and voting, of hatred in love."[4] While her reading captures the major themes of bodily affirmation[5] alongside the rejection of feudal hierarchy, Nussbaum overlooks the extent to which Whitman engages in an American reinterpretation of the mystical tradition of ascent in terms of selfhood.[6] Whitman's trope of the self as an ascending metempsychotic entity directly aligns him with Emerson's construction of the self. In the *First Series of Essays* (1841), Emerson similarly visualizes the transmigration of souls in terms of the evolution of consciousness in history. "To go over the whole ground" of history becomes the principal task of cognition—and Emerson repeatedly depicts this task with the imagery of the steps of a stairway or ladder: "We aim to master intellectually the steps, and reach the same height or the same degradation, that our fellow, our proxy, has done" (*W* 2: 7). The individual does not simply mount upward; in order to achieve a more perfect union, he must master the steps, which means descending into the series so as to know the path of history for himself before aspiring upward again and sublating the series in a heightened act of becoming. In "Love," which follows this assessment in "History," Emerson draws out the Neoplatonic and Idealist underpinnings of this ascending ladder: the "lover ascends to the highest beauty, to the love and knowledge of the Divinity, by steps on this ladder of created souls" (*W* 2: 106).

In "Circles" as well, Emerson celebrates individual power as a process that consists of climbing the ladder of ascent to reach the end of the

sequence: "Step by step we scale this mysterious ladder: the steps are ac-
tions; the new prospect is power." In scaling the ladder, the individual will
eventually come to the final step of the historical series with the soul's
power to realize a higher reality in nature: "There are no fixtures to men,
if we appeal to consciousness. Every man supposes himself not to be fully
understood; and if there is any truth in him, if he rests at last on the divine
soul, I see not how it can be otherwise. The last chamber, the last closet, he
must feel, was never opened; there is always a residuum unknown, unana-
lyzable. That is, every man believes that he has a greater possibility" (*W*
2: 182). Where, in "History" and "Love," Emerson depicts an individual's
ability to unite cognitively every step of the ladder as an initial poetic task,
in "Circles," he emphasizes how poetic creation ultimately takes place at
the end of the series. No longer determined by a preestablished sequence,
the individual comes "to rest at last on the divine soul." In short, he or she
has gained the power of the soul to realize "a greater possibility" in nature
and to extend the series outward into a more perfect inscription.

Contrary to Nussbaum's insistence upon "finitude" and a "descent of
love," Whitman's "Song of Myself" emphatically adapts Emerson's metem-
psychotic self in terms of a larger tradition of ascent. For Whitman, the
soul is not a nebulous entity or a substitute for the body; rather, it is an
agent of transformation and change. John T. Irwin captures part of this
understanding when he observes that "the physical is the pathway to the
metaphysical precisely because in [Whitman's] poetic vision the physical
is transformed into the metaphysical—man's body becomes his soul."[7]
Nussbaum similarly emphasizes the transformative power of Whitman's
poetry, but she merges soul and body together so that Whitman's descent
of love is ultimately an affirmation of the finite body, a counter-cosmology
in which Whitman "affirms the Aristotelian view that the body is the
soul."[8] But Whitman portrays a more complex soul/body relationship that
emphasizes how the soul takes on the body and lives through its sequence
until it comes to the end of that sequence fully fortified and strengthened
to enact the process again. In assuming identities and mounting the steps
of an ontological stairway, the poet gradually gains the power of creation
itself, achieved not simply in ascension, but in a spiritual culmination at
the top rung of the stair of being.

In section 44, Whitman uses the image of an ascending stairway to
illustrate the evolutionary aspiration of the self through time: "My feet
strike an apex of the apices of the stairs,/ On every step bunches of ages,
and larger bunches between the steps,/ All below duly travel'd, and still I
mount and mount" (44.1149–51). Combining the idea of the vast histori-
cal series of being with mystical ascent, Whitman portrays the movement
of the speaker through "bunches of ages" or multiple selves as a poetic

process culminating in new power. The emphasis upon the image of "feet," metrical measurements in poetry, indicates that he views the act of reading as a form of ascension, which eventually arrives at, or "strikes," an "apex," a point of spiritual culmination, which provides coherence and meaning in the emergent, presently unfolding scheme of individual and collective development:[9]

> For it the nebula cohered to an orb,
> The long slow strata piled to rest it on,
> Vast vegetables gave it sustenance,
> Monstrous sauroids transported it in their mouths and deposited it
>   with care.
>
> All forces have been steadily employ'd to complete and delight me,
> Now on this spot I stand with my robust soul. (44.1164–69)

Here, Whitman recasts the soul's experience of the entire series of days as an expressly poetic venture. Where Emerson often conceived of the soul's experience of the stairway of being as a phenomenological inquiry, Whitman imagines the soul's relation to the series much more precisely as a structural component of his own poetry. It is not simply "the long slow strata" of ascending geological formations or the "monstrous sauroids" that transport the soul from one height to another, but also the metric sequence itself that serves as the physical template upon which the poet ascends upward in a spiritual strengthening that takes place at the top of the stairway of being. Here, it is important to observe that the soul is readying itself to refigure the body in a "superior circuit" that is not yet manifest, but will eventually be stamped or imprinted as a textual character. In short, the soul has been increased and strengthened by its experience of metempsychosis. By living through, and absorbing the whole series of being, it has achieved self-awareness and now possesses a poetic, self-fashioning power, at once freed from the series and yet mastering the ability to constitute the series' future, robust ground.

While Whitman announces himself as the poet of both the soul and the body, the soul nonetheless possesses a very particular distinction in "Song of Myself." Whitman repeatedly imagines ascension as the arduous quest of metempsychotic integration in order to attain an unmediated relationship with the soul. In Section 25, it is precisely this art of ascension that wards off the psychological limitations of the human body and allows the poet to access the eternal energy of the soul. In order to overcome the killing rays of the sun, the poet must do more than assume bodies; he must propel himself upward toward renewal: "We also ascend dazzling and tremendous as the sun,/ We found our own O my soul in the calm and cool of the daybreak" (25.562–63). Harold Bloom calls this "movement from I, the persona of Walt Whitman, to We, self and soul together" a "triumph" of the "American sublime," a "transcendence" of the traditional "limitation of finding [one's] own soul unknowable."[10] From a more precise vantage point, Whitman instills the mystical delineations of ascent into his poetry, especially Emerson's conviction that the soul's power is finally made manifest at the end of the historical series of being. In "Song of Myself," therefore, the poet climbs history's preestablished sequence, finding at long last an express mutuality with his soul, which ever-compels the poet "to continue beyond":

> This day before dawn I ascended a hill and look'd at the crowded
> heaven,
> And I said to my spirit *When we become the enfolders of those orbs,*
> *and the pleasure and knowledge of every thing in them, shall we be*
> *fill'd and satisfied then?*
> And my spirit said *No, we but level that lift to pass and continue be-*
> *yond.* (46.1220–22)

Integrating the ascension of Section 25 and the robust soul of Section 44 into a conversation between self and soul, Whitman asks if his metempsychotic assimilation has been completed and the soul answers that the movement upward must continue perpetually. The poet has thereby learned to converse directly with his soul by virtue of ascending the historical series of being. He no longer sees through the eyes of the dead; he has overcome the mimetic crisis, and his perception is no longer mediated by matter. At every plateau, he assimilates the materiality he sees and attains the long-promised "origin of all poems." It is not a process achieved in spiritual isolation. Whitman evokes the process in direct relation to his readers, who will attempt to mount the series for themselves so as to assume what the poet assumes, as the second line of the poem indicates.

"On the Extremest Verge"

In the 1855 preface to *Leaves of Grass*, Whitman has prepared his readers to imagine their relationship with him in terms of ascent. Indeed, the movement upward toward robust power is not an occasional metaphor; it constitutes Whitman's poetic challenge to his audience to become poets in turn. If the reader fails to respond, fails to constitute a new vista of experience beyond the preestablished sequence he or she inherits, he has, so to speak, missed his metempsychotic apprenticeship and must "merge in the general run and wait his development," simply remaining a reader who is as-yet unable to exceed or transcend the sequence provided and has to wait for another incarnation in which to manifest his poetic power. In Emersonian terms, the reader will have not learned "self-trust" or "self-reliance" and must thereby ceaselessly perceive the textual series without contributing or registering his or her own inscription: "If [the poet] does not flood himself with the immediate age as with vast oceanic tides" and does not make "the present spot the passage from what was to what shall be [. . .]—let him merge in the general run and wait his development" (1855: 705–19). Here, "the present spot" anticipates the stairway of being in "Song of Myself," for the privileged place between past and future that Whitman announces in the preface expressly prefigures "this spot" on which "I stand with my robust soul." Whitman thereby gives two choices to his audience—the first being a deferral of poetic maturation and the other, a metempsychotic integration of history into the self, a process in which the spiritual aspires upward through history's vast sequence until it transforms these materials into the promise of the present moment: the "eternity [. . .] rises up from its inconceivable vagueness and infiniteness in the swimming shape of today."

Whitman invites his readers to watch the "greatest poet" ascend the ladder or stairway of being so as to climb through the textual series and disappear beyond the last word. In witnessing the spectacle, the reader is compelled either to follow the poet or to remain behind among all the cultural forms over which he still has no power: "The greatest poet does not dazzle his rays over character and scenes and passions . . . he finally *ascends* and finishes all . . . he exhibits the pinnacles that no man can tell what they are for or what is beyond . . . he glows a moment *on the extremest verge*. He is wonderful in his last half-hidden smile or frown . . . by that flash of the moment of parting the one that sees it shall be encouraged or terrified afterward for many years" (1855: 311–18; emphasis added). To gain the power of the poet, "to glow on the extremest verge," is, to a large extent, the central preoccupation of the 1855 edition of *Leaves of Grass*. On the final rung of the historical series of being, the poet at last glows, becomes a flash of light before disappearing—and Whitman equates this spectacle with the experience of ascent, a sublime, evolutionary process from or to which the reader either shrinks or turns.

Whitman's depiction of the poet's disappearance or "moment of part-ing" that leaves the reader "encouraged or terrified" can also be under-stood as a direct response to Emerson's articulation of the future poet as "an object of awe and terror." In Emerson's "The Poet" (1844), the reader must consider if he appears "a man to all eyes" (W 3: 21), or whether the poet—who has a fuller experience of the stairway or ladder of ascent and, thus, has undergone a greater development or evolution on it—perceives the reader from another, higher evolutionary vantage point. In the 1855 preface, Whitman intensifies this relationship between reader and poet by imagining his own poetic form as an ascending series on which two prospective identities play: the reader ascending through the textual sequence and the poet hovering just above or beyond the series, having already assimilated and transcended the sequence, yet nevertheless descending into the series once again to aid the reader in his progress. Once the reader has witnessed the poet on "the extremest verge" of the ascending poetic series transcending the last word, the reader musters the courage to attempt such transcendence, but he does not achieve this feat alone; he is aided by the poet who now "takes" the reader with "firm sure grasp" into "living regions previously unattained":

> The touch of him tells in action. Whom he takes he takes with firm sure grasp into live regions previously unattained. . . . thenceforward is no rest. . . . they see the space and ineffable sheen that turn the old spots and lights into dead vacuums. The companion of him beholds the birth and progress of stars and learns one of the meanings. Now there shall be a man cohered out of tumult and chaos. . . . the elder encourages the younger and shows him how . . . they two shall launch off fearlessly together till the new world fits an orbit for itself and looks unabashed on the lesser orbits of the stars and sweeps through the ceaseless rings and shall never be quiet again. (1855: 741–51)

In a very specific manner, Whitman adapts traditional transcendence and makes it applicable to the reading and writing process; he presents it as a form of physical love and intimacy whose upward and downward gravities find an express mutuality and union: the elder descends into the series so as to take hold of the younger and help him ascend toward new creation, so that they can "see the space and ineffable sheen" of new life. The elder's instruction allows the younger to "behold [for himself] the birth and progress of stars," and this pedagogical, poetic, and erotic project is transformed from one which initially contains an implicit power structure—the elder grasping the younger and leading him upward—to one of emergent equality. Once the "elder encourages the younger and shows him how" to perceive the prospect of new creation, the two of them "launch off fearlessly together" to engender this "new world." Fittingly, Whitman's pronouncement of future unity—"Now there shall be a man cohered out of tumult and chaos"—possesses a necessary ambiguity. The exact identity of this prospective man remains unclear; he is neither the elder nor the younger, but both together; their partnership has allowed a new entity to cohere out of division and chaos. What was, on one level, a pedagogical lesson in reading poetry has led to the emergence of a new individual unity, which repeats the universe's push outward on an even higher and more fortified ontological level.

What began, then, as a simple reading process soon becomes a tangible "touch" between reader and poet, a process that both transcends and simultaneously affirms the very physicality of "the new world." Perception prepares for creation, since the companions' journey into this new region entails the organ of sight, but the emphasis on the "firm sure grasp" of actual, physical friendship or homoerotic love along this journey is Whitman's own, a decidedly human touch that binds and coheres what was always prospective or even impossible in Emerson. The delineations of Emerson's metempsychotic self inform the way that Whitman presents the end of the stairway as the spot on which two energies, one coming from below and the other from above, coalesce "to launch off fearlessly [. . .] till the new world fits an orbit for itself." But Whitman much more fully imagines such a spiritual reshaping of the self as a decisive part of the reading process, which offers the most intimate of experiences, the ecstatic bond between master and apprentice, reader and poet, lover and beloved, a process much more reminiscent of the actual stages of Platonic ascent.

In Plato's *Symposium*, for instance, Diotima's pupil does not just see the Good or the Beautiful; the disciple's ascent is an arduous path where persistent and wide-ranging study eventually leads the student to become a master-creator in his own right: perception gives way to touch, a perceptual physicality that may be either lost or emphasized according to the dialogue's translator. In Percy Shelley's translation of the *Symposium*, one of the translations most readily available to Whitman, the movement toward creation is explicit and does not evoke a conventional or stereotypical Platonism where soul simply throws off the body. Rather, Diotima assures Socrates that "earnest Love is a tendency towards eternity"[11] and that the pregnancy of the body can lead to an even more potent pregnancy of the soul.[12] Subsequently, the pupil is told not to enslave himself to one or another form if he "would turn towards the wide ocean of intellectual beauty, and *from the sight of the lovely and majestic forms which it contains, would abundantly bring forth his conceptions.*"[13] Shelley captures the physicality that is a decisive part of this process, since the ascent employs sexual images in describing the eventual pregnancy of the soul wishing to procreate upon the beautiful, which comes in its highest manifestation to entail *touch*: "When any one, ascending from a correct system of Love, begins to contemplate this supreme beauty, he already touches the consummation of his labor."[14]

Contrary to Nussbaum's insistence upon the "descent of love," Whitman's 1855 preface and "Song of Myself" emphatically depict the empowerment and expansion of the self in terms of the robust soul, an ascending spiritual fortification, which possesses a further Emersonian and Idealist angle of interpretation. In an 1842 journal, Emerson conceives of the robust soul in terms of dialectic, a simultaneous movement downward to material singularity and upward to unified multiplicity: "A spark of fire is infinitely deep, but a mass of fire reaching from earth upward into heaven, this is the sign of the *robust, united, burning, radiant soul.*" In "Love" (1841), Emerson interprets this fiery dialectic in relation to the ladder of ascent from Plato's *Symposium*. He integrates the notion of Platonic Forms into a project of perpetual cognitive transformation by showing how the ladder of being becomes the locus upon which opposing gravities play: a "celestial rapture falling out of heaven" takes root in the "private heart" of one individual and soon passes its "spark" to others "until it warms and beams upon multitudes of men and women, upon the universal heart of all, and so lights up the whole world and all nature with its generous flames" (*W* 2: 100, 102).[15] For Emerson, the soul's circular movement downward out of heaven and upward in a mass of fire is not a one-time activity, but constituted and informed by multiple journeys up and down the ladder of being, its reascent characterized by the fact that it has already descended into matter.[16]

Emerson's conception of the soul's descent and ascent toward robustness echoes a well-established Neoplatonic tradition in England. With its unmistakable, although somewhat ephemeral emphasis upon the double movement of the soul, Floyer Sydenham's eighteenth-century translation of Plato's *Symposium*, *The Banquet: A Dialogue of Plato Concerning Love* (1767), depicts the Platonic ladder as one of ascent and descent. The soul in moving up the rungs toward the Sovereign Beauty remembers that it has inhabited these steps before, albeit under an opposing gravity, and is now not liable to destruction since its present movement upward rejuvenates it and asserts its inward power against decay.[17] Whitman's implicit adaptation of Emerson's robust soul captures this Platonic notion of ascent in the *Symposium*, particularly Diotima's final step on the ladder of ascent on which the soul is physically strengthened and increased so that it will be capable of seeing and touching the beautiful. Like Whitman later, the English Platonists emphasize the physicality of the soul approaching the highest vision of beauty on the ladder of ascent. In Thomas Taylor's influential 1804 revision of the Sydenham edition of the *Symposium*, the description of the soul fully fortified at the end of this ascent is translated as follows: "till thus being strengthened and increased, he perceives what that one science is which is so singularly great."[18] In his 1818 translation of the *Symposium*, Percy Shelley who knew well the Sydenham and Taylor editions translates the passage as follows: "until, strengthened and confirmed, he should at length steadily contemplate one science."[19] The actual

Greek word surprisingly provides an even surer ground for comparison since, in Greek, this strengthening is *rhōstheis*, as close as one can get to "robust" in English. In Whitman, moreover, the word "robust" appears in the final versions of the poem, not in the original 1855 edition where we simply have: "Now I stand on this spot with my soul" (1168). Whitman's later added emphasis upon the strengthening of the much-labored soul indicates a striking affinity with the stages of ascent in Emerson and the mystical tradition he intensively studied and transformed for an American audience.[20]

The Flash of the Eye on the Page

Whitman's adaptation of Emerson's metempsychotic self with its ascending and descending order entails a startling integration of this structure into a heightened awareness of language. Where in the Renaissance there was a new emphasis "on human action, on man's role in completing God's creation and bringing the cosmos to its full nature,"[21] in Whitman's writing, the poet attempts to fulfill the unrealized promise of God's creation through words. The new poetic form of *Leaves of Grass* democratizes the Protestant Reformation value of *sola scriptura,* but more than this, it makes the poetic sequence the site in which an individual may seek for a greater understanding of history and open its structures and language to the discourse of the present and, more mysteriously, the future. While Romanticism emphasized the human being's expressive powers to transfigure the world of sense impressions by accessing an inner source,[22] Whitman goes much further than this in expressing the metaphysical underpinnings of the modern self as a process that is consummated in poetry.[23]

Both Emerson and Whitman depict selfhood by radically transforming the traditional ladder of ascent into an ontological and poetic structure of power, and they locate this power in the site of textuality. In "Goethe" (1850), Emerson depicts representative personality not simply as past materials that need to be assimilated by a current self; rather, the reading process evokes a relationship between perceiver and poet, which imbues the textual frame with a vital form of energy that it does not ordinarily possess:

> It makes a great difference to the force of any sentence, whether there be a man behind it, or no. In the learned journal, in the influential newspaper, I discern no form, only some irresponsible shadow, oftener, some monied corporation, or some dangler, who hopes in the mask and robes of his paragraph, to pass for somebody. But, through every clause and part of speech of a right book, I meet the eyes of the

most determined of men: his force and terror inundate every word:
the commas and dashes are alive; so that the writing is athletic and
nimble, can go far and live long. (*W* 4: 162)

Emerson's repeated desire to inhabit all points of view becomes, in this
instance, a reader's face-to-face meeting with the poet beyond the immedi-
ate parameters of the individual body. Peering into the face of the "right
book," the reader seeks to "meet the eyes of the most determined of men"
whose "force and terror inundate every word." Here, the mimetic dilemma
that inevitably haunts the textual process has been overcome. Instead of
having to see through an "irresponsible shadow" or, in Whitman's words,
the "eyes of the dead," the reader finds that the text may yield a living in-
timacy: two eyes meeting each other through the textual medium so that
even the "commas and dashes are alive."

Whitman's self-described effort "to put a whole living man in the ex-
pression of a poem, without wincing"[24] is certainly a grand figuration
of Emerson's insistence above that the "right book" can evoke a form of
intense intimacy. At the same time, there is a radical sense in Whitman
that any poetic relationship is and will be irreconcilably scattered into a
perpetually changing relationship with language. What makes Whitman's
writing particularly modern is that the democratic pact between poet and
reader uneasily pivots upon a shared textuality, whose poetic arrange-
ment resonates with all of its history. In Section 48 of "Song of Myself," the
speaker sees a world imbued with the divine presence of God and realizes
that all the forms of the world are discarded letters of the divine, a lan-
guage that the speaker, in turn, adopts and discards for those who come
after him:[25] "In the faces of men and women I see God, and in my own
face in the glass,/ I find letters from God dropt in the street, and every
one is sign'd by God's name,/ And I leave them where they are, for I know
that wheresoe'er I go,/ Others will punctually come for ever and ever"
(48.1285–88). Whitman implicitly underscores the metempsychotic order
as a model for textuality itself. The poet is initially a reader; he assumes a
language—"letters"—which provides a prehistory of the sequence of which
he is a part, and like God who has already passed through this series, he
leaves the letters for others to read. As Whitman immediately continues,
life itself is composed of many such dead letters, and identity can be under-
stood as a successive taking on and throwing off of being and its language:
"And as to you Life I reckon you are the leavings of many deaths,/ (No
doubt I have died myself ten thousand times before)" (49.1297–98). The
individual thereby uses his eyes to transmigrate through every *leaf*—every
word and letter—and, in this metempsychosis, he learns to unite himself
with the greater community.

The closing sections of "Song of Myself" illuminate this uneasy, ecstatic bond between individual and community. On the one hand, every step in the textual sequence is always the domain of one, ever-changing self: "The past and present wilt—I have fill'd them, emptied them,/ And proceed to fill my next fold of the future" (51.1319–20). On the other hand, each step in the textual series is a new individual entity whose relationship to the ones before and those who come after it populate the world of the text and allow it to stand for the larger American nation.[26] To achieve another transmigration, Whitman's poetry requires other individuals to populate it. After all his assumptions, the poet of "Song of Myself" thus enacts a process of sundering and comes to "wait on the door-slab" (51.1327) for the reader to speak and translate the poet's dead corpse—now letters on a page—into the new life of the soul.[27] Here, at the close of the process, the trajectories of ascent and descent implicitly reemerge, but the whole process is swayed by a different gravity. The poet has already achieved spiritual robustness; he no longer needs to ascend upward; rather, he "bequeaths [himself] to the dirt" (52.1339), to the textual materials below, "under your boot-soles." Even at the close of the poetic process, the reader is actually beginning his journey into the text; he does not yet need to ascend through the textual materials; he currently occupies a privileged position not simply outside the text, but above it: "Listener up there! What have you to confide to me?" (51.1321). Like the stalwart heir of the 1855 preface, the reader approaches the threshold, which is now an explicitly textual domain, and his role is to descend into the series by using his perception to endow the textual inscriptions with new life.

In "Crossing Brooklyn Ferry," Whitman accomplishes what "Song of Myself" initiated: the metempsychotic movement beyond one self into another expresses itself as both a central preoccupation and a formal order with Whitman as both the changing material body and the spirit that pours itself from one generation to the next: "What is more subtle than this which ties me to the woman or man that looks in my face?/ Which fuses me into you now, and pours my meaning into you?" (8.96–97). In "Crossing Brooklyn Ferry" (1856), the command of "Song of Myself" to "look in my face" is, once again, a poetic foundation for democratic and poetic union—"I see you face to face!" (1.1)—implicitly echoing the religious overtones that Emerson so prominently espoused in the first paragraph of his most famous essay, "Nature" (1836): "The foregoing generations beheld God and nature face to face; we, through their eyes. Why should not we also enjoy an original relation to the universe?" As God once spoke "*face to face*" with Moses and made a covenant with him,[28] Whitman promises to restore this sacred and elect ability to *all* his readers. What was once a living testament between God and his people is thereby transformed into a democratic challenge that cannot simply be written down upon blocks of stone or stamped upon leaves of paper. The poetic sequence itself has become the face of the poet with Whitman seeking to unite himself with his future readers, even those who come "hundreds" of years later.[29]

The passage of the speaker "from shore to shore" is implicitly akin to meeting his future audience "face to face" in a strange, metempsychotic realization of a present, perceiving self who, although unified, has nevertheless to experience itself not simply through succession, but different bodies. The possibility of a robust fulfillment in which speaker and reader unite is the unfulfilled promise of Whitman's poetic ritual. Somehow, two sets of eyes may yet meet through the medium of the textual frame, thereby linking a vast sequence from past to future:

> Consider, you who peruse me, whether I may not in unknown ways
>   be looking upon you;
> Be firm, rail over the river, to support those who lean idly, yet haste
>   with hasting current;
> Fly on, sea-birds! fly sideways, or wheel in large circles high in the air;
> Receive the summer sky, you water, and faithfully hold it till all
>   downcast eyes have time to take it from you!
> Diverge, fine spokes of light, from the shape of my head, or any one's
>   head, in the sunlit water! (9.112–16)

Here, the fantastical Emersonian image of two sets of eyes meeting through the medium of the textual frame takes on added complexity and coherence in Whitman's apostrophe of the future. The act of perception—"you who peruse me"—is diffused into, or refracted through many temporal avenues and selves. The reader's activity is mirrored by the poet's perception so that what is seen is not simply words on a page, but the reflective waters that buoy and sweep the ferry from shore to shore and capture the looks of those who "lean idly" by the river, the sea-birds who fly or wheel far above the waters, and "all downcast eyes," which themselves are a medium that reflects "the summer sky." The image of "fine spokes of light" diverging from the poet's head into the sunlit water emphasizes the centrality and divinity of a self that reverberates throughout time as a continual act of perception and self-constitution, connecting one life to many others in open-ended metempsychotic sequence.

Whitman's poetic form universalizes itself not simply through sentiment or imagery, but through the realization that reading and writing constitute a shared process that bestows a whole tradition, fragmentary though it may appear, upon the participant. Whitman calls upon his reader to become self-aware and to enjoy and love the poet who has thus shaped the textual cosmos. If self-fashioning or self-constitution is the ever-deferred aim of Emersonianism, then it is the achievement of Whitman's poetry to elicit a heightened self-awareness in the reader so that he may yet learn to look through his own eyes and not through the eyes of the dead. Where in Emerson's "Circles," the "flash of his eye [. . .] converts statues into fiery men" (*W* 2: 184), so in "Crossing Brooklyn Ferry," Whitman teaches his readers how to convert mere shapes or remembrances—"dumb, beautiful ministers"—into living, ensouled entities:[30]

> You have waited, you always wait, you dumb, beautiful ministers,
> We receive you with free sense at last, and are insatiate
>   hence-forward,
> Not you any more shall be able to foil us, or withhold yourselves from
>   us,
> We use you, and do not cast you aside—we plant you permanently
>   within us,
> We fathom you not—we love you—there is perfection in you also,
> You furnish your parts toward eternity,
> Great or small, you furnish your parts toward the soul. (9.126–32)

In the first version of the poem, the ensouling image of "downcast eyes" that descend like sunrays into the "dumb, beautiful ministers" is even more emphatic: "We descend upon you and all things—we arrest you all;/ We realize the soul only by you, you faithful solids and fluids;/ Through you color, form, location, sublimity, ideality;/ Through you every proof, comparison, and all the suggestions and determinations of ourselves" (12.136–39). In both versions, the principal value that Whitman champions is the conversion of mere matter or externality into a world of selves, each of which are not simply husks or coverings, but immanent aspects of humanity's inner life: "we plant you permanently within us." This form of visual ensoulment outlines the vastness of the poet's task, accomplished through the bond that allows sequence and historical progression, an affirmation not of the linearity of consciousness in time, but of the work of consciousness to synthesize and bestow its own invented order upon what it sees and loves.

Deceptions of the Thrush

In the ancient world, metempsychosis most often indicated the alienation of the soul in matter. "I wept and wailed when I saw the unfamiliar land," Empedocles proclaims in one of the fragments that remain of his work, underscoring the loneliness and estrangement the soul feels upon entering the material world.[31] In Book 7 of the *Republic*, Plato proposes how the human being can overcome his or her material entrapment; the eye accesses "the indwelling power of the soul" through turning itself around, converting itself to the light until it "is able to endure the contemplation of essence and the brightest region of being."[32] In Whitman, this spiritual process underlies the act of seeing so that presence and absence, life and death, soul and body, are connected through the bonds of language and these divisions in the self can be healed. To do this, one must attempt to convert material objects or to turn them around to the light, which Whitman often imagines as a descent into matter and a simultaneous ascent, a chiastic process in which the body educates the soul and the soul vitalizes the body. Gone are many of the mythologies of the past, yet there is another emergent modern value, built upon the back of many mystical traditions, that seeks to console the individual that his nature is capable of renewal.

Where Whitman attempts to heal the dilemma of Emerson's double consciousness by removing "the distinction between the reflections within the mind and things in the world,"[33] in the work of many modern poets the double consciousness vigorously reemerges. Indeed, part of the energy and ritual of modernism can be located in this desire for self-directed robust renewal and the simultaneous fear that the self is unable to accomplish such a spiritual feat, that it is forced to repeat a pattern already laid out for it. In the third episode of *Ulysses* (1922), James Joyce formulates the question of metempsychosis for a modern audience in just this context. Molly Bloom's query seems simple enough: "Metempsychosis?" she asks her husband. The explication, however, points beyond Molly's desire for a description in "plain words." The mystical term—one that Molly has singled out in her book—indicates a relationship directly involving, yet gesturing beyond, the domain of words and their supposed meanings to the question of self—or, in Molly's case, the lack of self. What Molly cannot know is that she is a textual pattern meticulously crafted in relation to Homer's comedic cycle, *The Odyssey*; she is a character, a metempsychotic recreation of the past, mirroring and repeating a formation set out millennia ago. As a figure constructed out of words, she must forever remain unaware of the law that has set her down in language and authored her fate. As a recreation of life, bearing the outlines of human nature, however, she invariably imitates the need to question her identity and to understand her place in a series of relations.

Joyce's dramatic irony establishes itself, therefore, on the self-referential problem of identity, implicitly directing Molly's question of metempsychosis to the reader who must consider the larger ramifications of what it may mean, not as a doctrine reduced to a worn-out, archaic metaphysics, but as a phenomenological predicament that interrupts the cool separation of reader and page.[34] Indeed, Molly's question is not so strange; as we have seen, it echoes the earlier Romantic desire to preserve the freedom of the soul in relation to an emerging understanding of the vastness of the historical record and of how this record determines consciousness. For both Emerson and Whitman, a man may embrace his own historical emergence, first, by making himself the self-aware locus of the historical series of being and, second, by writing himself anew, but he more often is "forced to accept an irresistible dictation" that makes him but "a link in a chain" (*W* 6: 2, 12). In short, his being, his very biology, is already written by the historical series that props up his emergence in time.

The central predicament in so much of Emerson's oeuvre is precisely this failure—and the perpetual hope—to constitute the self more fully. It is an implicit angst that accompanies the very idea of self-knowing spirit and its capacity to salvage the project of Enlightenment humanism in the looming face of modernity and materialism. After all, Emerson champions both self-knowing and *self-trust*[35]—as though he were secretly unsure of his own immanence and perpetually projecting this doubt onto every map of the private and social self. That is why, in the domain of the double consciousness, the individual has to go in search of himself, in search of the soul that exists both within and in the future. The spiritual emphases of both Emerson and Whitman center, therefore, on the capacity of the self to renew its material nature and, in so doing, heal the divisions to which consciousness continually succumbs. In the work of many modern poets, this double consciousness, with its ancient and esoteric underpinnings, continues to resonate uneasily. While modernism entails, on one level, a rejection of transcendentalism and its humanist conception of self and history, it nonetheless retains the very divisions of the self with which Romanticism struggled.

During the modernist period, there was indeed a sweeping condemnation of American transcendentalism.[36] T. S. Eliot's remark that "the essays of Emerson are already an encumbrance"[37] has become representative of a generation's distain for what Irving Howe described as "the whole complex of Emersonianism" and its "individualism of vaporous spirituality." The "major critics of this period were concerned primarily with discrediting the Emerson whom their forebears had enshrined and showed little interest in exploring the possibility that he might support alternate readings."[38] In "Cousin Nancy" (1917) and particularly in "Sweeney Erect" (1920), Eliot directly mocks the Emersonian belief in personality:[39] "The lengthened shadow of a man/ Is history, said Emerson/ Who had not seen the silhouette/ Of Sweeney straddled in the sun."[40] Clearly, Eliot's Sweeney—the ignorant modern man—is incompatible with Emerson's vision of "representative men" spanning the evolutionary arc of history. More specifically, Eliot's objection to Emerson is driven by his express distaste for

Romanticism's underlying metaphysical understanding of reality. As he acknowledges in "Tradition and the Individual Talent" (1920), the "point of view which I am struggling to attack is perhaps related to the metaphysical theory of the substantial unity of the soul."[41]

For the early Eliot, moreover, the question of soul is even more vexing and psychologically confusing than it was Emerson or Whitman. Where Emerson laments the possibility of ever uniting material understanding with the future life of the soul, for Eliot, the soul or loss of soul forms the site upon which the modern self's psychological drama pivots. "Preludes" (1917) offers a touchstone for the type of spiritual dilemma that preoccupies Eliot in his early poetry. The speaker of the poem suffers from a psychological schism similar in outline to Emerson's double consciousness, one side all externality and the other an internal fancy that at once comprises the emotional center of the subject and yet causes him to feel an irreconcilable sense of displacement in the world. Where Emerson portrayed the Sphinx's metempsychotic quest through a "thousand natures," Eliot describes a soul "constituted" by "a thousand sordid images," a pollution he places squarely upon the reader, the "you" who spends the night entertaining a type of perverse metempsychotic cinematic projection upon the ceiling above:

> You tossed a blanket from the bed
> You lay upon your back, and waited;
> You dozed, and watched the night revealing
> The thousand sordid images
> Of which your soul was constituted;
> They flickered against the ceiling.[42]

Eliot intensifies the psychological split between the immanent self and the world by projecting the dirtiness associated with the "masquerades" of time upon the reader and preserving the wish for spiritual constancy as an internal fancy of the self. The only time that this self—*the I*—speaks is in a meditation upon the instability of immanent consciousness, now an emotion that the individual apprehensively preserves: "I am moved by fancies that are curled/ Around these images, and cling:/ The notion of some infinitely gentle/ Infinitely suffering thing."[43] This self who speaks tentatively from the first-person perspective is not moved by anything definite at all; rather, the immanent domain of the soul, that gentle infinite thing, is an abstract fancy, a mere "notion," curled about the definite images of the poem.

In "Preludes," the transcendental doubt of Emerson's "Experience" is pitched headlong into the despair and confusion of modernity. Eliot ascertains as much in the final lines of the poem, immediately displacing the hesitant emergence of internality with the jeering image of the reader wiping his mouth after an act of consumption. Indeed, the self's spiritual reservoir has been emptied of its sustenance, perhaps even carelessly and crassly consumed by the reader himself or herself: "Wipe your hand across your mouth, and laugh;/ The worlds revolve like ancient women/ Gathering fuel in vacant lots."[44] Eliot's meaning is at once suggestively open to interpretation and plainly clear. Ancient women gathering fuel in empty lots replays the principal strategy of transcendentalism in a much different key, for the soul's continual effort to absorb the materials with which it will compose its material sequence in time has become an empty formula. To be sure, Eliot has already preset the context, for "the grimy scraps of withered leaves about your feet" imply that the poetic sequence itself, composed of metric feet and leaves of paper, is polluted and dead, the internal moral compass directing the process at hand simply the "conscience of a blackened street/ Impatient to assume the world."[45] The self's transcendental desire to absorb everything around it in a robust spiritual strengthening has thus become an exhausted, potentially sinister ritual. In short, the lots are empty, despite the continuation of poetic rites that indicate otherwise.

"Preludes" thus exhibits not a departure from transcendentalism, but a deepening anxiety about the schism within the self that transcendentalists like Emerson and Whitman problematized and attempted to heal. In the opening of "Burnt Norton" (1935), the first part of the *Four Quartets*, Eliot endeavors to come to terms with this schism; in doing so, he portrays a structure of subjectivity directly dependent upon the Idealist tradition. Eliot powerfully repositions the unreal fancy of the self in "Preludes" as the internal architecture of the mind that the speaker and his readers must collectively confront. "What might have been is an abstraction/ Remaining a perpetual possibility/ Only in a world of speculation," Eliot writes, indicating that consciousness' internal abstraction is nonetheless intimately intertwined with material history, for both together comprise what is present: "What might have been and what has been/ Point to one end, which is always present."[46] Just as Emerson used ancient mystical cosmologies as maps of the internal, cognitive structure of consciousness, so Eliot depicts the poetic process as an explicitly internal journey. The action of "Burnt Norton" takes place both in relation to the page itself and within the mind, for Eliot expressly situates the metric feet or footfalls that measure the poetic pace in the mind:

Footfalls echo in the memory
Down the passage which we did not take
Towards the door we never opened
Into the rose-garden. My words echo
Thus, in your mind.[47]

Eliot evokes a poetic process that promises a reintegration of history and memory with the immanent life of the soul. In Emersonian and Whitmanian terms, the effort to restore the fire and splendor of immanence requires awakening consciousness in the order of time to realize that the soul has already departed, has already evacuated this structure of being. Thus, the words of the departed poet—who already formed the material structure of the poem—echo in the mind of the reader. The poet's voice is not completely present; the world that he created, the sequence that is not yet our own and requires us to enter into it for the first time, is emptied of the immanent life that we must now somehow restore through our gaze.

While figuring the prospect of immanence, Eliot thus cannot wholly affirm the soul. The soul, like the poet's voice, is known only as an echo presently requiring a journey into the dead materials of the poem, an attempt to retrace the poetic sequence: "But to what purpose/ Disturbing the dust on a bowl of rose-leaves/ I do not know."[48] The journey within to the rose garden immediately reveals that the leaves—the very pages of the poem—are dead. Nor can the poet assure his readers that their journey has a clear, pragmatic purpose. The voice of the speaker wavers, displayed with a sudden visual breaking of the stanza form. The speaker now asks his readers to follow him, which at once entails a deepening of the psychic ties that unite one life to another and yet displaces the assurance and the unity of the speaking voice. Other echoes inhabit the garden, and suddenly the speaker is in the position of the reader, having to follow out a pattern that he does not fully understand and that he implicitly doubts: "Other echoes/ Inhabit the garden. Shall we follow?/ Quick, said the bird, find them, find them,/ Round the corner. Through the first gate,/ Into our first world, shall we follow/ The deception of the thrush?" As the reader retraces the poetic sequence, the bird—the traditional image of the winged soul—appears as a guide who will direct both poet and reader deeper into the imaginary garden of consciousness. In Whitman's "Song of Myself," the reader follows the poet, retracing the leavings of many deaths, but, in Eliot, the poet is immediately displaced as an authority. Nor can the poet assure his reader, for he too doubts the poetic pattern even though he is compelled to follow the bird. Indeed, the bird itself potentially represents a "deception," the soul not at all an image of assurance, but one that casts doubt upon the very structure that it makes.

While doubt tinges the experience of the mind's rose garden, nonetheless, the experience itself cannot be denied. In retracing the self-reflexive pattern, the poet and reader vertiginously affirm a structure by the very virtue of participating in it. Disturbing the dust on the leaves of the poem is thereby akin to journeying into the recesses of the mind in search of something that, while it writes itself, was never wholly present. The problem of double consciousness, the mimetic crisis itself, that Emerson posed and Whitman attempted to solve through the fluid assimilating motions of the metempsychotic self, is that individual consciousness has already been structured by the precepts of the past and that it pursues liberty, a pathway beyond mediation, the key to which hides from view, disappearing in its many vanishing points. Despite their doubts, modern poets are just as adamant as their transcendental, Romantic precursors that, through poetic practice, the self may yet learn to heal itself. This process is imagined explicitly in textual visualizations. By gaining the robust power of the soul, the self can reinfuse the dead body of the poem, the metempsychotic strategy of Emerson and Whitman reemerging as one of the dominant desires of the modernist poetic psyche.

In Eliot's "Burnt Norton," retracing being's historical series and the simultaneous movement into the immanent domain of the self are not simply part of an elaborate formal ritual; this practice is meant to transform the external delineations of the poem from a dead mimetic object into an ensouled, self-constituting reality. The poet and reader thereby follow the bird through the "first gate" into the "first world" of consciousness to find that the echoes have now taken on a fuller immaterial stature: "There they were, dignified, invisible,/ Moving without pressure, over the dead leaves."[49] Where, from a completely external vantage point, reality can only be understood in mimetic terms, now within the deeper layers of the psyche, those mimetic echoes constitute themselves into spiritual entities hovering just above the language of the poem. For Eliot, this relationship forms a complex pattern of vision, the ensouling eyebeam no longer positioned from one reading perspective, but becoming dialectical and acquiring a multiplicity of vantage points: "And the bird called, in response to/ The unheard music hidden in the shrubbery,/ And the unseen eyebeam crossed, for the roses/ Had the look of flowers that are looked at."[50] The process is highly symbolic, resonating largely in metaphysical terms, for once the echoes are transformed into dignified monads hovering above the dead leaves, the bird begins a conversation with a music now emanating from the garden. In this context of emergent dialectic, the rose garden, which was dead at the beginning of the journey, has somehow been reborn. For Eliot, as with the whole Idealist tradition, it is in an act of dynamic perception that such restoration takes place, the unseen eyebeam restoring the possibility of immanence in the image of a now living garden of the mind. It is not the reader alone who sees, moreover; his perception opens itself to a dynamic range of possibilities with Eliot subtly punning on the relationship between the perceiver and perceived with his use of the word "look." Indeed, the reader's eyebeam is not the only constituting power. The roses take on the "look" of flowers that are "looked at," suggesting that

that the roses themselves have become capable of sight, of looking back, of turning themselves around, in Neoplatonic terms, so as to be capable of seeing the light of being. In being seen by the reader, the roses cause themselves to see, so that "the unseen eyebeam crosses" and a dialectic of perception is achieved, two sets of eyes seeking each other out through the textual medium and, in the process, restoring the living beauty of the internal garden.

Eliot thereby presents a methodology of reading, echoing at once the Neoplatonic conception of eyesight and its many Romantic adaptations. The question is not whether one doubts or believes in the soul's existence; the act of perception already promises "secondsight" and imagines its relationship with the object in terms of a grander model of consciousness. Emerson and Whitman's respective conceptions of mystical descent and ascent particularly help to clarify this dialectic of the unseen eyebeam in the opening of "Burnt Norton." Where perception by virtue of the ensouling eyebeam descends into the object, the object in being seen begins to ascend upward, a pattern that involves not simply conversion, turning itself around to the light, but self-constitution, integrating the divine light of the soul into being. In Eliot, the same pattern is operative, for once the unseen eyebeam crosses, the reader, poet, and the invisible monads "look down" into an empty pool, which is immediately filled with water out of sunlight, giving rise to a pattern of natural and symbolic ascent in the image of a lotos flower:

> So we moved, and they, in a formal pattern,
> Along the empty alley, into the box circle,
> To look down into the drained pool.
> Dry the pool, dry concrete, brown edged,
> And the pool was filled with water out of sunlight,
> And the lotos rose, quietly, quietly,
> The surface glittered out of heart of light,
> And they were behind us, reflected in the pool.[51]

The second epigraph of "Burnt Norton"—Heraclitus's famous fragment, "the way up and the way down are one and the same"—anticipates this meditation upon perception with the insistence that both directions, up and down, are not simply necessary, but part of one flowing system. Indeed, the emphasis upon the spatiality of perception, the eyebeam's procession downward into matter and its conversion in a self-constituting movement upward, underscores an accompanying temporal complexity. Here, the sheer linearity of poetry's sequence is transformed into an activity where the architecture of both mind and world expands with a multiplicity of possible configurations. As we have seen, the act of reading, repossessing the poetic sequence in time, entails not just a journey from left to right along the static characters of the page, but a journey inward into the mind or psyche. Eliot intensifies this twofold pattern with a metaphysical analogy for perception highly reminiscent of American transcendentalism's metempsychotic self: the soul in the figure of the eye journeys downward into materiality, into the drained pool, and suddenly through the life of the eye which brings with it the light of the sun a new entity coalesces and begins its ascent upward. Eliot also complicates these spatial and temporal strands with the dizzying imagery of ensoulment and reflection. The invisible dignitaries who look down into the pool are vertiginously repositioned; they stand at once "behind" consciousness and yet remain reflected on the sunlit textual medium.

Eliot's depiction of a "moment of mystical ecstasy" achieves a symbolic overlapping of religious traditions. Indeed, "the lotos, the sacred flower of Buddhism, replaces the expected rose"—with Eliot emphasizing not simply Christianity's symbol of transcendent beauty, but also the Eastern notion of selfhood.[52] Just as crucial to this experience is the mystical phenomenology of the greater Idealist tradition. Plotinus captures something definitive about the Platonic privilege of vision in his portrayal of the eyes as "sun-formed" (*helio-eides*),[53] a conception that finds new expression centuries later in Jacob Böhme's description of the soul as "a life awakened out of the eye of God, its original is in the fire and the fire is its life."[54] Emerson's claim that "the glance of [the] eye has the power of sunbeams" (*W* 6: 16) is itself a dynamic adaptation of this heritage. The poetic structure of "Burnt Norton" is similarly dependent on this tradition of thought, for the eye-beam does more than disturb the dust on a bowl of rose leaves; it too has the power of sunbeams and bestows fresh life onto the leaves and makes them capable of celebration: "Go, said the bird, for the leaves were full of children,/ Hidden excitedly, containing laughter."[55] Here, the sunlight of perception awakens the dead leaves back to life and restores the power of immanent consciousness so that "all is always now," as Eliot claims in the fifth and final section of "Burnt Norton." This too is the central claim of early modern Idealism, Hegel's self-knowing spirit existing in an eternal present and Emerson's metempsychotic self enacting its progression in the "Here and Now" (*W* 2: 7).

With the restoration of true sight, the initial temporal crisis of "Burnt Norton"—"If all time is eternally present/ All time is eternally unredeemable"—has been experienced in a new way. "Only through time time is conquered,"[56] Eliot writes, indicating that consciousness' experience of time is a vital dimension of the eternal present. On one level, every moment in time exists "at the still point of the turning world [. . .] where past and future are gathered." In this eternal present where nothing is lost, since every step in the sequence of time exists forever, there is "Neither movement from nor towards,/ Neither ascent nor decline."[57] But, on another level, in the individual experience of consciousness, which is forced by its nature to accept one pathway, ascent and descent again emerge. Thus, Eliot urges his readers onward through the poetic sequence, at once downward—"Descend lower, descend only/ Into the world of perpetual solitude"—and upward on the ladder of ascent: "The detail of the pattern is movement,/ As in the figure of the ten stairs."[58] Here, Eliot opens the final stanza of "Burnt Norton" with the image of the ten stairs from St. John's *Dark Night of the Soul*. Like almost all other mystical models of ascent, the ten stairs comprise a pathway of love, a structure upon which the soul can reachieve its union with God. In Eliot, this figure of ascent reaffirms the promise of the soul that we participate in a pattern over which we possess some command. We may yet overcome Molly Bloom's bewilderment at her inscribed existence and attain the power of the robust soul, which is the original assurance and continuing consolation of the Western self.

At the End of the Mind

A number of critics have understood Eliot's best poetry as "a play between opposites that moves forward by spiraling back (a return) and up (a transcendence)." Like Emerson's double consciousness, Eliot's pattern of descent and ascent "goes beyond Hegel [. . .] in resisting linearity, eschewing mentalism, and evading synthesis."[59] Wallace Stevens, whose early journals are filled with Emersonian passages and whom Harold Bloom has called "the involuntary heir of Whitman,"[60] embraces a similar type of unsettled dialectic in his poetry. In the estimation of Helen Vendler, "Neither the unbodied nor the embodied engages Stevens for long; he is engrossed in 'a voyaging up and down, between two elements,' and the emphasis should be on the 'between.'"[61] Indeed, poetry, for Stevens, "is an extended inquiry into new possibilities of transition," an attempt "to think beyond the received imperatives of thinking."[62] Stevens's poetry continually oscillates between doubt and revelation, a form of poetic vertigo that challenges the reader's sense of balance in the forceful figurations of transition and becoming.[63] At the same time, it is not enough to shuffle off every mythology, to empty one's breast of windy conceits, as Emerson writes in "Fate." At the heart of Stevens's poetic project is a much older metaphysical and religious desire. It is the same mystical concern with renewal that preoccupies Eliot throughout his career, but in Stevens's poetry, it is much more explicitly American. Indeed, the crisis of transcendentalism's metempsychotic self, both its psychic split and the promise of healing that is best identified in the imagery of the robust soul, is part of the poetic legacy that Stevens transforms into a radically new meditation upon language.

In his first long poem, *The Comedian as the Letter C* (1922), Stevens takes up the theme of metempsychosis and uses it in direct relation to the discovery and subsequent colonization of America. Some earlier critics have argued that the poem "traces the growth of a writer arriving and settling in America." Crispin, the protagonist of the poem, if you can call him such, is accordingly "the European come to America," the "would-be father of a new literature."[64] Harold Bloom helps to clarify Crispin's elusiveness as a character, calling the poem in which he is set a parody that "almost undoes the High Romantic quest-poem."[65] Indeed, *The Comedian as the Letter C* ironically locates itself as an irreverent adaptation of Romantic values, and it does so by making metempsychosis more than a theme, but a pattern of poetic order, the very title of the poem emphasizing the open-ended sequence in which the soul is set. The letter C and its place in the alphabet signal that there is no real beginning or ending to the poem, since the sequence is already underway. In a similar vein, Crispin the Comedian, an alliterative pun on the C classification that Stevens ironically, even mockingly elaborates, possesses very few real characteristics at all. In the first section, Stevens gives Crispin so many personages and titles that he is best understood as a protean figure in perpetual transition from one name to another.

Some critics have emphasized the difficulty of locating the speaking voice of the poem. Is the third-person narrator an older Crispin recounting his epic journey? Helen Vendler insists that Crispin is dead.[66] At the end of the first section, there can be no absolute answer. Crispin is both living and dead, a self in perpetual transition. In attempting to cross the Atlantic Ocean from France to Carolina, he has been stripped of the many names and monikers that Stevens gives him. On one level, Crispin has become "the sovereign ghost," the Plotinian "intelligence of his soil" of the first stanza, but without the authority that such a title bestows. Like many of Emerson's metempsychotic depictions, Crispin cannot fully constitute himself in any one name and begins to dissolve until he is virtually nothing but an outline of being. As such, Crispin is not a real entity, but a modernist adaptation, even a parody of the metempsychotic self:

Just so an ancient Crispin was dissolved.
The valet in the tempest was annulled.
Bordeaux to Yucatan, Havana next,
And then to Carolina. Simple jaunt.
Crispin, merest minuscule in the gales,
Dejected his manner to the turbulence.

> The salt hung on his spirit like a frost,
> The dead brine melted in him like a dew
> Of winter, until nothing of himself
> Remained, except some starker, barer self[67]

In the mythology-stripping imagery of Crispin's disembodiment, we see part of the allure that has allowed some critics to call Stevens's poetic practice postmodern. The myriad, absurd titles that define Crispin are taken away. As Stevens affirms, the "last distortion of romance/ Forsook the insatiable egotist. The sea severs not only lands but selves." Yet, amid these deconstructing pressures that dissolve the possibility of Crispin as a spiritual continuity manifested in one flesh or another, the hope for a self cannot be entirely wiped away. The "starker, barer self" shorn of its flesh becomes a glimmer of metempsychotic continuity, one that is carried over into the New World despite the opposing pressures of the imagination and reality. "Here was no help before reality," Stevens continues, "Crispin beheld and Crispin was made new./ The imagination, here, could not evade,/ In poems of plums, the strict austerity/ Of one vast, subjugating, final tone." At the moment when every belief has ceased to convince the believer, there is still the preservation of an idea of self, even if this self is simply a question mark, a placeholder for something impossible to determine:

> What was this gaudy, gusty panoply?
> Out of what swift destruction did it spring?
> It was a caparison of wind and cloud
> And something given to make whole among
> The ruses that were shattered by the large.[68]

Stevens thus reimagines the "sovereign ghost" presiding over the soil, over the network of its own material existence. The ghost is now an ephemeral and volatile placeholder that somehow has survived all the other ruses, deceptions or self-deceptions that reality eventually breaks down. The preservation of this provisional self pivots, moreover, on a tacit, ever-elusive phenomenology. Crispin beholds; he sees and thus he is made new. Accordingly, Crispin's effort to find a "new continent in which to dwell" and "to make a new intelligence prevail" can begin again.[69]

This desire for renewal through perception also comprises much of the poetic energy of Stevens's later work. In *Notes Toward a Supreme Fiction* (1947), Stevens echoes some of the principal characteristics of metempsychotic perception—from the Platonic dialectic of perception, two eyes exchanging an eyebeam, to Plotinus's presentation of the self-reflexive medium of eyesight, to Whitman's poetic declaration that he can assume other bodies through the power of the eye. For Stevens, the power of perception unfixes the static words on the page so that they are "changing essences," for the movement of the eye "on the blank" is "a will to change, a neces-sitous/ And present way, a presentation, a kind/ Of volatile world, too con-stant to be denied."[70] The singular reader is reunited with other selves so that the "eye of a vagabond in metaphor [. . .] catches our own," allowing the reader in his efforts to recognize that the "freshness of transformation" is his own and that he "is poor without the poet's lines."[71] In this setting, metempsychotic vision provides the modern reader with the unsettled and shifting ground he requires to see beyond his own single inscribed and in-scribing shape. This order is not just a function or semiology of language. It arises as a transmission from poet to poet, individual to individual, each of whom share their materials and revelations, but turn their faces away so that the reader, like the reader in Whitman's 1855 preface, looks toward the series' end and finds that he can follow out these material threads and become self-fashioning in turn.

While many critics have attempted to de-idealize his poetry, Stevens does not so much demythologize as reconstitute the mystical poetic tradi-tion he inherited. In "The Woman in Sunshine" (1950), Stevens expresses a variant form of the robust soul. Here, however, Stevens's imagery under-scores an even more unstable enterprise, for it immediately gives way to a more volatile way of understanding the relationship between soul and matter, poet and reader, and reader and textual shapes. Stevens compares the movement of writing and reading, inscribing and reconstituting, to the image of a moving psyche (soul) and/or woman and, thereby, complicates any simple interpretation of the poem, since the process is in movement and must reformulate itself in each of the reader's apprehensions:

It is only that this warmth and movement are like
The warmth and movement of a woman.

It is not that there is any image in the air
Nor the beginning nor end of a form:

It is empty. But a woman in threadless gold
Burns us with brushings of her dress

And a dissociated abundance of being,
More definite for what she is—

Because she is disembodied,
Bearing the odors of the summer fields,

Confessing the taciturn and yet indifferent,
Invisibly clear, the only love.[72]

Stevens suggests that our movement as readers does not begin or end in the poem; nor is it based upon an immutable essence ("an image in the air"). Instead, Stevens formulates the uneasy, ever-changing chiastic relationship between emptiness and presence into a self-reflexive model—and the reader, in turn, has to follow out the poet's already established textual series, a "threadless gold" that burns him and makes him feel something that is not present to him. Stevens thereby focuses upon the process of thinking itself, namely, how, in perceiving the world, we formulate an abstract image that can stand for our experience. The woman in sunshine is an object of thought that arises from textual shapes, inscribed or perceived, an idea whose dimensions take on a "definite" reality when animated by the sunshine of our perception, but Stevens is careful to indicate the slippage of the whole process, since the woman in the poem is neither reducible to the sequence at hand, nor a permanent essence of which the sequence is but a copy. Stevens thereby indicates that the cognitive synthesis of this warmth and movement is not fully material or entirely present at all, but a dissociated abundance of being that reconstitutes itself in each of our successive perceptions, even while recapitulating one continually changing idea. On another level, although they cannot meet, poet and reader are paradoxically held together, even united, by this dissociation of being. Emptiness separates every step in the series and thereby allows something outside the text to fill it, to grasp and transform it through the sunshine of perception's mystical power.

Like Emerson's orders of genesis and time, the two sides of this dialectical relation—poet and reader, writing and reading, soul and matter—fall into each other without ever fully touching, and the reader becomes conscious of this by inhabiting a series, the extremes of which run out of sight. This is after all Emerson's emphasis in "Experience" when he writes that a "man is a golden impossibility," unable to hold the two poles of his individual and universal life together, but having nonetheless to attempt the feat by ceaselessly reconstituting himself in new forms. For Whitman, this superhuman effort of self-constitution can only be provisionally achieved through the scattering of the self and an impossible repossessing of all these lives in reading. In "Large Red Man Reading" (1950), moreover, Stevens poeticizes perception's power not only to transfigure the material world but also to renew the possibility of immanence itself. The very title identifies a paradoxical type of metempsychotic coexistence, the pun on "red" suggesting that the man reading in the poem is simultaneously the object being perceived, his own self-constitution dependent on the activity of a reader beyond the poem. Stevens intensifies this image of duality between the living, infusing gaze of the reader and the dead letters of the page with the intimation that a "red" blood now circulates through the organs of the poem. The very first lines of the poem follow this theme with the dual activity of reading and speaking now calling ghosts to earth so that the poem can become a nexus of life:

> There were ghosts that returned to earth to hear his phrases,
> As he sat there reading, aloud, the great blue tabulae.
> They were those from the wilderness of stars that had expected more.
> There were those that returned to hear him read from the poem of
> life,
> Of the pans above the stove, the pots on the table, the tulips among
> them.[73]

Stevens ritualizes the reading process so that the ordinary world—the book, "the pans above the stove," "the pots," and "the tulips among them"—swells with a new mysterious energy. The poem has taken on religious, spiritual proportions; it has the power to call the dead to earth so as to hear the reader speak aloud the poetic phrases of the text. At the same time, Stevens only allows the transformative power of poetry to resonate with a conditional and tenuous allure: "They were those that *would* have wept to step barefoot into reality,/ That *would* have wept and been happy, have shivered in the frost/ And cried out to feel it again."[74] Similar to the way Whitman uses the incongruence between words and being to evoke a textual energy, Stevens depicts how poetic reading is an act in which the metaphysical and physical come into contact without touching. The ghosts only *would* have become real, but they have not yet consummated the feat.

In hearing the man reading from the "poem of life," the ghosts tenuously achieve a life of their own: they "would [. . .] have run fingers over leaves/ And against the most coiled thorn, have seized on what was ugly/ And laughed."[75] Here, they mimic the activity of the reader who touches the leaves or pages of the poem. Stevens again heightens the desire to assume a poetic language with religious intensity, for "the most coiled thorn" recalls the crown of thorns placed on Jesus's head during his passion and crucifixion. While the unreal ghosts cling to a type of conditional existence, a transformation *has* taken place: the ghosts who would have seized the thorn have been pierced by it nonetheless; a "red" blood now infuses the "blue tabulae," two colors mixing together to produce the sacred and priestly color of purple:

> [. . .] as he sat there reading, from out of the purple tabulae,
> The outlines of being and its expressings, the syllables of its law:
> *Poesis, poesis*, the literal characters, the vatic lines,
>
> Which in those ears and in those thin, those spended hearts,
> Took on color, took on shape and the size of things as they are

And spoke the feeling for them, which was what they had lacked.[76]

Poetic form thus charts the "outlines of being and its expressing," its "literal characters" becoming real by referring both to the physical reality of the text and the "vatic lines" (priestly and prophetic) of an architecture beyond literality. In "Large Red Man Reading," therefore, Stevens captures the unsettled energy that emerges when words themselves become the center of focus—when in their relationship to each other and to the reader they not only assume preeminence but also break the ordinary ties between language and life. Yet Steven's poem is not simply an attempt "to achieve epiphany by deranging reference—to give power to symbols by taking language beyond discourse."[77] It is an attempt to heal the split in consciousness and to transform dead words on a page into a living cognitive process. Like Emerson's stone statues, Whitman's dumb beautiful ministers or Eliot's dead rose leaves, all of which are transformed by the sunlight of an ensouled eyebeam, the page or stone tabulae only come alive when they are properly planted *within* the human being, for it is within the "thin and spended hearts" of the ghosts that the literal characters of the poem take on color and the size and shape of things as they are. Here, Stevens gives a much truer depiction of what self-knowing meant in the nineteenth century, not in-itself the totalizing gesture that many scholars assume today, but the experience by which remembrances or abstract abbreviations are transformed into pure being, by which, in other words, they come alive.

Like Emerson and Whitman, Stevens also imagines this epiphanic process to be a form of poetic maturation achieved on the extremest verge of the series. In what has become one of his signature poems, "Of Mere Being" (1954), Stevens writes of a "palm at the end of the mind,/ Beyond the last thought" and a "wind" that "moves slowly in its branches."[78] Recalling Emerson's metempsychosis of nature where the individual attempts to live through the whole series of being in order to arrive at the last step, Stevens situates this last step both in the mind and in nature, creating his own type of natural inwardness. Like the rose garden of "Burnt Norton," the palm at the end of the mind is a place precariously present. The whole process leans upon a rich archive of metaphysical and poetic thought, for there is nothing "mere" about the being Stevens is attempting to represent. In addition, Whitman's evocation of the "firm sure grasp" of poetic creation that is paradoxically achieved at the end of the robust soul's ascent reemerges in Stevens's poem. With Stevens, as with Platonism and other forms of alchemical and esoteric thought, the dominant image is that of fire. Indeed, the "gold-feathered bird" in "the palm" at the furthest stretches of consciousness sings "without human meaning,/ Without human feeling."

Here, the duality of being and soul, that which is human and that which is beyond human, is brought together in the physicality of the palm and its capacity to grasp the deepest and furthest reaches of thought.

With the sun-colored bird singing in its branches, the palm comes to resonate with a mysterious, symbolic power: it is at once an actual tree, the biblical tree of life, a network of words, and a hand ready to grasp the meaning of the series and to inscribe the future with a quill of fire: "The palm stands on the edge of space./ The wind moves slowly in the branches./ The bird's fire-fangled feathers dangle down." As with the robust soul on the ladder of ascent, which becomes "a mass of fire reaching from earth upward into heaven," the movement beyond transfigures itself into touch, into a taking on of materials, so that the imagination and the real merge without the reader being entirely sure how such a union is achieved. Whitman's "Democratic Vistas" prefigures the process, for the "soaring flight" or "interior consciousness, like a hitherto unseen inscription, in magic ink, beams out its wondrous line to the senses."[79] In these imagined spaces, the simultaneity of ascent and descent, the esoteric dictum "as above, so below," resonates with a very particular creative energy, the order of time now flowing into the order of genesis. So, in Stevens's "Of Mere Being," the bird's fire-fangled feathers dangle down like a quill descending toward the page—a soul at the end of the mind ready again to take on another body. Even the rhythm of the poem begins to be born in the alliteration of this process of creation, both a memory of an entire tradition and a powerful prolepsis of what has not yet come to be.

Conclusion

In the ancient world, the various types of metempsychosis that we see in Hinduism, Buddhism, Pythagoreanism, Platonism, and Neoplatonism are part of a cosmological scheme in which the soul or the self undergoes successive incarnations or transformations. The ultimate goal of the transmigrations that the soul undertakes is either escape from the wheel of rebirth through a recovery of its larger memory, as in Buddhism or Hinduism, or *anamnesis* in Platonism, or the achievement of a transformative likeness to the divine by a conversion of consciousness, as in Neoplatonism. In Emerson, these traditions assume a distinctively modern figure, tinged with the Kantian supposition that nothing exists outside of consciousness. Emerson, as we have seen, adopts metempsychosis to bridge the growing modern gap between scientific objectivity and subjective consciousness. As a result, Emerson does not necessarily insist that the individual human being has experienced past lives; successive rebirth characterizes thinking itself or consciousness' phenomenological ground. This modern view, interestingly enough, both rejects much of the metaphysical baggage of the past and simultaneously transforms a theory of soul and its destiny into the structure of individual consciousness, even while problematizing it as an emergent, provisional method of discovery.

Emersonian metempsychosis as well as Whitman's adaptation of it into a poetic medium thereby emerges not as a comprehensive theory about everything that exists, but instead as a dilemma or enigma that each individual must face in attempting to understand his or her own historical emergence. One discovers in both Emerson and Whitman a radical awareness of incompleteness: the self-constituting ground somehow upholding psychic and perceptual consciousness is provisional and lives each of its moments to incorporate the shifting field of its perception into a type of expansive, indeterminate, and highly temporal order. The Neoplatonic triad of abiding, procession, and conversion becomes in Emerson's conception of metempsychotic perception a process of individual self-constitution. The modern emphasis upon perception comes yet again to be reborn in Emerson from the multivalent traditions of his own reading: Plato, Plotinus, Kant, Böhme, Swedenborg, Goethe, Hegel, and others. At the same time, the experience of perception—that in Plotinus and others hovers over several indeterminacies and finds itself only partially capable of constituting itself—becomes in Emerson the ground of human unsettledness itself, the scattering of a self that is unable to constitute itself fully in its own metempsychotic reading, a peculiarly existential take upon the Neoplatonic view that corporeal entities are incapable of complete self-constitution. This metempsychotic stratagem in both Emerson and Whitman ensures that in each moment of experience, an individual attempts to become a more conscious whole, yet is unable to bring himself or herself into full presence. Consequently, the ceaseless urge to reconstitute or renegotiate the self into another shape is not simply a formal order, but an ongoing and unsettled dilemma that each individual must brave.

Here, in rather unfamiliar form, we witness the play—and emerging lament—of American poetic consciousness, a method by which the "faith" of the past (in fact, of many pasts) may be used to construct a coherent ground, even while subjecting it to radical scrutiny. For Harold Bloom and Jonathan Levin, the quintessential Emersonian belief is a belief in power as transition. In Emerson's own words, "Power [. . .] resides in the moment of transition from a past to a new state, in the shooting of a gulf, in the darting to an aim" (W 2: 40). While Bloom argues that Whitman embraces this verdict more fully than any other American poet,[1] Levin sees such a formulation as the cornerstone upon which the "antifoundationalist" precepts of American pragmatism along with its "politically progressive consequences" are based.[2] As I have shown, Emerson's power of transition—the self-reflexive movement from "a past to a new state"—is emphatically a metempsychotic project, modernized and formalized into a system that makes questioning identity and language a principal part of its poetic episteme. As a structure of power, moreover, Emerson's metempsychotic self is a form of assimilation by which everything that is foreign to the subject can at last be absorbed in a heightened process of self-knowing.

In Emerson, this prospect is not simply individual; it is also a model for nationhood. Emerson heralds the future poet—who lies just beyond the series' end—as the individual most capable of questioning and revitalizing the materials of the past so as to found a new American nation: "I am ready to die out of nature, and be born again into this new yet unapproachable America I have found in the West" (*W* 3: 41). Emerson's future poet, however, must first live through numerous identities, for the question of a new and fitter American individual formulates itself in bridging the private life with the public life of a nation. In "Fate" (1860), Emerson's solution for the dilemma of double consciousness—the private and public, the individuation of the soul and its dispersal into the life of the community— recognizes the individual, corporeal self, yet advocates an individual "rallying" himself to the Deity that lives in all:

> One key, one solution to the mysteries of human condition, one solution to the old knots of fate, freedom, and foreknowledge, exists, the propounding, namely, of the double consciousness. A man must ride alternately on the horses of his private and his public nature, as the equestrians in the circus throw themselves nimbly from horse to horse, or plant one foot on the back of one, and the other foot on the back of the other. So when a man is the victim of his fate, has sciatica in his loins, and cramp in his mind; a club-foot and a club in his wit; a sour face, and a selfish temper; a strut in his gait, and a conceit in his affection; or is ground to powder by the vice of his race; he is to rally on his relation to the Universe, which his ruin benefits. Leaving the daemon who suffers, he is to take sides with the Deity who secures universal benefit by his pain. (*W* 6: 25–26)

As with so much of Emerson's writing, the unsettled, aerobatic formulation of identity—being thrown or throwing oneself "nimbly from horse to horse"—underscores a metempsychotic paradigm whereby an individual realizes himself not simply in his own singular "ruin," but also in transcending his lot by rallying his "relation to the Universe" and embracing the journey into other selves in accordance with a law that "dissolves persons" and "vivifies nature" (*W* 6: 27).

Such a metempsychotic ethos of American individuality is original, but by no means an isolated occurrence in the antebellum period. Robert Montgomery Bird's recently republished book, *Sheppard Lee, Written by Himself* (1836), initially received high praise for its use of "metempsychosis" by Edgar Allan Poe who himself wrote various tales of metempsychosis throughout his career.[3] First published anonymously, *Sheppard Lee* "is famous for asking, in a chapter with this title, 'What is an American?'"[4]—a difficult question to answer in a narrative where the speaker repeatedly transmigrates from one body to another. Indeed, the very question of identity in Bird's picaresque novel runs the gamut of America's social classes. Bird gives his audience a sly wink at the beginning of his narrative with the admission that "the importance of any single individual in society,

especially one so isolated as myself, is so little, that it can scarcely be sup-
posed that the community at large can be affected by his fortunes, either
good or evil, or interested in any way in his fate."[5] Accordingly, Bird adopts
a witty, if not uncanny, remedy: the main character will matter to his audi-
ence because he will become his audience; he will journey through their
myriad identities, at times wealthy, poor, free, enslaved—the only constant
being his continual metempsychosis through American society.

In Emerson and Whitman's writings, the individual is similarly subject
to such unsettled transmigrations, but with an aim that Bird's novel does
not possess. For both transcendentalists, the elusive figure of the poet rep-
resents the primary, half-expressed work of American nationhood. Emer-
son himself does not just simply accept the Romantic privilege of the poet;
rather, the poet's preeminence lies in his very ability to live through and
unite all the metempsychotic identities of the past in order to achieve a
new and fitter individuation and to help others, in turn, achieve their own.
For Whitman, the poet's metempsychotic acceptance of the American
spirit—of its millions of individual identities—is the chief reason that he
may speak for his nation. In *Still the New World* (1999), Philip Fisher sug-
gests the appropriateness of this metempsychotic paradigm without using
the term: "Behind Whitman's words 'I am the man, I suffer'd, I was there,'
lies the staggering fact that these resonant words are spoken not about a
proud moment of his own experience, but out of his claim to be able to be
someone else."[6] Whitman's poetry promises its readers that they will be
able to transcend their own individual limits and to experience the life of
someone else and, in accordance with this metempsychotic principle, the
more abundant promise of a youthful and teeming nation.

Whitman's radical adaptation of Emerson's metempsychotic self is most
palpable in making the poetic text the medium through which individu-
alism and the public life of a nation may not simply express themselves,
but coexist side by side or "face to face" as Whitman writes in "Song of
Myself" and "Crossing Brooklyn Ferry." Whereas many critics see this
"face to face" meeting as a secular trope, it is patently mystical, being not
only biblical but one of the sacred figurations of Hermetic and alchemi-
cal forms of thought. Where Emerson idealized his poet as the man who
could evoke "awe and terror" in his readers by drawing them through
successive transmigratory perceptions to a future point of culmination,
Whitman most ably fulfills Emerson's fantastical vision of the poet as seer
and prophet who finds an undiscovered, unpeopled land and beckons his
readers to fill it. Just as Emerson's metempsychotic dialectic is most tan-
gible as a textual pattern, so too is Whitman's dialectic between nation and
individual a poetic challenge, one enacted between eye and page. Meter,
rhyme, eloquence—none of these are required when the poetic series itself,

dead letters on a page, provides an invitation and challenge for consciousness to find in this mimetic or discarded sequence its own aspiring height and to become a "robust soul."

In Whitman's poetry, therefore, metempsychosis emerges both as a central theme and as a poetic technique in which the relationship between eye and page resonates with a whole tradition of mystical thought. As with Neoplatonism and various esoteric forms of thought influenced by it, the eye projects a spiritual power into the objects around it. This is not a one-way linear activity, for it takes place from a number of vantage points—in relation to the sun that bestows light, the eye that receives the light and issues it forth, and the object that constitutes itself in being seen. For Emerson, perception can convert dead statues into fiery men, and in Whitman's "Crossing Brooklyn Ferry," this ensouled power becomes a vast textual trope with the dumb, beautiful ministers of the page becoming alive, now planted firmly inside the new American individual who sees no longer through the eyes of the dead, but with his own eyes. In Whitman's poetry, this wish to overcome mediation is paramount. In his 1855 preface to the *Leaves of Grass*, Whitman, in fact, promises that he will remove such cumbersome impediments to his mutual understanding with his readers: "I will not have in my writing any elegance or effect or originality to hang in the way between me and the rest like curtains. I will have nothing hang in the way, not the richest curtains" (1855: 344–46). Overcoming the mediated space between poet and reader is by no means a simple or even possible feat. Yet, under Whitman's tutelage, the reader becomes aware of his or her own relation to the series he or she apprehends, thereby reanimating a discarded sequence and, accordingly, using his or her eyes to transmigrate through each of its moments. All the while, Whitman reminds his readers that he has already prepared for them; they will have to accept the process of figuring a song of self by living through the poet's discarded figurations and coming at last to stand on their own robust ground.

The reader's pursuit of the poet through all his substitutions, evasions, and disappearances thereby relies on the sharing of materials, even though Whitman provocatively announces that such an embrace occurs without a shred of himself: "What I experience or portray shall go from my composition without a shred of my composition. You shall stand by my side and look in the mirror with me" (1855: 342–54). Whitman's evocation mystifies for an express purpose, suggesting a bodily coexistence in which no bodies actually touch. Whitman takes on the role of priest and prophet, inviting his readers to receive the dead bodies of the past, abbreviated into a textual sequence, to live for a fixed duration in or with each one and, subsequently, to discard each signature, "leav[ing] them where they are," as Whitman writes in Section 48 of "Song of Myself," "for others who punctually come for ever and ever" (48.1287–88). In a thoroughly new fashion, Whitman's poetry is religious, as with the lines above of a God leaving letters behind in the street which will be perpetually adopted and discarded in time, not just by Whitman and the present reader, but by all those who come "for ever and ever," the emphasis no longer upon an eternal God beyond being, but upon the daily lives of men and women.

While Whitman joyfully adapted Emerson's metempsychotic self as a method of overcoming the physiological limits of the self through poetry, his adaptation nonetheless bears the inevitable tensions of modernity's emerging ontological awareness of finitude. Friedrich Nietzsche, who praised Emerson's philosophy of self-reliance, but subverted the metaphysical foundations that shape his individualism, is another touchstone for this emerging anxiety. In his first book, *The Birth of Tragedy* (1872), Nietzsche employs the ancient notion of the dialectical tearing apart of the one into the many as a form of metempsychotic order in his explanation of the Apollonian and Dionysian forces that lie at the root of drama. Where, in "History," Emerson presents the genius "watch[ing] the monad through all his masks as he performs the metempsychosis of nature" (*W* 2: 8), Nietzsche argues that "Greek Tragedy in its oldest form dealt only with the sufferings of Dionysus, and for a long time Dionysus was the only theatrical hero [. . .] Prometheus, Oedipus and so on—are merely masks of that original hero."[7] From this vantage point, tragedy comprises a type of metempsychotic performance in which "a divinity lurks behind all these masks," and Nietzsche lays out the changing aesthetics of "how the Homeric myths are reborn in a different form, and in this metempsychosis show that Olympian culture too has been vanquished by an even deeper vision of the world."[8]

While Nietzsche utilizes metempsychosis, he essentially rejects the spiritual evolution implicit in Emerson and Whitman's conception of the series. By contrast, Nietzsche argues that the "metempsychosis" of tragedy eventually championed the illusory, Apollonian attempt to sublimate the suffering Dionysiac individual through the arts. In opposition to the Apollonian aesthetic, Nietzsche heralds a type of epiphanic perception that cuts through all the cultural, metempsychotic layers of drama to recognize the human being in all his or her continuing finitude, which philosophy and art have tried to apotheosize, redeem and console. Nietzsche's later philosophy of eternal return, developed particularly in *The Gay Science* and *Thus Spoke Zarathustra*, implicitly critiques the aspiring, metempsychotic series with its underlying dialectical method and seeks to amend its evolutionary focus. While Emerson and Nietzsche's systems are quite obviously at odds with each other, nonetheless, they unite in heralding the necessity of metempsychotic perception as a precursor for epiphany. Whereas, for Emerson, removing the veil of the series reveals that the human being is not yet himself, that he always requires a greater arc with which to constitute himself, for Nietzsche, removing this veil is the strongest and bravest individual act precisely because it demystifies the whole metempsychotic project to reveal the suffering, finite form of the human being that lies beneath all the cultural forms that have tried to amend, mythologize, or perfect him.

In *The Anxiety of Influence* (1973), Harold Bloom explores these metempsychotic threads in direct relation to Romantic poetic consciousness. "A philosophy of composition," Bloom insists, "is a genealogy of imagination necessarily, a study of the only guilt that matters to a poet, the guilt of indebtedness."[9] In Bloom, the metempsychotic order regains its Emersonian coherence, but with a more emphatic emphasis upon struggle and guilt. In the Romantic ethos, Bloom argues, the poet's true self "lies through the precursor's subject," and the poet thereby "transform[s] himself through the purgations of his revisionary stance," revealing in the process that he "is the direct descendant of every Orphic adept who rolled in mud and meal so that he might be raised out of the fury and the mire of being merely human." "All poetic ecstasy, all sense that the poet steps out from man into god [. . .] begins as the dark doctrine of metempsychosis and its attendant fears of devouring a former version of the self."[10]

In this setting, Bloom recapitulates "the dark doctrine of metempsychosis" with a decidedly Nietzschean twist, since the order primarily unfolds through poetic influence, effectively replacing the soul's bodily transmigrations with an intertextual process that emphasizes the poet's sublimation of his poetic ancestors in monumental, culturally and individually constructed events. Accordingly, Bloom identifies Nietzsche as "the true psychologist of this guilt" of "indebtedness" precisely because he is first to psychoanalyze, as it were, the "terrible vision of 'the relationship between living men and their forebears'" and to anticipate Freud's "mechanisms of defense in sublimation."[11] Bloom, however, makes an important distinction in addressing the American Sublime, instituted most powerfully through Emerson's evocation of perception. In Emerson and Whitman, Bloom argues, ascetic practice, the latent psychological property of purging the self of its guilt, takes a different form than that of their Romantic precursors or contemporaries: "The eye, most tyrannous of the bodily senses, from which nature freed Milton, and from which Wordsworth freed nature, is in American poetry a rage and a program. Where the eye dominates, without curtailment, *askesis* tends to center on the self's awareness of other selves."[12] Whereas Bloom asserts that one inevitable consequence of

"Emersonian seeing" is a deepened solipsism, he nonetheless recognizes that another consequence conversely offers itself as a linguistic openness, which incorporates and adapts past structures in order to place a new emphasis upon the role of poetic transmission, either in the figure of the poet or reader struggling for self-constitution not only in isolation, but in communion with a greater community or tradition.

It is in the emergence of poststructuralism and its overthrowing of New Criticism's confidence in the relatively invariant structures of the text that metempsychosis reenters the critical field with what may look like a decidedly Whitmanian force, but is arguably more like the elimination of the evolutionary double consciousness in favor of a deconstructive epistemology. In 1968, Roland Barthes proclaimed the death of the author and the birth of the reader: "The birth of the reader must be at the cost of the death of the Author."[13] In subsequent works, however, notably *The Pleasure of the Text* and *Sade, Fourier, Loyola*, the force of this manifesto was somewhat more nuanced. The author is dead "as institution," Barthes writes; "his person [. . .] has disappeared [. . .] but in the text, in a certain way, I desire the author: I need his figure."[14] This desire of the author (lower case) *in* the text, as opposed to the death of the Author (upper case) *behind* the text, suggests a form of metempsychotic slippage from the older, more traditional privileged subject to a different nonsubject assimilation. This author turns out to have, in Barthes's words, "no unity: he is a simple plural of 'charms,' the site of a few tenuous details" that give pleasure when "the literary text [. . .] transmigrates into our life, when another manages to write fragments in our own dailiness, in short, when there occurs co-existence."[15] So instead of the metempsychosis of a person/soul/subject, here in Barthes we find the transmigration or *metemsomatosis* only of the author and the scattered, fragmented text in what Barthes calls "the twisted dialectic . . . destroyer of every subject."[16]

The birth of poststructuralism, at least in this form, appears to involve the author's return from decomposition as another's writing not "behind" a unitary text, but as somatic dispersion—"biographemes" or written fragments—in a fantasy of transmigratory coexistence. While it is true that the metempsychotic self of Emerson and Whitman, as well as the whole metaphysical tradition with which it spoke and wrestled, has lost part of its spiritual preeminence, nonetheless poststructuralism is itself constrained to inhabit a heritage whose subjectivity it can only admit under quasi-personified transmigratory forms. Even the new architecture cannot escape the memory of the old forms: the reader's approach to the text is still an approach to the series, to an archive, which holds within it the history of subjects and selves whose death and afterlife are played out in the current customs of reception. We may find, therefore, that the very thought of the modern self gives way, under a particular interpretative pressure, to a mystical subtext that underwrites the ways in which we understand our everyday experience. It is a question not of demystifying ourselves, but of understanding that this very possibility hinges upon an older metaphysical cosmology irreconcilably woven into modern consciousness.

Notes

Introduction

1. Metempsychosis, transmigration of the soul, or the passage of soul from one body to another (broadly speaking, [a] either from human to human body; [b] from human to other animal or plant body or, again, [c] through a serial succession of different kinds of bodies metamorphically as in the case of Proteus in Homer's *Odyssey* Book 4, or [d] through a vertical succession of different qualitative bodies, e.g., physical, pneumatic, lunar, solar, astral, etc. in descent into the cosmos or in ascent up through the cosmos and beyond (as in Porphyry, *Sentences* 29) is the belief that the soul (or principle of animation of a body) undergoes a series of rebirths, perhaps, but not always, with the aim of escaping the wheel of rebirth and subjection to the cycle of opposites and/or as a result of some primal mistake, fall, or decision. This complex view is found in the Eastern traditions of Hinduism, Jainism, and Buddhism, particularly in the *Bhagavad Gītā, The Vedas, The Upanishads*, and the *Dhammapada*, and also in the Western world, starting, as far back, according to what later testimonies report, as Pherecydes, Pythagoras (c. 582–507 BCE), and the devotees of Orpheus (known as Orphics), then later in Empedocles (490–430 BCE), Plato (427–347 BCE), Plotinus (204–270 CE), Porphyry, Iamblichus, Proclus, etc. From these later thinkers (e.g., Plotinus to Proclus), collectively known as Neoplatonic thinkers, who were in fact the inheritors and developers of the entire ancient thought-heritage, this view was transmitted, first, into Jewish, Arabic, and Christian thought (transmigration of the soul is to be found, for instance, in Origen of Alexandria and in his later Christian followers) and later into the broader complex heritage of Hermetic, Neopythagorean, and Neoplatonic thinkers who helped in some measure to develop the modern world (among them: Ficino, Giordano Bruno, Pico della Mirandella in the Italian Renaissance; Copernicus, Kepler, and Newton in the development of physical science; Goethe, Hegel, and Schelling in German Idealism; Wordsworth, Coleridge, and Shelley in English Romanticism) and to transmit this mosaic to the New World (on this see Carl Huffman, "Pythagoreanism," *The Stanford Encyclopedia of Philosophy*, March 29,

2006, last modified June 14, 2010, http://plato.stanford.edu/archives/sum2010/entries/
pythagoreanism/; and, more generally, Alexandre Koyre, *From the Closed World to
the Infinite Universe* [Baltimore, MD: Johns Hopkins University Press, 1968]; Paolo
Rossi, *The Birth of Modern Science*, Trans. Cynthia De Nardi Ipsen [Malden, England:
Blackwell Publishers Ltd., 2001]). The term metempsychosis occurs in Alexander of
Aphrodisias (*De An.* 17, 18), Porphyry (*De Abst.* 4.16), Proclus (in *Rempublicam* 2.340),
and is related to the cognate terms *metemsomatosis/metemsomatesthai*, "transmigra-
tion" and "to be put into another body," which can be found in Plotinus, *Enneads* I,
1, 12; II, 9, 6; IV, 3, 9. The English terms "reincarnation" and "transmigration" come
from the Latin. The Greek or Latinized Greek word "metamorphosis," the changing of
forms or biological development from one form to another, is not synonymous with
metempsychosis, though Ovid's placing of Pythagoras's speech prominently at the
conclusion of his *Metamorphoses*, Bk. XV, explicitly presents Pythagoras's philosophy
of metempsychosis as a perennial philosophy of cyclical return in the midst of Hera-
clitean flux and, therefore, again implicitly as a prototype of metamorphosis itself. On
reincarnation generally, see the *Encyclopedia of Religion*, Macmillan, vol. 11 or 12, and
the *Routledge Encyclopedia of Philosophy*, vol. 8, under "reincarnation." Generally, on
Pythagoras, see Iamblichus, *Life of Pythagoras*, trans. Thomas Taylor (Rochester, VT:
Inner Traditions International, Ltd., 1986); and Christoph Riedweg, *Pythagoras: His
Life, Teaching, and Influence*, trans. Steven Rendall (Ithaca, NY: Cornell University
Press, 2005); on Plato, Aristotle, and Neoplatonism, R.T. Wallis, *Neoplatonism*, 2d ed.
(London: Duckworth, 1995); Kevin Corrigan, *Reading Plotinus: A Practical Guide to
Neoplatonism* (West Lafayette, IN: Purdue University Press, 2004) (see conclusion,
chapter 5.2 for the story of the "afterlife" from Plotinus to the contemporary period).
For the Orphics and Pherecydes, see G. S. Kirk and J. E. Raven, *The Pre-Socratic Phi-
losophers* (Cambridge: Cambridge University Press, 1966), 37–72; for testimonies on
Pythagoras (and the Egyptians), ibid., 222–24; and for Empedocles, Diels-Kranz, frag-
ments B 112, 115, 117, 118, 121, 127, 127, 146, 147.

2. Mark Vernon, "Reincarnation in Jewish Mysticism and Gnosticism," *Shofar: An
Interdisciplinary Journal of Jewish Studies* 24.1 (2005): 174. For another example of
how Jacob's dream was being interpreted according to Philo's Jewish Mysticism as
well as Platonic sources, see John Smith, *Select Discourses* (London: Rivingtons and
Cochran, 1821). John Smith (1618–52), the prominent Cambridge Platonist, examines
Jacob's dream as a specific form of inspired prophesy, outlined by Philo who "sailing
between Cabbalism and Platonism, gropes after an allegorical and mystical meaning."
Jacob's ladder exemplifies, Smith argues, the *"anima mundi*, or 'universal soul,' as it is
described by the Pythagoreans and Platonists," and understood by Philo who outlined
this form of prophesy: "'When our rational faculty, being moved together with the
soul of the world, and filled with a divinely-inspired fury, doth predict those things
that are to come'" (200).

3. For the "golden chain," see Homer's *Iliad* Book 8, Verses 10–27, where an angry
Zeus threatens to cast down the other gods to Hades so that even a golden chain hang-
ing down from the heavens would never drag him down nearer to them "from sky to
earth." In Plato's *Theaetetus* 153c-d, Socrates argues that this golden chain is nothing
other than the sun whose revolution guarantees the existence and survival of gods
and human beings. For this chain of being that both separates and yet connects the
entire series of emanations from the One to matter or the golden chain of pedagogi-
cal transmission in later thought, especially in the later Neoplatonists (from Plotinus

through Iamblichus to Proclus), see Macrobius, *Commentary on* [Cicero's] *the Dream of Scipio* I 14. 15; Marinus, *Life of Proclus* 19.26; Proclus, *Commentary on Plato's Parmenides*, 791, 28–795, 8 (a classic text for the series of different senses of nature) and for an overall view see especially the introduction to Algis Uzdavinys, *The Golden Chain: An Anthology of Pythagorean and Platonic Philosophy*, foreword by John F. Finamore (Bloomington, IN: World Wisdom, Inc., 2004), xi–xxviii. See also Emery Edward George, *Holderlin and the Golden Chain of Homer: Including an Unknown Source* (Lewiston, NY: Edwin Mellen Press Ltd., 1992). For Goethe, see Paul Bishop, *Analytical Psychology and German Classical Aesthetics: Goethe, Schiller and Jung* (New York: Routledge, 2009).

4. See Arthur Versluis, *The Esoteric Origins of the American Renaissance* (Oxford: Oxford University Press, 2001), 124–46. In his chapter on Emerson, Versluis makes the claim that Emerson widely disseminated mystical and esoteric thought accordingly to a distinctively American manner. Also see Mitch Horowitz, *Occult America: White House Séances, Ouija Circles, Masons, and the Secret Mystic History of Our Nation* (New York: Bantam Books Trade Paperbacks, 2009), 48–49. Horowitz argues that the success of the theosophist movement of Madame Blavatsky in the latter part of the nineteenth century could never have been achieved without the earlier foundations of American transcendentalism: "The ideas and interests of Ralph Waldo Emerson, Henry David Thoreau, Bronson Alcott, and the venerable Yankee Mystics played a decided role in introducing magical philosophies into American thought."

5. James Freeman Clarke, *Ten Great Religions Part II: A Comparison of All Religions* (Boston: Houghton, Mifflin and Company, 1895), ix. See also Chapter 1, note 7 for additional context on the origins of the term monad and its use in American transcendentalism.

6. Ralph Waldo Emerson, *The Collected Works of Ralph Waldo Emerson*, 6 volumes, ed. Robert E. Spiller, Alfred R. Ferguson, Joseph Slater, Douglas Emory Wilson, Jean Ferguson Carr, Wallace E. Williams, Philip Nicoloff, Robert E. Burkholder, and Barbara L. Packer (Cambridge, MA: Harvard University Press, 1971–2003)—hereafter, *W* 2: 14; *W* for Collected Works, 2 for volume number followed by page number.

7. For self-transformation in relation to William Blake, see Laura Quinney, *William Blake on Self and Soul* (Cambridge, MA: Harvard University Press, 2009), 23. Quinney argues that the "call for change is more radical than Rousseaustic, Christian, or even Gnostic psychologies propose, for self-purification in itself is inadequate. It is not a question of returning to, or recalling, a lost self. You must altogether remake yourself or, more pointedly, remake your self."

8. Harold Bloom, *Where Shall Wisdom Be Found?* (New York: Riverhead Books, 2004), 194.

9. Jonathan Levin, *The Poetics of Transition: Emerson, Pragmatism and American Literary Modernism* (Durham, NC: Duke University Press, 1999), ix.

10. Perry Miller, ed., *The Transcendentalists: An Anthology* (Cambridge, MA: Harvard University Press, 2001), 25.

11. Ibid., 55.

12. Ibid., 54.

13. Aristotle, *De Anima* III, 4 429a.

14. See Barbara Packer, *The Transcendentalists* (Athens: University of Georgia Press, 2007), 27 for Reed; and 20–31 for greater context.

15. P. Miller, *Transcendentalists*, 54.

16. Amos Bronson Alcott, *Table-Talk* (Boston: Roberts Brothers, 1877), 176, 177.

17. Ralph Waldo Emerson, *The Later Lectures of Ralph Waldo Emerson*, 2 volumes, ed. Ronald A. Bosco and Joel Myerson (Athens: University of Georgia Press, 2001)—hereafter, *LL* 2: 97; *LL* for *Later Lectures*, 2 for volume number followed by page number.

18. Frances A. Yates, *The Rosicrucian Enlightenment* (London and New York: Routledge Classics, 2002), 157.

19. See Algis Uzdavinys, *Philosophy and Theurgy in Late Antiquity* (San Rafael, CA: Sophia Perennis, 2010); and Gregory Shaw, *Theurgy and the Soul: The Neoplatonism of Iamblichus* (University Park: Pennsylvania State University Press, 1995).

20. Jacob Böhme's *The Signature of All Things* in *Essential Writings of Christian Mysticism: Medieval Mystic Paths to God* (St. Petersburg, FL: Red and Black Publishers, 2010), 43–45.

21. Walt Whitman, *Leaves of Grass and Other Writings*, ed. Michael Moon (New York: W. W. Norton, 2002), line numbers 1–2.

22. Whitman, *Leaves of Grass and other Writings*, Section 33, line 831—hereafter, 33.831.

1 / The Metempsychotic Mind

1. David L. Smith summarizes this critical turn, arguing that the "new critics point us toward an Emerson whose religious center of gravity lies in neither faith nor skepticism, theism nor naturalism, but in the space opened up by their interplay." See David L. Smith, "The Open Secret of Ralph Waldo Emerson," *The Journal of Religion* 70.1 (1990): 23. More recently, Louis Menand emphasizes the curious fact that Emerson's contemporaries found his thought consoling and reassuring, even though Emerson "plays continually with the limits of thought, and his greatest essays are efforts to get at the way life is held up, in the end, by nothing. Except in the mingled intensity and detachment of their unfolding, those essays are deeply unconsoling." See Louis Menand, *The Metaphysical Club: The Story of Ideas in America* (New York: Farrar, Straus and Giroux, 2001), 18. Similarly, Lawrence Buell contends that Emerson can be seen more as "a performance artist who favored a highly imaginative, improvisational style of expression" and "kept returning lifelong to his core idea; yet he was forever reopening and reformulating it, looping away and back again, convinced that the spirit of the idea dictated that no final statement was possible" (Lawrence Buell, *Emerson* [Cambridge, MA: The Belknap Press of Harvard University Press, 2003], 2).

2. See Lawrence Buell, "The Emerson Industry in the 1980's: A Survey of Trends and Achievements," *ESQ* 30.2 (1984): 117–36. Buell argues that throughout the 1940s, 1950s, and 1960s much scholarship dealt with Emerson's thought and poetry in an uncharitable and dismissive manner. It was not until the 1970s that scholars began to make a case for the "sophistication" of Emerson's "aesthetic and prose style" (131), and with the rise of "deconstructionist analysis" that charted "the elements of indeterminacy and discontinuousness in Emersonian rhetoric" (133) in the late 1970s and early 1980s, scholarship began to consider Emerson seriously as a thinker, leading to watershed years in Emersonian criticism. Since Buell's article, many critics have taken up the effort to consider Emerson in a postmodern manner, one of the most notable being Michael Lopez who argues for a post-Idealist, posttranscendental Emerson who adopts, to a certain extent, Hegel's dialectical system, but rejects his final

synthesis, presenting instead a system always on the brink of disclosing unity. See Michael Lopez, "De-Transcendentalizing Emerson," *ESQ* 34.1–2 (1988): 77–139; and Michael Lopez, *Emerson and Power: Creative Antagonism in the Nineteenth Century* (DeKalb: Northern Illinois University Press, 1996), 187–89. In addition, see Eric Wilson, *Emerson's Sublime Science* (New York: St. Martin's Press, 1999), 14.

3. In scholarship, Emerson's view of metempsychosis is almost completely absent. Some earlier criticism dismissively notes metempsychosis in the larger context of Emerson's evolutionary program. In *Spires of Form*, for instance, Vivian Hopkins argues that, while Emerson touches upon the doctrine of metempsychosis, he does so in an ironic fashion and prefers to focus upon the more serious conception of evolution: [. . .] he entertained the Pythagorean concept of metempsychosis with something more than irony, frequently noting a wolf's fangs or a fox's teeth beneath the human countenance of certain individuals. The fact remains that his concept of evolution is simply a gradual refinement of natural forms, following a spiral upward movement" (Vivian C. Hopkins, *Spires of Form: A Study of Emerson's Aesthetic Theory* [Cambridge, MA: Harvard University Press, 1951], 123). Most recently, Len Gougeon underlines some of the dynamics of Emersonian metempsychosis—without using the term itself—by noting the "myth of eternal return" and "the cycle of rebirth." See Len Gougeon, *Emerson & Eros: The Making of a Cultural Hero* (Albany: State University of New York Press, 2007), 63.

4. Arthur Versluis, *American Transcendentalism and Asian Religions* (Oxford: Oxford University Press, 1993), 60–61.

5. Ralph Waldo Emerson, *The Early Lectures of Ralph Waldo Emerson*, 3 volumes, ed. Stephen E. Whicher, Robert E. Spiller, and Wallace E. Williams (Cambridge, MA: Harvard University Press, 1959–72)—hereafter, *EL* 1: 136; EL for *Early Lectures*, 1 for volume number followed by page number.

6. Stanley Cavell, *Emerson's Transcendental Etudes*, ed. David Justin Hodge (Stanford: Stanford University Press, 2003), 193.

7. The term monad—probably derived from Neopythagorean number theory (see Kenneth Guthrie and David R. Fideler, *The Pythagorean Sourcebook and Library* [Grand Rapids, MI: Phanes Press, 1987], 20–24), although it is used by both Plato and Aristotle—signifies in later Neoplatonism (e.g., Proclus) all the members of a particular series preunified in one single reality. See, for example, Proclus, *Elements of Theology*, proposition 21. Here, Emerson brings together the monad and the drama enacted in its unfolding multiplicity.

8. See James R. Guthrie, *Above Time: Emerson's and Thoreau's Temporal Revolutions* (Columbia: University of Missouri Press, 2001), 10.

9. Lawrence Buell argues that Emerson's modernity lies in his view that truth, along with our contemplation of it, is not separable from action: "What especially gives Emerson his modern look, whether Jamesean or Nietzchean, is his conviction that the way truth matters for individuals is through acts of thinking, of expression, of living. That became the key reason why he found it impossible to maintain the critical distance between contemplation and action that he sought initially to posit in his theories of Self-Reliance and of intellectual work generally" (Buell, *Emerson*, 237–38). In "The American Scholar," Emerson states that, without action, "thought could never ripen into truth" (*W* 1: 59). Only through spontaneous activity can thought become productive, correlating to Emerson's formulation of *Man Thinking* who in "the right state [. . .] is the delegated intellect—as opposed to the degenerate thinker who merely

parrots "other men's ideas" (W 1: 53). See also Kenneth Sacks, *Understanding Emerson: "The America Scholar" and his Struggle for Self-Reliance* (Princeton, NJ: Princeton University Press, 2003). Sacks notes that Emerson never attempted philosophy in any traditional sense: "He was not, literally speaking, a lover of wisdom"; rather, he was "a lover of the spontaneous insight his own experience could provide" (125). Harold Bloom also emphasizes a similar point, which he calls an "obvious truth [that] always needs restating": "Emerson is an experiential critic and essayist, not a Transcendental philosopher" (Harold Bloom, ed., *Bloom's Modern Critical Views: Ralph Waldo Emerson*, updated ed. [New York: Chelsea House Publishers, 2007], 1). For David Jacobson, "authentic individual activity" comprises the heart of Emerson's early humanism (David Jacobson, *Emerson's Pragmatic Vision: The Dance of the Eye* [University Park: Pennsylvania State University Press, 1993], 64).

10. Emerson's progression from perception to creation is particularly Romantic. The "Romantic discovered excitement in the *making of meaning*. Romantic transcendence cannot be explained wholly in terms of the particular point of departure and arrival it employed. The sublime dramatized the rhythm of transcendence in its extreme and purest form, for the sublime began where the conventional systems, reading of landscape or text, broke down, and it found that in the very collapse the foundation for another order of meaning" (Thomas Weiskel, *The Romantic Sublime: Studies in the Structure and Psychology of Transcendence* [Baltimore, MD: Johns Hopkins University Press, 1976], 22). While Weiskel argues that the three phases, from reading to crisis to creation, culminate when "the mind recovers the balance of outer and inner by constituting a fresh relation between itself and the object" (24), in Emerson's "History," the pattern is the same, but less tenuous, for the individual's perception must be heightened before he can produce meaning by virtue of cultivating a new relation between the mind and its object. Weiskel's description of the process, however, is instructive, since it illuminates transcendence as a method of refashioning material relations.

11. Ralph Waldo Emerson, *The Journals and Miscellaneous Notebooks of Ralph Waldo Emerson*, 16 volumes, ed. William H. Gilman and Ralph H. Orth et al. (Cambridge, MA: Harvard University Press, 1960–82)–hereafter, *JMN* 2: 400; *JMN* for Journals and Miscellaneous Notebooks, 2 for volume number followed by page number.

12. By "transcendence" here I mean the view in Platonism generally that the Good or First Principle is wholly "beyond" everything (e.g., "beyond intellect" or "being," *Republic* 6) or in Christianity and Judaism that God is wholly other than creation. Hinduism provides a similar, yet contrasting model, since the First Principle is beyond creation and is creation simultaneously.

13. The major figures of this tradition that Emerson cites or refers to are Socrates, Plato, Plotinus, Porphyry, Iamblichus, and Proclus. Early to mid-twentieth-century criticism tended to explore Emerson's acceptance of many Neoplatonic teachings, particularly through the well-known Cambridge Platonist, Ralph Cudworth (1617–88). See John S. Harrison, *The Teachers of Emerson* (New York: Sturgis and Walton Company, 1910); Vivian C. Hopkins, "Emerson and Cudworth: Plastic Nature and Transcendental Art," *American Literature* 23.1 (1951): 80–98. For a later account, see Stanley Brodwin, "Emerson's Version of Plotinus: The Flight to Beauty," *Journal of the History of Ideas* 35.3 (1974): 465–83. For a concise summary of Emerson's immersion in Neoplatonism and Neopythagoreanism, see especially Robert Richardson, *The Mind on Fire* (Berkeley: University of California Press, 1995), 345–48.

14. Compare generally Plotinus, *Enneads* IV, 7 (on the immortality of the soul); see Plotinus, *The Enneads*, 7 volumes, trans. A. H. Armstrong (Cambridge: Loeb Classical Library, 1966–88).

15. Compare Heraclitus, *Diels-Kranz*, fragments B1–2. See H. Diels and W. Kranz, *Die Fragmente Der Vorsokratiker*, 6th edition, 3 volumes (Dublin and Zurich: Weidmann, 1951–52).

16. For Plato and the later Neoplatonists, there are essentially two kinds of memory: (1) historical memory (*mneme*) as a function of everyday existence; and (2) a transcendental memory, recollection/reminiscence or *anamnesis* as a power either to recall eternal truths (as in Plato's *Meno*) or past lives (as in Plato's *Phaedrus*). In Plotinus, these two memories can become separated after death (e.g., the soul does not need a lower memory when it lives in the intelligible world; see Enneads IV 3–IV, 4), but nonetheless transcendental memory or *anamnesis* is an integral function of the soul's historical existence (see Ennead V, 8, 2). These two functions of memory work together in Emerson in different ways, but are implicitly traditional in the sense I have just outlined, for Emerson asserts famously that "life has no memory"—the soul possesses no material residue of the lives that it has lived; rather, it exists in-itself; it knows only itself—yet in its embodiment, the soul may realize the transcendental capacity to realize the series anew and, therefore, to become a full embodiment of history itself.

17. Russell B. Goodman, "East-West Philosophy in Nineteenth-Century America: Emerson and Hinduism," *Journal of the History of Ideas* 51.4 (1990): 626–27.

18. Versluis, *American Transcendentalism and Asian Religions*, 60.

19. See William Bysshe Stein, *Two Brahman Sources of Emerson and Thoreau* (Gainesville, FL: Scholars' Facsimiles and Reprints, 1967). In one of the main Brahman sources of Emerson, *A View of the History, Literature, and Mythology of the Hindoos* (1822), William Ward summarizes the tradition of how Greek philosophy and Indian religion are intertwined and how the modern work of science has been to restore this involved, interconnected tradition: "The system adopted by Pythagoras, in certain particulars, approaches nearest to that of the brahmins, as appears from his doctrine of metempsychosis, of the active and passive principles in nature, of God as the soul of the world, from his rules of self-denial and of subduing the passions [. . .]. In all these respects, the Hindoo and Pythagorian systems are so much the same, that a candid investigator can scarcely avoid subscribing to the opinion 'that India was visited, for the purpose of acquiring knowledge, by Pythagoras, Anaxarchus, Pyrrho, and others, who afterward became eminent philosophers in Greece. That which is said of Pythagoras, that he was possessed of the true idea of the solar system, revived by Copernicus, and fully established by Newton, is affirmed of the Hindoo philosophers, nor does it seem altogether without foundation" (118).

20. Charles Grant, *A Poem on the Restoration of Learning in the East* (Salem, MA: Cushing & Appleton, 1807), 19, 21.

21. Ibid., 20.

22. Ibid.

23. Goodman, "East-West Philosophy," 627.

24. Victor Cousin, *Lectures on the True, the Beautiful and the Good*, trans. Orlando Williams (New York: D. Appleton & Company, 1870), 36.

25. Ibid., 33.

26. Victor Cousin, *Course of the History of Modern Philosophy*, trans. O. W. Wight (New York: D. Appleton & Company, 1872), 368–72.

27. Goodman, "Emerson and Hinduism," 627–28.

28. *Bhagavad Gītā,* trans. with an introduction by Juan Mascaro (New York: Penguin Books, 1962), Section 2, Line 58.

29. Ibid, 2.61.

30. Ibid., 4.5.

31. *Upanishads,* trans. with an intro. by Patrick Olivelle (Oxford: Oxford University Press, 1996), 1.4.8.

32. Ibid., 1.4.9.

33. While phenomenology is certainly modern, Hindu thought repeatedly emphasizes that the soul is a type of greater perception. From "Southey's notes to *The Curse of Kehama,* [Emerson] first encountered a portion of Jones's translation of *The Laws of Manu,* which anticipates Emerson's own self-oriented metaphysics: 'The soul itself is its own witness; the soul itself is its own refuge; offend not thy conscious soul, the supreme witness of men!'" (Goodman, "East-West Philosophy," 627).

34. Versluis, *American Transcendentalism and Asian Religions,* 58.

35. Friedrich Wilhelm Joseph Von Schelling, *Ages of the World,* trans. Jason M. Wirth (Albany: State University of New York Press, 2000), 4.

36. Here we can usefully distinguish serial metempsychosis (as in the individual soul inhabiting different bodies) and vertical metempsychosis (in which the soul inhabits a series of different body-stages—e.g., lunar, solar, astral bodies—in its ascent to or descent from the intelligible world). Emerson's metempsychosis is neither serial nor vertical in these senses, yet it combines both by being simultaneously dynamic, developmental, and historical, as we shall see.

37. For an analysis of *metamorphosis* in relation to Emerson's poetics, see Leonard Neufeldt, *The House of Emerson* (Lincoln: University of Nebraska Press, 1982). Neufeldt examines what he terms "the Emersonian mode" (48), "a process of metamorphosis in tropes, context, and reference. Such a process, in which metaphor is principal and agent, arrives at not a philosophic explanation but an artistic solution. Thus, the philosophic problem [of observing or understanding the past] is transmuted into artistic process and the literary enactments into a truth-making" (49–50). For Emerson's conception of *metamorphosis* in relation to Goethe, see Wilson, *Emerson's Sublime Science,* 70–75.

38. The wording is slightly different, however. In 1841, since Emerson largely emphasizes the "metempsychosis of nature" as an act of mind, he uses the word "mind" to indicate the Intellect and its activity, whereas, in his 1837 journal entry, he postulates this conception as an act of individual soul: "Every soul has to learn the whole lesson for itself. It <has> must go over the whole ground. What it does not see[,] what it does not live it will not know. What the former age has epitomized into a formula or rule for manipular convenience, it will lose all the good of verifying for itself by means of the wall of that Rule. Sometime or other, somewhere or other, it will demand & find compensation for that loss by doing the work itself" (*JMN* 5: 384). Although Emerson often uses soul or mind interchangeably, the word change stresses the work of mind, a process of conscious deliberation.

39. From its origins, Emersonian scholarship has generally accepted the fact that Emerson's work develops a pre-Darwinian concept of evolution. Moncure Daniel Conway, Emerson's friend and admirer, was one of the first to initiate the explicit relation between the theory of evolution and Emerson's thought, proclaiming Emerson to be Darwinism's precursor in his two autobiographical works, *Emerson at Home and*

Abroad and *Autobiography, Memories and Experience.* In "Emerson and Evolution," *University of Toronto Quarterly* 3 (1934): 474–97, Joseph Warren Beach continues this claim, laying many of the modern scholarly foundations for the contention that Emerson's thought was expressly evolutionary. See Laura Dassow Walls, *Emerson's Life in Science: The Culture of Truth* (Ithaca, NY: Cornell University Press, 2003), 166–75, for one of the most recent and definitive accounts of Emerson's development of a theory of evolution. See Guthrie, *Above Time*, for a notable exception to this critical tendency. Guthrie argues that Conway was responsible for initiating a historical fallacy (31–33), since Emerson like his two friends, Lyell and Agassiz, "resisted Lamarck's contention that over time, one species could metamorphose into another" (187). For Guthrie, Emerson accepted Goethe's botanical metamorphosis and comprehended materialistic change as a process "that was more spiritual than mechanical" (187). Emerson was thereby more predisposed, insists Guthrie, "to accept Hegel's developmentalism because the ascending, expanding model of consciousness it postulated complemented his own progressive, upward-spiraling idealism" (30). As Richardson argues, however, there is no evidence that Emerson accepted Agassiz's position at all, even though they were friends (*Emerson: Mind on Fire*, 546). In fact, Emerson was much more predisposed to Lamarck and Robert Chambers's pre-Darwinian conceptions so that when Emerson finally read Darwin's *On the Origin of Species*, he saw it as "perfectly unsurprising" (Walls, *Emerson's Life in Science*, 66).

40. Thus, the eye of the intelligent, scientific observer performs an *anamnesis* or recollection-memory discernment of geological history as a way of representing the "memory of God." *Anamnesis* becomes a form not of spiritual philosophy, but of scientific observation. For some additional context on the problem of memory in Emerson's later life, see Richardson, *Emerson: Mind on Fire*, 543–46.

41. See Leon Chai, *The Romantic Foundations of the American Renaissance* (Ithaca, NY: Cornell University Press, 1987). Chai demonstrates how Emerson was also influenced by the revitalization of classification as a method in the rise of the biological and geological sciences (141–45). For instance, Louis Agassiz, a friend of Emerson, developed Georges Cuvier's system of classification, arguing that previous systems merely amassed and systemized facts, while Cuvier realized that a principle of interrelation was needed to understand the conditions of existence. Thus, since "nothing can exist if it does not unite the conditions which render its existence possible, the different parts of each being should be coordinated in such a manner as to render possible the complete being, not only in itself, but in its relations with those who surround it" (143). As Chai goes on to argue, this view of classification "suggests a certain view of the world and of physical nature. It suggests that the essence of such a world is to be grasped by defining the relations between its parts" (145). See also Lee Rust Brown, *The Emerson Museum: Practical Romanticism and the Pursuit of the Whole* (Cambridge, MA: Harvard University Press, 1997), for a richly detailed work on the influence of scientific methods of classification on Emerson's thought.

42. Richardson, *Emerson: Mind on Fire*, 171. For one of the most definitive accounts of Emerson's early quest to combine science and metaphysics, see also Walls, *Emerson's Life in Science*, 68–166.

43. "This was what Goethe sought in his Metamorphosis of plants. The Pythagorean doctrine of transmigration is an Idea; the Swedenborgian of Affections Clothed, is one also. Let the Mind of the <observer> student be in a natural, healthful, & progressive state[;] let him in the midst of his most minute dissection, not lose sight of

the place & relations of the subject. Shun giving it a disproportionate importance but speedily adjust himself & study to see the thing through with added acquaintance of its <proximate> intimate structure under the sun & in the landscape as he did before. Let it be a point as before. Integrate the particulars" (*JMN* 4: 288).

44. Similar to Emerson's understanding of the soul's successive incarnations in matter, Swedenborg's "order from the Lord is successive from first things to last, and in the order itself there is nothing but what is Divine" (Sig Synnestvedt, ed., *The Essential Swedenborg: Basic Religious Teachings of Emanuel Swedenborg* [New York: Swedenborg Foundation Inc., 1981], 47). This conception of the soul's journey into matter entails a process of adaptation, although matter itself has no adaptive features except in relation to the shaping influence of the divine: "The order is for the celestial to inflow into the spiritual and adapt it to itself; for the spiritual . . . to inflow into the rational and adapt it to itself; and for the rational . . . to inflow into the memory-knowledge [of men] and adapt it to itself" (47).

45. Raimonda Modiano, *Coleridge and the Concept of Nature* (London: The MacMillan Press Ltd., 1985), 101.

46. Goethe's influence certainly helped to temper Emerson's initial disregard of matter, an earlier intellectual position that has been termed by some scholars the "Platonic strain in Emerson's idealism" (Gustaaf Van Cromphout, *Emerson's Modernity and the Example of Goethe* [Columbia: University of Missouri Press, 1990], 42). While this critique reflects only one narrow view of the Platonic tradition, much of Emerson's earliest writing presents the general Platonic view that matter is a degradation of ideal Form or that the material world is a reality that human beings need to overcome, whereas "Goethe's critique showed Emerson that it was possible to validate nature without denying spirit" (43). Goethe's insistence "that the idea achieves its fullness only *through phenomenal realization*" (44) offered Emerson a current model, one similarly upheld by Hegel and Cousin, facilitating Emerson's movement beyond his early belief in "the absolute self-sufficiency of the mind" (*EL* 2: 146). This steady transition is particularly evident in his journals during 1833 and 1834. Whereas much of his emphasis in 1833 rests upon the dark certainty of matter—when quoting Carlyle, Emerson bemoans "striking the electric chain wherewith we are darkly bound" and laments how "hard [it is] to command or [. . .] solicit the soul" (*JMN* 4: 28)—the following year, Emerson quotes Goethe's definition of genius as a "power which by working & doing gives laws & rules" so as to underscore the necessity of matter to the activity of understanding and communication: "If any eye rest on this page let him know that he who blotted it, could not go into conversation with any person of good understanding without being presently gravelled" (*JMN* 4: 354).

47. Also see Guthrie, *Above Time*, 29–30, 180; and Buell, *Emerson*, 201.

48. Lopez, "De-Transcendentalizing Emerson," 118. At the same time, Lopez sees Emerson as a transitional figure, away from German Idealism and Romanticism to modern and even postmodern concerns: "What defines Emerson's thought is not its success as an organic, omnisynthetic philosophy or cosmic vision [. . .] but its significance as a post-Hegelian, post-idealist or post-Transcendental philosophy of will" (118).

49. G. W. F. Hegel, *The Philosophy of History*, trans. J. Sibree (Mineola, NY: Dover Publications, Inc., 2004), 73.

50. Ibid., 78.

51. Hegel, *Phenomenology of Spirit*, trans. A. V. Miller with analysis by J. N. Findlay (Oxford: Oxford University Press, 1977), 17.

52. Here we see the driving force of Hegel's dialectical enterprise: out of thesis emerges antithesis which leads to the destruction of both in their present form, and the simultaneous "sublation" or *"Aufhebung"* of their content into a new form or thesis, out of which a new dialectic progresses. See Howard P. Kainz, *Hegel's Phenomenology, Part I: Analysis and Commentary* (Tuscaloosa: University of Alabama Press, 1976).

53. Hegel, *Phenomenology of Spirit*, 55.

54. Ibid., 56.

55. The notion that identity is fluid and that both bodily and psychic identity are in a constant flux or ebb is not only a modern notion, developed in Emerson as a proto or para-Darwinian theory, but an ancient one both in Heraclitus (See Diels-Kranz, fragment B91) and prominently in Plato (*Symposium* 207eff.; *Gorgias* 493aff.). See also Ovid, *Metamorphoses*, trans. A. D. Melville with intro. and notes by E. J. Kennedy (Oxford: Oxford University Press, 1998). In the last book of the *Metamorphoses*, Ovid provides an influential, if not definitive example of flux in direct relation to metempsychosis or the doctrines of Pythagoras: "Now since the sea's great surges sweep me on,/ All canvas spread, hear me! In all creation/ Nothing endures, all is in endless flux" (XV. 179–81). "Each wandering shape" within this ceaseless flux, according to Ovid, searches to revitalize itself, for "time flies on and follows, flies and follows,/ Always, for ever new. What was before/ Is left behind; what never was is now;/ And every passing moment is renewed" (182–91).

56. In Kantian terms, they are a priori forms of embodied spiritual existence. But Emerson's view is not Kantian as such, but more Neoplatonic in so far as the causal conditions of our existence lie in the being of all things (are indwelling), revealing a causal, hierarchical order—all the steps of a series, such as being, life, and intelligence, to which we must turn in order to realize their expression. For this notion of preexistence, see Proclus, *Elements of Theology* 118; and more generally, 103. See Proclus, *The Elements of Theology*, 2d ed., ed. and trans. E. R. Dodds (Oxford: Clarendon Press, 1963). For more on Proclus and science, see Lucas Siorvanes, *Proclus: Neo-Platonic Philosophy and Science* (New Haven, CT: Yale University Press, 1996). In terms of Emerson scholarship, Eric Wilson, *Emerson's Sublime Science*, shows how the "science of electricity [. . .] convinced Emerson that nature is a presentation of vast, perpetual, infinite forces" (47). Plotinus's conception—"everywhere there is all, and each is all" —and "Pascal's intuitions," so vital to the development of Romanticism, were being "scientifically shown [. . .] for the first time in the history of thought" (47).

57. Here again, as Richardson argues in *Emerson: Mind on Fire*, Emerson was indebted to Goethe who introduced him to an "open, outward-facing working method of sympathetic appropriation and creative recombination of the world's materials" (173). For a much more definitive account, see Wilson, *Emerson's Sublime Science*, which examines Emerson's immersion in European Romanticism's hermeneutical roots and its preoccupation with alchemy (50–75) as well as his study of Humphry Davy and Michael Faraday's scientific experiments with electromagnetism as a method of explaining not only natural phenomena, but also the composition of natural bodies (76–97). As Faraday's discoveries proposed, "The forms of natural bodies depend upon different arrangements of the same particles of matter; that possibly the world shall be found to be composed of oxygen and hydrogen; and that even these two elements are but one matter in different states of electricity" (12–13). In this respect, Coleridge

and Goethe's fascination with new considerations of alchemy prepared Emerson for his later scientifically influenced belief that the sequence of material forms throughout history was creative rearrangements of the same key natural elements. Importantly, Wilson argues that "the only times Emerson uses alchemical imagery in substantial detail is to describe his composing process, the practice by which he symbolizes his thoughts" (73). In this respect, metamorphosis becomes a template with which to understand creation, especially artistic creation.

58. For the major features of this chain, see the classic study by Arthur O. Lovejoy, *The Great Chain of Being: A Study in the History of an Idea* (Cambridge, MA: Harvard University Press, 1936).

59. The human being is first an effect, produced by a cause he cannot fathom—until he learns to unite himself with the origin or cause in the act of creation. Nonetheless, Emerson is quite specific that genius is, initially, a product of nature: "But nature never pauses. Whilst we admire and exaggerate one genius, and, perhaps, after a century or two, have learned to appreciate it, she throws into our neighborhood another and another to be the study and astonishment of other times and distant eyes" (*EL* 3: 361). In *Emerson's Pragmatic Vision*, David Jacobson gives an account on how Emerson gradually transforms the relationship between nature and man from one that values the human being as the active locus of nature to an antihumanism where "Man remains the principal fact and the greatest phenomenon of nature, the terminal where nature is manifest, but is no longer the depth and purpose of nature. Man remains the eyes of nature; but now decentered and partial, Man is a passive monitor" (100). An impersonal force that works in combination with nature produces the human being—and the will to make and create becomes an expression of a power of which he is but an effect.

60. The idea of coupling or linking in sequence cause and effect in a complex series is also strikingly characteristic of Plotinus on providence, *Enneads* III, 2–3,—especially the notion of a coupling *logos* (*logos synapton*). See III, 3, 4, 9–13, for the distinction between a "making" *logos* (*poietikos*) and a linking (*synapton*) *logos*.

61. That is, respectively, Ovid's *Metamorphoses*, Apuleius's *Golden Ass*, or Homer's *Odyssey*, Bk. 4 (Proteus) on one hand, and the *Vedas* and the *Bhagavad Gītā*, together with Hindu mythology, on the other.

62. Guthrie, *Above Time*, 27.

63. See, for example, the emphasis upon *paideia* or education in the central books of the *Republic*; the goal of dialectic in *Republic* 7, 537c, is to see as a whole (*synoptikos*). Compare *Symposium* 210a–212b and especially the *7th Letter*, 344b. See also Werner Wilhelm Jaeger, *Paideia: The Ideals of Greek Culture* (Oxford: Oxford University Press, 1965), 99ff.

64. See, for example, Ennead 6, 7, 32, 34–39; 5, 1, 1, 4; 2, 4, 5, 27–37.

65. See Plotinus, Ennead IV, iii, 3, 8, 9. For comparison, see Stephen Mackenna, *The Essence of Plotinus: Extracts from the Six Enneads and Porphyry's Life of Plotinus* (New York: Oxford University Press, 1948), 266.

66. Emerson repeatedly uses the imagery of a bird moving from one material fixture to another as a trope for spirit's time-bound existence. For instance, in his 1848 lecture, "The Spirit of the Times," he states, "This age is ours; is our world. As the wandering sea-bird which crossing the ocean alights on some rock or islet to rest for a moment its wings, and to look back on the wilderness of waves behind, and onward to the wilderness of waters before, so stand we perched on this rock or shoal of time,

arrive out of the immensity of the past, and bound and road-ready to plunge into immensity again" (*LL* 1: 124).

67. This notion of a power that abides never simply in any one individual or even in all of them in a series but only in itself so that it comes to be manifest differently in all lies at the basis of Neoplatonism and its most famous triad: *mone* (abiding), *prohodos* (outpouring/outgoing), *epistrophe* (conversion/reversion-dance/turning). See, for example, Proclus, *Elements of Theology*, propositions 25–39.

68. "As the sun is conceived to have made our system by hurling out from itself the outer rings of diffuse ether, which, slowly have condensed into earths and moons;—by a higher force of the same law, the mind detaches minds, and a mind detaches thoughts or intellections. These, again, all mimic in their sphericity the first mind, and share its power" (*LL* 2: 75–77).

69. As we have seen, Goethe's principle of fusion between the ideal and the actual, expressed in both his poetic and scientific works, influenced Emerson immensely, and, in the earlier esoteric thought of Emanuel Swedenborg (1688–1772), Emerson saw a familial urge to formulate a new metaphysical science, which he both affirms and conversely finds lacking. As he wrote in 1850, Swedenborg's best work "was written with the highest end, to put science and the soul, long estranged from each other, at one again" (*W* 4: 63). And earlier in an 1834 letter to Thomas Carlyle, Emerson professed that "the new faith which must arise out of all" (*SL*: 137) owes its most modern expression to Swedenborg and his followers. Accordingly, Emerson saw Swedenborg as much more than a scientist or Christian theologian; he was the poetic heir of "Dante, Shakespeare and Milton" (*EL* 3: 361) and had given timely expression to a faith that was in the process of revealing itself.

70. See James Perrin Warren, *Culture of Eloquence: Oratory and Reform in Antebellum America* (University Park: Pennsylvania State University Press, 1999), 34.

71. See Menand, *Metaphysical Club*, 89.

72. More generally, see Versluis, *Esoteric Origins*, 133–34.

73. This emphasis on will also relates to Schopenhauer's "irrational, impersonal Will" and anticipates Nietzsche's will to power. See Robert Solomon, *Continental Philosophy Since 1750: The Rise and Fall of the Self* (Oxford: Oxford University Press, 1988) for Schopenhauer, 75–85; and Nietzsche, 115–26. See also Lucretius, *On the Nature of Things*, trans. Martin Ferguson Smith (Indianapolis, IN: Hackett Publishing Company, Inc., 2001), Bk. 2, 245–84. See also Plato *Republic* 9 on how the individual will swerves the destiny operating on it from without and Plotinus's conception of the free will of the One, *Ennead* VI, 8.

74. Emerson puts a new emphasis on willpower that by 1860, nineteen years after his *First Series of Essays* and ten years after this assessment of Swedenborg, comes to be the principal power by which the human being both enables and resists the dictates of fate: "A breath of will blows eternally through the universe of souls in the direction of the Right and Necessary. It is the air which all intellects inhale and exhale, and it is the wind which blows the worlds into order and orbit" (*W* 6: 15).

75. Emerson formulates this type of metempsychotic passage in numerous ways. Here, it is explicitly mystical, although he is perfectly ready to translate its meaning into different frameworks. For instance, in an 1848 lecture, he portrays this process as an evolutionary one, where soul and matter continually emit more complexly arranged emergent properties out of their older, cruder organizations: "The gracious lesson taught by science to this Century is that the history of nature from first to last

is *melioration*, incessant advance from less to more, from rude to finer and finest organization, the globe of matter thus conspiring with the principle of undying Hope in man" (*LL* 1: 123).

76. See J. Bussanich, *The One and its Relation to Intellect in Plotinus* (Leiden, Netherlands: Brill, 1988), 172ff., 231–36; and R. T. Wallis, *Neoplatonism*, 2d ed. (London: Duckworth, 1995), 82–90 (Plotinus); 118–37 (Iamblichus); and 141–57 (Proclus).

77. Ralph Waldo Emerson, *Collected Poems and Translations*, ed. Harold Bloom and Paul Kane (New York: Library of America, 1994), 5–8.

78. See Gougeon, *Emerson & Eros*, on the "myth of eternal return" and "the cycle of rebirth," 63.

2 / The Double Consciousness

1. Bloom, *Bloom's Modern Critical Views: Ralph Waldo Emerson*, 5.

2. George Kateb, *Emerson and Self-Reliance* (Totowa, NJ: Rowman & Littlefield, 2002), 8.

3. By this term with a very complex history, which we cannot treat here, Emerson means something like what Plotinus and the Neoplatonists appear to mean, i.e., the whole of all that is real, whole in itself and whole in each of the parts, though each part participates only to the extent of its own power or potential. For Plotinus, see especially *Ennead* VI, 4–5, on the simultaneous omnipresence of being.

4. This unsettled, double structure has been treated differently by critics, although most criticism has ignored Emerson's specific inferences of the double consciousness and concentrated upon dialectic. From the 1960s to the 1980s, some criticism tended to portray the concept of "irreconcilable conflict" as a prevailing pattern in Emerson's thought. In *Emerson's Fall: A New Interpretation of the Major Essays* (New York: Continuum International Publishing Group, 1982), Barbara Packer upholds "Experience" as the essay that fully realizes this paradox where "experience and consciousness are indeed in perpetual conflict." See also, Evan Carton, *The Rhetoric of American Romance: Dialectic and Identity in Emerson, Dickinson, Poe, and Hawthorne* (Baltimore, MD: Johns Hopkins University Press, 1985), for the treatment of doubleness as dialectic. For the most part, it has been understood as a paradox or a shifting emphasis from Emerson's early to later writings (see, for instance, Sharon Cameron, *Impersonality: Seven Essays* (Chicago: University of Chicago Press, 2007), 79–107. However, in *Emerson*, Lawrence Buell notes that Emerson's complex, shifting conception of God is not simply paradoxical. In fact, he quotes William James to illuminate the relationship between "the platonic belief that the foundation of things is an overarching Reason" and "radical individualism" (163). Buell takes this a step further and argues that "the oscillation between the one and the many in Emerson's metaphysics applies to his thinking on other subjects too" (163). Here, this double character—Platonic Form and ontological consciousness—can be understood as conflictual and dialectical, composing in its movement a consistent, although always unsettled methodology or way of thinking, comprising at once ancient thought and the modern problem of subjectivity.

5. Emerson's reluctance to abandon the philosophers of transcendence elicits other critical responses as well. In the assessment of Barbara Packer, Emerson remained attached to the Western Idealist tradition because he needed a panacea for grief, a soothing spell for melancholy: "Idealism as a doctrine was more than philosophically important for Emerson; it was emotionally important as well" (Barbara L. Packer,

"The Curse of Kehama," *Bloom's Modern Critical Views: Ralph Waldo Emerson*, updated ed. [New York: Infobase Publishing, 2007], 74). The deaths of his first wife, Ellen Louisa Tucker, in 1831 and his first son, Waldo, in 1842 certainly reinforced Emerson's attempts to reconcile the claims of materialism with his lifelong hunger for the soul. Accordingly, Emerson found reassurance in Idealism and developed, as a result, a voracious appetite for Idealist thinkers to keep the darkness of his moods at bay: "No wonder Emerson seized eagerly upon every philosopher whose system tended toward idealism of one kind or another: Plato, Plotinus, Berkeley, Kant, Fichte, Schelling" (74). Sharon Cameron argues that Emerson primarily espoused transcendent views for the rhetorical purposes of ravishing his listeners so as to affect a climactic flourish on Idealist peaks. For Cameron, the trope of the ever-moving soul creates an intentional lack of balance, preparing readers for "that influx of the Divine mind into our mind," which Emerson characterizes "consistently as 'enthusiasm,' 'ecstasy,' 'trance,' or 'inspiration,' and 'in the case of remarkable persons like Socrates, Plotinus, George Fox, and Behmen,'" he employs "ravishment," which is precisely what his "essays attempt to dramatize" (Cameron, *Impersonality*, 92–93).

6. Dialectic, of course, means many things even in Plato's dialogues: "conversation" or "reflexive self-knowledge" (in *Alcibiades* I) or conversation together with a method for testing hypotheses (e.g., in different ways in the *Phaedo, Republic, Sophist, Parmenides*) or ladder of ascent (in the *Symposium*). For Plotinus, see Ennead I, 3; and for Hegel see note 7 below and further in this chapter. For Emerson, see also Carl Stauch, "Emerson's Sacred Science," *PMLA* 73.3 (1958): 237–50; and Carton, *Rhetoric of American Romance*.

7. "The double consciousness" or the uneasy relationship between "the understanding and the soul" in Emerson is a complex phenomenon in the history of thought relating to the gap between the human city and the City of God in Augustine's *City of God*, Book 1 ("both as it exists in this world of time, a stranger among the ungodly, living by faith, and as it stands in the security of its everlasting seat"), or between different levels of being in a single individual, as between the intelligible world and the self as *nous*, on the level of understanding, and the historical-sensible world and the self as soul, on the level of perceptible experience, as in Plato, Plotinus, and Proclus. This uneasy relation also maps onto the structure of self-consciousness itself, not only in Plato—in the *Alcibiades* I, where self-knowledge is described as a reflexive relationship between two selves or sets of eyes in which the seer's own image is reflected back into his eyes—but especially in Plotinus and later still in Hegel. For Plotinus, seer and seen, knower and known, have to become one in two if the seer is really to see; otherwise, we only have a subject looking at an object—a kind of external consciousness, whereas real self-consciousness as the purest form of thinking is a doubled-unity. See *Enneads* III, 8; V, 8; V, 3 especially. For Hegel, self-consciousness is a peculiar form of doubling in that each pole of self-consciousness is itself self-consciousness, providing a form of doubled self that can only be mediated by a sublation of its content into a higher synthesis as, for instance, initially in the Master-Slave dialectic. Hegel, of course, ultimately wants to purge self-consciousness of anything alien to it. But in every relation (particularly from a Platonic viewpoint), this cannot be achieved; consciousness always retains its shadow, whether positive or negative. And so the self and its shadow are characteristic of Emerson and Plato, but not so much of Hegel. This is the reason why so much recent criticism tends to portray Emerson as a thinker who rejects absolute unity. For example, in *The Emerson Effect: Individualism and Submission in*

America (Chicago: University of Chicago Press, 1996), Christopher Newfield argues that Emerson presents "a double legacy" where "both sides of his thought are in continual operation" (26) and are not reducible to an absolute privilege. The continual doubleness of his thought is, in this context, not a lack of systemization, but the embracing and avowal of an unsettled order.

8. Packer, *Transcendentalists*, 24.

9. Ibid.

10. *W* 3: 41. See particularly the notion of peopling a new land through reversal or conversion; Stanley Cavell, *This New Yet Unapproachable America* (Albuquerque, NM: Living Batch Press, 1989), 92–93.

11. In America, the far-reaching question of metempsychosis is most powerfully posed in direct relation to book or print culture—the origins of which are already discernible in Benjamin Franklin's famous epitaph, which he penned at the age of twenty-two, sixty-two years before his death: "The body of Benjamin Franklin, Printer, like the cover of an old book, its contents torn out and stripped of its lettering and gilding, lies here, food for worms; but the work shall not be lost, for it will, as he believed, appear once more in a new and more elegant edition, revised and corrected by the Author." Franklin's sentiment strikes a humorously prosaic note with its third-person omniscient voice reflecting on the underlying religious role of Franklin's own profession as printer, which seeks to perfect the human text from one edition or age to another. Franklin's epitaph illuminates the vital intermingling of religion with an emerging culture of mass production, a method of spiritualizing or humanizing the printer's profession and making it vital to the American project of personal and national amelioration.

12. Washington Irving, *The Legend of Sleepy Hollow and Other Stories*, intro. and notes by William L. Hedges (New York: Penguin Books, 1999), 61.

13. Ibid., 61, 63; emphasis added.

14. Bayard Taylor, *The Poetical Works of Bayard Taylor* (Boston: Houghton, Mifflin and Company, 1907), 39.

15. Ibid., 39.

16. Ibid., 40.

17. Ibid., 41.

18. Ibid.

19. Ibid., 41–42.

20. Stanley Bates, "The Mind's Horizon," in *Beyond Representation: Philosophy and Poetic Imagination*, ed. Richard Thomas Eldridge (Cambridge: Cambridge University Press, 1996), 164.

21. Hans-Georg Gadamer, *Hegel's Dialectic: Five Hermeneutical Studies*, trans. P. Christopher Smith (New Haven, CT: Yale University Press, 1976), 78.

22. The interpretation of Plato's theory of Forms is a vexed question since elements of the "theory" are only proposed in different dialogues (and never by Plato directly) and the only dialogue in which it comes up in an extended discussion between Zeno, Parmenides, and Socrates (*Parmenides*), it is rigorously subjected to most of the major criticisms later leveled against it (for instance, by Aristotle in the *Metaphysics*). In other words, Plato appears to deconstruct his own theory in the dialogues.

23. Plato, *Symposium*, 211a.

24. For a contemporary, influential treatment of many figures in this tradition from Plato to Whitman, Proust, and Joyce, see Martha Nussbaum, *Upheavals of*

Thought: The Intelligence of the Emotions (Cambridge: Cambridge University Press, 2001).

25. Plato, *Symposium*, 211a5–b.

26. Ibid., 210c7–211a.

27. See George Kateb, *Emerson and Self-Reliance*, 131–33. Kateb calls Emerson's adaptation of Platonic ascent a "super-Platonized picture of the metamorphoses of sexual love" (131). While arguing that Emerson's love is decidedly unsexual, Kateb similarly catches Emerson's emphasis upon dialectical ascent and descent: "The lover should try to climb to a love of the ideal itself and descend again to a particular love, but now enlightened by an understanding of the nature of love" (132).

28. Yet, at the same time, he manages to be true to the Platonic spirit insofar as the "ladder of created souls" (which is not in Plato) reflects the reflexive aspect of each step in Plato, that is, *logos* and the nurturing of *logos* between two human beings. See *Symposium* 210 a 7–8, c 1–2; etc. and so on for each step.

29. This notion of dissatisfaction has been influentially treated by Stanley Cavell who stresses Emerson's writing/thinking as a process of aversion—turning away from in order to turn back to, conversion or transformation. In *Conditions Handsome and Unhandsome* (Chicago: University of Chicago Press, 1990), Cavell expresses it in this way: "Emersonian Perfectionism requires that we become ashamed in a particular way of ourselves, of our present stance, and that the Emersonian Nietzsche requires, as a sign of consecration to the next self, that we hate ourselves [. . .]. So that the mission of Perfectionism generally, in a world of false (and false calls for) democracy, is the discovery of the possibility of democracy, which to exist has recurrently to be (re)discovered" (16–17).

30. Cf. the title of Goethe's work, *Elective Affinities* (translation of *Die Wahlverwandschaften*).

31. The Stoics called the soul "*scintilla aetheris*," a spark or smoldering ember of ether (See *Stoicorum Veterum Fragmenta*, index). Emerson transforms this image by combining it with Plato's "wandering cause," a condition of unpredictability in the *Timaeus* (see 47eff.), thereby transforming both into his own complex image.

32. See especially *Enneads* III 8; V 8; III 3, 7, 9–24.

33. See Walls, *Emerson's Life in Science*, 187–93; Menand, *Metaphysical Club*, 177–200; and David William Bates, *Enlightenment Aberrations: Error and Revolution in France* (Ithaca, NY: Cornell University Press, 2002), 248–49.

34. As a complex union of *anamnesis* and historical memory, Emerson's reminiscence is explicitly more metempsychotic than Plato's, although as we saw in Chapter 1, Emerson argues that Plato's theory of reminiscence is metempsychotic. Plato emphasizes how the soul remembers its higher life and, thus, feels the need to reclaim its lost eminence, while Emerson incorporates a number of traditions into his notion of memory, particularly the Hindu conception of enlightenment entailing a full memory of all one's pervious lives.

35. See Pamela Schirmeister, *Less Legible Meanings: Between Poetry and Philosophy in the Work of Emerson* (Stanford: Stanford University Press, 1999). Schirmeister examines Emerson's conception of representariness "as the very interruption of exemplarity, as written, exposed, and public, but also as risk" (163). In this respect, Emerson's *Representative Men* continues his earlier project of writing as "openendedness," since writing and representation operate in the context of limit and simultaneous absence. "To exist at all, community must be written, marked, but neither

it nor its writing can complete themselves as a project" (162). Schirmeister argues in this context that Emerson proceeds to find fault with each of his representative men precisely because he resists "the closure of communication" (162). Emerson argues that "Plato has no system" since Plato and all the other representative men provide themselves as "partial and fragmentary indications of a vocation, that is, of a work exposed and calling to us" (162). Stanley Cavell is influential in providing the opening of this branch of criticism, particularly in terms of constitutional and individual negotiation. He argues that Emerson's conception of representation brings into question and contention the relation of self to the materials or exemplifications which we inherit, the process by which we construct identity or "'my constitution,' meaning for [Emerson] simultaneously the condition of the body, his personal health (a figure for the body or system of his prose), and more particularly his writing (or amending) of the nation's constitution" (*Conditions Handsome and Unhandsome*, 11). In this respect, Emerson asks his reader "to picture what constitutes such journeying (Emerson's word for it is taking steps, say walking, a kind of success(ion), in which the direction is not up but on, and in which the goal is decided not by anything picturable as the sun, by nothing beyond the way of the journey itself" (10). Emerson, therefore, teaches "that we are to see beyond representativeness, or rather see it as a process of individuation" (10). Representation, therefore, isn't just limit or absence—it becomes the site in which an individual negotiates himself in relation to a greater social body or "its glimpse of perfectionist aspiration as calling on, or remembering, the wish for participation in the city" (18): "If there is a perfectionism not only compatible with democracy but necessary to it, it lies not in excusing democracy for its inevitable failures, or looking to rise above them, but in teaching how to respond to those failures, and to one's compromise by them, otherwise than by excuse or withdrawal" (18). For a recent article building on these foundations, see Hans von Rautenfeld, "Thinking for Thousands: Emerson's Theory of Political Representation in the Public Sphere," *American Journal of Political Science* 49.1 (2005): 184–97. Here, Rautenfeld argues that the "value at the heart of Emerson's conception of democracy is the ability of all persons to shape their lives through thinking and thus to exercise their capacity for self-government" (184).

36. As noted previously, some critics see Plato's philosophy as one which Emerson would largely overcome (see Van Cromphout, *Emerson's Modernity and the Example of Goethe*, 42–44). Many critics from the 1990s onward stress the vital importance of Platonic thought to Emerson's thinking. In *Emerson: Mind on Fire*, for instance, Richardson states that "Emerson's interest in Plato would become a major preoccupation" throughout his lifetime. Although Emerson could read Greek, he worked largely with translations, and Richardson describes the "seven discernable stages" by which Emerson acquainted himself with Plato (65–66).

37. See also Kevin Corrigan and John D. Turner, *Platonisms: Ancient, Modern, and Postmodern* (Leiden, Netherlands: Brill, 2007), 4–5. Emerson's argument strikingly anticipates Alfred North Whitehead's judgment that "Plato's personal endowments, his wide opportunities for experience [. . .], his inheritance of an intellectual tradition not yet stiffened by excessive systematization, have made his writing an inexhaustible mine of suggestion."

38. One might argue that this is an essential, if mostly overlooked, feature of Platonism itself, namely, its capacity for "well-meaning" refutation built into dialectic. See, for example, Plato, *7th Letter*, 342e–343c.

39. Cf. Plato, *Philebus* 26d; 27b; 53d–54d; Aristotle, *Parts of Animals* 645a23–36; 641b31–32.

40. See, for example, Plotinus, *Ennead* III, 9, 3, for the priority of soul to its "image."

41. As Plato famously argues in *Republic* 10, the poet does not perceive truth, for his poem is an imitation only. He does not, therefore, deal with true existence, but only with appearance: "The imitator or maker of the image knows nothing of true existence; he knows appearances only." His artwork remains an imitation of an imitation and is, therefore, twice removed from the ideal form. Mimesis, however, does not need to be interpreted as entirely negative in the *Republic* or other dialogues, since all forms of expression are mimetic and, while defective, they are still forms of expression through which we may catch glimpses of something real.

42. In such a scheme, one can see the precise nature of the privilege that Emerson gives to poetry. Since the poet's activity deals more directly than any other activity with an ideal, timeless form, his work is the least derivative and, therefore, possibly the most transcendent product in creation. As Emerson writes in 1836, poetry is the birthplace of all language: "As we go back in history, language becomes more picturesque, until its infancy, when it is all poetry" (*W* 1: 19). Poetry possesses the distinct quality of being a more perfect language because it is closest to the ideal Form that generated it. At root, then, Emerson's conception of language is clearly Platonic, since material objects—whether natural forms or words—are reflections of higher, incorporeal Forms. As with Platonism, Emerson employs a scale of ascension or derivation: the nobler objects are the ones closer to the Forms they express, while conversely, the further removed from their essential Forms, the more depraved or degraded the material objects thus become. In "Nature," Emerson's critique of derivative writing follows just such a formula, for he faults writers who cannot express original ideas, using only the language of others to trick audiences into accepting their authority: "Hundreds of writers may be found in every long-civilized nation, who for a short time believe, and make others believe, that they see and utter truths, who do not of themselves clothe one thought in its natural garment, but who *feed unconsciously upon the language created by the primary writers of the country*, those, namely, who hold primarily on nature" (*W* 1: 20; emphasis added). Reflecting Plato's critique of poetry in *The Republic*, Emerson presents his own argument that these authors use a language twice-removed from truth, since their words are not the "natural garment" of truth, but merely imitations of other words. While Emerson plainly relies upon the classical, Platonic-Aristotelian conception of form and matter, his emphasis is decidedly different than Plato's in Books 2, 3, and 10 of *The Republic*. Emerson's critique points to an implicit hierarchy of poetic consciousness. It is only men of lesser capacity that are imitative; they cannot see beyond the copy: "Impure men consider life as it is reflected in opinions, events, and persons. They cannot see the action, until it is done" (*W* 3: 57). Because they function on an unconscious level, such writers degrade the language they use, for it is not the fault of language but the "corruption of man [which] is followed by the corruption of language" (*W* 1: 20).

43. In this context, Emerson's early essays from 1836 to 1844 possess a particular ambivalence toward nature and her symbols. In "Nature" (1836), for instance, he maintains the concept of fallen nature, however much he praises nature in other contexts. In one of the essay's concluding statements, Emerson proclaims the priority of spirit over matter and asks his audience to imagine history from the point of view of the eternal soul, asserting that history itself is a process of degradation: "The

foundations of man are not in matter, but in spirit. But the element of spirit is eternity. To it, therefore, the longest series of events, the oldest chronologies are young and recent. In the cycle of the universal man, from whom the known individuals proceed, centuries are points, and *all history is but the epoch of one degradation*" (*W* 1: 42; emphasis added). In this manner, Emerson relegates the universe's expansive chronology to a manageable mimetic formula: history is simply an imperfect addition to spirit, a mere derivative likeness of an original essence. And since the human being is part of history, he is "a god in ruins" (*W* 1: 42). Issued forth from a universal source, he has lost his original innocence, and the penalty exacted for this loss is, as in the Judeo-Christian account of *Genesis*, death. In this context, Emerson muses that when men recover their innocence, they will not only live longer, but also transcend the bonds of matter with greater ease: "When men are innocent, life shall be longer, and shall pass into the immortal, as gently as we awake from dreams" (*W* 1: 42).

44. See Nancy Lewis Tuten and John Zubizaretta, eds., *The Robert Frost Encyclopedia* (Westport, CT: Greenwood Publishing Group, 2001), 93.

45. See Stephen E. Whicher, *Freedom and Fate: An Inner Life of Ralph Waldo Emerson* (Philadelphia: University of Pennsylvania Press, 1971), 74–76; Hugh H. Witemeyer, "'Line' and 'Round' in Emerson's 'Uriel'," *PMLA* 82.1 (1967): 98; Buell, *Emerson*, 159–69; Menand, *Metaphysical Club*, 18–20; Peter Field, *Ralph Waldo Emerson: The Making of a Democratic Intellectual* (Lanham, MD: Rowman & Littlefield Publishers, Inc., 2002), 121–25; and especially Patrick J. Keane, *Emerson, Romanticism, and Intuitive Reason* (Columbia: University of Missouri Press, 2005), 325–50.

46. Emerson's rejection of authority can be seen as a component of his Unitarian anti-institutionalism; such a position was also preset as an emerging tenet, as it were, of continental transcendentalism itself, particularly Hegelian dialectic. As Hegel writes in the *Philosophy of History*, "Custom is activity without opposition, for which there remains only a formal duration; in which the fullness and zest that originally characterized the aim of life are out of the question—a merely external sensuous existence which has ceased to throw itself enthusiastically into its object" (74–75).

47. Emerson, *Collected Poems and Translations*, 15–16.

48. Guthrie, *Above Time*, 108.

49. Ibid., 109.

50. See Immanuel Kant, *Critique of Pure Reason* (Unified ed.), trans. Werner S. Pluhar and intro. by Patricia Kitcher (Indianapolis, IN: Hackett Publishing Company, Inc., 1996). For Kant, time and space are the a priori, inner and outer forms of intuition or grounds for consciousness: "Time and space [. . .] are two sources of cognition" (92: B 55). In short, creation cannot be understood outside of consciousness. Since "the concept of change requires the perception of some existent [being] and of the succession of its determinations; hence it acquires experience" (94: B 58), creation in some sense depends upon the experience and perception of being.

51. John Milton, *Paradise Lost* (Oxford: Oxford University Press, 2008), Book III, Line 690.

52. Edward Emerson, ed., *The Complete Works of Ralph Waldo Emerson*, volume 9 (Boston and New York: Houghton, Mifflin, and Company/The Riverside Press, 1904), 408–9. Edward Emerson also provides a metempsychotic context for "Uriel," writing that the poem attempts to move beyond the concept of "Eternal Return": the young gods "only see the Circle, not the Spiral which is Advance combined with Return,

adding the element of Progress" (409). To illustrate further this concept of transmigration as an evolutionary principle, Emerson draws extensively upon the Neoplatonic tradition. Quoting Proclus, Emerson provides the Pythagorean doctrine of transmigration as a circular path the soul must eternally take: "Every partial soul must make periods of ascent from and descent into generation, and this forever and ever" (410). Quoting a well-known Plotinian passage, Emerson also notes, "There are two kinds of souls that descend into the world of matter, the higher order, like so many kinds, associating with the governor of all things, become his colleagues in the general administration of the world. They descend for the sake of causing the perfection of the universe. The second class of souls descend because they are condemned to suffer punishment" (410).

53. Witemeyer, "'Line' and 'Round' in Emerson's 'Uriel'," 103.

54. By the phrase "Plato's *logos*" here I do not signify any particular use of the word *logos* in any of the dialogues, but rather the whole order of genesis—or substance (*ousia*) as the *Philebus* puts it—that depends upon and derives from the World of Forms or intelligible *kosmos*, however we are to conceive this.

55. On the history of procession and conversion generally, see Wallis, *Neoplatonism* and, for Plotinus specifically, see K. Corrigan, *Reading Plotinus*, 28–34, 149–51.

56. Witemeyer, "'Line' and 'Round' in Emerson's 'Uriel'," 101.

57. On the poem or text as a cosmological recreation (e.g., Plato's *Timaeus*), see Pierre Hadot, *The Veil of Isis: An Essay on the History of the Idea of Nature*, trans. Michael Chase (Cambridge, MA: The Belknap Press of Harvard University Press, 2006).

58. Hegel, *Science of Logic*, trans. by A.V. Miller with analysis by J. N. Findlay (Atlantic Highlands, NJ: Humanities Press International, INC., 1990), 51.

59. Ibid., 71.

60. Ibid.

61. Hegel, *Philosophy of History*, 73.

62. The phoenix is a traditional image with which to represent the metempsychotic progression. In the last book of *Metamorphoses*, Ovid uses the phoenix as one of the central images to show how the soul continually seeks to renew herself (XV. 392–408). Importantly, however, Ovid uses the phoenix to differentiate between forms of reincarnation: "These creatures all derive their first beginnings/ From others of their kind. But one alone,/ A bird, renews and re-begets itself" (XV. 392–94). Whereas other souls fall from animal to human and back into animal again as is the more general understanding of Pythagorean metempsychosis, the phoenix's pattern reveals itself to be a self-propelling, sacred act: "When time has built his strength/ With power to raise the weight, he lifts the nest—/ The nest his cradle and his father's tomb—/ As love and duty prompt, from that tall palm/ And carries it across the sky to reach/ The Sun's great city, and before the doors/ Of the Sun's holy temple lays it down" (XV. 401–7). Here, the soul does not arbitrarily engender herself; rather, she seeks herself in accordance with "love and duty" and enacts a familial progression, from father to son, ever-seeking to heighten and renew her materials by the light of heaven.

63. Hegel, *Philosophy of History*, 73.

64. Here we have an implicit Hegelian critique of Kant's a priori and a posteriori, which signal a divide between two worlds, the *noumenal* world of "things in themselves" (i.e., a supersensible world about which we can know nothing in itself) and a *phenomenal* world of fluctuating appearances. See Daniel Bonevac, "Kant's Copernican Revolution" from Robert C. Solomon et al. *The Age of German Idealism* (London:

Routledge, 1993), 45–46. For Hegel, the *noumenal* is present implicitly in the whole phenomenology of spirit. As Hegel concludes in the introduction to the *Science of Logic*, "The abstract forms of the *a priori* and the *a posteriori*" must be integrated into the system so as to comprehend them according to their "specific content" (64). Also see Charles Taylor, *Hegel* (Cambridge: Cambridge University Press, 1975), for background on the rise of Kantian transcendentalism and its subsequent critique by Hegel, 3–51.

65. Hegel, *Philosophy of History*, 79.

66. The importance of the circle-image in Neoplatonism cannot be underemphasized. See especially *Ennead* VI, 8, 18. For the circle image in Emerson, see Gougeon, *Emerson & Eros*, 73, 152–53, 161.

67. Self-reliance is, of course, one of the principal values of Emerson's thought. As he writes in the essay of the same name (1841), "To believe your own thought, to believe that what is true for you in your private heart, is true for all men,—that is genius" (*W* 2: 27). In this respect, Emerson advocates that, amid the volatile experience of life, an individual must avoid imitation and instead look into himself in order to find the spiritual law that steadies him. For more on Emerson's development of the term and individualism itself, see Peter S. Field, *Ralph Waldo Emerson: The Making of a Democratic Intellectual* (Lanham, MD: Rowman & Littlefield Publishers, Inc., 2002), 219–22. Also for self-reliance in relation to Platonism as a dilemma pertinent not just for an individual, but for a nation, see David Justin Hodge, *On Emerson* (Wadsworth, UK: Thomson Learning, Inc., 2003), 53–58. In addition, see Christopher Newfield, *The Emerson Effect: Individualism and Submission in America* (Chicago: University of Chicago Press, 1996), on Cornell West and Stanley Cavell, 21–22.

68. This is true insofar as Hegel's express effort is to reveal consciousness' eventual, absolute self-knowledge, not necessarily unity, but the inseparability of all the elements in the process of consciousness coming to know itself without anything alien to it. There is, certainly, considerable disagreement about Hegel's method. Some critics argue that, for Hegel, "there is no limit for thought, and every limit as drawn, as thought, is already transcended" (William Desmond, *Beyond Hegel and Dialectic: Speculation, Cult and Comedy* [Albany: State University of New York Press, 1992], 186). Indeed, in *The Opening of Hegel's Logic: From Being to Infinity* (West Lafayette, IN: Purdue University Press, 2006), Stephen Houlgate defends Hegel from critics who claim that he presupposes the absolute outcome of his dialectical system. Houlgate contends that this is a misinterpretation of Hegel "because the whole point of the Logic is to seek to discover—without taking for granted—whether the presumed opposition between categories such as 'finitude' and 'infinity' is definitive or not" (37–38). Houlgate goes on to argue that Hegel's method in his *Science of Logic* is based upon presuppositionless thinking and does not ascribe an absolute end, but validates and emphasizes itself as an open-ended process (45).

69. Emerson removes any final, determination from his metaphysical system. Thus, while, from one perspective, his dialectic resembles Hegel's system, Emerson rejects Hegel's systematization of consciousness. In Hegel's *Phenomenology of Spirit*, for instance, the greatest weight is placed not upon the initial stages of the dialectic, but upon the latter stages: "Just because the form is as essential to the essence as the essence is to itself, the divine essence is not to be conceived and expressed merely as essence, i.e. as immediate substance of pure self-contemplation of the divine, but likewise as form, and the whole wealth of the developed form" (11). Hegel aims at the

whole wealth of the developed form, which is the full actuality of spirit, not simply its development: "The True is the whole. But the whole is nothing other than the essence consummating itself through its development. Of the Absolute it must be said that it is essentially a result, that only in the end is it what it truly is; and that precisely in this consists its nature, viz. to be actual, subject, the spontaneous becoming of itself" (11). While Emerson clearly accepts many of the dynamics of Hegel's dialectic, his striking difference to Hegelianism is that, although man properly discovers himself in developing a higher consciousness, there is no end to his nature and development. For Hegel, this terminus of history is a principal, albeit future prospect, but, for Emerson, the future promise, the whole wealth of the system, has value particularly as an undiscovered potentiality, "the last chamber," which realization will only degrade.

70. See Alan Hodder, *Emerson's Rhetoric of Revelation: Nature, the Reader, and the Apocalypse Within* (University Park: Pennsylvania State University Press, 1989). Hodder makes the important point that Emerson is actually very consistent through the many stages of his career. The shift from theology to science that many critics argue was so instrumental "is actual based on hearsay. It never took place. What is fashioned as a shift in values was really only a change in vocabulary, Emerson being fond of such changes" (38).

71. In "Fate," Emerson quotes Quetelet to explain that the "most casual and extraordinary events [. . .] become matter of fixed calculation" (*W* 6: 9). In this respect, all social phenomena can be explained with the "new science of Statistics." From this perspective, even genius is not an anomaly or a divine grace, but a material certainty if one possesses enough data about a population. For a recent and illuminating history of how Probability Theory or the Law of Errors influenced New England from the 1850's onward, see Menand, *Metaphysical Club*, 177–200.

72. Again compare Plotinus, *Ennead* III, 3, 6, 8–17: "Since the universe is a living thing, one who contemplates the things that come to be in it contemplates at the same time the origins and the providence which watches over it [. . .] so he contemplates things which are mixed and continually go on being mixed; and he cannot distinguish providence and what is according to providence clearly on the one side, and on the other the substrate and all that it gives to what results from it. The discrimination is not for a human being [. . .] a god alone could have this privilege."

3 / Reading the Metempsychotic Text

1. Harold Bloom, *The Anxiety of Influence: A Theory of Poetry*, 2d ed. (Oxford: Oxford University Press, 1997), 132.

2. Jacobson, *Emerson's Pragmatic Vision*, 34.

3. In "The Instructing Eye: Emerson's Cosmogony in 'Prospects'," *Emerson's Nature: Origin, Growth, Meaning*, ed. Merton M. Sealts Jr. and Alfred R. Ferguson (Carbondale: Southern Illinois University Press, 1979), Barbara Packer's examination of perception reveals the slippery ground of Emerson's privilege of vision—and her scholarship, in general, influenced criticism's reassessment of Emerson not as a philosopher of "truth," but as one of paradox, dislocation, and slippage. Previous criticism tended to interpret Emerson's vision as a unitary act. For instance, see Sherman Paul, *Emerson's Angle of Vision: Man and Nature in American Experience* (Cambridge, MA: Harvard University Press, 1965). Paul argues the "higher knowledge of value would come, Emerson believed, when seeing became a unitary act involving

both the emotional and intellectual responses of man. Perception, then, could not be too narrowly accounted for as the passive reception of sense-impressions, and their consequent accumulation as knowledge. A fuller description was needed, emphasizing the active contribution of man's total nature, his *desire* for unity, and the ways and means by which this desire was fulfilled" (38). By contrast, Packer interprets the "transparent eyeball" as a principal site of paradox: "The transparent eye-ball passage is chiefly composed of paradoxes ('I am nothing, I see all'). Here Emerson approaches the subject through negation" (220). In this respect, the exuberance of Emerson's early articulations of vision reveals, under close scrutiny, the evocation of a dilemma, rather than the establishing of a solution.

4. Bloom, *Anxiety of Influence*, 132.

5. In *The Emerson Museum*, Brown argues that perception is the quintessential Emersonian trope: "If among Emerson's many refrains there is a single dominating image, an image at once so common and synoptic as to seem ubiquitous, it is that of an opening eye. I can say without exaggeration that all I have been doing, in looking at Emerson's approaches to natural and mental life, to reading and writing, and to the frontier between the Old and New Worlds, has been to consider how he managed to conceive of opening the eye. This is a practical task as much as a stirring image, and it needs readers and listeners in order to take place" (202).

6. M. H. Abrams examines the central Romantic trope of the poet as divine creator, arguing that Plotinus provided a reinterpretation of Plato's cosmos that allowed the artist to reattain his preeminence. The artist is not simply a translator or imitator, but he creates according to a divine pattern: "Plotinus, for one, showed how a philosopher might retain the frame of Plato's cosmos and yet avoid Plato's derogation of the arts simply by allowing the artist to by-pass the sensible world in order to imitate the Ideas at first hand. By this sleight, the work of art is conceived to reflect the ideal more accurately than does imperfect nature itself. [. . .] The artist, from being a craftsman, became (in a momentous new aesthetic metaphor) a creator, for it was sometimes said that of all men the poet is likest God because he creates according to those patterns on which God himself has modeled the universe" (Abrams, *The Mirror and the Lamp: Romantic Theory and the Critical Tradition* [Oxford: Oxford University Press, 1971], 42).

7. As Emerson writes in "The Naturalist" (1836), one of his earliest lectures, "It is fit that man should look upon Nature with the eye of the Artist, to learn from the great Artist whose blood beats in our veins, whose taste is upspringing in our own perception of beauty, the laws by which our hands should work that we may build St. Peter'ses or paint Transfigurations or sing Iliads in worthy continuation of the architecture of the Andes, [of] the colors of the sky and the poem of life" (*EL* 1: 73).

8. Emerson soon indicates in "Circles" that the eye's emanation through creation operates according to the inner power of the soul, which ever-escapes material imprisonment to burst outward eternally: "But if the soul is quick and strong, it bursts over that boundary on all sides, and expands another orbit on the great deep, which also runs up into a high wave, with attempt again to stop and to bind. But the heart refuses to be imprisoned; in its first and narrowest pulses, it already tends outward with vast force, and to immense and innumerable expansions" (*W* 2: 181).

9. See Jacobson, *Emerson's Pragmatic Vision*, 1999, for an interpretation of "Circles" as a decisive expression of Emerson's early humanism: "The identity of the individual is raised through the articulation of a new circle. To see beyond is to see truly, and in this sense self-reliance, being in the upright posture, is to dare to think" (41).

For Jacobson, this movement beyond, different from the attitude of de-centering in later essays, is ultimately a method of reclaiming the transparence and permanence of nature and "man" at every turn: "If deep unto deep discloses a vast affirmative, then that affirmative names the permanent principle in Emerson's early method, consisting in the affirmation of Man" (41–42).

10. So in Plato (*Republic* 6–7) and Plotinus (*Ennead* III, 8, 11), the eyes' own proper light is "good-formed" (*agatho-eides*) or "sun-formed" (*helio-eides*).

11. For the image of life in itself as *self-direction*, i.e., not "in" anything else at all but in itself and therefore capable of being present to everything else, see Plotinus, *Ennead* III, 8, 8, and *Ennead* VI, 4–5, on the omnipresence of being.

12. Shadi Bartsch, *The Mirror of the Self: Sexuality, Self-Knowledge, and the Gaze in the Early Roman Empire* (Chicago: University of Chicago Press, 2006), 62.

13. See Versluis, *Esoteric Origins*, 139–40.

14. See Hadot, *Plotinus*, 40–42.

15. For a famous similar emphasis upon the nontranslatable character of hieroglyphics, see Plotinus, *Ennead* V, 8, 6. Also, for a critical work that focuses largely on the hieroglyph in Emerson's oeuvre, see William J. Scheick, *The Slender Human Word: Emerson's Artistry in Prose* (Knoxville: University of Tennessee Press, 1978), 10–25.

16. Hadot, *Veil of Isis*, 202.

17. Ibid., 203. See also Plotinus, *Ennead* II 3, 7, for the view that stars are like letters "always being written upon the heavens" and that "all things are full of signs, and it is the wise person who can learn about one thing from another."

18. See Buell, *Emerson*, 118.

19. For nature as the artwork of God, see Walls, *Emerson's Life in Science*, 42–55.

20. This theme of the great book of Nature has its origins in Judeo-Christian Scripture, as Augustine's treatment of Scripture, particularly in *Confessions* 12, attests and also in ancient philosophy, as one can see in Plotinus, *Enneads* III, 2–3. The idea of a scale of signs in nature or the text (from the literal to the allegorical and mystical) is to be found in Philo and Origen of Alexandria and has perhaps its finest expression in Dante (cf. *Letter to Can Grande*). Also, for the early modern relationship between nature and text, see Hadot, *Veil of Isis*, 216–29.

21. For nature as utility—"as a mere tool" (80), see Lopez, *Emerson and Power*, 79–86.

22. John T. Irwin, *American Hieroglyphics: The Symbol of the Egyptian Hieroglyphics in the American Renaissance* (New Haven, CT: Yale University Press, 1980), 13.

23. Swedenborg's doctrine of correspondences is generally accepted as a Neoplatonic inspired formulation. In *Melancholy Dialectics: Walter Benjamin and the Play of Mourning* (Amherst: University of Massachusetts Press, 1993), Max Pensky argues that there "is a genealogy that runs from this most esoteric expression of Renaissance Neoplatonism through Swedenborg to Baudelaire's doctrine of natural correspondences" (176). In addition, see Stanley Brodwin, "Emerson's Version of Plotinus: The Flight to Beauty," *Journal of the History of Ideas* 35.3 (1974): 465–83. Also, Walls, *Emerson's Life in Science*, outlines Emerson's scientific involvement in ideas of polarity in the context of Plato and Swedenborg, 163–65.

24. Hadot, *Plotinus*, 36; for Plotinus's influence on Goethe, see 40–41.

25. For Plotinus, see *Ennead* VI, 5, 8, 30–35 where he argues that "it was necessary for the same thing to become many and *to flee from itself* in order that it might be so multiple and something might participate of the same thing many times." This is

precisely a conception of a *fugitive essence* that not only has to flee from itself in order to be apprehended by many, but also has to go in search of itself.

26. Compare the rather different versions of the circle image in Emerson and Plotinus, *Ennead* VI, 8, 18. Cf. also Plato's description of the circles of the same and the different in the making of the World Soul, *Timaeus* 34a–40d.

27. For the desire to "unfix" language, see Buell, *Emerson*, 119.

28. Moved by a Platonic worldview and having expressed this pattern as the "metempsychosis of nature" in 1841, Emerson argues in 1850 that natural facts do not necessarily merge into wholeness, but comprise "successive platforms" and that the power of the intellect, while tracing their development, apprehends therein the sequence's dynamic openness to the prospect of self-generating and always unsettling expansion. Emerson is sure, moreover, to highlight that perception moving beyond the scope of human vision draws out the ulterior meaning of the series and recognizes the series' path to be circular and indeterminate, not linear and univocal: "These expansions or extensions consist in continuing the spiritual sight where the horizon falls on our natural vision, and by this secondsight discovering the long lines of law which shoot in every direction. Everywhere he stands on a path which has no end, but runs continuously round the universe. Therefore, every word becomes an exponent of nature. Whatever he looks upon discloses a second sense, and ulterior senses" (*W* 4: 46).

29. Jacob Böhme, *The Signature of All Things* (London: J. M. Dent and Sons, 1912), 261.

30. Ibid., 261.

31. See Plato's *Symposium* 211a. As Socrates recounts, "He who has been instructed [. . .] in the things of love [. . .] has learned to see the beautiful in due order and succession" and "when he comes to the end will suddenly perceive a nature of wondrous beauty" and so transcend "growing and decaying, or waxing and waning" for what is "everlasting."

32. The *First Series of Essays* (1841) uses this imagery as a dominant figurative arrangement. In "History," which initiates the collection, the eye must roll through all the architecture of the past and bring them into a present, living state. In "Art," which concludes the book, Emerson returns again to this imagery by using sculpture as an analogy of soul's movement through all creation. A pupil may learn the indwelling secret of form and the manner by which the soul translates itself into an object, but the created object does not yet possess a life of its own and, consequently, requires an activity to move through it so that it can realize its own life: "Sculpture may serve to teach the pupil how deep is the secret of form, how purely the spirit can translate its meaning into that eloquent dialect. But the statue will look cold and false before that new activity which needs to roll through all things, and is impatient of counterfeits, and things not alive" (*W* 2: 216). Artistic objects are in themselves lifeless and counterfeit, mere imitations of life and thereby fragmented features of the universe at a particular fallen stage in its gestation. But creation "needs" a new activity to unify the statue with all the other wreckages of creation and banish their fragmentation and disunity: "A true announcement of the law of creation, if a man were found worthy to declare it, would carry art up into the kingdom of nature, and destroy its separate and contrasted existence" (*W* 2: 217). This new activity or, in this case, true announcement of the law of creation makes art part of nature. The statue ceases to be lifeless and, although it has become a mimetic document, it can find a new, abundant fullness within an ensouled sequence of forms when a human being apprehends it as a living object

of study. For the image of sculpting in relation to the soul and to the emergence of the self, see also Plato, *Phaedrus*, 252d, and Plotinus, I, 6, 9.

33. In *Emerson's Pragmatic Vision*, David Jacobson asserts that the "strictly philosophical evolution" of Emerson's work "begins amid a philosophical context that has abandoned a narrow lexicon or taxonomy of reason and replaced it with an understanding of reason as the amorphous and fluid activity of spirit" (29). In Jacobson's view, Emerson's depiction of the individual's perception of nature corresponds to Hegel's "recognition of the reciprocity of thought and action, which gives reason a practical rather than contemplative, an historical rather than synchronic, foundation" (29).

34. Jacob Böhme, *Forty Questions of the Soul*, trans. by John Sparrow (Whitefish, MT: Kessinger Publishing, 1992), 91.

35. Hegel, *Phenomenology of Spirit*, 17.

36. Ibid., 17.

37. See Evan Carton, *The Rhetoric of American Romance: Dialectic and Identity in Emerson, Dickinson, Poe, and Hawthorne* (Baltimore, MD: Johns Hopkins University Press, 1985). Carton provides insightful context on how Emerson interprets language as "a potential that finds its precarious existence in the tension between Kantian and Hegelian alternatives, self-exile and self-subsumption" (20). In relation to Hegel's view that "romantic art" whose "medium is language" is the penultimate step to self-realization, Emerson develops a similar pattern that upholds the use of signs as transitional surfaces upon which a "precarious dialectic" can play (19–21).

38. Irwin, *American Hieroglyphics*, 13.

39. As Schelling argues in his epic philosophical poem, *The Ages of the World*, only the internal power of perception can make sense of the historical series, for imitation so overwhelms the individual that he cannot trace out or piece together the sequence of history: "Imitation, rather than the inner drive, leads to a research that confuses the senses as if by an inevitable fate. Hence, inner fortitude is necessary in order to keep a firm hold of the interrelation of movement from beginning to end" (3). The difficulty of arranging and keeping "a firm hold of the interrelation" of abbreviated shapes is that each perceptive act requires a creative composition. For the present perceiver, there is no correct, linear sequence from beginning to end whose meaning will be elicited in simply following out its sequence; rather, he or she must invent the cognitive pathways capable of comprehending each successive shape within an ever-expanding network of relations.

40. I have explored the attention of the eye as a Plotinian conception; however, it has a particular bearing in modernity. See Jonathan Crary, *Suspensions of Perception: Attention, Spectacle, and Modern Culture* (Cambridge, MA: MIT Press, 2001). Crary argues that the problem of attention arises in the nineteenth century due to a new awareness of the physiology of perception itself: "Attention becomes a specifically modern problem only because of the *historical* obliteration of the possibility of thinking the idea of presence in perception; attention will be both a simulation of presence and a makeshift, pragmatic substitute in the face of its impossibility" (4).

41. First, for Kant, the world does not exist outside of the mind, since the mind, in fact, constitutes the world. Second, all the determinations of consciousness appear disparate only to the phenomenal ego, while the capacity to unite this seemingly unconnected array of phenomena preexists a priori as transcendental ego-consciousness: "For the manifold presentations given in a certain intuition would not one and all be

my presentations, if they did not one and all belong to one self-consciousness, i.e., as my presentations (even if I am not conscious of them as being mine), they surely must conform necessarily to the condition under which alone they can stand together in one universal self-consciousness, since otherwise they would not thoroughly belong to me. [. . .] only because I can comprise the manifold of the presentations in one consciousness, do I call them one and all my presentations. For otherwise I would have a self as many-colored and varied as I have presentations that I am conscious of. Hence synthetic unity of the manifold of intuitions, as given a priori, is the basis of the identity itself of apperception, which precedes a priori all my determinate thought" (CPR, 178–79: B 132–34).

42. CPR, 43–44: B 1.

43. See Dagobert Runes, ed., *The Dictionary of Philosophy* (New York: Kessinger Publishing, 2006), 18.

44. Ibid., 15. See especially Kant, *The Foundations of the Metaphysic of Morals*, for the various forms of the categorical imperative.

45. Jacobson, *Emerson's Pragmatic Vision*, 28.

46. Walls argues that Plato's *Timaeus* provided Emerson with a "theory of vision" in which the eyes are an active creative force, not univocal, but emanating forth from the "fire within" to meet their "like" in the external world (*Emerson's Life in Science*, 68–69). In this, vision becomes the essential, even sole human organ that seeks integration and union between the inner world and the external. For the *Timaeus*, see 45b–47c.

47. *Phaedrus* 255c.

48. Ibid., 255c–d.

49. As Socrates argues, this pattern of perception is a spiritual practice, which prepares for the ascension of the soul into a more liberated existence: "And so, if the victory be won by the higher elements of mind guiding them into the ordered rule of philosophical life, their days on earth will be blessed with happiness and concord, for the power of evil in the soul has been subjected, and the power of goodness liberated; they have won self-mastery and inward peace. And when life is over, with burden shed and wings recovered they stand victorious [. . .] nor can any nobler prize be secured whether by the wisdom that is of man or by the madness that is of god" (Phaedrus 256b).

50. *Republic* 7 518b.

51. *Republic* 7 518c; emphasis added.

52. If, for Plato, the eye must turn itself around to the Good to escape from the cave and mimetic representations, in doing so, it becomes *synoptikos*. In the *Alcibiades I*, the eye reflected in the pupil of the other is the true medium of self-knowledge. In the *Seventh Letter* (and elsewhere), the flash of understanding that illuminates soul's perception is "sudden" (*exaiphnes*), an epiphanic moment in the midst of phenomena (344b), so in Hinduism, the greatest of men is "the man of vision" who uses his love for the One to pierce through the external "world of shadows" (7.14) to find himself in aspiring relation to the One: "The greatest of these is the man of vision, who is ever one, who loves the One. For I love the man of vision, and the man of vision loves me" (7.17). In *The Bhagavad Gītā*, Krishna tells the soldier Arjuna that the formation of such spiritual sight is produced after many transmigrations: "At the end of many lives the man of vision comes to me. 'God is all' this great man says. Such a spirit sublime how rarely is he found!" (7.19).

53. See Wallis, *Neoplatonism*, 65–66.

54. According to *Ennead* IV 6, 1, 14–18, perception takes place where the object is.

55. "Actual seeing is double; take the eye as an example, for it has one object of sight which is the form of the object perceived by the sense, and one which is the medium through which the form of its object is perceived, which is also itself perceptible to the eye; it is different from the form, but is the cause of the form's being seen; it is seen together in and with the form; this is the reason why it affords no clear perception of itself, since the eye is directed to the illuminated object; but when there is nothing there but the medium, the eye sees it by an instantaneous immediate perception, though even then it sees it based upon something different, but if it is alone and not resting on something else the sense is not able to grasp it. But if someone said that the sun was all light, [this might help] . . . for the sun will then be light which is in no form belonging to other visible things, and will be, perhaps, purely visible . . . This then is what the seeing of Intellect is like" (V, 5, 7; adapted).

56. Plato, *7th Letter*, 343a–344b.

57. For the Platonic and Neoplatonic influence on Goethe, see Friedrich Meinecke, *Historicism: The Rise of a New Historical Outlook* (New York: Routledge, 1972), 422–23; and Dennis Sepper, *Goethe Contra Newton: Polemics and the Project for a New Science of Color* (Cambridge: Cambridge University Press, 1988), 93.

58. Hadot, *Plotinus*, 41.

59. Ibid., 40.

60. Walls interprets "Goethe" as Emerson's final critique in *Representative Men* whose "individual essays [. . .] tend to be patterned across polar structures." Where Plato joins "these opposing 'gods of the mind,' enhancing the power of each and so realiz[es] 'a balanced soul,' who could see 'two sides of thing,'" Goethe offers another conception of synthesis as "the man through whom nature 'reports' or 'self-registers'" (*Emerson's Life in Science*, 163–64). Also, see Sepper, *Goethe Contra Newton*, 88–91, for how Goethe uses polarity as a schema with which to explain color-phenomena.

61. Sepper, *Goethe Contra Newton*, 158.

62. Herbert Hensel, "Goethe, Science, and Sensory Experience," *Goethe's Way of Science: A Phenomenology of Nature*, ed. David Seamon and Arthur Zajonc (Albany: State University of New York Press, 1998), 75.

63. Ibid.

64. David Seamon and Arthur Zajonc, eds., *Goethe's Way of Science: A Phenomenology of Nature* (Albany: State University of New York Press, 1998), 3.

65. Frederick Burwick, *The Damnation of Newton: Goethe's Color Theory and Romantic Perception* (New York: Walter de Gruyter, 1986), 15.

66. Johann Wolfgang von Goethe, *Theory of Colours*, trans. Charles Lock Eastlake (Cambridge, MA: MIT Press, 1970), lii–liii.

67. See P. F. H. Lauxtermann, "Hegel and Schopenhauer as Partisans of Goethe's Theory of Color," *Journal of the History of Ideas* 51.4 (1990): 599–624.

68. See Van Cromphout, *Emerson's Modernity*, 26–27.

69. See Burwick, *Damnation of Newton*, 10–12; and Seamon, *Goethe's Way of Science*, 5.

70. Sepper, *Goethe Contra Newton*, 90.

71. Ibid., 3.

72. Ibid., 74.

73. Goethe, *Theory of Colours*, liv.

74. Hensel, "Goethe, Science, and Sensory Experience," 74–75.

75. Burwick, *Damnation of Newton*, 11.

76. As Burwick argues, "Goethe's experiment was subjective: with the prism before his eyes the light that was blocked by the narrow bar in the window appeared to radiate in bands of violet and blue on one side, red and yellow on the other side" (*Damnation of Newton*, 11).

77. Ibid., 11.

78. Hensel, "Goethe, Science, and Sensory Experience," 75.

79. Jonathan Crary, *Techniques of the Observer: On Vision and Modernity in the Nineteenth Century* (Cambridge, MA: MIT Press, 1990), 70.

80. Ibid., 68.

81. Ibid., 68, 71.

82. Ibid., 70.

83. Goethe himself sees this relationship between the light within and the light without as a decisive part of Greek philosophy. Thus, he presents his theory of sight by explicitly quoting Empedocles of the Ionian school—and Plato's perception in *Republic* 7. See Goethe, *Theory of Colours*, liii.

84. *Ennead* V, 5, 7.

85. Goethe, *Theory of Colors*, liii.

86. Ibid., liii.

87. *Ennead* V, 5, 7.

88. Sepper, *Goethe Contra Newton*, 91.

89. Compare Plotinus, *Ennead* I, 6, generally. The soul must awake another mode of seeing and in becoming that vision, a pure vision, it not only sees what is beyond itself in love (cf. VI, 7, 35) but becomes a cogenerator of being, i.e., of its own being.

90. Note here the double emphasis on sight and touch. Both are characteristic of Neoplatonism, and perhaps touch even more so since "intellect" at its highest for Plotinus is a sight "not seeing," but "touching" (cf. VI, 9; V, 3, 11). Brown argues a similar position: "Emerson's picture of mental life revives the manual sense of grasping or taking (*capere*) buried in the word 'perception.' Vision has a hands-on dimension, as it were, in which worker and material come together" (*Emerson Museum*, 172–73).

91. Evan Carton argues that reading and writing share a similar foundation or an overlapping concern, for "reading necessarily involves representation; otherwise 'readings' never could be transformed into knowledge or "transcribed into new writings." Moreover, "conjoined once by their receptivity, reading and writing are conjoined again by their creativity. This double relation describes the precarious aesthetic that Emerson requires and struggles to articulate—an aesthetic of creative reading or receptive writing that accommodates both the originality of the inventive self and the originality of the changeless Origin" (*Rhetoric of American Romance*, 34).

92. Cameron, *Impersonality*, 141.

93. *7th Letter*, 343a–344b; or as Plotinus writes in V 5, 7, "the seeing of Intellect [. . .] is all light."

94. Emerson, *Collected Poems*, 15–16.

95. Stanley Cavell interprets this passage in relation to the notion of rebirth as a reversal, arguing that "Emerson's writing is (an image of promise of, the constitution for) this new yet unapproachable America: his aversion is a rebirth of himself into it (there will be other rebirths); its presence to us is unapproachable, both because there is nowhere *else* to go to find it, we have to turn toward it, reverse ourselves; and because

we do not know if our presence to it is peopling it" (*This New Yet Unapproachable America*, 92–93). Cavell denotes a type of implicit dialectic that requires a reversal (inversion) of one's previous perspective or grounds so as to be reborn into what is already there. At the same time, this is no solipsistic effort, for this turning is not simply an individual's rebirth, but potentially a way of peopling a new land and, thus, writing a new constitution for experience. One can hear, as it were, a Platonic strain in Cavell's argument, especially if one considers Plato's conception of using the eyes to turn the whole body around, as I have shown. It is this turn that allows an approach to creation, to realizing what was not there before; it is not an extension, linearly in any simple sense, but a revolution of consciousness.

96. Michael Lopez argues that Emerson does not avoid failure: "Victory required defeat. True success was impossible without failure. Health was the overcoming, not the avoidance, of disease. Power lay in the use, not the transcending, of loss and weakness" (*Emerson and Power*, 107). Emerson uses failure, therefore, as the true ground of his art: "The essays provided the arena in which Emerson's search for power could take place, where "the antagonizing mind" could discover and admit its fears and casualties and could them into the expressive force that was his art" (116).

97. The process is reminiscent of Socrates's description of the slow realization of a reversal of vision in the *Phaedrus*: "Like one who has caught a disease of the eye from another, he cannot account for it, not realizing that his lover is as it were a mirror in which he beholds himself" (Phaedrus 255d).

98. Emerson's concept of metempsychotic perception as a whole host of perspectives anticipates the "social principle" of pragmatism. For instance, Louis Menand describes Charles Peirce's desire to reveal the mistaken belief of nominalism. Peirce applied the law of errors to an examination of perception: an individual may observe a phenomenon, but his own singular observation is insufficient for "an accurate and objective knowledge of reality. But the aggregate beliefs of many individual minds is another matter" (*Metaphysical Club*, 228). Thus, for Peirce, reasoning "inexorably requires that our interests shall not be limited. They must not stop at our own fate, but must embrace the whole community" (229). Emerson's metempsychotic perspective, in this respect, underscores both the individual character of perception and the greater polyphonic perspective, one that transcends the fate of one individual so as to expand society's body of knowledge.

99. For the emphasis upon the "drive to link text-building with world-building" as a recurring romantic desire that can only be, for Emerson, "approximated," not fulfilled, see Buell, *Emerson*, 114.

100. Emerson's prosaic form comes to emphasize "artistic expression [. . .] as anticipation rather than achievement" (ibid., 114).

101. Ibid., 114, for the emphasis upon the "drive to link text-building with world-building" as a recurring romantic desire that can only be, for Emerson, "approximated," not fulfilled.

102. The *Bhagavad Gītā* provides an important context for this metempsychotic plurality. On the one hand, an individual can attain a vision of the diversity of things without comprehending their unity: "But if one merely sees the diversity of things, with their divisions and limitations, then one has impure knowledge" (18.21). On the other hand, vision, in its purest and most transcendent form, consists of a full recollection of the numerous transmigrations of soul that has turned itself inward to ponder itself, but not simply as a withdrawal or even "renunciation" (18.49) of the

work to be done, but as a joyful undertaking: "There is wisdom which knows when to go and when to return, what is to be done and what is not to be done, what is fear and what is courage, what is bondage and what is liberation—that is pure wisdom" (18.30). This undertaking finds itself in and out of numerous bodies and is a necessary act of purification. In this context, Emerson utilizes this tradition of unifying all the transmigrations of soul into an abundant consciousness, but he stresses it always as an incomplete, evolving pattern, oscillating between the knowledge of "all eyes" and the solitary perspective, which sees this heightened, multiperception with awe and fear, since it is only a sublimity hovering ghostlike at the end of the series, both in and out of being.

103. See Schirmeister, *Less Legible Meanings*, 119–46. The movement of "Experience" is, according to her, one of risk and provisionality, gesturing to the future arrangement both of community and self therein: "Our experience is at risk, an adventure into an unforeseeable future, but a future for which we are nonetheless responsible at every step" (145).

4 / Writing the Metempsychotic Text

1. See V. K. Chari, *Whitman in the Light of Vedantic Mysticism* (Lincoln: University of Nebraska Press, 1964); T. R. Rajasekharaiah, *The Roots of Whitman's Grass* (Madison, NJ: Fairleigh Dickinson University Press, 1970); and Nagendra Kr Singh, *Encyclopedia of Hinduism* (New Delhi, India: Anmol Publications PVT. LTD., 1997), 1802–30.

2. See David Kuebrich, *Minor Prophecy: Walt Whitman's New American Religion* (Indianapolis: Indiana University Press, 1989); and Versluis, *Esoteric Origins*, 157–70.

3. Versluis, *Esoteric Origins*, 158.

4. Harold Bloom, ed., *Bloom's Modern Critical Views: Walt Whitman*, updated ed. (New York: Chelsea House Publishers, 2006), 239.

5. Ibid., 238.

6. Walt Whitman, *Notes and Fragments*, ed. Richard Maurice Bucke (Folcroft, PA: Folcroft Library Editions, 1972), 57.

7. Michael Robertson, *Worshipping Walt: The Whitman Disciples* (Princeton, NJ: Princeton University Press, 2008), 5.

8. Cavell, *This New Yet Unapproachable America*, 92–93. See also Kerry C. Larson, *Whitman's Drama of Consensus* (Chicago: University of Chicago Press, 1989). Larson contends that poetry is the ground upon which such a negotiation takes place and argues that Whitman offers a different form of "transaction" than "those forms of exchange that regulate society at large" (44); Whitman "is at pains to circumvent by insisting that his verse does not favor one side of a given transaction (neither owner nor owned; creditor nor debtor), but travels between both positions so as to incarnate the dynamic of giving and receiving itself" (44–45). Whitman's text provides a structure that defers ownership, thereby positing relations without valuing one over the other. For Jay Grossman, a critical approach to either Emerson or Whitman can lead to the recovery of this oppositional space, since, as representatives of their age, these thinkers "provide sites and particularities in and through which to discover the elusive traces and wholesale recurrences–textual, political, performative, and cultural–of the nation's Founding dilemmas" (*Reconstituting the American Renaissance: Emerson, Whitman, and the Politics of Representation* [Durham, NC: Duke University Press, 2003], 8).

9. Philip Fisher, *Still the New World* (Cambridge, MA: Harvard University Press, 1999), 56. See also Alan Ackerman, *The Portable Theater: American Literature & the Nineteenth-Century Stage* (Baltimore, MD: Johns Hopkins University Press, 1999). Ackerman analyzes the dramatic, theatrical underpinnings of Whitman's endeavor and argues that Whitman's poetry integrates a social energy, vital to the experience of theater itself, so that "the often antagonistic opposition between performer and audience" transforms itself into "an electrical harmony" (82). In this space or upon this vast, "visible stage," Ackerman writes, "a great performance can transform the character of the audience, not only in the theater but also in a more lasting way" (81, 82). In witnessing drama, the members of an audience may become more than simple spectators; they may yet aspire toward a communal as well as a personal activity and thereby come to experience and participate in the drama of nationhood and identity (85–86).

10. While this chapter largely attempts to illuminate Whitman's incorporation of Emerson's metempsychotic order in the pre-Civil War editions of *Leaves of Grass*, I have used the deathbed edition (1891–92) for Whitman's poetry on the assumption that this final edition remains the fullest and most mature expression of Whitman's early vision. David Cavitch sets a sound precedent for exploring the early period in this manner, arguing that "despite his loss of fresh creativity, his years of writing increased his skill as a reader and editor of his own poems" so that the "final versions" of his poetry "are poetically superior" (*My Soul and I: The Inner Life of Walt Whitman* [Boston: Beacon Press, 1985], xv–vi).

11. Joel Myerson, ed., *Whitman in His Own Time: A Biographical Chronicle of His Life, Drawn from Recollections, Memoirs, and Interviews by Friends and Associates* (Iowa City: University of Iowa Press, 2005), 17.

12. Philip Callow, *From Noon to Starry Night: A Life of Walt Whitman* (Chicago: Ivan R. Dee, 1992), 272.

13. See Jerome Loving, *Walt Whitman: The Song of Himself* (Berkeley: University of California Press, 1999), 157.

14. Richardson, *Emerson: Mind on Fire*, 529.

15. For a concise, if hypothetical, account of Emerson's influence on Whitman beginning in 1842 to the early 1850s, see Loving, *Walt Whitman*, 156–72. See also Callow, *From Noon to Starry Night*, 84–85.

16. Loving, *Walt Whitman*, 162.

17. Walt Whitman, *Leaves of Grass and Other Writings*, ed. Michael Moon (New York: W. W. Norton, 2002), 637–38.

18. For a fuller account of these events, see Carlos Baker, *Emerson Among the Eccentrics: A Group Portrait* (New York: The Penguin Group, 1996), 368; and Kenneth Price, "Whitman on Emerson: New Light on the 1856 Open Letter," *American Literature* 56.1 (1984): 83–87.

19. Emerson's influence on, and friendship with Whitman are, of course, complex issues, which should not be minimized or reduced to simple lines of cause and effect. The 1856 edition of *Leaves of Grass* undoubtedly solidified and complicated Emerson and Whitman's relationship both publicly and privately, since Whitman included, without permission, Emerson's letter of praise in the 1856 edition. Criticism has treated this event in different ways. Jerome Loving describes how "Emerson had suddenly become mute after Whitman published his private letter of praise" and only "broke his silence in 1863" to write letters of introduction for Whitman so that he could gain employment, an effort that was unsuccessful (*Walt Whitman,*

18), and Carlos Baker recounts how Emerson's initial high praise was followed by some minor reservations which were undoubtedly bolstered by the widespread consensus around him that the overt sexuality in Whitman's poetry was profane (*Emerson Among the Eccentrics*, 367–70). The Emerson biographer, Richardson, stresses a different interpretation, asserting that Emerson never withdrew his full support of Whitman or faulted him for publishing his private correspondence; instead, Emerson worked diligently to bolster Whitman's reputation to all those he knew (*Emerson: Mind on Fire*, 526–31). There can be no dispute, however, that, from 1860 onward and especially after the Civil War, Whitman became much more ambivalent about Emerson, even going so far as to deny Emerson's influence upon him. See Walt Whitman, *Specimen Days & Collect* (New York: Dover Publications, Inc., 1995), 319–22; and Maurice O. Johnson, *Walt Whitman as a Critic of Literature* (New York: Haskell House Publishers Ltd., 1970), 62–64. This ambivalence partially transpired because of Emerson's advice to Whitman to censor much of the "sexually offending" passages of his poetry for the third edition. Michael Moon puts the matter succinctly and reveals Whitman's criticism of Emerson on this score (*Disseminating Whitman: Revision and Corporeality in Leaves of Grass* [Cambridge, MA: Harvard University Press, 1991], 139–40).

20. Michael Moon identifies Whitman's letter to Emerson as a second preface for the *Leaves of Grass* (*Leaves of Grass*, 637n1).

21. For an account of the differences between Emerson's oeuvre and Whitman's 1856 letter, particularly Whitman's foregrounding of the body, see Grossman, *Reconstituting the American Renaissance*, 106–15.

22. While Emerson certainly appreciated Whitman's poetry, Emerson was never absolutely sure how to appraise it. In relation to the 1855 *Leaves*, Emerson was actually most struck and excited by Whitman's prose preface, whereas he was more doubtful about the poetry, often seeking advice as to its power or whether it was too lurid. See Richardson, *Emerson: Mind on Fire*, 526–31.

23. Whitman, *Specimen Days & Collect*, 331.

24. Ibid., 322.

25. Chari argues that although Whitman "came unwittingly to exhibit such marked affinities with Hindu thought" (*Whitman in the Light of Vedantic Mysticism*, 9), his poetic method reveals fundamental differences from "the method of the dialectic" advocated by Fichte, Schelling, and Hegel (17), one particularly highlighted by his striking depiction of the self's journey as metempsychosis: "The self is not [. . .] the dialectical being of the Germans, torn by an inner differentiation and caught in an endless web of relationships. [. . .] It is not the 'many in one' of Hegel but an 'identity,' the soul identified with the infinite *Brahman*, the eternal self which remains immutable through the processes of metempsychosis" (81). While this is not altogether true in the sense that Whitman sees the self's development as its basic, fundamental purpose, Whitman's depiction of the self submitting itself to the series of being is undoubtedly a metempsychotic process, particularly seen in relation to Emerson's conception of this ancient Eastern and Western doctrine. While some criticism discusses metempsychosis in relation to Whitman, there has been no consistent analysis of it, especially not in terms of the Emersonian influence.

26. Theodore Parker, *Ten Sermons of Religion* (Boston: Little, Brown and Company, 1855), 144.

27. Ibid., 143.

28. Ibid., 143–44.

29. Tenney Nathanson, *Whitman's Presence* (New York: New York University Press, 1992), 31.

30. Fisher, *Still the New World*, 60.

31. Donald E. Pease, *Visionary Compacts: American Renaissance Writings in Cultural Context* (Madison: University of Wisconsin Press, 1987), 129.

32. Ibid., 149.

33. D. J. Moores, *Mystical Discourse in Wordsworth and Whitman: A Transatlantic Bridge* (Leuven, Belgium: Peters Publishers, 2006), 69.

34. See Len Gougeon, "Emerson, Whitman, and Eros," *Walt Whitman Quarterly Review* 23 (2006): 126–46. Gougeon explores the nineteenth-century construction of a "sanitized and stilted view of Emerson" (127) and its problematic influence on literary criticism. Unlike many critics who distance Whitman and his sensuality from Emerson, Gougeon moves decisively to emphasize that Emerson not only approved of Whitman's notion of the body, but pursued a very similar conception of the body's relationship to the soul: "Emerson and Whitman sought to achieve a dynamic balance between body and soul that enhanced both entities tremendously. As a result, they were able to offer a vision of unity and spontaneous spiritual and physical life to an ailing and fragmented society" (142). Whereas many critics attempt to separate Whitman's notion of the self from an ostensibly ascetic and spiritual Emerson, we can see, in this context, that Whitman's adaptation of Emerson's metempsychotic self underscores precisely this process of achieving balance between body and soul and bringing both aspects into synthesis.

35. Bloom, *Bloom's Modern Critical Views*, 238.

36. See Michael Sowder, *Whitman's Ecstatic Union: Conversion and Ideology in Leaves of Grass* (New York: Routledge, 2005). Sowder contends that although Whitman's evocation of the great American poet "often uses future tenses and the subjunctive mood," nonetheless "the predominant tense of the Preface is the present tense, a kind of proleptic present indicating that the coming poet is so imminent that future tenses are inadequate to describe him" (47).

37. See M. Wynn Thomas, *The Lunar Light of Whitman's Poetry* (Cambridge, MA: Harvard University Press, 1987). Thomas interprets Whitman's concept of the soul as the promise of such completion: "The loss of the conception of the complete human being is what Whitman vehemently charges his society with, and he exhorts it to make good that loss. The nebulous word 'soul' is invoked to communicate to others his conviction that they have allowed themselves to be devalued, silently demoralized by accepting the current market prices for their lives and by relying on the crude descriptive terms of social classification for their self-identity" (13).

38. Larson presents an alternative, yet corresponding interpretation of this process of poetic expression and democratic consensus. Larson argues that "the risks and rewards of constitution-making as they are acted out in" Whitman's writings "do not seek to master a meaning so much as to bring to pass the 'common ground' in which a meaningful exchange may take place" (*Whitman's Drama of Consensus*, xxii–xxiii). In this sense, the ground of exchange belongs to the poem itself, not so that meaning is confirmed or "safely assumed," but "scrutinized" (xxiii).

39. See James Dougherty, *Walt Whitman and the Citizen's Eye* (Baton Rouge: Louisiana State University Press, 1993). Dougherty argues that the mystery of the eyesight—its elusive double structure—operates as a shared process between poet and

reader. The "poem achieves its understanding with the reader not by naming objects but by reminding him of a familiar process" (185).

40. Alan Trachtenberg, "Whitman's Visionary Politics," in *Walt Whitman of Mickle Street: A Centennial Collection*, ed. Geoffrey M. Sill (Knoxville: University of Tennessee Press, 1994), 103.

41. Bloom, *Anxiety of Influence*, 133.

42. Ibid., 132.

43. In the first edition of *Leaves of Grass*, Whitman "offers an alternative metaphor for the status of his body, his self, 'his life,' in the text [...] 'His whole work, his life, manners, friendship, writings, all have among their leading purposes an evident purpose to stamp a new type of character, namely his own, and indelibly to fix it and publish it, not for a model but an illustration, for the present and future of American letters and American young men'" (Moon, *Disseminating Whitman*, 72). On the one hand, the text becomes a "conduit" for the "affectionate physical presence between males," which includes the "reader's body being enfolded in the text" (72–73). On the other hand, "the desire to imbue a text with full physical presence and the recognition of the impossibility of doing so [are] the generative contradiction at the heart of *Leaves of Grass*" (73).

44. The opening of Whitman's "Song of Myself" informs the reader as to what his or her own role will be in the course of the reading: "what I assume you shall assume." As Tenney Nathanson observes, "Whitman's play on 'assume' confounds intellectual and atomic priority: it is not only the poet's ideas but also his atoms that we will put on, a conflation that works to make language and self indistinguishable from the order of nature" (*Whitman's Presence*, 396). In this respect, the reader's activity is a multiplicity of activities, literal and highly figurative, that establish a metempsychotic project of taking on bodies and/or words.

45. According to Mark Bauerlein, "The attempt to be a poet and the raw materials of poetry threaten the very singularity of self-hood" so that Whitman's presence, as it were, diffuses itself both into the textual series itself and yet eludes it, a division that perception itself enacts by apprehending something both "seen and unseen" ("Reading," in *Bloom's Modern Critical Views: Walt Whitman*, updated ed., ed. Harold Bloom [New York: Chelsea House Publishers, 2006], 168, 162).

46. The 1855 preface "at first summon[s] an essentially descriptive, visualist poetry reciting the grandeur of the continent and the vitality and diversity of human life in the democracy that flourished there" (1), a visual apparatus that quickly gives way, even in signaling a restored, whole human form, to the dilemma of identity (Dougherty, *Walt Whitman and the Citizen's Eye*, 2–35).

47. George B. Hutchinson calls this a "visionary technique," which "raises the consciousness of the audience—'entrains' our participation through the rapid, dizzying catalogue—and then immerses us, once prepared, in the sort of experiences that evoke feelings of union and patriotism" (*The Ecstatic Whitman: Literary Shamanism & the Crisis of the Union* [Columbus: Ohio State University Press, 1986], 86). The "origin of this technique" he argues, "is in Whitman's journalistic glorification of the founding fathers and his approval of contemporary heroics, which he viewed in the light of revitalizing Revolutionary values" (86). Nathanson contends that "Whitman's poetry is a sustained if troubled effort to conceive of naming as an act of mastery and transformation." Whitman's lists are a "hypnotic" address that diffuses the poet's presence into language. These "catalogues typically mobilize the vocative power of the word [...],

retrieving things from the dispersed exterior space in which they have hitherto been isolated and immersing them in the fluid, somaticized realm these litanies suggest" (*Whitman's Presence*, 30).

48. Highlighting this passage from section 2 of "Song of Myself," Ackerman argues that Whitman presents himself to his readers "as a kind of challenge" emphasizing "responsibility of the individual in a collective aesthetic/political experience" (*Portable Theater*, 86).

49. See also Whitman's 1856 letter to Emerson, which explicitly describes mimesis as anathema to the health and poetic vitality of the republic. America's youth will recognize the poet who leads them away from imitation with the revitalizing power of nature: "The young men will be clear what they want, and will have it. They will follow none except him whose spirit leads them in the like spirit with themselves. Any such man will be welcome as *the flowers of May*. Others will be put out without ceremony" (1856: 213–17). As nature refurbishes itself in springtime, the approaching poet will fertilize the old institutions that they may be included in the larger arc and development of an expansive, democratic nation. And in revealing how his poet can overcome the mimetic order, Whitman puts the burden of mimesis—"all second-hand, or third, fourth, or fifth-hand"—on the hierarchical and unjust organization of society, rebuking the institutions that permit the "imitators of fashion" to flourish on the backs of others' work and invention: "How much is there anyhow, to the young men of These States, in a parcel of helpless dandies, who can neither fight, work, shoot, ride, run, command—some of them devout, some quite insane, some castrated—*all second-hand, or third, fourth, or fifth-hand*—waited upon waiters, putting not his land first, but always other lands first, talking of art, doing the most ridiculous, smirking and skipping along, continually taking off their hats—no one behaving, dressing, writing, talking, loving, out of any natural and manly tastes of his own, but each one looking cautiously to see how the rest behave, dress, write, talk, love—pressing the noses of dead books upon themselves and upon their country—favoring no poets, philosophs, literates here, but dog-like danglers at the heels of the poets [. . .]. Of course they and the likes of them can never justify the strong poems of America" (1856: 217–34). The experience of creation's mimetic burden implies, for Whitman, a social and political quandary, not merely a poetic one. America's youth must avoid reinstilling the values of feudalism whose institutions support a class of "castrated" men who can never overcome a "second-hand, or third, fourth, or fifth-hand" experience of life due to their inherited and adopted values of wealth and privilege. These men press "dead books upon themselves and their country" for their very existence underscores a mimetic crisis at odds with democracy's great project to liberate all men and women.

50. Michael West argues that Whitman's "underlying temperament of Romantic irony" makes his poetry truly original with "a unique ability to unsettle the most sophisticated reader" (*Transcendental Wordplay: America's Romantic Punsters and the Search for the Language of Nature* [Athens: Ohio University Press, 2000], 400–401). Whitman's poetry thereby underscores a process of linguistic engagement and deferral reflecting a "casual, ever-shifting, self-cancelling organization" (400). In this sense, Whitman's poetry is a conflictual record where the linguistic process at once engages and yet defers meaning. The "exaltation of process and denial of any terminus committed him to the paradoxical subversion of his own authority" (401), meaning that Whitman offers himself as the full poetic voice at once gathering and yet subverting

its own plenitude toward the future, approaching readers who will, in turn, undergo a similar affirmation and subversion.

51. Cavitch contextualizes the reader's burden in relation to the totalitarian aspect of Whitman's poetry. Whitman comes to possess a singular authority; "overmastering" his audience, he "demands that we acknowledge and yield to his external administration of our feelings and thoughts as he explicitly anticipates and defines what we must accept as our own responses formed in him" (*My Soul and I*, 45–46).

52. For many critics, Whitman's self is a divided being. See, for instance, James Miller Jr., *Leaves of Grass: America's Lyric-Epic of Self and Democracy* (New York: Twayne Publishers, 1992). Miller sees the division between soul and body in terms of sexual play, "the soul holding the body in a kind of sexual thrall, the interpenetration and interfusion suggesting the inseparability of the self's two dimensions" (11).

53. For a succinct crystallization of this divided, conflicted tension from a political, social perspective, see James M. Killingsworth, *The Growth of Leaves of Grass: The Organic Tradition in Whitman Studies* (Columbia, MO: Camden House, Inc., 1993). As he notes, "increasingly at odds with the culture's advancing division of labor and rationalization of social relations [. . . ,] Whitman appears to have felt and expressed the typical self-conflicts of this age as an alternate desire to be, on the one hand, original and different, and, on the other hand, representative and one with the common American self. Two concepts of poetic genius warred within him—the Romantic view of the genius alienated from the historical context and the older, bardic view of the genius who consummates and contains his culture and age" (10).

54. Mark Maslan, *Whitman Possessed: Poetry, Sexuality, and Popular Authority* (Baltimore, MD: Johns Hopkins University Press, 2001), 52, 54.

55. Ibid., 142–43.

56. In this early model for Greek and Judeo-Christian philosophy, Empedocles's *Purifications* proposes one of the earliest known conceptions of a metempsychotic order, which includes the concepts of both alienation and advantage. On the one hand, this order consists of the degradation of the "divine spirit" through "bloodshed," a category of which Empedocles counts himself a part ("Of this number am I too now"). The divine spirit is exiled, doomed to assume many different shapes as a punishment for his crime: "There is an oracle of Necessity, an ancient degree of the gods, eternal, sealed fast with broad oaths, that when one of the divine spirits whose portion is long life sinfully stains his own limbs with bloodshed, and following Hate has sworn a false oath—these must wander for thrice ten thousand seasons far from the company of the blessed, being born throughout the period into all kinds of mortal shapes, which exchange one hard way of life for another. For the mighty Air chases them into the Sea, and the Sea spews them forth onto the dry land, and the Earth (drives them) towards the rays of the blazing Sun; and the Sun hurls them into the eddies of the Aether. One (Element) receives them from the other, and all loathe them. Of this number am I too now, a fugitive from heaven and a wanderer, because I trusted in raging hate" (DK Frg. B 115). Thus, does the divine, fallen spirit take on various embodiments—"For by now I have been born as boy, girl, plant, bird, and dumb sea-fish" (Frg. B 117)—but spirit gradually develops itself through its embodiments toward greater consciousness: "At last they become seers, and bards, and physicians, and princes among earth-dwelling men, from which (state) they blossom forth as gods highest in honor" (Frg. B 163). See J. B. Wilbur and H. J. Allen eds., *The Worlds of the Early Greek Philosophers* (Buffalo, NY: Prometheus Books, 1979).

57. For many critics, this concept of being "in and out of the game" is a touchstone for Whitman's uneasy, unsettled dualism of identity. Cavitch interprets this passage biographically to show that the two selves in Whitman's poetry can be understood as a familial tension underscoring Whitman's "habitual pattern of relating to others while preserving vivid separateness" (*My Soul and I*, 12). In another vein, Grossman writes that "Whitman's polemic [. . .] pronounces the ambiguous status of the figure of the representative, what Whitman characterized in another context as 'both in and out of the game.'" Whitman blurs "the line between speaking *for* and speaking *with*," revealing "the central unresolved feature of American representative praxis and the virtuality at/as its core." Being both a part of the nation and yet separate from it, the settled figure of the representative begs "fundamental questions" about representative democracy: "What is the nature of political representation? Who shall speak, and for whom?" (*Reconstituting the American Renaissance*, 10–11).

58. Bromwich crystallizes the critical consensus on Whitman's avocation of a physically grounded identity: "Our usual mistake about immortality, as Whitman sees it, is to imagine our survival as the extension of a single entity. We can avoid this, he thinks, by supposing that we continue in time only as an author's words continue in the minds of his readers. [. . .] This side of Whitman's thinking seemed to D.H. Lawrence praiseworthy beyond all the rest since it released us from the tiresome superiority of the soul" ("A Simple Separate Person," 143).

59. Criticism judges Whitman's later period in very different ways. The most common understanding—one which follows Whitman's own conception of his poetic maturation—is that Whitman attempts a new, more spiritualized poetry after the Civil War. For instance, Killingsworth interprets Whitman's later poetic period as illustrating "a new effort to invigorate the body by controlling it, by spiritualizing it, by essentially denying it." Whitman thus struggles "to regain a hope of expansion. He had emerged from the quicksand years [during and after the Civil War] a very different poet, a soul poet, a poet of death and the beyond" (*Whitman's Poetry of the Body: Sexuality, Politics and the Text* [Chapel Hill: North Carolina University Press, 1989], 134). Many critics see this later period as ineffectual compared to the poetry of the first four editions of *Leaves of Grass*. As James Warren observes, the "negative view of Whitman's late poetry is pervasive," providing an extensive list of critics in this camp (*Walt Whitman's Language Experiment* [University Park: Pennsylvania State University Press, 1990], 194–95).

60. Whitman, *Specimen Days & Collect*, 68.

61. Ibid., 276.

62. Ibid., 277.

63. See Ed Folsom and Kenneth M. Price, *Re-Scripting Walt Whitman: An Introduction to His Life and Work* (Malden, England: Blackwell Publishing, 2005), 119–20.

64. See Paul Zweig, *Walt Whitman: The Making of a Poet* (New York: Basic, 1984), 324. In addition, Moon sets his analysis of the fourth edition of *Leaves of Grass* in this context: "Matters of gender and sexuality in this text are extremely highly charged, arising as they do in relation to the desire(s) of or for bodies that are no longer capable of being perceived as whole, 'healthy,' and labile" (*Disseminating Whitman*, 174–75).

65. Whitman, *Specimen Days & Collect*, 256.

66. This postwar crisis of bodily and national proportions, expressed in 1871 as "the highly artificial and materialistic bases of modern civilization" (Whitman, *Specimen Days & Collect*, 256), relates to Whitman's earlier political arguments against the

materialist greed of America's economic system, a position that led Whitman eagerly to anticipate the war and then to appreciate the bitter cost it had on the nation. See Moon, *Disseminating Whitman*, 171–72.

67. Kenneth Price observes a similar dynamic in his analysis of "Calamus" number 27, arguing that although "Whitman labels as 'dead' the past self that he 'was for years,' he is not rid of his identity, since in self-divided fashion he looks at that part of himself that he would—but cannot fully—disengage from" (*To Walt Whitman, America* [Chapel Hill: North Carolina University Press, 2004], 60).

68. Whitman, *Specimen Days & Collect*, 68.

69. The pervasive negative estimation of Whitman's later period falls decisively upon Whitman's highly spiritualized poetics. Although this elegy is often praised by critics, nonetheless, this image of the soul, apart and transcendent, presents a theme that becomes a subject of ridicule for many critics. As Thomas summarizes, "The soul [. . .] in his later poetry" is "used as part of a vapid vocabulary of spiritual transcendence" (*Lunar Light of Whitman's Poetry*, 13).

70. Whitman, *Specimen Days & Collect*, 68.

71. See Betsy Erkkila, "The Poetics of Reconstruction: Whitman the Political Poet after the Civil War," in *Leaves of Grass and Other Writings*, ed. Michael Moon (New York: W. W. Norton, 2002), 892–94.

72. See Harold Aspiz, *So Long! Walt Whitman's Poetry of Death* (Tuscaloosa: University of Alabama Press, 2004), 223.

73. Whitman, *Specimen Days & Collect*, 256.

74. Ibid., 255.

75. Ibid., 253.

76. In the later 1870s, Whitman also comes to question and criticize Emerson's influence upon America's psyche. Whitman never abandons his central support of Emerson; as Whitman told Horace Traubel in 1888, "Emerson was the whole horizon—Ralph Waldo Emerson, the gentle, noble, perfect, radiant, consolatory, Emerson" (Myerson, *Whitman in His Own Time*, 241). By this time, Whitman was even disposed to forgive Emerson his arguments for Whitman's self-censorship, telling Traubel that Emerson admitted that "a man who does not live according to his lights—who trims his sails to the current breeze is already dead, is as many times dead as he is untrue" (241). At the same time, in these later years, Emerson's spirit of enlightenment—of throwing off all the beliefs and conventions of the past and believing only in the self—now seemed an ineffectual recipe to Whitman, no longer required as a cure for the situation at hand: "[Emerson's] final influence is to make his students cease to worship anything—almost cease to believe in anything, outside of themselves. These books will fill, and well fill, certain stretches of life, certain stages of development [. . .]. But in old or nervous or solemnest or dying hours, when one needs the impalpably soothing and vitalizing influences of abysmic Nature, or its affinities in literature or human society, and the soul resents the keenest mere intellection, they will not be sought for" (*Specimen Days & Collect*, 320). One of the principal implications of this criticism is Whitman's insistence that Emerson's thought invigorates the young and mature, but does not pertain to the stage of infirmity and dying, which confronts, from 1863 onward, the entire national consciousness.

77. Whitman, *Specimen Days & Collect*, 255.

78. Ibid., 233.

79. As Louis Martz explained a generation ago, the charge against Whitman runs so: Whitman's "tendency to make abstract assertions about the future grew, until he weakened his essential poetic power, his ability to deal concretely and dynamically with the world about him" (*The Poem of the Mind: Essays on Poetry* [New York: Oxford University Press, 1966], 85).

5 / The New Poetry

1. Walt Whitman, *Leaves of Grass and Other Writings*, ed. Michael Moon (New York: W. W. Norton, 2002), Section 42, Lines 1138, 1136–hereafter, 42.113, 1136.

2. Martha Nussbaum, *Upheavals of Thought: The Intelligence of the Emotions* (Cambridge: Cambridge University Press, 2001), 656–61; also for another reading of Whitman's counter-cosmology, see Moon, *Disseminating Whitman*, 60–61.

3. Nussbaum, *Upheavals of Thought*, 658.

4. Ibid., 658.

5. D. H. Lawrence's criticism of Whitman captures some of the ambivalence that Whitman's poetry receives from modern writers and scholars who praise Whitman's avowal of the body and disdain his metaphysics of presence or his all-encompassing spiritual unity. Lawrence argues that, while the Christian impulse sought to spiritualize the human being and rid him of the body, Whitman has attempted to reverse this in a thoroughly "self-conscious" manner and achieve a "spiritual triumph" where the body makes the spirit more powerful: "Whitman enters on the last phase of spiritual triumph. He really arrives at that stage of infinity which the seers sought. By subjecting the deepest centers of the lower self, he attains the maximum consciousness in the higher self: a degree of extensive consciousness greater, perhaps, than any man in the modern world" (Whitman, *Leaves of Grass*, 825). At the same time, Lawrence criticizes the goal of Whitman's thought, for "Whitman's way to Allness [. . .] becomes a hideous tyranny once he has attained his goal of Allness. His One Identity is a prison of horror, once realized" (826).

6. Not very many critics have explored the Platonic strains in Whitman's oeuvre, especially since it has been supposed that Whitman's knowledge of the classics was quite minimal, especially in the 1840s and 1850s leading up to the first edition of *Leaves of Grass*. As a result, most criticism contextualizes Platonism in Whitman's poetry in a general way. For instance, for an interpretation of Whitman from a conventional Platonic-Romantic perspective, see Thomas who argues that Whitman incorporates the defense of poetry paradigm into his poetic method; "the prevailing mode" of Whitman's poetry thereby operates as a social service that idealizes the nation to show how "indispensable the powers of poetry after all are to the human condition" (*Lunar Light of Whitman's Poetry*, 8). "By imputing to contemporary, everyday American life a full measure of the ideal qualities he wishes it to possess, he represents it as already being the virtual embodiment of its Platonic conception of itself. This is, of course, one of the most ancient of those services the poet has rendered his community [. . .]. When, however, the term 'poetry of praise' has been applied to Whitman's work its meaning has tended to be confided to the broadly religious or spiritual realm, whereas if the social features of traditional praise-poetry were to be recalled, Whitman's achievements in this style would be much more fully appreciated. In fact, it would be useful to regard Whitman's praise of the spiritual order of the natural universe as a concealed form of inspirational

praise of the premises upon which, in his view, the particular social and political order of the United States is based" (9–10).

7. Irwin, *American Hieroglyphics*, 38.

8. Nussbaum, *Upheavals of Thought*, 660.

9. Importantly, the 1855 version of the poem even more explicitly emphasizes the divine process involved in the maturation of individual consciousness on the "apices of the stairs," for "God carried me through the lethargic mist" (1155), signaling that the God is intimately and actively involved in a maturing, evolving individuation. The very context of the poem in the relation to the process of ascent makes Whitman's later omission of this line clearly understandable, since the context already implies the divine's presence at every level of the development on being's stairway.

10. Harold Bloom, *How to Read and Why* (New York: Simon and Schuster, 2001), 92.

11. Percy Bysshe Shelley, trans., *The Symposium of Plato*, ed. David K. O'Connor (South Bend, FL: St. Augustine's Press, 2002), 208b.

12. Shelley, 208e–209a.

13. Shelley, 210d.

14. Shelley, 211b.

15. In "Love," moreover, the soul as a spark of fire falls from heaven and has to develop itself in every possible position and combination in nature, climbing through the material order until it spiritually purifies itself into a golden ray of light. But the process does not end here; the "immutable lights" (*W* 2: 110) at the end of "Love" (1841) must be swept up in a dialectical sequence that has no apparent end.

16. Again, in an 1869 speech, Emerson highlights not so much the spiritual, but the intellectual or educational aspect of this robust soul, echoing the emphasis of eighteenth- and nineteenth-century English Neoplatonism upon the apprenticeship along the Platonic ladder as a pedagogical journey, a process that powerfully strengthens the mind or intellect: "All education is to accustom him to trust himself, discriminate between his higher and lower thoughts, *exert the timid faculties until they are robust*, and thus train him to self-help, until he ceases to be an underling, a tool, and becomes a benefactor. I think wise men wish their religion to be all of this kind, teaching the agent to go alone, not to hang on the world as a pensioner, a permitted person, but an adult, self-searching soul, brave to assist or resist a world: only humble and docile before the source of the wisdom he has discovered within him" (*CW* 11; emphasis added). In this context, Emerson shows that the faculties of the "self-searching soul" are brought to robustness so as to overcome mimesis, for the ladder only mounts upward when consciousness retraces the path of genesis. At every stage of ascent, the individual must overcome the downward trajectory of objects long separated from their source. Only at the highest level—in the vision of the beautiful itself—does the individual touch upon or see true images themselves. The man of learning is no longer "an underling, a tool," but a "benefactor," truly self-reliant as "an adult, self-searching soul, brave to assist or resist a world."

17. See Floyer Sydenham, *The Banquet: A Dialogue of Plato Concerning Love, The Second Part* (London: W. Sandby, 1767), 223. "Hitherto the Aſcent to the Supreme Beauty, and the ſeveral Steps in that Aſcent, have been deſcribed at large. *Plato* is now proceeding to give a *Summary View* of thoſe Steps, by way of *Recapitulation*. But not a Word has been mentioned all along concerning a *Deſcent*. The word re-aſcending therefore in this place is very remarkable. It carries with it a Suggeſtion, that the

Human Soul had been with this Supreme Beauty before its Acquaintance with thofe lower Forms, and had defcended from Mind into Body. [...] On Purpofe therefore to prevent the Error of confounding the Human Soul with thefe Forms; and to give us to underftand, that She partakes of the Sovereign Beauty in a Manner different from Them; that Her Generation is not fimilar to Theirs, and Her Being is not, like Theirs, liable to Deftruction; but particularly with a View to what follows, concerning this very point, near the Conclufion of the Speech, and by way of Preparation to it, the *Defcent* of the Soul feems to be here fignified, and fhown by Implication, in this Mention of its *Re-afcent*."

18. Thomas Taylor and Floyer Sydenham, trans., *Plato: The Symposium* (Somerset, England: The Prometheus Trust, 2002), 210d–e.

19. Shelley, 210d.

20. Richardson, *Emerson: Mind on Fire*, 346–48.

21. Charles Taylor, *Sources of the Self: The Making of Modern Identity* (Cambridge, MA: Harvard University Press, 1989), 200.

22. In the beginning of *A Defense of Poetry* (1821, 1840), Shelley argues that the imagination is that faculty which draws together or unifies the series into an inward whole: "Man is an instrument over which a series of external and internal impressions are driven, like the alternations of an ever-changing wind over an Aeolian lyre, which move it by their motion to ever-changing melody. But there is a principle within the human being, perhaps within all sentient beings, which acts otherwise than in the lyre" (*A Defence of Poetry*, ed. Mrs. Shelley [Indianapolis, IN: The Bobbs-Merril Company, 1904], 13). Accordingly, Shelley concludes that the poetic legislator overcomes the chaos of the world: "Poetry defeats the curse which binds us to be subjected to the accident of surrounding impressions. And whether it spreads its own figured curtain, or withdraws life's dark veil from before the scene of things, it equally creates for us a being within our being. It makes us the inhabitant of a world to which the familiar world is a chaos" (42).

23. Taylor argues that the making of epiphany in modern poetry cannot be seen as a simple inheritance or rejection of the Romantic notion of self-hood, nature, and creative expression. The modern turn inward has changed; the identification of human expression with nature can no longer exist in its Romantic clarity (*Sources of the Self*, 417); rather, modern inwardness tends to focus on the human being's relationship with an artistic medium: "What underlay this separation [between Romantic and modern] was the sense that the revelatory power of the symbol depends on a break with ordinary discourse. Mallarmé speaks of the poet as 'ceding the initiative to words' and allowing the poem to be structured by their inherent, interacting forces, 'mobilized by the shock of their inequality'. [...] Here the Romantic contrast between the symbolic and the referential has intensified into the attempt to achieve epiphany by deranging reference—to give power to symbols by taking language beyond discourse. [...] What was united in the Romantics [expression and its medium] is rigorously opposed. So the principle of unity of Pound's *Cantos* is utterly different from that of Wordsworth's *Prelude*. It is no longer narrative, but the interlocking images, which unify" (426). According to Taylor, moreover, the modern rejection of Romantic epiphany lies in "a decentring of the subject" (456). Previous epiphany celebrated the creative powers of the individual, but the modernist strain, while obviously preserving this aspect in certain forms, places "the centre of interest onto language" (456).

24. Myerson, *Whitman in His Own Time*, 17.

25. Whereas Emerson's integration of Hegel remains more ambiguous, Whitman's adoption of Hegelianism is explicit, especially after the Civil War. For instance, in *Democratic Vistas*, Whitman writes about the "forms of beauty and majesty" that stand "along the great highways of time" and reckons "Kant and Hegel" the nearest to his time (*Specimen Days & Collect*, 240–41). The work of the new American poets must realize the system of Hegel, for these poets must be "possess'd of the religious fire and abandon of Isaiah" and be "consistent with the Hegelian formulas" (Whitman, *Specimen Days & Collect*, 253). But it is in Whitman's "Song of Myself" that one sees an explicit Hegelian context. In the *Phenomenology of Spirit*, Hegel describes the path that the individual pursues in the wake of World-Spirit who successively embodies and discards itself so as to attain the "goal" or "insight into what knowing is" (17). As a result, the individual's own ascendancy in Hegel is, in part, less onerous than that of the World-Spirit, "since all this has already been *implicitly* accomplished; the content is already the actuality reduced to a possibility, its immediacy overcome, and the embodied shape reduced to abbreviated, simple determinations of thought" (17). The individual thereby takes on the "enormous effort of world-history" (17) as a recollection—"the *recollected in-itself*"—and must assume the discarded shapes of World-Spirit in order to achieve the greater "insight" of the whole. Whitman follows this model with the reader and all those who come after him forever retracing the leavings of God and the creator poet. All these figures are united by their apprehension and transmigration through the historical series of being—although in Whitman the whole process is explicitly textual, for it is his poetry that outlines the sequence and bids the reader adopt it.

26. This relationship between poet and reader as constituting poetic structure is generally assumed by critics. As Larson argues, by "placing his auditors at the center stage of his verse, Whitman hopes to bring forward and actualize the movement from isolated individuality ('the simple, separate person') to affirmed unanimity ('the word Democratic, the word En-Masse' captured within the 'common ground' of the poem itself" [*Whitman's Drama of Consensus*, 6]). What I suggest, however, is that this common ground is itself a development of a double, metempsychotic order whose polarity—oscillating gravities—uncovers a methodology of reading, the structure of which is undoubtedly a metaphysics formalized as a phenomenal project, retaining its history not as settled matter, but as a structure requiring scrutiny, particularly realized in such a present framework.

27. Aspiz also describes this double movement at the close of "Song of Myself." On the one hand, "it is his body that must be abandoned to facilitate the setting forth of his spirit." On the other hand, "he bestows his spirit-self on the earth, the grass, the human heart, and the universe" (*So Long!* 75). Moreover, Aspiz sees another "major transformation" occurring in this finale. As the speaker once translated "the converging objects of the universe," now he has become "one of the translated," requiring a new subject to translate him (75).

28. Exodus 33:11; Deuteronomy 34:10.

29. "Crossing Brooklyn Ferry" is a "poem most clearly about reading," establishing "a comforting, stable identification between the way future generations [. . .] perceive the scene and the way Whitman does" (Bauerlein, "Reading," 163).

30. Michael Moon calls the concluding movement "a poetic demonstration of the power of appearances—'dumb, beautiful ministers'—to affirm the soul" (Whitman, *Leaves of Grass*, 135n1). Also, see M. Wynn Thomas, who argues that in this passage Whitman

celebrates "his newfound power to read the sign of the times, to decipher and thus uncover the secret meanings of the material, temporal order" ("Representatives and Revolutionists: The New Urban Politics Revisited," in *Whitman East & West: New Contexts for Reading Walt Whitman*, ed. Ed Folsom [Iowa City: University of Iowa Press, 2002], 151).

31. See Wilbur and Allen, *Worlds of the Early Greek Philosophers*; and Chapter 4, footnote 56.

32. Plato, *Republic* 7 518c.

33. Pease, *Visionary Compacts*, 129.

34. See James Ramey, "Intertextual Metempsychosis in *Ulysses*: Murphy, Sinbad, and the 'U.P.: up' Postcard," *James Joyce Quarterly* 45.1 (2007): 97–114. Ramey coins Joyce's process "intertextual metempsychosis" and argues that it is "intrinsic to Joyce's methodology" since the "metatextual dynamics of Ulysses [. . .] recalls the transmigration of characters from ancient to modern texts" (97).

35. As Emerson famously writes in "Self-Reliance" (1841), "Trust thyself: every heart vibrates to that iron string."

36. See Martin Halliwell, "American Romanticism: Approaches and Interpretations," in *Encyclopedia of the Romantic Era: 1760–1850*, ed. Christopher John Murray (New York: Routledge, 2003), 17.

37. See Robert G. Cook, "Emerson's 'Self-Reliance,' Sweeney, and Prufrock." *American Literature* 42.2 (1970): 222.

38. Charles E. Mitchell, *Individualism and its Discontents: Appropriations of Emerson, 1880–1950* (Amherst: University of Massachusetts Press, 1997), 7.

39. Cook, "Emerson's 'Self-Reliance,' Sweeney, and Prufrock," 221–26.

40. T. S. Eliot, *Collected Poems: 1909–1962* (New York: Harcourt Brace & Company, 1968), 34.

41. T. S. Eliot, *Selected Essays: 1917–1932* (New York: Harcourt Brace & Company, 1932), 9.

42. Eliot, *Collected Poems 1909–1962*, 24–25.

43. Ibid., 24–25.

44. Ibid., 25.

45. Ibid., 23, 24.

46. Ibid., 189.

47. Ibid.

48. Ibid.

49. Ibid., 190.

50. Ibid.

51. Ibid.

52. Alan Williamson, "Forms of Simultaneity in The Waste Land and Burnt Norton," in *T. S. Eliot: The Modernist in History*, ed. Ronald Bush (Cambridge: Cambridge University Press, 1991), 162.

53. Plotinus, *Ennead* III, 8, 11.

54. Böhme, *Forty Questions of the Soul*, 91.

55. Ibid., 190.

56. Ibid., 192.

57. Ibid., 191.

58. Ibid., 193, 195.

59. See Jewel Spears Brooker, *Mastery and Escape: T.S. Eliot and the Dialectic of Modernism* (Amherst: University of Massachusetts Press, 1994), 3.

60. Bloom, *Walt Whitman: Bloom's Modern Critical Views*, 2.

61. Helen Hennessy Vendler, *On Extended Wings: Wallace Stevens' Longer Poems* (Cambridge, MA: Harvard University Press, 1969), 47. Vendler makes her assessment in relation to Randall Jarrell's estimation of Steven's poetry; see, for instance, Charles Doyle, ed., *Wallace Stevens: The Critical Heritage* (New York: Routledge, 1997), 328–39.

62. Levin, *Poetics of Transition*, 182.

63. David R. Jarraway sees Stevens's poetry as an inquiry that makes headway "through a constant stripping away of different versions of reality." Indeed, "by moving out from under the finite paradigms of presence in classicism and romanticism, Stevens's modernism offers us their opposite. His poetry thus becomes a model of infinite absence, hence a rhetoric of limitless expressiveness." See Jarraway, "Stevens and Belief," *The Cambridge Companion to Wallace Stevens*, ed. John N. Serio (Cambridge: Cambridge University Press, 2007), 200.

64. Eleanor Cook, "Wallace Stevens: The Comedian as the Letter C," *American Literature* 49.2 (1977): 192.

65. Harold Bloom, *Wallace Stevens: The Poems of Our Climate* (Ithaca, NY: Cornell University Press, 1980), 70.

66. Vendler, *On Extended Wings*, 41.

67. Wallace Stevens, *The Collected Poems of Wallace Stevens* (New York: Vintage Books, 1990), 29.

68. Ibid., 30.

69. Ibid., 37.

70. Ibid., 397.

71. Ibid., 397, 407.

72. Ibid., 445.

73. Ibid., 423.

74. Ibid., 423–24; emphasis added.

75. Ibid., 424.

76. Ibid.

77. Taylor, *Sources of the Self*, 426.

78. Wallace Stevens, *The Palm at the End of the Mind*, ed. Holly Stevens (New York: Vintage Books, 1990), 398.

79. Whitman, *Specimen Days & Collect*, 233.

Conclusion

1. "What is urgent for Walt is the *crossing*, Emerson's metaphor for darting to a new aim" (Bloom, *Walt Whitman*, 238).

2. See Levin, *Poetics of Transition*, xii; see also pages 45–90.

3. Robert Montgomery Bird, *Sheppard Lee, Written by Himself*, intro. by Christopher Looby (New York: New York Review Books, 2008), xvi.

4. Ibid., xxxviii.

5. Ibid., 7.

6. Fisher, *Still the New World*, 60.

7. Friedrich Nietzsche, *The Birth of Tragedy: Out of the Spirit of Music*, trans. Shaun Whiteside and ed. Michael Tanner (New York: Penguin Books, 2003), 51.

8. Ibid., 52–53.

9. Bloom, *Anxiety of Influence*, 117.

10. Ibid., 116–17.

11. Ibid., 117–18, 119.

12. Ibid., 132.

13. Roland Barthes, *Image—Music—Text*, trans. Stephen Heath (New York: Hill & Wang, 1978), 148.

14. Roland Barthes, *The Pleasure of the Text*, trans. Richard Miller (New York: Hill & Wang, 1975), 27.

15. Roland Barthes, *Sade, Fourier, Loyola*, trans. Richard Miller (Berkeley: University of California Press, 1976), 7–8.

16. Ibid., 8–9.

Bibliography

Abrams, M. K. *The Mirror and the Lamp: Romantic Theory and the Critical Tradition.* Oxford: Oxford University Press, 1971.

Ackerman, Alan. *The Portable Theater: American Literature & the Nineteenth-Century Stage.* Baltimore, MD: Johns Hopkins University Press, 1999.

Alcott, Amos Bronson. *Table-Talk.* Boston: Roberts Brothers, 1877.

Aspiz, Harold. *So Long! Walt Whitman's Poetry of Death.* Tuscaloosa: University of Alabama Press, 2004.

———. *Walt Whitman and the Body Beautiful.* Urbana: Illinois University Press, 1980.

Baker, Carlos. *Emerson Among the Eccentrics: A Group Portrait.* Introduction and epilogue by James R. Mellow. New York: The Penguin Group, 1996.

Barthes, Roland. *Image—Music—Text.* Trans. Stephen Heath. New York: Hill & Wang, 1978.

———. *The Pleasure of the Text.* Trans. Richard Miller. New York: Hill & Wang, 1975.

———. *Sade, Fourier, Loyola.* Trans. Richard Miller. Berkeley: University of California Press, 1976.

Bartsch, Shadi. *The Mirror of the Self: Sexuality, Self-Knowledge, and the Gaze in the Early Roman Empire.* Chicago: University of Chicago Press, 2006.

Bates, David William. *Enlightenment Aberrations: Error and Revolution in France.* Ithaca, NY: Cornell University Press, 2002.

Bates, Stanley. "The Mind's Horizon." In *Beyond Representation: Philosophy and Poetic Imagination.* Ed. Richard Thomas Eldridge. Cambridge: Cambridge University Press, 1996.

Bauerlein, Mark. "Reading." In *Bloom's Modern Critical Views: Walt Whitman,* updated ed. Ed. Harold Bloom. New York: Chelsea House Publishers, 2006.

Beach, Joseph Warren. "Emerson and Evolution." *University of Toronto Quarterly* 3 (1934): 474–97.

Bhagavad Gītā. Translated with an introduction by Juan Mascaro. New York: Penguin Books, 1962.

Bird, Robert Montgomery. *Sheppard Lee, Written by Himself.* Introduction by Christopher Looby. New York: New York Review Books, 2008.

Bishop, Jonathan. *Emerson on the Soul.* Cambridge, MA: Harvard University Press, 1964.

Bishop, Paul. *Analytical Psychology and German Classical Aesthetics: Goethe, Schiller and Jung.* New York: Routledge, 2009.

Bloom, Harold. *The Anxiety of Influence: A Theory of Poetry.* 2d ed. Oxford: Oxford University Press, 1997.

———, ed. *Ralph Waldo Emerson: Bloom's Modern Critical Views.* Updated ed. New York: Chelsea House Publishers, 2007.

———. *Wallace Stevens: The Poems of Our Climate.* Ithaca, NY: Cornell University Press, 1980.

———, ed. *Walt Whitman: Bloom's Modern Critical Views.* Updated ed. New York: Chelsea House Publishers, 2006.

———. *Where Shall Wisdom Be Found?* New York: Riverhead Books, 2004.

———. "Whitman's Image of Voice: To the Tally of My Soul." In *Agon: Towards a Theory of Revisionism.* Oxford: University Press, 1982.

Böhme, Jacob. *Forty Questions of the Soul.* Translated by John Sparrow. Whitefish, MT: Kessinger Publishing, 1992.

———. *The Signature of All Things.* London: J. M. Dent and Sons, 1912.

Böhme, Jacob, and Meister Eckhart. *Essential Writings of Christian Mysticism: Medieval Mystic Paths to God.* St. Petersburg, FL: Red and Black Publishers, 2010.

Brodwin, Stanley. "Emerson's Version of Plotinus: The Flight to Beauty." *Journal of the History of Ideas* 35.3 (1974): 465–83.

Bromwich David. "A Simple Separate Person." In *Bloom's Modern Critical Views: Walt Whitman,* ed. Harold Bloom. New York: Chelsea House Publishers, 2006.

Brooker, Jewel Spears. *Mastery and Escape: T.S. Eliot and the Dialectic of Modernism.* Amherst: University of Massachusetts Press, 1994.

Brown, Lee Rust. *The Emerson Museum: Practical Romanticism and the Pursuit of the Whole.* Cambridge, MA: Harvard University Press, 1997.

Buell, Lawrence. *Emerson.* Cambridge, MA: The Belknap Press of Harvard University Press, 2003.

———. "The Emerson Industry in the 1980's: A Survey of Trends and Achievements." *ESQ* 30.2 (1984): 117–36.

Burwick, Frederick. *The Damnation of Newton: Goethe's Color Theory and Romantic Perception.* New York: Walter de Gruyter, 1986.

Bussanich, J. *The One and its Relation to Intellect in Plotinus.* Leiden, Netherlands: Brill, 1988.

Callow, Philip. *From Noon to Starry Night: A Life of Walt Whitman*. Chicago: Ivan R. Dee, 1992.

Cameron, Sharon. *Impersonality: Seven Essays*. Chicago: University of Chicago Press, 2007.

———. "The Way of Life by Abandonment: Emerson's Impersonal." In *Bloom's Modern Critical Views: Ralph Waldo Emerson*, ed. Harold Bloom. New York: Chelsea House Publishers, 2007.

Carton, Evan. *The Rhetoric of American Romance: Dialectic and Identity in Emerson, Dickinson, Poe, and Hawthorne*. Baltimore, MD: Johns Hopkins University Press, 1985.

Cavell, Stanley. *Conditions Handsome and Unhandsome: The Constitution of Emersonian Perfectionism*. Chicago: University of Chicago Press, 1990.

———. "Emerson's Constitutional Amending: Reading 'Fate.'" 2003. In *Bloom's Modern Critical Views: Ralph Waldo Emerson*. Updated ed. New York: Infobase Publishing, 2007.

———. *Emerson's Transcendental Etudes*. Ed. David Justin Hodge. Stanford: Stanford University Press, 2003.

———. *This New Yet Unapproachable America*. Albuquerque, NM: Living Batch Press, 1989.

Cavitch, David. *My Soul and I: The Inner Life of Walt Whitman*. Boston: Beacon Press, 1985.

Chai, Leon. *The Romantic Foundations of the American Renaissance*. Ithaca, NY: Cornell University Press, 1987.

Chari, V. K. *Whitman in the Light of Vedantic Mysticism*. Lincoln: University of Nebraska Press, 1964.

Clarke, James Freeman. *Ten Great Religions Part II: A Comparison of All Religions*. Boston: Houghton, Mifflin and Company, 1895.

Cook, Eleanor. "Wallace Stevens: The Comedian as the Letter C." *American Literature* 49.2 (1977): 192–205.

Cook, Robert G. "Emerson's 'Self-Reliance,' Sweeney, and Prufrock." *American Literature* 42.2 (1970): 221–26.

Corrigan, Kevin. *Reading Plotinus: A Practical Introduction to Neoplatonism*. West Lafayette, IN: Purdue University Press, 2005.

Corrigan, Kevin, and John D. Turner. *Platonisms: Ancient, Modern, and Postmodern*. Leiden, Netherlands: Brill, 2007.

Cousin, Victor. *Course of the History of Modern Philosophy*. Translated by O. W. Wight. New York: D. Appleton & Company, 1872.

———. *Lectures on the True, the Beautiful and the Good*. Translated by Orlando Williams. New York: D. Appleton & Company, 1870.

Crary, Jonathan. *Suspensions of Perception: Attention, Spectacle, and Modern Culture*. Cambridge, MA: MIT Press, 2001.

———. *Techniques of the Observer: On Vision and Modernity in the Nineteenth Century*. Cambridge, MA: MIT Press, 1990.

Desmond, William. *Beyond Hegel and Dialectic: Speculation, Cult and Comedy.* Albany: State University of New York Press, 1992.

Dickinson, Emily. *The Complete Poems of Emily Dickinson.* Edited by Thomas H. Johnson. Boston: Back Bay Books, 1961.

Diels, H., and W. Kranz. *Die Fragmente Der Vorsokratiker,* 6th ed., 3 volumes. Dublin and Zurich: Weidmann, 1951–52.

Dougherty, James. *Walt Whitman and the Citizen's Eye.* Baton Rouge: Louisiana State University Press, 1993.

Doyle, Charles, ed. *Wallace Stevens: The Critical Heritage.* New York: Routledge, 1997.

Eliot, T. S. *Collected Poems: 1909–1962.* New York: Harcourt Brace & Company, 1968.

———. *Selected Essays: 1917–1932.* New York: Harcourt Brace & Company, 1932.

Emerson, Ralph Waldo. *Collected Poems and Translations.* Ed. Harold Bloom and Paul Kane. New York: Library of America, 1994.

———. *The Collected Works of Ralph Waldo Emerson.* 6 volumes. Ed. Robert E. Spiller, Alfred R. Ferguson, Joseph Slater, Douglas Emory Wilson, Jean Ferguson Carr, Wallace E. Williams, Philip Nicoloff, Robert E. Burkholder, and Barbara L. Packer. Cambridge, MA: Harvard University Press, 1971–2003.

———. *The Early Lectures of Ralph Waldo Emerson.* 3 volumes. Ed. Stephen E. Whicher, Robert E. Spiller, and Wallace E. Williams. Cambridge, MA: Harvard University Press, 1959–72.

———. *The Journals and Miscellaneous Notebooks of Ralph Waldo Emerson.* 16 volumes. Ed. William H. Gilman and Ralph H. Orth et al. Cambridge, MA: Harvard University Press, 1960–82.

———. *The Later Lectures of Ralph Waldo Emerson.* 2 volumes. Ed. Ronald A. Bosco and Joel Myerson. Athens: University of Georgia Press, 2001.

———. *The Selected Letters of Ralph Waldo Emerson.* Ed. Joel Myerson. New York: Columbia University Press, 1997.

Emerson, Edward, ed. *The Complete Works of Ralph Waldo Emerson.* Volume 9. Boston and New York: Houghton, Mifflin and Company/The Riverside Press, 1904.

Emilsson, E. K. *Plotinus on Sense-Perception: A Philosophical Study.* Cambridge: Cambridge University Press, 1988.

Erkkila, Betsy. "The Poetics of Reconstruction: Whitman the Political Poet after the Civil War." *Leaves of Grass and Other Writings.* Ed. Michael Moon. New York: W. W. Norton, 2002.

———. *Whitman the Political Poet.* New York: Oxford University Press, 1989.

Field, Peter S. *Ralph Waldo Emerson: The Making of a Democratic Intellectual.* Lanham, MD: Rowman & Littlefield Publishers, Inc., 2002.

Field, Susan L. *The Romance of Desire: Emerson's Commitment to Incompletion.* Madison, WI: Fairleigh Dickinson University Press, 1997.

Fisher, Philip. *Still the New World: American Literature in a Culture of Creative Destruction.* Cambridge, MA: Harvard University Press, 1999.

Folsom, Ed, and Kenneth M. Price. *Re-Scripting Walt Whitman: An Introduction to His Life and Work*. Malden, England: Blackwell Publishing, 2005.

Foucault, Michel. *The Order of Things: An Archaeology of the Human Sciences*. New York: Vintage Books, 1973.

Fromm, Harold. "Overcoming the Oversoul: Emerson's Evolutionary Existentialism." *The Hudson Review* 57.1 (2004): 71–95.

Gadamer, Hans-Georg. *Hegel's Dialectic: Five Hermeneutical Studies*. Translated by P. Christopher Smith. New Haven, CT: Yale University Press, 1976.

———. "Man and Language." In *Philosophical Hermeneutics*. Translated and edited by David E. Linge. Berkeley: University of California Press, 1977.

———. *Truth and Method*. New York: The Seabury Press, 1975.

George, Emery Edward. *Holderlin and the Golden Chain of Homer: Including an Unknown Source*. Lewiston, NY: Edwin Mellen Press Ltd., 1992.

Goethe, Johann Wolfgang von. *Theory of Colours*. Translated by Charles Lock Eastlake. Cambridge, MA: MIT Press, 1970.

Goodman, Russell B. "East-West Philosophy in Nineteenth-Century America: Emerson and Hinduism." *Journal of the History of Ideas* 51.4 (1990): 625–45.

Gougeon, Len. *Emerson & Eros: The Making of a Cultural Hero*. Albany: State University of New York Press, 2007.

———. "Emerson, Whitman, and Eros." *Walt Whitman Quarterly Review* 23 (2006): 126–46.

Grant, Charles. *A Poem on the Restoration of Learning in the East*. Salem, MA: Cushing & Appleton, 1807.

Grossman, Jay. *Reconstituting the American Renaissance: Emerson, Whitman, and the Politics of Representation*. Durham, NC: Duke University Press, 2003.

Guthrie, James R. *Above Time: Emerson's and Thoreau's Temporal Revolutions*. Columbia: University of Missouri Press, 2001.

Guthrie, Kenneth Sylvan, trans., and David R. Fideler, ed. *The Pythagorean Sourcebook and Library: An Anthology of Ancient Writings Which Relate to Pythagoras and Pythagorean Philosophy*. Grand Rapids, MI: Phanes Press, 1987.

Hadot, Pierre. *Plotinus, or The Simplicity of Vision*. Translated by Michael Chase. Chicago: University of Chicago Press, 1993.

———. *The Veil of Isis: An Essay on the History of the Idea of Nature*. Translated by Michael Chase. Cambridge, MA: The Belknap Press of Harvard University Press, 2006.

Halliwell, Martin. "American Romanticism: Approaches and Interpretations." In *Encyclopedia of the Romantic Era: 1760–1850*. Ed. Christopher John Murray. New York: Routledge, 2003.

Harrison, John S. *The Teachers of Emerson*. New York: Sturgis and Walton Company, 1910.

Hegel, G. W. F. *Phenomenology of Spirit*. Translated by A. V. Miller with analysis by J. N. Findlay. Oxford: Oxford University Press, 1977.

———. *The Philosophy of History*. Translated by J. Sibree. Mineola: Dover Publications, Inc., 2004.

———. *Science of Logic.* Translated by A.V. Miller with analysis by J. N. Findlay. Atlantic Highlands, NJ: Humanities Press International, Inc., 1990.

Hensel, Herbert. "Goethe, Science, and Sensory Experience." In *Goethe's Way of Science: A Phenomenology of Nature,* ed. David Seamon and Arthur Zajonc, pp. 71–82. Albany: State University of New York Press, 1998.

Hodder, Alan D. *Emerson's Rhetoric of Revelation: Nature, the Reader, and the Apocalypse Within.* University Park: Pennsylvania State University Press, 1989.

Hodge, David Justin. *On Emerson.* Wadsworth, England: Thomson Learning, Inc., 2003.

Hopkins, Vivian C. "Emerson and Cudworth: Plastic Nature and Transcendental Art." *American Literature* 23.1 (1951): 80–98.

———. *Spires of Form: A Study of Emerson's Aesthetic Theory.* Cambridge, MA: Harvard University Press, 1951.

Horowitz, Mitch. *Occult America: White House Séances, Ouija Circles, Masons, and the Secret Mystic History of Our Nation.* New York: Bantam Books Trade Paperbacks, 2009.

Houlgate, Stephen. *The Opening of Hegel's Logic: From Being to Infinity.* West Lafayette, IN: Purdue University Press, 2006.

Huffman, Carl. "Pythagoreanism." *Stanford Encyclopedia of Philosophy.* Ed. Edward N. Zalta. March 29, 2006, last modified June 14, 2010, http://plato. stanford.edu/archives/sum2010/entries/pythagoreanism/.

Hutchinson, George B. *The Ecstatic Whitman: Literary Shamanism & the Crisis of the Union.* Columbus: Ohio State University Press, 1986.

Iamblichus. *Life of Pythagoras.* Translated by Thomas Taylor. Rochester, VT: Inner Traditions International, Ltd., 1986.

Irving, Washington. *The Legend of Sleepy Hollow and Other Stories.* Introduction and notes by William L. Hedges. New York: Penguin Books, 1999.

Irwin, John T. *American Hieroglyphics: The Symbol of the Egyptian Hieroglyphics in the American Renaissance.* New Haven, CT: Yale University Press, 1980.

Jacobson, David. *Emerson's Pragmatic Vision: The Dance of the Eye.* University Park: Pennsylvania State University Press, 1993.

Jaeger, Werner Wilhelm. *Paideia: The Ideals of Greek Culture.* Oxford: Oxford University Press, 1965.

Jarraway, David R. "Stevens and Belief." In *The Cambridge Companion to Wallace Stevens,* ed. John N. Serio, pp. 193–206. Cambridge: Cambridge University Press, 2007.

Johnson, Maurice O. *Walt Whitman as a Critic of Literature.* New York: Haskell House Publishers Ltd., 1970.

Kainz, Howard P. *Hegel's Phenomenology, Part I: Analysis and Commentary.* Tuscaloosa: University of Alabama Press, 1976.

Kant, Immanuel. *Critique of Pure Reason* (Unified ed.). Translated by Werner S.

Pluhar and introduction by Patricia Kitcher. Indianapolis, IN: Hackett Publishing Company, Inc., 1996.

Kateb, George. *Emerson and Self-Reliance*. Totowa, NJ: Rowman & Littlefield, 2002.

Keane, Patrick J. *Emerson, Romanticism, and Intuitive Reason: The Transatlantic "Light of All Our Day."* Columbia: University of Missouri Press, 2005.

Killingsworth, M. Jimmie. *The Growth of Leaves of Grass: The Organic Tradition in Whitman Studies*. Columbia, MO: Camden House, INC., 1993.

———. *Whitman's Poetry of the Body: Sexuality, Politics and the Text*. Chapel Hill: University of North Carolina Press, 1989.

Kirk, G. S., and J. E. Raven. *The Pre-Socratic Philosophers*. Cambridge: Cambridge University Press, 1966.

Koyre, Alexandre. *From the Closed World to the Infinite Universe*. Baltimore, MD: John Hopkins University Press, 1968.

Kuebrich, David. *Minor Prophecy: Walt Whitman's New American Religion*. Indianapolis: University of Indiana Press, 1989.

Larson, Kerry C. *Whitman's Drama of Consensus*. Chicago: University of Chicago Press, 1989.

Lauxtermann, P. F. H. "Hegel and Schopenhauer as Partisans of Goethe's Theory of Color." *Journal of the History of Ideas* 51.4 (1990): 599–624.

Levin, Jonathan. *The Poetics of Transition: Emerson, Pragmatism & American Literary Modernism*. Durham, NC: Duke University Press, 1999.

Levinas, Emmanuel. *Otherwise than Being or Beyond Essence*. Translated by Alphonso Lingis. Pittsburgh, PA: Duquesne University Press, 1998.

Lewis, R. W. B. "Walt Whitman: Always Coming Out and Coming Out." In *Bloom's Modern Critical Views: Walt Whitman*, ed. Harold Bloom. New York: Chelsea House Publishers, 2006.

Lopez, Michael. "De-Transcendentalizing Emerson." *ESQ* 34.1–2 (1988): 77–139.

———. *Emerson and Power: Creative Antagonism in the Nineteenth Century*. DeKalb: Northern Illinois University Press, 1996.

Lovejoy, Arthur O. *The Great Chain of Being: A Study in the History of an Idea*. Cambridge, MA: Harvard University Press, 1936.

Loving, Jerome. *Walt Whitman: The Song of Himself*. Berkeley: University of California Press, 1999.

Lucretius. *On the Nature of Things*. Translated with introduction and notes by Martin Ferguson Smith. Indianapolis, IN: Hackett Publishing Company, Inc., 2001.

MacGregor, Geddes. *Reincarnation in Christianity: A New Vision of the Role of Rebirth in Christian Thought*. Wheaton, PA: Quest Books, 1978.

Mackenna, Stephen. *The Essence of Plotinus: Extracts from the Six Enneads and Porphyry's Life of Plotinus*. New York: Oxford University Press, 1948.

Martz, Louis L. *The Poem of the Mind: Essays on Poetry*. New York: Oxford University Press, 1966.

Maslan, Mark. *Whitman Possessed: Poetry, Sexuality, and Popular Authority.* Baltimore, MD: Johns Hopkins University Press, 2001.

Matthiessen, F. O. *American Renaissance: Art and Expression in the Age of Emerson and Whitman.* London: Oxford University Press, 1941.

McMillin, T. S. *Our Preposterous Use of Literature: Emerson and the Nature of Reading.* Urbana and Chicago: University of Illinois Press, 2000.

Meinecke, Friedrich. *Historicism: The Rise of a New Historical Outlook.* New York: Routledge, 1972.

Menand, Louis. *The Metaphysical Club: The Story of Ideas in America.* New York: Farrar, Straus and Giroux, 2001.

Miller, James E., Jr. *Leaves of Grass: America's Lyric-Epic of Self and Democracy.* New York: Twayne Publishers, 1992.

Miller, Perry, ed. *The Transcendentalists: An Anthology.* Cambridge, MA: Harvard University Press, 2001.

Milton, John. *Paradise Lost.* Oxford: Oxford University Press, 2008.

Mitchell, Charles E. *Individualism and its Discontents: Appropriations of Emerson, 1880–1950.* Amherst: University of Massachusetts Press, 1997.

Modiano, Raimonda. *Coleridge and the Concept of Nature.* London: The MacMillan Press Ltd., 1985.

Moon, Michael. *Disseminating Whitman: Revision and Corporeality in Leaves of Grass.* Cambridge, MA: Harvard University Press, 1991.

Moores, D. J. *Mystical Discourse in Wordsworth and Whitman: A Transatlantic Bridge.* Leuven, Belgium: Peters Publishers, 2006.

Myerson, Joel. Ed. *Whitman in His Own Time: A Biographical Chronicle of His Life, Drawn from Recollections, Memoirs, and Interviews by Friends and Associates.* Iowa City: University of Iowa Press, 2005.

Nathanson, Tenney. *Whitman's Presence: Body, Voice, and Writing in Leaves of Grass.* New York: New University Press, 1992.

Neufeldt, Leonard. *The House of Emerson.* Lincoln: University of Nebraska Press, 1982.

Newfield, Christopher. *The Emerson Effect: Individualism and Submission in America.* Chicago: University of Chicago Press, 1996.

Nietzsche, Friedrich. *The Birth of Tragedy: Out of the Spirit of Music.* Translated by Shaun Whiteside, and edited by Michael Tanner. New York: Penguin Books, 2003.

Norton, Robert E. *The Beautiful Soul: Aesthetic Morality in the Eighteenth Century.* Ithaca, NY: Cornell University Press, 1995.

Nussbaum, Martha. *Upheavals of Thought: The Intelligence of the Emotions.* Cambridge: Cambridge University Press, 2001.

Ovid. *Metamorphoses.* Translated by A. D. Melville, with introduction and notes by E. J. Kennedy. Oxford: Oxford University Press, 1998.

Packer, Barbara L. "The Curse of Kehama." 1982. In *Bloom's Modern Critical Views: Ralph Waldo Emerson,* updated ed. New York: Infobase Publishing, 2007.

———. *Emerson's Fall: A New Interpretation of the Major Essays.* New York: Continuum International Publishing Group, 1982.

———. "The Instructed Eye: Emerson's Cosmogony in 'Prospects'." In *Emerson's Nature: Origin, Growth, Meaning,* 2d ed., ed. Merton M. Sealts Jr. and Alfred R. Ferguson. Carbondale: Southern Illinois University Press, 1979.

———. *The Transcendentalists.* Athens: University of Georgia Press, 2007.

Parker, Theodore. *Ten Sermons of Religion.* 2d ed. Boston: Little, Brown and Company, 1855.

Paul, Sherman. *Emerson's Angle of Vision: Man and Nature in American Experience.* Cambridge, MA: Harvard University Press, 1965.

Pease, Donald E. *Visionary Compacts: American Renaissance Writings in Cultural Context.* Madison: University of Wisconsin Press, 1987.

Pensky, Max. *Melancholy Dialectics: Walter Benjamin and the Play of Mourning.* Amherst: University of Massachusetts Press, 1993.

Plato. *The Collected Works of Plato.* Ed. Edith Hamilton and Huntington Cairns. New York: Pantheon Books, 1966.

Plotinus. *The Enneads,* 7 volumes. Translated by A. H. Armstrong. Cambridge, MA: Loeb Classical Library, 1966–88.

Porter, David. *Emerson and Literary Change.* Cambridge, MA: Harvard University Press, 1978.

Price, Kenneth M. *To Walt Whitman, America.* Chapel Hill: University of North Carolina Press, 2004.

———. "Whitman on Emerson: New Light on the 1856 Open Letter." *American Literature* 56.1 (1984): 83–87.

Proclus. *The Elements of Theology,* 2d ed., edited and translated by E. R. Dodds. Oxford: Clarendon Press, 1963.

Quinney, Laura. *William Blake on Self and Soul.* Cambridge, MA: Harvard University Press, 2009.

Rajasekharaiah, T. R. *The Roots of Whitman's Grass.* Madison, NJ: Fairleigh Dickinson University Press, 1970.

Ramey, James. "Intertextual Metempsychosis in *Ulysses*: Murphy, Sinbad, and the 'U.P.: up' Postcard." *James Joyce Quarterly* 45.1 (2007): 97–114.

Rautenfeld, Hans von. "Thinking for Thousands: Emerson's Theory of Political Representation in the Public Sphere." *American Journal of Political Science* 49.1 (2005): 184–97.

Richardson Jr., Robert. *Emerson: The Mind on Fire.* Berkeley: University of California Press, 1995.

Riedweg, Christoph. *Pythagoras: His Life, Teaching, and Influence.* Translated by Steven Rendall. Ithaca, NY: Cornell University Press, 2005.

Roberts, Julian. *German Philosophy: An Introduction.* Atlantic Highlands, NJ: Humanities Press International, Inc., 1988.

Robertson, Michael. *Worshipping Walt: The Whitman Disciples.* Princeton, NJ: Princeton University Press, 2008.

Robinson, David. *Apostle of Culture: Emerson as Preacher and Lecturer.* Philadelphia: University of Philadelphia Press, 1982.

———. *Emerson and the Conduct of Life: Pragmatism and Ethical Purpose in the Later Work.* Cambridge: Cambridge University Press, 1993.

Rossi, Paola. *The Birth of Modern Science.* Translated by Cynthia De Nardi Ipsen. Malden, England: Blackwell Publishers Ltd., 2001.

Runes, Dagobert D., ed. *The Dictionary of Philosophy.* New York: Kessinger Publishing, 2006.

Sacks, Kenneth S. *Understanding Emerson: "The America Scholar" and his Struggle for Self-Reliance.* Princeton, NJ: Princeton University Press, 2003.

Scheick, William J. *The Slender Human Word: Emerson's Artistry in Prose.* Knoxville: University of Tennessee Press, 1978.

Schelling, Friedrich Wilhelm Joseph Von. *Ages of the World.* Translated by Jason M. Wirth. Albany: State University of New York Press, 2000.

Schirmeister, Pamela. *Less Legible Meanings: Between Poetry and Philosophy in the Work of Emerson.* Stanford: Stanford University Press, 1999.

Seamon, David. "Goethe, Nature and Phenomenology: An Introduction." In *Goethe's Way of Science: A Phenomenology of Nature*, ed. David Seamon and Arthur Zajonc, pp. 1–14. Albany: State University of New York Press, 1998.

Sepper, Dennis L. *Goethe Contra Newton: Polemics and the Project for a New Science of Color.* Cambridge: Cambridge University Press, 1988.

Shaw, Gregory. *Theurgy and the Soul: The Neoplatonism of Iamblichus.* University Park: Pennsylvania State University Press, 1995.

Shelley, Percy Bysshe. *A Defence of Poetry.* Ed. Mrs. Shelley. Indianapolis, IN: The Bobbs-Merril Company, 1904.

———, trans. *The Symposium of Plato.* Ed. David K. O'Connor. South Bend, IN: St. Augustine's Press, 2002.

Singh, Nagendra Kr. *Encyclopedia of Hinduism.* New Delhi, India: Anmol Publications PVT. LTD., 1997.

Siorvanes, Lucas. *Proclus: Neo-Platonic Philosophy and Science.* New Haven, CT: Yale University Press, 1996.

Smith, David L., "The Open Secret of Ralph Waldo Emerson." *The Journal of Religion* 70.1 (1990): 19–35.

Smith, John. *Select Discourses.* London: Rivingtons and Cochran, 1821.

Solomon, Robert C., and Kathleen M. Higgins, eds. *The Age of German Idealism.* London: Routledge, 1993.

———. *Continental Philosophy Since 1750: The Rise and Fall of the Self.* Oxford: Oxford University Press, 1988.

———. *From Hegel to Existentialism.* New York: Oxford University Press, 1987.

Sowder, Michael. *Whitman's Ecstatic Union: Conversion and Ideology in Leaves of Grass.* New York: Routledge, 2005.

Stauch, Carl F. "Emerson's Sacred Science." *PMLA* 73.3 (1958): 237–50.

Stein, William Bysshe. *Two Brahman Sources of Emerson and Thoreau.* Gainesville, FL: Scholars' Facsimiles and Reprints, 1967.

Stevens, Wallace. *The Collected Poems.* New York: Vintage Books, 1990.

———. *The Palm at the End of the Mind.* Ed. Holly Stevens. New York: Vintage Books, 1990.

Sydenham, Floyer, trans. *The Banquet, A Dialogue of Plato Concerning Love, The Second Part.* London: W. Sandby, 1767.

Synnestvedt, Sig, ed. *The Essential Swedenborg: Basic Religious Teachings of Emanuel Swedenborg.* New York: Swedenborg Foundation Inc., 1981.

Taylor, Bayard. *The Poetical Works of Bayard Taylor.* Boston: Houghton, Mifflin and Company, 1907.

Taylor, Charles. *Hegel.* Cambridge: Cambridge University Press, 1975.

———. *Sources of the Self: The Making of Modern Identity.* Cambridge, MA: Harvard University Press, 1989.

Taylor, Thomas, and Floyer Sydenham, trans. *Plato: The Symposium.* Somerset, MA: The Prometheus Trust, 2002.

Thomas, M. Wynn. *The Lunar Light of Whitman's Poetry.* Cambridge, MA: Harvard University Press, 1987.

———. "Representatives and Revolutionists: The New Urban Politics Revisited." In *Whitman East & West: New Contexts for Reading Walt Whitman,* ed. Ed Folsom. Iowa City: University of Iowa Press, 2002.

Trachtenberg, Alan. "Whitman's Visionary Politics." In *Walt Whitman of Mickle Street: A Centennial Collection,* ed. Geoffrey M. Sill. Knoxville: University of Tennessee Press, 1994.

Tuten, Nancy Lewis, and John Zubizaretta, eds. *The Robert Frost Encyclopedia.* Westport, CT: Greenwood Publishing Group, 2001.

Upanishads. Translated with an introduction by Patrick Olivelle. Oxford: Oxford University Press, 1996.

Uzdavinys, Algis. *The Golden Chain: An Anthology of Pythagorean and Platonic Philosophy.* Foreword by John F. Finamore. Bloomington, IN: World Wisdom Inc., 2004.

———. *Philosophy and Theurgy in Late Antiquity.* San Rafael, CA: Sophia Perennis, 2010.

Van Cromphout, Gustaaf. *Emerson's Modernity and the Example of Goethe.* Columbia: University of Missouri Press, 1990.

Van Leer, David. *Emerson's Epistemology: The Argument of the Essays.* Cambridge: Cambridge University Press, 1986.

Vendler, Helen Hennessy. *On Extended Wings: Wallace Stevens' Longer Poems.* Cambridge, MA: Harvard University Press, 1969.

Vernon, Mark. "Reincarnation in Jewish Mysticism and Gnosticism." *Shofar: An Interdisciplinary Journal of Jewish Studies* 24.1 (2005): 173–75.

Versluis, Arthur. *American Transcendentalism and Asian Religions.* Oxford: Oxford University Press, 1993.

———. *The Esoteric Origins of the American Renaissance*. Oxford: Oxford University Press, 2001.

Waggoner, Hyatt H. *Emerson as Poet*. Princeton, NJ: Princeton University Press, 1974.

Wallis, R. T. *Neoplatonism*. 2d ed. London: Duckworth, 1995.

Walls, Laura Dassow. *Emerson's Life in Science: The Culture of Truth*. Ithaca, NY: Cornell University Press, 2003.

Warren, James Perrin. *Culture of Eloquence: Oratory and Reform in Antebellum America*. University Park: Pennsylvania State University Press, 1999.

———. *Walt Whitman's Language Experiment*. University Park: Pennsylvania State University Press, 1990.

Waters, William. *Poetry's Touch: On Lyric Address*. Ithaca, NY: Cornell University Press, 2003.

Weiskel, Thomas. *The Romantic Sublime: Studies in the Structure and Psychology of Transcendence*. Baltimore, MD: Johns Hopkins University Press, 1976.

West, Michael. *Transcendental Wordplay: America's Romantic Punsters and the Search for the Language of Nature*. Athens: University of Ohio Press, 2000.

Whicher, Stephen E. *Freedom and Fate: An Inner Life of Ralph Waldo Emerson*. Philadelphia: Pennsylvania University Press, 1971.

Whitehead, Alfred North. *Process and Reality*. New York: Macmillan, 1967.

Whitman, Walt. *Leaves of Grass and Other Writings*. Ed. Michael Moon. New York: W. W. Norton, 2002.

———. *Notes and Fragments*. Ed. Richard Maurice Bucke. Folcroft, PA: Folcroft Library Editions, 1972.

———. *Specimen Days & Collect*. New York: Dover Publications, Inc., 1995.

Wilbur, J. B., and H. J. Allen, eds. *The Worlds of the Early Greek Philosophers*. Buffalo, NY: Prometheus Books, 1979.

Williamson, Alan. "Forms of Simultaneity in *The Waste Land* and Burnt Norton." In *T.S. Eliot: The Modernist in History*, ed. Ronald Bush, pp. 153–68. Cambridge: Cambridge University Press, 1991.

Wilson, Eric. *Emerson's Sublime Science*. New York: St. Martin's Press, 1999.

Witemeyer, Hugh H. "'Line' and 'Round' in Emerson's 'Uriel'" *PMLA* 82.1 (1967): 98–103.

Yates, Frances A. *The Rosicrucian Enlightenment*. London and New York: Routledge Classics, 2002.

Zweig, Paul. *Walt Whitman: The Making of a Poet*. New York: Basic, 1984.

Index

Ackerman, Alan, 209n9, 213n48
agent, 74, 124, 138, 184n37, 218n16. *See also* reception
Agrippa, Cornelius, 6
alchemy, magic and occult science, 2, 3, 6, 9, 22, 28–29, 51, 164, 170, 187n57, 188n57
Alcott, Amos Bronson, 5, 135, 179n4, 180n16
Alexander of Aphrodisias, 178n1
America/American, 2–10, 12, 13, 41, 43, 44, 64, 68, 69, 83, 94, 96, 97, 103, 104, 105, 106, 108, 109–16, 128, 129, 130, 131, 133, 137, 140, 145, 147, 151, 157, 158, 159, 168, 179nn4–5, 192n11, 206n95, 208n2, 211n36, 212n43, 213n49, 214n43, 215n57, 216n66, 216n76, 217n6, 220n25; Adam, 3, 106; body, 128, 129, 132, 133, 194n35; consciousness/poetic, 109–14, 116, 130, 133, 168, 195n42, 216n76; metempsychosis *passim,* 159, 169–71, 192n11; nationhood, 43, 106, 115–16, 147, 168–169, 170; poet/poetry, 7, 103, 105, 116, 119, 131, 138, 168, 170, 173; Pragmatism, 168; psyche, 216n76; religion, 104; selfhood/individuality, 2, 9, 103, 115–16, 169–71, 214n53, 216n76, 220n25; solipsism, 113; sublime, 140, 173; Transcendentalism, 4, 20, 21, 41,

44, 61, 106, 107, 115, 151, 155, 157, 158, 179n4, 179n5, 181n4, 183n16, 184n34, 196n41, 198n64
Anaxagoras, 18
Apollonian/Dionysiac, 172
apprenticeship, 17–21, 140
Apuleius, 48, 188n61
Aquinas, Thomas, 137
Aristotle/Aristotelian, 4, 138, 178n1, 179n13, 181n7, 192n22, 195n39
ascendency (textual frame), 75–82
ascent (ladder of), 1–2, 6, 8, 40, 47–55, 63, 71–72, 79, 129, 134, 136–45, 156, 158, 164–65
Aspiz, Harold, 216n72, 220n27
Augustine of Hippo, 137, 191n7, 201n20

Bacon, Francis, 6
Baker, Carlos, 209n18, 210n19
Barthes, Roland, 174, 222n13, 222n14, 222n15
Bartsch, Shadi, 201n12
Bates, David William, 193n33
Bates, Stanley, 46, 192n20
Bauerlein, Mark, 212n45, 220n29
Beach, Joseph Warren, 185n39
beauty, 6, 47, 48, 49–53, 76, 84, 92, 93, 100, 120, 137, 143, 144, 156, 157, 182n13, 200n7, 201n23, 202n31, 218n17, 219n17, 220n25
Being, universal/individual, *passim,* 60, 73, 164, 187n56; abundance of, 159, 162;

all/complete, 13, 66, 185n41; being/
life/intelligence, 187n56; beyond, 128,
134, 172, 182n12; biology, 151; brightest
region of/heightened, 84, 110, 150;
chain/scale of, 6, 15, 29, 32, 36, 178n3,
188n58; currents of the Universal
Being, 73; dialectical, 210n25; discarded
shell of, 82; dissociation of, 162;
doorway of, 111; experience of, 127–28;
figure/game of, 127; foundation for, 11,
33; historical series of, 8, 15, 17, 20, 22,
23, 26, 27, 31, 36, 56, 76, 78, 80, 88, 95,
102, 108, 110, 112, 121, 130, 138–41, 144,
151, 155, 164; in/for itself, 27, 82; ladder
of, 8, 136, 138–41, 144; metempsychotic
unfolding of, 22; mimetic dilemma,
114–21, 128; multiple states of, 17, 34,
46, 101, 119; omnipresence of, 190n3,
201n11; and the One, 85; outline of, 159,
163, 164; perception of, 196n50; and
soul, 128, 156, 165; and words/speech,
113, 163
bird, 31–32, 51, 109, 129, 131–32, 136, 148,
154, 155, 159, 164–65, 188n66, 197n62,
214n56
Bird, Robert Montgomery, 169–70, 222n3
birth/rebirth, 4, 35, 58, 70, 117, 121, 126,
131, 142, 167, 174, 177n1, 181n3, 190n78,
206n95, 207n95; wheel of, 167, 177n1,
181n3, 190n78
Bishop, Paul, 179n3
Blake, William, vii, 1–2, 197n7
Bloom, Harold, 3, 73, 104, 110, 113, 140,
158, 159, 168, 173–74, 179n8, 182n9,
190n77, 190n1, 191n5, 199n1, 200n4,
208n4, 211n35, 212n41, 215n45, 218n10,
222n60, 222n65, 222n1, 222n9
Bloom, Molly, 150, 158
body, 3, 4, 7, 9, 18, 19, 25, 32, 33, 34, 35, 37,
40, 44, 45–46, 48, 49, 50, 53, 57, 60, 62,
69, 71, 72, 74, 81, 82, 84, 85, 91, 92, 98,
99, 109, 112, 114–15, 121, 124, 128, 129,
130, 134–39 passim, 143, 146, 147, 150,
155, 165, 177n1, 178n1, 184n36, 192n11,
194n35, 210n21, 211n34, 212n43,
214n52, 215n59, 217n5, 219n17,
220n27; American/politic, 128, 129,
132, 133, 194n35; dead, 114, 131, 155;
divine, 81, 82; and eye, 112; idealized
vs. dying, 129; poet of, 9; poetic,
45–46; pregnancy of, 143; textuality,
129, 155, 212n43; many, 9, 33, 177n1;
and soul, 5, 8, 22, 24–25, 34, 37, 39, 40,

46, 49–50, 57, 59–60, 62, 69, 71, 100,
109, 112, 124, 127, 128, 129, 134, 135,
150, 184n36
Böhme, Jacob, 7, 34, 74–75, 77, 78–79, 81,
83, 157, 168, 180n20, 202n29, 203n34,
221n54
Brodwin, Stanley, 182n13, 201n23
Bromwich, David, 215n58
Brontë, Emily, 137
Brooker, Jewel Spears, 221n59
Brown, Lee Rust, 185n41, 200n5, 206n90
Browne, Thomas, 75
Bruno, Giordano, 177n1
Buddhism and Confucianism, 12, 19, 157,
167, 177n1
Buell, Lawrence, 180nn1–2, 181n9, 186n47,
190n4, 196n45, 201n18, 202n27, 207n99
Burwick, Fredrick, 90, 205n65, 205n69,
206n75, 206n76
Bussanich, John, 190n76

Callow, Philip, 209n12, 209n15
camera obscura, 75, 88, 90–92
Cameron, Sharon, 93–94, 190n4, 191n5,
206n92
Carlyle, Thomas, 189n69
Carton, Evan, 190n4, 191n6, 203n37,
206n91
Cavell, Stanley, 13–14, 181n6, 192n10,
193n29, 194n35, 198n67, 206n95,
207n95, 208n8
Cavitch, David, 118, 209n10, 214n51,
215n57
Chai, Leon, 185n41
chain, 2, 6, 15, 29, 36, 54, 71, 79, 101, 115,
151, 178n3, 186n46, 188n58; of being,
15, 29, 36, 188n58; golden, 2, 6, 178n3;
material, 54
Chambers, Robert, 185n39
Channing, William Ellery, 3–4
Chari, V.K., 208n1, 210n25
Christ, Jesus, 125, 126, 128, 163
circle, 1, 7, 16, 60, 65, 66–68, 74, 77, 88,
96, 127, 135, 148, 156, 196n52, 198n66,
200n8, 200n9, 202n26; creation, 67; and
identity, 200n9; self-evolving, 66–68;
and Uriel, 68
Civil War, 106, 128–33, 209n10, 210n19,
215n59, 216n71, 220n25
Clarke, James Freeman, 2, 135, 179n6
classification (scientific), 24, 159, 185n41,
211n37
Colebrooke, Henry Thomas, 19

Coleridge, Samuel Taylor, 25, 41–42, 52, 177n1, 186n55, 187–88n57
Columbus, Christopher, 96
consciousness, 1–7, 12, 13, 14, 15, 17, 18, 20, 21, 23, 25–28, 33, 35, 36, 37, 38, 39–72 *passim*, 77, 78, 79, 81, 82, 85, 92, 94, 95, 99, 100, 101, 102, 103, 108, 109–14, 115, 116, 117, 174, 127, 128, 130, 133, 134, 135–36, 137, 138, 150–65 *passim*, 167, 168, 171, 173, 175, 185n39, 190n4, 191n7, 195n42, 196n50, 198n68, 198, 69, 203n41, 207n95, 208n102, 212n47, 214n56, 216n76, 217n5, 218n9, 218n16; American poetic, 109–14, 116, 130, 133, 168, 195n42, 216n76; a priori capacity of, 83; celestial, 36; conversion of, 167; dialectical, 49; double/divided, 5–7, 39–72, 77, 78, 85, 94, 95, 115, 150, 151, 152, 155, 158, 169, 173, 190n4, 191n7; ego-consciousness, 203n41; end of the mind, 158–65; evolution/emergence of, 36, 40, 50, 53, 54, 55, 61, 67–68, 102, 108, 136, 137, 173, 185n39; first world of, 155; fossil of, 117; future power, 79; garden of, 136, 154; historical, 14, 35, 49, 51, 54, 57, 65, 138, 151, 152, 157; immaterial/ heightened, 42, 199n69; individual, 15, 18, 23, 81, 82, 85, 100, 101, 155, 158, 167, 218n9; interconnectivity, 54; interior, 133, 134, 153, 165; material, 6, 41; metempsychotic dilemma/nature of, 43, 46, 108; modern, 12, 17, 21, 175; ontological, 62, 190n4; poetic, 116; phenomenology/philosophical, 21, 25–28, 65–68, 167, 185n39, 191n7, 198n68, 198n69; pre-consciousness, 45, 50, 52; reluctance of, 124; self-consciousness, 92, 191n7, 204n41; and soul, 5, 33, 35, 36, 41–47, 53–56, 68, 84, 134, 154, 184n33, 191n7; textual representation, 64. *See also* mind; soul
Constitution, U.S., 105, 116, 117, 206–7n95, 211n38
Cook, Eleanor, 222n64
Cook, Robert, 221n37, 221n39
Copernicus, Nicholas, 177n1, 183n19
Corrigan, Kevin, 178n1, 194n37, 197n55
cosmology, 1, 40, 56, 58, 62, 63, 77, 137, 138; chiastic, 56; counter-cosmology, 137, 138, 217n2; indeterminate, 63; spiritual, 1; static, 62
Cousin, Victor, 20, 183n24, 183n26, 186n46
Crary, Jonathan, 203n40, 206n79

crucifixion, 1, 127, 128, 163
Cudworth, Ralph, 83, 182n13
Cuvier, Georges, 23, 185n41

Dante Alighieri, 137, 189n69, 201n20
Darwin, Charles, 6, 8, 24, 70, 119, 184n39, 187n55. *See also* evolution
death, 7, 45, 66, 67, 109, 121, 122, 177n1
death/rebirth, 4, 66, 67, 121, 125, 126, 131
deceptions, 149–58
Dee, Ivan R., 209n12
Dee, John, 6
Della Porta, 75
Descartes, René, 83
Desmond, William, 198n68
determinism, 52, 69, 82, 100
dialectic, 41, 46, 49–50, 54, 57, 61–68, 78, 84, 86, 99, 115, 117, 121, 124, 126, 127, 128, 144, 155, 156, 158, 170, 172, 180n2, 187n52, 188n63, 190n4, 191n6, 191n7, 193n27, 194n38, 196n46, 198n68, 198n69, 199n69, 203n37, 207n95, 210n25, 218n15
Dickinson, Emily, 190n4, 203n37
Diels, H. and W. Kranz, 178n1, 183n15, 187n55
divided self, 105, 121–28, 131
doctrine of correspondences, 34, 51, 59, 75, 77, 201n23
Dodds, E.R., 187n56
double consciousness, 5–7, 39–72, 77, 78, 85, 94, 95, 115, 150, 151, 152, 155, 158, 169, 173, 174, 190n4, 191n7
Dougherty, James, 211n39, 212n46
Doyle, Charles, 222n61

Eldridge, Richard Thomas, 192n20
Eliot, Thomas Sterns, 136, 151–58, 164, 221nn40–52, 221n59; "Burnt Norton," 153–58, 164; "Cousin Nancy," 151; "Preludes," 152–53; "Sweeney Erect," 151; "Tradition and the Individual Talent," 152
emanation, 18, 19, 34, 74, 87, 178n3, 200n8
Emerson, Edward Waldo, 62
Emerson, Ralph Waldo, *passim*, but especially, 1–103, 105–9, 167–75, 179n4, 179n6, 179n9m 180n17, 180nn1–2, 181nn3, 5, 6, 7, 8, 9, 180nn10, 11, 13, 183nn16, 17, 19, 184nn27, 33, 36–42, 186nn44, 46–48, 187nn55–57, 188n59, 189nn, 69, 74, 75, 190n70, 190nn1–5, 191nn6–7, 193nn27–29, 31, 33–35,

194nn36–37, 195nn42–43, 196nn45–47, 52, 197nn53, 56, 198nn, 66, 67, 69, 199nn70–71, 199nn2–3, 200nn5, 7, 8, 9, 201n15, 19, 21, 33, 202nn26–28, 32, 203nn33, 37, 204nn45–46, 205n60, 206nn68, 91, 94, 95, 207nn96, 98–101, 208n102, 208n8, 209nn10, 14, 15, 18, 19, 210nn20–22, 25, 211n34, 213n49, 216n76, 218n16, 219n20, 220n45, 221nn35, 37–39, 222n1; "The American Scholar," 94, 181n9; "Art," 79–80, 86–87, 100, 164; "Beauty," 92–93; "Circles," 7, 36, 39, 45, 74, 77, 79, 80, 82, 87, 93, 117, 137, 138, 149, 164, 171, 200n8; college years, 17–21; *Conduct of Life*, 69; "Experience," 31, 42–43, 59, 64, 69, 71, 93–98, 152, 162, 168–69; "Fate," 69–72, 74, 98, 115, 135, 158, 169, 199n71; "Goethe," 145; "History," 2, 3, 7, 14–17, 22, 26, 28, 36, 37, 43, 51, 53, 67, 109, 112, 117, 136, 137, 138, 157, 172, 202n32; "Love," 47–55, 60, 63, 71, 87, 94, 95, 137, 138, 144; "The Naturalist," 76, 200n7; "Nature" (1836), 13, 60, 76, 79, 147; "Nature" (1844), 59, 69, 195n43; "The Poet," 57–60, 69, 74, 101–3, 113, 124, 141; *Representative Men*, 55, 78, 83, 85, 88, 93, 122, 193n35, 205n60; Science of mind, 34; "Self-Reliance," 198n67, 221n35; "The Sphinx," 37–38, 42, 152; "Swedenborg, or the Mystic," 34–37; "The Transcendentalist,» 41, 69, 100, 102; "Uriel,» 40, 60–69, 79, 94, 196n52; Whitman, 106–9, 209n15, 209n19

Empedocles, 74, 149, 177n1, 178n1, 206n83, 214n56

Empiricism, 69, 90

Enlightenment, 6, 44, 75, 90, 151

Erkkila, Betsy, vii, 216n71

esotericism, Christian mysticism (forms of), 8, 12, 19, 34, 47, 82, 104, 151, 164, 165, 170, 171

eternal return, 130, 172, 181n3, 190n78, 196n52

Euclid, 74

evolution, 12, 22, 34, 36, 48, 55, 68, 74, 107, 110, 129, 137, 138, 141, 172, 174, 181n3, 184n39, 185n39, 189n75, 197n52, 203n33

expansion, 4, 52, 55, 56, 59, 78, 85, 99, 104, 110, 113, 124, 130, 143–44, 200n8, 202n28, 215n59; germ/mind/self, 4, 55, 56, 124, 130,

143–44; mimetic, 59; perceptual, 99; unsettling, 202n28

experience, 3, 5, 8–10, 16, 17, 26, 27, 28, 31, 34, 37, 38, 39, 42–43, 52, 53, 54, 56, 59, 60, 61, 64, 65, 69, 71, 83, 86, 89, 91, 92, 93–98, 100, 101, 102, 105, 108, 109, 113, 118, 119, 120, 121, 124, 125, 127, 129, 130, 133, 135, 139, 140, 141, 143, 148, 152, 154, 157, 159, 162, 164, 167, 168, 170, 171, 175, 182n10, 190n4, 191n7, 194n37, 196n50, 198n67, 207n95, 208n103, 209n9, 212n47, 213n48, 213n49

eye/eyebeam, 7, 8, 9, 22, 23, 37, 38, 40, 46, 53, 70–82, 84, 85, 86, 87, 88–93, 95, 96, 97, 98, 99, 101, 102, 112, 113, 114, 118, 119, 120, 121, 123, 124, 130, 140, 145–49, 150, 155, 156, 157, 160, 161, 164, 170, 171, 173, 185n40, 186n46, 188n59, 191n7, 199n3, 200n3, 200n7, 200n8, 201n10, 202n32, 203n40, 204n46, 204n52, 205n55, 206n76, 207n95, 207n97, 208n102, 201n139; all eyes, 8, 101, 102, 113, 124, 141, 208n102; blind, 84; and brain, 71–72; of the dead, 118, 121, 140, 141, 149, 171; dialectic of perception, 85, 91, 102, 160; emanations of, 74; ensouled, 7, 84, 112, 114, 155, 160, 161, 164; flash of, 79–80, 81, 86, 87, 114, 145–49; of God, 81, 157; immanent, 74, 149–50; inward, 98; metempsychotic, 74; and the page, 145–49; pig-eye, 53; Plotinian, 78, 203n40; Proper, 37, 38, 201n10; right/left, 78; self-constituting, 85, 86, 88–93, 98; sun-formed, 157; transcendent power, 73, 79

Fall, the, 60–68, 126

Faraday, Michael, 187n57

fate, 28, 30, 36, 58, 60, 69–72, 74, 80, 96, 98, 115, 133, 135, 150, 158, 169, 170, 189n74, 196n45, 199n71, 203n39, 207n98

Ficino, Marsilio, 177n1

Field, Peter S., 196n45, 198n67

fire, 6, 7, 8, 18, 23, 52, 53, 81, 86, 115, 117, 118, 132, 133, 144, 154, 164, 165, 204n46, 218n15, 220n25; celestial, 6; of creation, 7, 8, 53, 81, 115, 117, 133; feathers fire-fangled, 165; fiery line, 93; love, 52, 218n15; quill of, 165; vital, religious, 132; of soul, 7, 18, 118, 132, 144, 157, 165; twofold (Böhme), 81

Fisher, Philip, 109, 170, 209n9, 211n30, 222n6
flash, 145–49. *See also* eye
flight, 44, 109, 123, 133, 134, 135, 165, 182n13, 201n23
Folsom, Ed, 221n30
Folsom, Ed and Kenneth M. Price, 215n63
Fox, George, 12–13, 191n5
Freud, Sigmund, 173
Frost, Robert, 60–61

Gadamer, Hans-Georg, 47, 192n21
George, Emery Edward, 179n3
Gnosticism, 178n2, 179n7
God, 1, 3, 7, 14, 19, 20, 21, 23, 34, 56, 6–63, 68, 71, 73, 75–80, 87, 94, 97, 108, 122, 137, 145, 146, 147, 158, 172, 183n19, 191n7, 201n9, 204n49, 204n52, 205n60, 213n56, 218n9; beyond being, 172; "cometh the god," 80, 87; creation from and to, 56, 78; eye of, 81, 157; fallen, 94; God carried me, 218n9; god in ruins, 60, 196n43; indwelling, 3, 21; I, particle of, 73; journey/ladder of mind to, 20, 76, 78, 122; love greater than, 34; madness of, 204n49; opposing gods of the mind, 205n60; and poet, 137, 173, 200n6; young gods, 62–65, 68, 196n52
Goethe, Johann Wolfgang von, 2, 12, 24–25, 28, 52, 55, 75, 76, 77, 83, 88–95, 97–98, 113, 168, 177n1, 179n3, 184n37, 185n39, 185n43, 186n46, 187n57, 188n57, 189n69, 193n30, 194n36, 201n4, 205n57, 205n61, 205nn61–62,nn64–67, nn69–73, 206n74, 206n76, 206n78, 206n83, 206nn85–88
Goodman, Russell B., 183n17, 183n23, 184n27, 184n33
Gougeon, Len, 181n3, 190n78, 198n66, 211n34
Grant, Charles, 19–20, 183n20
Great Chain of Being, 15, 29, 178n3, 188n55
Grossman, Jay, 208n8, 210n21, 215n57
Guthrie, James, 61, 181n8, 185n39, 186n47, 188n62, 196n48
Guthrie, Kenneth, 181n7

Hadot, Pierre, 75–76, 88, 197n57, 201nn14, 16, 20, 24, 205n58
Halliwell, Martin, 221n36
Harrison, John S, 182n13
Hegel, G.W.F., or Hegelianism, 5, 9, 12, 25–28, 31, 34, 40, 46–47, 55, 61–68, 74–75, 81–83, 90, 110, 157, 168, 177n1, 180n2, 185n39, 186n46, 186nn48–50, 187nn51–54, 191nn6–7, 192n21, 196n46, 197n58, 197n61, 197n63–64, 198nn64–65,nn68069, 203n33, 203nn35–37, 205n67, 210n25, 220n25; *Phenomenology of Spirit*, 26, 82, 187nn51–54, 198n64, 198n69, 203nn35–36, 220n25; *Philosophy of History, Lectures on*, 25, 66, 186nn49–50, 196n46, 197n61, 198n65; *Science of Logic*, 65, 66, 197nn58–60, 198n64, 198n68
Hensel, Herbert, 205n62, 206n74, 206n78
Heraclitus, 18–19, 156, 183n15, 187n55
hieroglyphics, 75–83, 88, 201n15, 201n22, 203n38, 218n7
Hinduism, 8, 12, 17, 19, 20, 21, 22, 24–25, 32, 35, 70, 71, 104, 109, 122, 167, 177n1, 182n12, 183n17, 183n19, 184n27, 184n33, 188n61, 193n34, 204n52, 208n1, 210n25; Atman, 19; *Bhagavad Gītā*, 20–21, 177n1, 184n28, 188n61, 204n52, 207n102; Brahman, 21; Brahmins, 24–25, 35, 101–2; reincarnation, rebirth or transmigration, 25, 36, 70, 71, 110, 167, 178nn1–2; *Upanishads*, 21, 177n1, 184n31
historical series, 9, 14, 16, 21, 23, 29, 30–38, 45, 50–51, 67, 80, 85, 89, 102, 111, 121, 122, 148, 172, 184n36
Hodge, David Justin, 181n6, 198n67
Hölderlin, Friedrich, 2, 179n3
Homer, 2, 150, 172, 177n1, 178n3, 179n3, 188n61
Hopkins, Vivian, 181n3, 182n13
Horowitz, Mitch, 179n4
Houlgate, Stephen, 198n68
Howe, Irving, 151
Huffman, Carl, 177n1
humanism, 5, 12, 151, 182n9, 200n9; antihumanism, 188n59
Hutchinson, George B., 212n47
Hutton, James, 3, 6

Iamblichus, 7, 33, 37, 177n1, 178n1, 179n3, 180n19, 182n13, 190n76
idealism (ancient, English and Continental forms of), 19, 20, 22, 25, 37, 69, 90, 104, 115, 136, 137, 144, 153, 155, 157, 177n1, 185n39, 186n46, 186n48, 190n5, 191n5, 197n64
imagination, 24, 160, 165, 173, 219n22; genealogy of, 173

immanence, 3, 13, 16, 18, 20, 49, 53, 68, 74, 79, 109, 110, 126, 128–34, 137, 140, 142, 149, 151–55, 158, 162, 182n12, 190n5, 216n69; and eye, 74, 155; subject, 99, 152, 157

industrialization, 43–47, 69

intellect, 4, 5, 14, 19, 31, 32–33, 36, 37, 38, 49, 55, 56, 83–87, 101, 181n9, 182n12, 184n38, 189n74, 190n79, 202n28, 205n55, 206n90, 206n93, 218n16; intellection, 42, 85–87, 189n68, 216n76; intellectual beauty, 143

intertextual, 40, 125, 173, 221n34

Irving, Washington, 43–44, 192n12

Irwin, John T., 76–77, 82, 138, 201n22, 203n38, 218n7

Jacob's ladder. *See* William Blake

Jacobson, David, 73, 83, 182n9, 188n59, 199n2, 200n9, 203n33, 204n45

Jaeger, Werner Wilhelm, 188n63

Jainism, 177n1

Jarraway, David R., 222n63

John of the Cross, Saint, 158

Johnson, Andrew, 132

Johnson, Maurice, 210n19

Jones, William, 19, 184n33

Joyce, James, 137, 150–51, 158, 192n24, 221n34

Judas, 125

Kainz, Howard , 187n52

Kane, Paul, 190n77

Kant, Immanuel, 19, 25, 61, 76, 83, 167, 168, 187n56, 191n5, 196n50, 197n64, 198n64, 203n37, 203n41, 204n44, 220n25

Kateb, George, 190n2, 193n27

Keane, Patrick J., 196n45

Kepler, Johannes, 96, 177n1

Killingsworth, M. Jimmie, 214n53, 215n59

Kirchweger, Anton Joseph (Golden Chain of Homer), 2

Kirk, G.S., and J.R. Raven, 178n1

Koyre, Alexandre, 178n1

Kuebrich, David, 104, 208n2

ladder or stairway of ascent, 1–2, 6, 8, 40, 47–56, 63, 71–72, 79, 129, 134, 136–45, 156, 158, 164–65

Lamarck, Jean-Baptiste, 185n39

Laplace, Pierre-Simon, 52, 69–70, 100. *See also* probability theory

Larson, Kerry C., 208n8, 211n38, 220n26

Lauxtermann, P.F.H., 205n67

law, 13, 15, 16, 23, 28, 29, 33, 40, 44, 48, 53, 56, 62, 65, 68, 72, 76, 83, 87, 90, 93, 98, 100, 117, 150, 163, 169, 186n46, 189n68, 200n7; beauty of, 4, 8, 53; of being, 163; categorical imperatives, 83; of creation, 202n32; laws of errors, 100, 199n71, 207n98; laws of form, 62; laws of nature, 28, 29, 33, 44, 76, 87, 117; "long lines of laws," 56, 202n28; omnipresence of, 98; secret, spiritual, 40, 68, 76, 198n67

Levin, Jonathon, 3, 168, 179n9, 222n62, 222n2

Lincoln, Abraham, 128, 131–32

line/linear, 13, 16, 22, 32, 37, 46, 56, 61, 62, 66, 71, 93, 95, 98, 100, 107, 108, 114, 133, 149, 156, 158, 161, 163, 164, 165, 171, 172, 196n45, 197n53, 197n56, 202n28, 203n39, 207n95; fiery line, 93

Locke, John, 4, 41–42

logos, 47, 62, 188n60, 193n28, 197n54

Lopez, Michael, 25, 180n2, 181n2, 186n48, 201n21, 207n96

love, 1, 6, 29, 30, 34, 36, 39, 40, 47–54, 59, 60, 63, 68, 71, 79, 81, 84, 87, 94, 95, 102, 119–20, 130, 131, 134, 136, 137, 138, 143, 148, 149, 158, 161, 182n9, 193n27, 197n62, 202n31, 204n52, 206n89, 207n97, 213n49, 218n15, 218n17; descent of, 137, 138, 143; homoerotic, 143; intermediate spirit, 50; ladder/ascent, 1, 47–54, 136; Platonic, 8, 48–54, 84, 102

Lovejoy, Arthur, 188n55

Loving, Jerome, 106, 209n13, 209nn15–16, 209n19

Lucretius, 189n73

Luther, Martin, 12–13

MacKenna, Stephen, 188n65

Mahler, Gustav, 137

Martz, Louis L., 217n79

Marsh, James, 41

matter, 14, 18, 20, 21–28, 32, 34, 38, 40, 44, 47, 49, 50, 53, 56, 57, 58, 59–60, 61, 63, 64, 65, 71, 79, 85, 100, 109, 129–30, 140, 144, 149, 150, 156, 161, 162, 178n3, 186n44, 186n46, 187n57, 189n75, 190n75, 195n42, 195n43, 196n43, 197n52; and form, 195n42; and soul, 49, 56, 57, 60, 61, 63, 64, 65, 71, 85, 129–30, 144, 149, 161,

162, 186n44; transformability of, 21–28

Maslan, Mark, 124, 214nn54–55

Materialism, 119, 129, 132, 151

Meinecke, Friedrich, 205n57

memory, 5, 17, 18–19, 20, 23, 33, 110, 153, 154, 165, 167, 174, 183n16, 186n44, 193n34; anamnesis/recollection, 167, 183n16, 185n40, 193n34; of God, 23; historical/transcendental, 183n16; and history, 17, 19, 154, 183n66, 185n40, 193n34. *See also* recollection

Menand, Louis, 180n1, 189n71, 193n33, 196n45, 199n71, 207n98

metamorphosis, 12, 14, 22–30, 33, 34, 89, 92, 125, 178n1, 184n37, 185n39, 185n43, 188n57

metempsychosis, *passim*, but especially, 11–38, 73–103, 104–34, 171n1, 181n3, 183n19, 184n36, 184n38, 187n55, 192n11, 193n34, 196n52, 197n62, 202n28, 207n98, 207n102, 209n10, 210n25, 211n34, 212n44, 214n56, 220n26, 221n34; absorption/ assimilation, 110, 124, 139, 140, 174; alchemy, 28, 30–38; alienation, 149–50; and America, 159, 169–71, 192n11; apprenticeship, 140; art of bookmaking, 44–45; ascent/descent, 2, 5, 7, 16, 22, 63, 70, 137; and being, 22, 134; cinematic, 132; classical theories, 21–26, 36, 101–2, 167, 177n1; and consciousness, 9, 14, 42, 43, 45, 46, 55, 108; divided self, 105, 121–28; ecstasy, 94; evolution, 2, 12, 14, 16, 22, 29, 61, 181n3; historical series, 9, 14, 16, 21, 23, 29, 30–38, 45, 50–51, 67, 80, 85, 89, 102, 111, 121, 122, 148, 172, 184n36; identity, 5, 14, 28, 170; intertextual, 221n34; journey, 16, 21, 40, 61, 74, 87, 94, 103, 108, 112, 130, 210n25; masks, 87, 88; and metamorphosis, 22, 30, 33, 34; metempsychotic decree of the gods, 214n56; mimesis, 7, 40, 55–60, 71, 79, 80, 81, 94; mind/intellect, 4, 12, 14, 17, 25, 31, 32, 33, 36, 39, 61, 108, 109; of nature, 3, 12, 15, 22, 23, 35, 39, 53, 79, 105, 108, 112, 164, 172, 184n38, 202n28; order of time/genesis, 53, 55–60, 61, 64, 80, 94, 96, 134, 136, 146, 172, 173, 209n10, 216n76, 214n56, 220n26; pedagogical project, 17; perception/vision/experience, 7–9, 12, 14, 64, 74–75, 83, 88, 94, 96–99, 103, 105,

113, 117, 160–61, 168, 172–73, 207n98; phoenix, 197n62; plurality, 207n102; poetry, 7–8, 70, 98–103, 111, 128, 136, 159, 184n37; reading, 73–103, 134, 168; recollection, 21, 45, 53, 82, 193n34; and science, 24, 34, 35; and self, 2, 4, 5, 9, 16, 38, 42, 44, 74, 100, 105, 110, 114, 121, 123, 136–38, 141, 143, 145, 147, 148, 155, 157, 158, 159, 168, 170, 174, 172, 211n34; and soul, 15, 87, 100, 123, 135, 138, 139, 149; and spirit, 67; structure/ pattern, 34, 38, 39, 44, 70–71, 75, 105, 128, 136, 159, 169, 184n37; textuality, 10, 23, 44, 61, 70, 73–103, 104–34, 168; unsettled/unsettling, 12, 30–38, 64, 75; writing, 104–34. *See also* birth/rebirth; reincarnation; soul; transmigration

Miller, A.V., 187n51, 197n58

Miller, James E. Jr., 214n52

Miller, Perry, 179nn10–12, 179n15

Miller, Richard, 223nn14–16

Milton, John, 48, 62–3, 173, 189n69, 196n51

mimesis, 40, 42, 46, 57–60, 63–71, 74, 79–80, 85, 86, 94, 114–21, 126, 128, 140, 146, 155, 171

mind, 4, 11–38, 39–72, 73, 76, 83, 86, 88, 92–93, 94, 97, 98, 102, 108–10, 112, 150, 153, 154, 155, 156, 157, 158–65, 182n10, 184n38, 185n43, 186n46, 189n68, 191n5, 203n41, 204n49, 205n60, 207n96, 207n98, 215n58, 218n16, 219n17; architecture, 153; end of, 158–65; garden of, 155; germ of expansion, 4, 55, 56, 124, 130, 143–44; journey into, 157; second sight, 92–93. *See also* consciousness; intellect; soul

Mitchell, Charles E., 221n38

modernism, 3, 136, 150, 151, 179n9, 221n59, 222n63

Modiano, Raimonda, 186n45

monad, 2, 15, 23, 38, 79, 88, 112, 155, 156, 172, 179n5, 181n7; and metempsychosis of nature, 23, 53, 67, 79, 112, 172; protean, 88; spiritual/invisible, 2, 156

Moon, Michael, 180n21, 209n17, 210nn19– 20, 212n43, 215n64, 216n66, 216n71, 217nn1–2, 220n30

Moores, D.J., 221n33

Myerson, Joel, 180n17, 209n11, 216n76, 219n24

mysticism/mystical, 1–12, 17–21, 31, 34–36, 37, 43, 59, 81, 88, 104, 110, 114, 135–40, 145, 150, 153, 156, 157, 158, 161, 162, 170,

171, 175, 178n2, 179n4, 189n75, 201n20,
210n25, 211n33

Nathanson, Tenney, 211n29, 212n44,
212n49
naturalism, 23–24
nature, metempsychosis of, 3, 12, 15, 22,
23, 35, 39, 53, 79, 105, 108, 112, 164, 172,
184n38, 202n28
necessity, 27, 69–72, 80, 97, 172–73, 186n46,
214n56; ring of, 69–72
Neoplatonism/Neoplatonic, 4, 6, 7, 8,
12, 18, 19, 20, 31–32, 33–34, 37, 40,
47, 62, 63, 64, 74, 75, 77, 78, 83–88,
89, 91–92, 94, 97, 109, 114, 115, 137,
144, 156, 160, 167, 168, 171, 178n1,
178n3, 181n7, 182n13, 183n66, 187n56,
189n67, 190n76, 190n3, 197n52, 197n55,
198n66, 201n23, 205n53, 205n57,
206n90, 218n16; abiding, procession
and conversion, 33, 56, 62, 85–87, 168;
ensouled eyebeam, 7, 46; intellect, 4, 14,
19, 32, 33, 37, 55–56, 86–87; light-eye
medium, 87, 91–92, 97, 160; procession,
conversion and self-constitution, 6,
62, 85–87, 93, 96, 97, 102–3, 115, 156;
second sight, 7, 56, 83, 85, 93, 156;
substance, 40; theurgy, 7
Neopythagoreanism, 177n1, 181n7, 182n13
Neufeldt, Leonard, 184n37
New Criticism, 174
Newfield, Christopher, 192n7, 198n67
Newton, Isaac, 90–91, 177n1, 183n19
New York Tribune, 106
Nietzsche, Friedrich, 172–73, 189n73,
193n29, 222n7
Novalis (Georg von Hardenberg), 90
Nussbaum, Martha, 136–38, 143, 192n24,
197nn2–3, 218n8

One, the, 6–7, 56, 60, 62, 63, 78, 85, 95, 115,
172, 178n3, 189n73, 190n76, 190n4,
204n5; and being, 85; and creation, 60,
62; free will of, 189n73; and love, 204n5;
and many, 190n4; and matter, 56,
178n3; procession/conversion, 62, 63,
95, 115; and soul, 6, 78
optics, 74, 75, 88, 89, 90, 95; Euclid, 74;
Goethe, 75, 88, 89, 90; Newtonian,
90. See also eye; eyebeam; perception;
vision
order of time/genesis, 40, 55–60, 61, 70,
80, 82, 85, 94, 96, 99, 115, 121, 136, 143,

146, 154, 159, 162, 165, 172, 173, 209n10,
214n56, 220n26; God's hierarchic
order, 62
Orpheus/Orphic, 2, 5, 173, 177n1, 178n1
Ovid, 36, 178n1, 187n55

Packer, Barbara, 41, 73, 179n6, 179n16,
190nn4–5, 192n8, 199n3, 200n3
Paracelsus (Philippus von Hohenheim), 75
Parker, Theodore, 108–9, 135, 210n26
Paul, Sherman, 199n3
Pease, Donald E., 109–10, 211n31, 221n33
Pensky, Max, 201n23
perception, 7–9, 12, 14, 64, 74–75, 83–88,
88–93, 93–98, 103, 105, 113, 117, 160–61,
168, 172–73, 207n98; dilemma of,
93–98; prototypes of, 83–93; self-
constituting eye, 88–93. See also eye;
eyebeam; vision
person/personal, 4, 5, 13, 16, 36, 39, 54, 55,
68, 76, 94, 99, 103, 117, 123, 128–34,
169, 174, 186n46, 191n5, 192n11,
194n35, 194n37, 195n42, 201n17, 209n9,
215n58, 218n16, 220n26; democratic,
105; first-person, 100, 152; impersonal,
188n59, 189n73; persona, 123, 140;
and poetics, 128–34; soul/subject, 174;
third-person, 159, 192n11
personal transcendence, 128–34
Petrarch, 48
Pherecydes, 177n1, 178n1
Philo of Alexandria, 2, 6
Phrenology, 70
Plato, 1–2, 4, 7, 32, 33, 35, 42, 48, 49, 51,
53, 55–57, 58, 75, 78, 83–88, 91, 92, 94,
102, 113, 137, 143, 144, 149, 168, 177n1,
178n1, 178n3, 179n3, 181n7, 182n13,
183n16, 187n55, 189n73, 191n5, 191n6,
191n7, 192n22, 192n23, 192n24, 193n25,
193n28, 193n31, 193n34, 194n35,
194n36, 194n38, 195n39, 195n41m
195n42, 197n54, 197n57, 200n6, 201n10,
201n23, 202n26, 202n31, 204n46,
204n52, 205n56, 205n60, 206n83,
207n95, 218n11, 218n17, 219n18,
221n32; Alcibiades I, 191n6, 191n7,
204n52; critique of poetry, 57–58;
Meno, 183n16; Parmenides, 191n6,
192n22; Phaedo, 191n6; Phaedrus,
84, 183n16, 204n47, 204n48, 207n97;
Philebus, 195n39, 197n54; Republic, 42,
57, 58, 84, 85, 92, 117, 149–50, 189n73,
191n6, 195n41, 201n10; Seventh Letter,

94, 205n56; *Sophist*, 191n6; *Symposium*,
1, 33, 47–50, 136–37, 143, 144, 187n55,
191n6 192n23, 192n25, 202n31, 218n11;
Theory of Forms, 47, 49–51, 54–59, 61,
89, 137, 144; *Timaeus*, 2, 83, 193n31,
197n57, 202n26, 204n46
Platonism /Platonic, 1–2, 4, 6, 8, 12, 18, 31,
40, 47, 48, 49, 50, 51, 53, 54, 55, 56, 57,
59, 61, 62, 74, 78, 83–88, 91, 92, 97, 114,
115, 136–37, 143, 144, 157, 160, 164, 167,
178n2, 179n3, 180n19, 182n12, 182n13,
186n46, 190n4, 191n7, 193n27, 193n28,
194n36, 194n37, 194n38, 195n42,
198n67, 202n28, 25n57, 207n95, 217n6
Plotinus, 7, 14, 31, 33, 52, 75, 77, 78, 83–89,
91–92, 115, 157, 160, 168, 177n1, 178n1,
178n3, 182n13, 183n14, 183n16, 187n56,
188n60, 188n65, 189n73, 190n76, 190n3,
191n5, 191n6, 191n7, 195n40, 197n55,
199n72, 200n6, 210n10, 201n11, 201n14,
201n15, 201n17, 201n20, 201n23,
201n24, 201n25, 202n26, 203n32,
205n58, 206n89, 206n90, 206n93,
221n53
Plutarch, 48
Poe, Edgar Allan, 169
poetics/poetry/poet, 3, 98–103, 128–34,
135–65, 184n37, 216n69; and alchemy,
28–31; emergent figure, 98–103;
metempsychotic structure, 128,
136, 184n37; new poetry, 135–65;
personal transcendence, 128–34; of
reading, 98–99; series, 64, 142, 170; of
transition, 3
Porphyry, 177n1, 178n1, 182n13, 188n65
Postmodernism/poststructuralism, 174
Pragmatism (American), 168
Price, Kenneth M., 209n18, 215n63, 216n67
probability theory or law of errors, 52,
69–70, 100, 199n71. *See also* Pierre-
Simon Laplace and Adolphe Quetelet
Proclus, 7, 33, 37, 177n1, 178n1, 179n3,
181n7, 182n13, 187n56, 189n67, 190n76,
191n7, 197n52
Protestant Reformation, 75, 145
Proust, Marcel, 137, 192n24
Pythagoras, 18, 19, 24, 32, 101–2, 177n1,
183n19, 187n55
Pythagorean/ism, 2, 8, 24, 25, 63, 74, 109,
167, 177n1, 178n1, 183n19

Quetelet, Adolphe, 52, 70, 100, 199n71. *See
also* probability theory

Quinney, Laura, 179n7

Rajasekharaiah, T.R., 208n1
Ramey, James, 221n34
Rautenfeld, Hans von, 194n35
reading (metempsychotic text), 73–103,
134, 142, 148, 162, 168, 182n10, 200n5,
206n91, 212nn44–45, 220n26, 220n29
reception, 16, 44, 46, 116, 117, 121, 123, 174,
200n3, 206n10
recollection, 21, 45, 53, 82, 193n34;
anamnesis, 193n34
Reconstruction, 128
redemption, 76
reincarnation. *See* metempsychosis
religion/religious, 2, 8, 12, 21, 63, 103, 108,
130, 132, 133, 137, 147, 157, 158, 163, 172,
180n1, 183n19, 217n6, 218n16, 220n25;
great religions/philosophies, 12, 20, 21,
110, 137, 157, 183n19; historicity of, 20;
new American, 103, 104; schisms, 83;
and science, 17, 199n70; spirituality, 133
resurrection, 7, 125, 132
Richardson Jr., Robert, 24, 182n13, 185n39,
185n40, 185n42, 187n57, 194n36,
209n14, 210n19, 210n22, 219n20
Robertson, Michael, 104, 208n7
robust soul, 136–40, 218n16
Romantic/Romanticism, 106, 145, 151, 152,
155, 156, 159, 170, 173, 177n1, 182n10,
185n41, 186n48, 187nn56–57, 196n45,
200n6, 203n37, 207n99, 207n101, 213n50,
214n53, 217n6, 219n23, 221n36, 222n63
Rossi, Paola, 178n1
Runes, Dagobert D., 204n43

Sacks, Kenneth S., 182n9
Scheick, William J., 201n15
Schelling, F.W.J., 22, 70, 90, 177n1, 184n35,
191n5, 203n39, 210n25
Schiller, Friedrich, 25, 179n3
Schirmeister, Pamela, 193n35, 208n103
Schopenhauer, Arthur, 90, 189n73, 205n66
Seamon, David, 205n69
Seamon, David and Arthur Zajonc,
205n62, 205n64
self/subjective, 2, 4, 5, 9, 16, 38, 42, 44, 74,
100, 105, 110, 114, 121, 123, 136–38, 141,
143, 145, 147, 148, 155, 157, 158, 159,
168, 170, 174, 172, 211n34
self-reflexivity, 3, 6, 46, 54, 74, 83, 101, 110,
136, 154, 160, 162, 168, 191n6, 191n7,
193n28

Sepper, Dennis L., 205n57, 205n60, 205n61, 205n70, 206n88
series/sequence, 9, 14, 16, 21, 23, 29, 30–38, 45, 50–51, 67, 80, 85, 89, 102, 111, 121, 122, 148, 172, 184n36
sex/sexuality, 50, 105, 120, 124, 126, 137, 143, 193n77, 201n12, 210n19, 214n52, 214n54, 215n39, 215n64
Shaw, Gregory, 180n19
Shelley, Percy, 143, 144, 177n1, 218nn11–14, 219n19, 219n22
Sibylline leaves, 50
Singh, Nagendra Kr, 208n1
Siorvanes, Lucas, 187n56
slavery, 116, 117, 129
Smith, Christopher P., 192n21
Smith, David L., 180n1
Smith, John, 178n2
Smith, Martin Ferguson, 189n73
sola scriptura, 75, 145
solipsism, 113, 174
Solomon, Robert C., 189n73, 197n64
soul, 1–10 *passim*, 11–17, 18–115 *passim*, 123, 124, 127, 128, 129–30, 132–65, 167, 177n1, 178n2, 179n7, 183n14, 183n16, 184n33, 186n44, 186n44, 189n69, 189n74, 189n75, 191n5, 191n7, 193n28, 193n34, 195n40, 195n43, 197n52, 197n62, 200n8, 202n32, 203n32, 204n49, 204n52, 205n60, 206n89, 207n102, 208n102, 210n25, 211n34, 211n37, 214n52, 215n58, 215n59, 216n69, 216n76, 218n15, 218n16, 219n13, 220n30; abundance, 31, 32; animating life, 100, 177n1; ascent/descent, 2, 10, 40, 47–56, 63, 129, 133, 136–45, 156, 158, 164, 197n62, 204n49; balanced, 205n60; beauty, 48, 49; and being, 128, 165; bird, 132, 154; and body, 5, 8, 22, 24–25, 34, 37, 39, 40, 46, 49–50, 57, 59–60, 62, 69, 71, 100, 109, 112, 124, 127, 128, 129, 134, 135, 150, 184n36; brooding, 64; and consciousness, 5, 33, 35, 36, 41–47, 53–56, 68, 84, 134, 154, 184n33, 191n7; conversion/inversion, 63, 85, 99; created, 6, 48, 49, 193n28; ensoulment/indwelling, 129, 149, 150, 155, 157, 164, 171, 202n32; and evil, 204n49; eye/perception, 73–74, 84, 85, 101, 155–57, 184n33, 204n52; eyebeam ensouled, 7, 84, 102, 112, 114, 160, 161; and

fate/necessity, 69–72; fire/spark, 7, 42, 128, 132, 193n31; future life, 152; ghostly/shadowy, 45, 46; and God, 78, 81, 134, 157, 158; and historical series, 12–17, 26, 31, 56, 64, 65, 67, 79, 82, 135, 151, 159, 183n16; hunger, 129–30, 191n5; individual/individuation, 78, 134, 167, 169, 174, 184n38, 197n52; and matter, 24, 25, 49, 57, 59–60, 61, 63, 65, 85, 109, 129–30, 132, 149, 161, 162, 186n44, 189n75, 195n43, 200n8; metempsychosis/transmigration, 2, 5, 11, 22, 25, 29, 31, 32, 33, 61, 63, 64, 87, 101, 114–15, 123, 129–30, 165, 167, 173, 174, 177n1, 183n16, 184n36, 186n44, 197n62, 207n102, 208n102; mimetic wake/sequence, 59, 85, 171; over-soul, 31; procession/journey, 2, 6, 8, 17–18, 21, 31, 34, 35, 40, 49, 61, 64, 68, 73–74, 76, 85, 99, 136, 161, 202n32; redemption, 76; robust, 60, 129, 135, 135–45, 155, 158, 166, 164, 165, 171, 200n8, 218n16; and self, 61, 69, 100, 191n7, 210n25, 218n16; soul of the poet, 215n59; sphericity, 97; swallowing, 109, 123; transcendent movement, 134, 183n16; and unity, 18, 43, 57, 152, 210n25; universal, 18, 178n2; unsettled, 11, 73, 136; volatile, 2, 11; world soul, 2, 18, 178n2, 183n19, 202n26. *See also* consciousness; mind
Southey, Robert, 19
Sowder, Michael, 211n36
Spinoza, Baruch de, 137
spiral, 1, 158, 181n3, 185n39, 196n52
spirit/spiritual, *passim*; American, 170; ascent/culmination, 136–47, 153; body/spirit union, 3–4, 23, 35, 36, 89, 115, 128, 134; crisis, 42; ecstasy of, 37; fire, 17; Form, ideal, 57; Guide, 136; light/sight/insight, 44, 52, 56, 65, 78, 79, 81, 83, 85; love, 50–51; origin, 47; power, 29, 32, 34, 54, 85, 128, 135, 171; and science, 6, 12, 23, 24, 28; self-knowing, 47, 135, 151, 157; Spirit in history, 25, 26, 31, 39, 46, 66–67, 74, 81–82; Spiritualism, 105; upspringing perception, 74; World-Spirit, 26, 81–82. *See also* consciousness; intellect; mind; soul
stalwart heir, 109–14
Stauch, Carl F., 191n6
Stein, William, 183n19

Stevens, Wallace, 136, 158–64; *The Comedian as the Letter C*, 159–60; "Large Red Man Reading," 162–64; *Notes Toward a Supreme Fiction*, 160–61; "Of Mere Being," 164; "The Woman in Sunshine," 161–62
Stoics, 193n31
subjectivity, 4, 16, 35, 36, 37, 74, 90, 92, 96, 153, 167, 174, 190n4, 206n76; and metempsychosis, 4, 35, 36, 174; and perception, 16, 90, 96
Swedenborg, Emmanuel, 4, 24–25, 34–37, 40, 55, 59, 77, 122, 168, 185n43, 186n44, 189n69, 189n74, 201n23
Sydenham, Floyer, 144
Synnestvedt, Sig, 186n44

Taylor, Bayard, 44–47, 192n14
Taylor, Charles, 198n64, 219n21, 219n23, 222n77
Taylor, Thomas, 83, 144, 178n1, 219n18
textuality, 10, 23, 44, 61, 70, 73–103, 104–34, 145, 146, 155, 212n43
Thomas, M. Wynn, 211n37, 216n69, 217n6, 220n30
Thoreau, Henry David, 179n4, 183n19
thrush, 149–58. *See also* bird
Trachtenberg, Alan, 112, 212n40
transcendence, 14, 18, 20, 49, 53, 68, 79, 109, 110, 128–34, 137, 140–42, 158, 182n10, 182n12, 190n5, 216n69; and eye, 73; personal, 128–34; self-transcendence, 14
Transcendentalism (New England, American), 4, 20, 21, 41, 44, 61, 106, 107, 115, 151, 155, 157, 158, 179n4, 179n5, 181n4, 183n16, 184n34, 196n41, 198n64
transmigration. *See* metempsychosis
Turner, John D., 194n37
Tuten, Nancy Lewis and John Zubizaretta, 196n44

Unitarianism, 3, 5, 41, 61, 196n46
Uriel, 40, 61–68, 69, 79, 94, 196n45, 196n52, 197n53, 197n55
Uzdavinys, Algis, 180n19

Van Cromphout, Gustaaf, 184n46, 194n36, 205n68
veil, 7, 75, 80, 87, 173, 219n22
Vendler, Helen, 158, 159, 222n61, 222n66
verge, extremest, 141–45

Vernon, Mark, 178n2
Versluis, Arthur, 11, 19, 20, 21, 104, 179n4, 181n4, 183n18, 184n34, 189n72, 201n13, 208n2, 208n3
vision, 2, 5, 7, 8, 15, 23, 25, 37, 47, 51, 73, 74–75, 78, 83–93, 94, 95, 97, 98, 99, 103, 105, 106, 113, 116, 118, 119, 134, 137, 138, 144, 151, 155, 157, 161, 170, 172, 173, 199n3, 202n28, 204n46, 204n52, 206n89, 206n90, 207n97, 207n102, 209n10, 211n74; of American poet, 103, 105, 119, 138, 170; of the beautiful, 8, 47, 144, 218n16; cosmic, 5, 25, 37, 186n48; democratic, 103; dialectic of, 78; of genius, 23; metempsychotic conception of, 88, 94, 105, 161; models of, 74–75, 83–93; pedagogy of, 89; and speech, 113. *See also* eye; eyebeam; perception

Wallis, R.T., 178n1, 190n76, 197n55, 205n5
Walls, Laura Dassow, 83, 185n39, 185n42, 193n33, 201n19, 201n23, 204n46, 205n60
Warren, James Perrin, 189n70, 215n59
Weiskel, Thomas, 182n10
West, Michael, 213n50
West, Cornell, 198n67
Whitehead, Alfred North, 194n37
Whitman, Walt, *passim*, but especially 104–65, 167–75, 180nn21–22, 192n24, 208nn1, 2, 4–8, 209nn9–13, 15–19, 210nn20–25, 211nn29, 33–34, 36–39, 212nn40, 43–47, 49, 213nn48, 50, 214nn51–55, 215nn57–66, 216nn67–78, 217n79, 217nn1–6, 218n9, 219n24, 220nn25–26, 29–30, 222nn60, 79, 222n1; 1855 preface, 105, 108, 110–12, 115–17, 125, 127, 128, 131, 132, 136, 140–43, 147, 171; "A Clear Midnight," 134; "As a Strong Bird on Pinions Free," 129; "Crossing Brooklyn Ferry," 147–49, 164, 171, 220n29; *Democratic Vistas*, 132–34; "Drum Taps," 129–31; Emerson/Whitman relationship, 106–9, 209n15, 209n19; *From Noon to Starry Night*, 134; *Leaves of Grass*, 103ff., 212n43,; "Rise O Days from Your Fathomless Deeps," 129; "Song of Exposition," 132; "Song of Myself," 105, 109, 112–14, 117–28, 129, 131, 135–41, 143, 146–47, 171–72, 212n44, 213n48, 220n25; "Spirit Whose Work Is Done," 130; "Starting from Paumanok," 130;

"There Was a Child," 103; unsettled identity, 215nn57–59; "When Lilacs Last in the Dooryard Bloom'd," 131–32; "The Wound-Dresser," 130–31
Wilbur J.B. and H.J. Allen, 214n56, 221n31
Williamson, Allen, 221n52
Wilson, Eric, 181n2, 184n37, 187n56, 187n57
Wilson, Douglas Emory, 179n6
Witemeyer, Hugh H., 196n45, 197n53, 197n56

Wordsworth, William, 173, 177n1, 219n23
writing (metempsychotic text), 104–34, 142, 146, 148, 151, 161, 162, 171, 174, 193n29, 193n35, 194n35, 194n37, 195n42, 200n5, 206n91, 206n95, 209n10, 211n38, 212n43, 213n49

Yates, Frances, 180n18

Zweig, Paul, 215n64